The Providence Steam Roller

The Providence Steam Roller
New England's First NFL Team

Greg D. Tranter

McFarland & Company, Inc., Publishers
Jefferson, North Carolina

ISBN (print) 978-1-4766-9494-8
ISBN (ebook) 978-1-4766-5340-2

Library of Congress and British Library
cataloguing data are available

Library of Congress Control Number 2024034791

© 2024 Greg D. Tranter. All rights reserved

No part of this book may be reproduced or transmitted in any form or by any means, electronic or mechanical, including photocopying or recording, or by any information storage and retrieval system, without permission in writing from the publisher.

Front cover: The Steam Roller team on offense in a 1928 home game at the Cycledrome in Providence, Rhode Island.

Printed in the United States of America

*McFarland & Company, Inc., Publishers
Box 611, Jefferson, North Carolina 28640
www.mcfarlandpub.com*

To all the players who donned the Steam Roller uniform,
left an indelible mark on pro football
and brought an NFL championship to Providence.
Your commitment, hard work, guile and sacrifice
helped build the great game of pro football that we know today.

Table of Contents

Acknowledgments	ix
Preface	1
Introduction: The 1920s and the Early NFL	3
One. Before the NFL Came to Providence	7
THE EARLY YEARS OF THE INDEPENDENT STEAM ROLLER	7
THE CYCLEDROME	18
Two. The Early Years (1925–1927)	22
1925—THE INAUGURAL SEASON	22
1926—EXCITEMENT TURNS TO DISAPPOINTMENT	38
1927—CONZELMAN ARRIVES AND FORTUNES CHANGE	52
Three. The NFL Champions (1928)	68
1928—THE TOP OF THE MOUNTAIN	68
Four. Aftermath and Demise (1929–1931)	95
1929—THE CHAMPIONSHIP HANGOVER	95
1930—THE STEAM ROLLER CONTENDS BUT ATTENDANCE FALLS OFF SHARPLY	109
1931—MORE GAMES, FEWER FANS, THE END IS NEAR	121
Epilogue: The End and the Steam Roller Legacy	135
A Steam Roller Who's Who	143
Appendix: Year-by-Year Results, Team Rosters and Statistics	227
Chapter Notes	257
Bibliography	263
Index	273

Acknowledgments

This book has been a true joy to write and has allowed me to pursue my passion for researching and writing about professional football, this time specifically about a truly unique franchise in the annals of NFL history. I would like to thank several people who were integral in bringing this book to fruition.

Doug Stark, for sparking my interest in the Steam Roller and for his constant encouragement and support once I made the decision to pursue the book. He volunteered to review the manuscript and provided thoughtful insights and perspective that made the final product much better. Doug also connected me to a few other sports history people in Providence who also proved very valuable.

Budd Bailey, a friend and colleague with whom I have co-authored two other books, for his complete and thorough review of this manuscript. Budd offered several suggestions and edits that made the manuscript more concise, an easier and better read and a more compelling book.

Robert Cvornyek for his insights and thoughtful ideas and suggestions. He also shared some great images and some additional historical context that have made their way into the book. Brian Hart for the excellent information about Steam Roller owner Charles B. Coppen. And a thank-you to Chris Willis, head of the Research Library at NFL Films, for the insightful oral history interview with Pearce B. Johnson from October 4, 1991.

Ray Brutti, of the Brown University Archives at the John Hay Library, provided the wonderful photos of several Steam Roller players who matriculated through Brown on their way to professional football with the Providence NFL franchise.

Bill Corey, sports editor of the *Providence Journal*, was very helpful in assisting in identifying images for the book and referring me to Gannett Co., Inc., and Kim Reis for licensing some of the images that appear here.

I'm also appreciative for all the great help and support from the Rhode Island Historical Society, where I spent countless hours going through their collection and accessing the *Providence Journal*. Especially helpful were Leigh Schoberth, reference librarian, Jennifer Galpern, research services manager, and Dana Signe K. Munroe, cabinet keeper and library collections manager, for all their guidance and direction, and J.D. McKay, digital imaging specialist and rights and reproductions manager, for providing the many images from the RIHS collection that appear in the book.

A special thanks to Jason Aikens and Jon Kendle from the Pro Football Hall of Fame for their help in providing access and assistance in navigating the Hall of Fame's Steam Roller collection and the use of the images from the Hall's collection that appear here.

A thank you to friend and sports historian colleague Gary Cobb for his many thoughtful suggestions that proved extremely valuable and made for a better book. And a thanks for important insight and perspective from fellow Professional Football Researchers Association member and colleague Ryan Christiansen for his input about early professional football history prior to the NFL.

For my wife, Tracy, for her continued unwavering support of my various writing endeavors and specifically on my first New England–related book adventure.

A big thank-you to Gary Mitchem, senior editor, and all the people from McFarland for believing in this project and bringing it to a wonderful conclusion with the publication of this book.

Preface

This book examines one of the most unusual franchises in NFL history, the Providence Steam Roller. The team toiled in the NFL from 1925 to 1931 after playing for nine years as an independent professional football team. The Steam Roller, though part of the league for only seven years, achieved many firsts in NFL history, and its place in the early evolution of professional football is significant. In addition, Providence won an NFL championship—the last franchise that no longer exists to have achieved that feat.

The book came about by complete happenstance. During the International Tennis Hall of Fame's enshrinement week in 2021, I was having a conversation with Doug Stark, former executive director at the Hall of Fame and also a friend and colleague. As always, we were talking sports, and on this particular day he asked an innocent question: Did I know why the Steam Roller(s) nickname had been used by so many Providence professional sports franchises over the years? My answer was no. But I was intrigued by the question, and it started me on a journey of research. The more research I did, the more intriguing the story became, especially where it concerned the initial Steam Roller team and its ascension to the NFL. After several more conversations with Doug and learning more about the team, I knew that someone needed to tell the complete story of this franchise. Since I now had the interest and had actively worked to assemble all the details, I decided that I was the one to pen the book.

The manuscript took 18 months of exhaustive research, involving countless trips to the Rhode Island Historical Society (RIHS), multiple visits to the Pro Football Hall of Fame in Canton, Ohio, and thousands of online searches.

The book covers in depth the NFL iteration of the Providence Steam Roller, which lasted from 1925 to 1931. It provides background context about the independent professional Steam Roller team that played from 1916 through 1924 and positioned itself for entry into the NFL. The Providence Cycledrome is also covered thoroughly as it was the distinctive home to the NFL team throughout its existence.

Preface

The collection at RIHS was invaluable in this pursuit. *The Steam Roller Story*, a 1989 self-published book written by Dick Reynolds that focused on the 1928 championship team, provided essential insight to that title-winning season. Pearce B. Johnson and Dick Reynolds's *Professional Football in Rhode Island and Its National Connection*, also self-published in 1989 and part of the RIHS collection, proved likewise to be a terrific resource. These two books are the only ones that have been written about the franchise, but neither provided a comprehensive history of the NFL team.

It was fortuitous that Johnson, the Steam Roller's assistant general manager for its entire existence, left much of his collection to the Pro Football Hall of Fame, which made the materials accessible for me. And Peter Laudati, a part owner of the team, left many of his personal papers and a scrapbook to the RIHS. These collections provided information that could not be uncovered anywhere else, preserving several facts that would otherwise have been lost to history.

Many books on the early years of the National Football League contained references to the Steam Roller, adding to the story. Many newspapers reviewed through Newspapers.com provided coverage of the Steam Roller, much of it from the opponents' viewpoint. The RIHS provided access to the *Providence Journal*, which was full of so much rich information about the team and the community. Also, reading through the Steam Roller game programs at the Pro Football Hall of Fame and RIHS was fascinating. I even acquired several for my collection while doing the research.

I also tapped the brains of a few Providence sports historians who very willingly shared their knowledge. The Professional Football Researchers Association was helpful as several stories had been written about the Steam Roller in the association's newsletter, *The Coffin Corner*. Pro Football Archives and Pro Football Reference provided much basic information, including rosters and win-loss records, as well as player statistics of all sorts.

Brown University's John Hay Library Special Collections offered a treasure trove of great images from the 1920s. And the Brown University Athletic Hall of Fame provided great insight into the many Bears who played for the Steam Roller.

And, of course, just searching the internet for anything and everything Providence Steam Roller turned out to be very helpful as I found many excellent additional sources of information.

Researching and writing a book about a story nearly 100 years old takes a lot of patience, not to mention diligence in digging for details that seem somehow determined to remain buried. But truth be told, I enjoyed much of the work, which ultimately uncovered a remarkable story—one that I'm pleased to share with readers.

Introduction:
The 1920s and the Early NFL

This is the story of the Providence Steam Roller—an ancient and defunct National Football League franchise in the Renaissance City that brought major league sports to Rhode Island for the first time. It thrilled thousands of fans at a bicycle arena known as the Cycledrome. For one glorious season the team sat atop the pro football world, and then a few short years later it was gone to history. With the 100th anniversary of its first NFL season almost upon us, the in-depth story of the Providence Steam Roller is worth telling. Many who wore the team's uniform played professional football not for the money but for the love of the game and to represent the city of Providence while they worked other jobs to support their families.

The National Football League in the 1920s was not the high-powered, $18 billion enterprise that it is today. It was a fledgling hodge-podge league trying to survive and gain a foothold on the American sporting landscape. Its brand of football was thought to be brutal, offering little entertainment value; the true game, fans believed, was played at the college level.

The NFL, which began play as the American Professional Football Association (APFA) in 1920, was a loosely configured league in its early days. The APFA began with 14 teams in 1920 and, after a name change in 1922, saw its membership rise and fall unpredictably, from a high of 22 teams in 1926 to a low of 10 in 1928. Teams came and went as the league tried to attract fans and generate interest so that it could sustain itself. There was no broadcasting revenue to prop it up. With no standardized schedule, the teams played differing numbers of games, and league championships were awarded by winning percentage—or at times even by a vote of the team owners. Four of the first six championships were decided in postseason arguments among the owners. "The national press treated pro football like a raggedy stepchild while trumpeting the exploits of such teams as Dartmouth and the University of Washington," wrote David S.

Neft and Richard M. Cohen in their book *Pro Football: The Early Years: An Encyclopedic History 1895–1959*.[1]

Cities of all shapes and sizes entered the fray, with the league centered in the Midwest until the owners realized that for long-term survival they needed the franchises to be in major metropolitan markets. Some of the early NFL champions were in Akron, Ohio; Canton, Ohio; Frankford, Pennsylvania; and Green Bay, Wisconsin. Thirty-seven teams began play and then folded during the decade.

It was an easy league to join with no real criteria. You just needed the entrance fee, usually $100, a performance bond somewhere between $100 and $500, a stadium (or be a travel team) and players and a couple of coaches to put on the field.

When Providence entered the NFL in 1925, it was an unstable league, though it boasted 20 teams. However, that number shrank to 10 within three years. Compared with many of the other cities in the circuit, Providence had a lot going for it. It was a relatively wealthy city at the time, had a good sports reputation and was larger than many cities already in the league. Providence also had an ownership group that had money and connections, and it had an independent professional football team that had been successful for nine years, consistently fielding one of the best squads in the Northeast.

The game itself was not the pass-happy, wide-open offensive display that fans experience in today's NFL. The ball was leather and mostly round. It was easy to drop-kick but difficult to throw. Passing was typically limited to catch-up scenarios, end-of-game situations, or a periodic surprise move. The kickoff was at the 40-yard line and all 22 men on the kickoff teams stayed in the game. In the 1920s football was a single-platoon game with very little substitution. Even when players were injured, they stayed on the field unless it was extremely serious (broken arm, leg, etc.). Punting was key to the outcome of most games. The path to victory was not to possess the ball but to pin the opponent deep in its own territory and force it to make mistakes that your team could turn into points. Many punts came on early downs, as teams played for field position.

It was a game of tenacity, toughness and power with points at a premium. The 1922 champion Canton Bulldogs averaged 15.3 points per game but allowed only 15 points during the entire season as they finished with a 10–0–2 record. The 1920 champion Akron Pros averaged 13.7 points and the 1921 champion Chicago Staleys scored 11.6 per game.

The games had 12-minute quarters and usually lasted about two hours. They evolved into 15-minute quarters later in the decade. There were some unusual rules, at least in comparison with the modern game. When a team scored, for instance, it could choose to receive the ensuing kickoff, and many teams did. When a player carrying the ball went out of bounds, the next play had to start at that point, where he stepped out. The ball was not moved to the middle of the field, so in most instances the next offensive play was to run the ball to the center of the field. All field goal and extra-point attempts were dropkicks. The quarterback had to be five yards behind the line of scrimmage to throw a legal pass. There was a five-yard penalty if a team threw two incomplete passes in a row. And any incomplete pass thrown into the end zone was ruled an automatic touchback and the offensive team lost possession of the football. There were only three officials—an umpire, linesman and a referee—and they kept the time on the field.

The single-wing and the Notre Dame box were the dominant offenses of the era, both predominantly rushing attacks. Coaching was prohibited from the sidelines, though many coaches also played and rosters were limited to only 18 players. Many players wore leather helmets, but wearing headgear was optional.

The game of pro football was not popular with the broader public and had been "cast in the shadow of disrepute for so long, professional football's very birth has become a question," wrote Harold Claassen, assistant sports editor with the Associated Press and author of five books.[2] It had "the double burden of fan ennui and the outright hostility of the leaders in the then dominate collegiate version of the game."[3] It was not until Harold "Red" Grange became a professional player in 1925 and barnstormed across America that the public began to reconsider its view of the pro game.

The dominant sports of the era were professional baseball, with the incomparable slugging exploits of Babe Ruth; college football, with "Red" Grange and Ernie Nevers along with the superior Notre Dame teams of the legendary Knute Rockne; and boxing with Jack Dempsey and Gene Tunney collecting the headlines. As people had more leisure time that could be devoted to entertainment, athletes joined actors and musicians who became household names. Standout NFL players of the 1920s became stars, among them Grange, Guy Chamberlin, LaVern Dilweg, Nevers, Jim Thorpe, Paddy Driscoll, Joe Guyon, George Halas, Curly Lambeau and Jimmy Conzelman.

The Roaring Twenties were a frolicking, prosperous, fun-loving time in America, following World War I. Leisure activity exploded during the decade and by 1928 almost 25 percent of the national income was spent on fun activities. What better time to bring a pro football franchise to Providence?

This is the story of that team and those owners and players who made an indelible mark on the gridiron from 1925 to 1931. They produced many firsts in NFL history, such as playing on the first team that used a singular nickname (causing confusing that has stretched to this day). The Steam Roller is the last franchise to win an NFL championship and then go out of business. This book chronicles the exploits, highs and lows of that team. Enjoy the ride, just like the diehard fans who went to the Cycledrome to see their heroes way back when.

Chapter One

Before the NFL Came to Providence

At the turn of the 20th century, Providence, Rhode Island, was the 20th-largest city, with a population of 175,597, and one of the wealthiest municipalities in the United States. The state capital was one of the first in the country to industrialize and became noted for its textile manufacturing, jewelry, silverware and precision toolmaking. Companies like Gorham Manufacturing, Nicholson File, Brown & Sharpe, Fruit of the Loom and Corliss Steam Engine called Providence home and helped drive both the city's economy and the transformation of America into an industrial powerhouse.

Providence, founded in 1636 by Puritan theologian Roger Williams, is one of the oldest cities in America. Rhode Island was the first of the 13 colonies to renounce its allegiance to the British Crown, doing so on May 4, 1776, and the last to ratify the Constitution, as the vote was taken once the Bill of Rights was included, on May 29, 1790.

The city continued to grow and prosper from 1900 through the 1920s, a period in which professional sports was taking hold across America. Major League Baseball doubled in size with the addition of the American League, and two other major sports leagues, the National Football League and the National Hockey League, got their start. The NFL began as the American Professional Football Association in 1920 and was renamed the National Football League in 1922. The NHL began play in 1917.

As it tried to gain a foothold on the sporting landscape, the early NFL was populated by franchises in smaller cities, including Canton, Ohio; Columbus, Ohio; Dayton, Ohio; Duluth, Minnesota; Frankford, Pennsylvania; Pottsville, Pennsylvania; and Rochester, New York.

The Early Years of the Independent Steam Roller

The Providence Steam Roller joined the National Football League in 1925, but the team was founded several years earlier, in 1916, by Charles

B. Coppen. A physically small man who had played four years of football at Brown without earning a letter, Coppen was the sports editor of the *Providence Journal,* and he founded the team in the newspaper's offices on Westminster and Eddy Streets in downtown Providence. Pearce B. Johnson, who wrote high school sports stories for the paper, had suggested the idea to him and his assistant Ed Whelan.

"My football involvement goes back to 1912," Johnson said years later.[1] "I started as a waterboy for the Pawtuxet A.C. in Warwick. I was writing schoolboy sports for the *Journal* ... and I got to know the sports editor there very well. I approached him one night in 1916 and I said, 'You know, there are an awful lot of good football players in high school who never get to go to college.' I said to him, 'Somebody should start a professional team here.' He liked the idea so he and his assistant were the money men and they started the team."[2] Johnson was only 18 years old at the time, but after seeing semipro teams attracting 3,000 to 4,000 fans on a Sunday, he thought that football in Providence was a good idea. Soon Providence was on the professional football map.

"Those guys were the perfect fit for the franchise," said Chris Willis of NFL Films. "That's how a lot of teams got started in the 1920s. A group of sports-minded men, people who really cared about the game of football, would come together and try to get a team going."[3]

Coppen, at age 17, had joined the army during the Spanish-American War and earned the rank of sergeant. Matriculating at Brown in

Charles B. Coppen was the founding owner of the Providence Steam Roller in 1916 and remained an owner through the franchise's demise in 1932 (*Providence Journal*—USA TODAY NETWORK).

One. Before the NFL Came to Providence

1898, he graduated four years later, soon accepting a position as assistant headmaster of Abbott School in Farmington, Maine, where he remained until he joined the *Providence Journal* as a sports reporter in 1906. Coppen was promoted to sports editor in 1909 and served at that post until 1930. He left the newspaper to pursue a legal career, after having been admitted to the Rhode Island bar in 1924. Coppen practiced law until his death in 1950. He also served terms on the Board of Aldermen and City Council in his beloved Providence.

Coppen, a sports enthusiast, was part owner of the Steam Roller throughout the team's existence. He also managed the business of the franchise and was involved in player contract negotiations. Before his involvement with the football team, he was the chief organizer and president of the Colonial Baseball League, a minor league that was connected to the renegade Federal League in 1914 and 1915. Also, for several years he was involved in boxing. In addition, Coppen was a broadcaster for Brown University football and baseball games for many years.

Johnson did publicity for the team from the outset, writing the pregame stories and the game accounts that were distributed to the media outlets that covered the Steam Roller. In addition, he was a writer for the *Providence Journal*. A few years later he was appointed the team's business manager, a role that included securing opponents and arranging the schedule. Johnson eventually became the assistant general manager, serving in that capacity throughout the team's time as an NFL franchise. "I did most of my scouting from newspapers I'd get from around the country. There was a store in Providence that would get them a day or so late but I'd be there to pick them up. Believe it or not, we were able to sign some good players," Johnson said years later.[4] Following his career with the Steam Roller, he was actively involved in other independent pro football franchises that played in Providence along with other New England football-related activities, and he became a football historian for the Pro Football Researchers Association. Johnson also had a 37-year career as a department manager for the Ballou, Johnson & Nichols Company, a wholesale dealer and manufacturers' agent. Much of Johnson's personal memorabilia collection from the Steam Roller years is in the Pro Football Hall of Fame.

At the dawn of the franchise, Coppen brought two other very important people into the ownership group—James E. Dooley, the attorney for the franchise who was a local judge and state legislator, and Peter A. Laudati, Sr., a real estate developer and sports promoter.

Dooley was a leading sports figure in Rhode Island for decades. He was one of the founders of the Canadian-American Hockey League in 1926 and the sole owner of the Providence Reds, the state's first professional hockey team. Dooley also was president of the CAHL, today's American Hockey League, for six years. He owned the Reds until selling the team to Louis A.R. Pieri in 1938. Pieri, by the way, was a part owner of the Boston Celtics in the 1950s and 1960s.

Dooley was a judge for only one year before resigning but served in the Rhode Island General Assembly for several years. As a legislator, he fought for approval of a horse racing pari-mutuel gambling bill for the state. Dooley was the chief proponent and spokesperson of legalized horse racing beginning in 1919, and a law finally passed on May 18, 1934. Later that year, on August 1, Narragansett Park opened for thoroughbred horse racing in Pawtucket. Dooley was appointed racing secretary and in 1938 was named president of the track, a position he held until his death in 1960. Under his leadership, Narragansett Park became one of the most famous and successful horse racing venues in the country.

Laudati, in addition to his part ownership in the Steam Roller, was a real estate developer and promoter of diverse sports ventures. He owned and ran the Peter A. Laudati and Son real estate business in downtown Providence for 60 years until his retirement in 1970. In 1925, with the popularity of bicycle racing, he built and owned the Cycledrome on North Main Street. It became a popular bicycle track from 1925 through 1934 and it was also the home of the Steam Roller during its entire time in the NFL. When bicycle racing lost some of its popularity, he tore down the Cycledrome and built the E.M. Lowe's Drive-In Theatre on the same spot that opened in

Pearce B. Johnson suggested the idea to start a pro football team in Providence to Charles B. Coppen, *Providence Journal* sports editor, leading to the creation of the Steam Roller. Johnson served as assistant general manager for the duration of the franchise's existence (author's collection).

1937. It was the third drive-in theater in the country and the first that used large amplifiers for sound.

Laudati also built the former Kinsley Park in 1921. The facility was the home of the Steam Roller during its independent pro seasons of 1921–1924; the Providence Grays of baseball's Eastern League called it home in the 1930s. Laudati also attracted Babe Ruth and Lou Gehrig to play an exhibition game at the park in 1927.

Providence's new football franchise was in good hands with this high-quality ownership group. Coppen and his partners were serious about putting a competitive team on the field. The players were paid right from the outset as the Steam Roller compensated its head coach $10 per game, the backfield players $5, and the linemen $2.50. As Johnson said, "The players were happy as a lark."[5] This was not big money by any means, but it was extra money for the players, who also worked full-time jobs.

The start-up team played nine games throughout the fall of 1916 with Melrose Park, on Adelaide Avenue, serving as its home field. The park was also the home of the Providence Grays in that era, with Babe Ruth playing for the Boston Red Sox affiliate during part of one season. The first meeting of the football players occurred on September 27 at the *Providence Journal* offices. Some of the players on hand for that first meeting were captain and coach Jack McDonough, Hunk Jordan, George Kowalski, Eric Lee, Dan Mahoney (the only player to play all nine seasons with Providence before the team joined the NFL in 1925), Walter "Pard" Pearce and Everett Robertson.

The team practiced for only a few days prior to the opening game with Fort Adams of Newport, Rhode Island, on September 30. Providence defeated Fort Adams 14–0 in front of 1,000 curious onlookers at Melrose Park. Kowalski, a former University of Notre Dame player, scored the first touchdown in franchise history on a five-yard run that capped off a nine-play, 40-yard drive midway through the first quarter. Pearce, fresh out of Classical High School in Providence, scored the second touchdown on a dazzling 18-yard run on the first play of the fourth quarter.

An interesting note—two players who played in that first-ever game against Fort Adams also played for the NFL version of the Steam Roller in 1925: Pearce and Spike Staff.

The new football team was first named the Providence Professionals, but it picked up a more permanent name completely by accident. Coppen, while getting a hot dog in the concession line, overheard a fan say that Providence's opponent was getting "steamrolled." He loved the idea of that name for his team and immediately ordered the change to Providence Steam Roller. Though the game at which Coppen overheard the conversation is uncertain, it was likely Providence's second game of the season, held on October 7. The Rhode Island squad thrashed Orient Heights from Boston, holder for several years of the New England championship, by a score of 58–0. Shortly after that game, on October 19, the name Steam Roller appeared in the *Providence Journal* in connection with the team for the first time. It was used often when referring to the squad for the rest of its history. Providence was the first team to omit the traditional "s" from the end of its nickname. And Coppen was very staunch about the nickname not being used in a plural form would show his annoyance when it did occur. Therefore, the Steam Roller "paved the way," so to speak, for future sports team nicknames like the New Orleans/Utah Jazz, Tampa Bay Lightning and Colorado Avalanche.

The newly christened Steam Roller finished with a 7–2 record, highlighted by a 7–0 victory over Apponaug on December 9 with the help of eight Syracuse University football players. A week earlier Providence had lost 6–0 against Apponaug when its opponent used nine players from Tufts University. So Coppen thought he would get back at them by signing the Syracuse players. Apponaug again used Tufts players in the rematch, but the Steam Roller prevailed with a little extra help of its own. "In 1916 when we started, there was plenty of gambling. Gambling between this team and ourselves. I think the first game we played in the pool was $1,000. The second game it went to $2,000. That's the time we used the Syracuse boys, and they used the Tufts boys. Yes, that's the only time, truly, that I ever saw it. I knew it existed," Pearce B. Johnson said in a 1991 NFL Films interview.[6]

A department store in Providence, the Outlet Company, sponsored the team in 1917 and supplied uniforms and equipment. Instead of being called the Providence Steam Roller, the team formally adopted the name of the department store and was known as the Outlet Steam Roller. This was not an unusual practice in 1917. Many independent pro teams adopted the names of their company sponsors. And even when the NFL was formed, two teams' nicknames were their original company sponsors—the Green Bay Packers and Decatur Staleys. The Packers' name came from the original sponsor of the team in 1919, the Indian Packing Company. When they were later bought out by Acme Packing, the Packers name continued to be used to promote the new company. The Decatur Staleys' nickname came from Staley Starch Company in Decatur, Illinois, as it sponsored the team in its earliest years until the team's move to Chicago in the early 1920s. There they were renamed the Bears.

The Outlet Steam Roller, coached by former Brown University player Spike Staff and assisted by former Brown star Fritz Pollard, finished with a 5–3–1 record. Pollard became the first Black assistant football coach in professional football history and in 1921 he became the first Black head coach in NFL history when he co-coached the Akron Pros with Elgie

One. Before the NFL Came to Providence

Tobin. The Steam Roller's loss to American Chain of Bridgeport, Connecticut, by a score of 21–2 on November 25 enabled the Chain to claim the 1917 mythical New England championship. The Chain would be a nemesis to the Steam Roller for years to come.

With World War I still raging in Europe and many American young men fighting in the war, the Steam Roller played only two games in 1918 before calling off the season, finishing with a 1–1 record. The team had all but one player from 1917 serving in the military.

In 1919 and 1920, the Steam Roller played somewhat as a vagabond team, with five different home parks (Berkeley Oval in Massachusetts, Hope Field in Providence, Melrose Park in Providence, Weston Field in Cranston and the Clinton Oval in Woonsocket). Providence finished with a 6–2 record in 1919, highlighted by wins over Roslindale American Legion twice (19–0 and 7–0), the Cambridge A.A. Bulldogs (12–6) and the Dorchester American Legion. The Steam Roller's two losses were both inflicted by one of the best teams in the Northeast, the Williams team from New Haven, Connecticut, by 34–0 and 20–0 scores. The 1920 version of the Rollers was known as the "Scoreless Wonders" as the team never scored a point in its six games, finishing with a 0–2–4 record. The highlight of the season was a 0–0 tie with Clay Hills of Connecticut. The *Hartford Courant* reported that the game was "one of the best and cleanest football games ever seen here."[7] Pieri, longtime owner of the Rhode Island Auditorium, played on the 1920 team.

Part-owner Laudati had had enough of his team's vagabond ways at this point and built a stadium in 1921 at the corner of Kinsley Avenue and Acorn Street, across from the Nicholson File Company Mill Complex, in Providence. It was called Kinsley Park. This became the home for the Steam Roller and also played host to the Providence Grays baseball team and an American Soccer League squad, the Providence Clamdiggers/Gold Bugs. Despite the new digs, the Steam Roller finished with a 2–3–3 record for 1921. It defeated Quincy Athletic Association 7–0 on November 6 and a week later beat Pawtuxet 6–0 for its only two victories.

The Steam Roller started to become a Northeast powerhouse in 1922, finishing the season with an 8–2–2 record. Providence had an impressive win over Bridgeport (American Chain), 22–3, their first in six years over the perennial power; a 7–0 win over a quality New Britain, Connecticut, squad; and easy victories over several teams—the Ambulance quintet of Pawtucket 35–7, the Torpedo Station 27–6, Quincy A.A. 28–0 and the Harris A.C. team of Worcester, Massachusetts, 35–7. The Steam Roller also battled the impressive Cleveland Panthers to a scoreless tie in front of 7,000 on Thanksgiving Day at Kinsley Park.

The Steam Roller made sports history on October 1, 1922, when the team participated in the first-ever professional baseball-football doubleheader. At Kinsley Park, the baseball Boston Tigers played the Providence Colored All Stars for the colored baseball title of New England. It was Game 3 after each team had won a game. The Colored All Stars defeated the Tigers 5–3. Immediately following the baseball game, the Steam Roller hosted the Newport Torpedo Station in a professional football game. The hard-fought contest ended in a 0–0 tie.

Providence continued to upgrade its schedule and its roster for the 1923 season. The Steam Roller sported an overall 12–1 record, allowing only 19 points. Its only loss was at Bridgeport in a 3–0 defensive battle. But four weeks later, Providence bested the once-beaten Bridgeport squad 16–0 before 4,000 at Kinsley Park to lay claim to the professional football championship of New England.

The Steam Roller also had impressive victories over Boston Fitton A.C. 13–0 and Williams of New Haven 16–0, two wins over New Britain by scores of 10–7 and 10–0 and a 33–3 beatdown of All-Hartford. The Providence squad was led by Chick Burke, 1922 Dartmouth captain; Dutch Connor, 1921 New Hampshire College captain; Archie Golembeski, former Holy Cross star; Burt Shurtleff; Joe Braney; Pinky Lester; local schoolboy star Swede Vreeland; and future Baseball Hall of Famer Mickey Cochrane.

Cochrane did not play with the Roller in 1924, as instead he cast his lot with Portland of baseball's Pacific Coast League. He played so well for the Beavers that his minor league baseball contract was purchased by the Philadelphia Athletics on November 17, 1924, and he made his major league debut in 1925. After a sterling 13-year career, he was enshrined in the Baseball Hall of Fame in 1947.

At the NFL's 1924 summer league meetings, Providence made an inquiry to become a member of the league in 1925. The NFL was inclined to grant a franchise, knowing that Providence had a solid squad, but wanted to know whether the fan support would be good enough. The Steam Roller responded by significantly upgrading its schedule for the 1924 season, adding games with six NFL teams. (Such games between NFL and non-league teams were fairly common in those days.) The ownership group thought that would help show the franchise's ability to be successful both on the field and at the gate, as five of the NFL opponents would be coming to Providence to play.

Braney, a former college player at Fordham and Syracuse, became the Steam Roller's player-coach. The team's roster was dotted with several former local college stars, including Curly Oden, Shurtleff, Jack Spellman, Staff and Fred Sweet—all from Brown—Joe Kozlowsky from Boston College and Golembeski from Holy Cross. They were joined by players from other northeastern schools including Burke of Dartmouth, Connor of

One. Before the NFL Came to Providence

New Hampshire and Jim Laird of Colgate. All 11 of these players played key roles on the 1924 Steam Roller squad and would help the team transition into the NFL in 1925.

Braney's forces warmed up for the season by winning their first two games against overmatched opponents. They defeated Newport Naval Training Station 66–0 and South Weymouth, Massachusetts, by a 53–0 count. The Steam Roller then reeled off three consecutive impressive wins over perennial high-quality opponents before playing its first NFL team.

Providence defeated the New Haven Blues 21–0 on October 5, as the defense held the opposition to only one first down. A week later at Fenway Park in Boston, the Steam Roller defeated Pere Marquette 7–0 on a 60-yard punt return touchdown by Oden. A day later, Providence beat its nemesis, Bridgeport American Chain, 13–0. Dave Mullen recovered a fumble in the end zone and Laird scored on a short run to account for the two touchdowns, while the defense stymied the Bridgeport attack.

The 5–0 Steam Roller hosted the NFL's Columbus Panhandles on October 19 at Kinsley Park in its first battle against a big-league squad. The Panhandles, led by quarterback Sonny Winters, posed a real challenge for the home team. But the Providence defense rose to the occasion and shut out the Panhandles in front of 6,000 fans. However, the size of the Columbus defensive line at times overwhelmed the Roller offense and it was held scoreless as the game ended in a 0–0 tie. Providence gained nine first downs to seven for the visitors. Shurtleff's late-fourth-quarter interception, his second of the game, off Winters halted the final scoring chance for the Panhandles and secured the tie for the Steam Roller.

It wasn't a bad outcome for Providence. "Capt. Braney's stalwarts deserve no end of praise for the great fight which they made against a team crowded with stars who have made football history on gridirons in the Middle West. If the Steam Roller had an arena with adequate seating capacity for crowds of from 10,000 to 20,000 persons ... the management could berth the eleven in the National League and operate on a far more extensive scale," reported the *Providence Journal*.[8] Columbus would finish its NFL schedule with a 4–4 record.

The Steam Roller starting lineup for the first-ever game played in Providence against an NFL opponent was:

LE—Pinky Lester
LT—Jack Spellman
LG—Firpo Avedesian
C—Bert Shurtleff
RG—Joe Braney
RT—Dave Mullen

RE—Bulger Lowe
QB—Curly Oden
LH—Jim Laird
RH—Swede Vreeland
FB—Babe Tonry

The following week, Providence traveled to Frankford, Pennsylvania, to play one of the NFL's best teams. (Frankford is now part of the city of Philadelphia.) The Yellow Jackets jumped on the Steam Roller right from the outset by scoring three first-quarter touchdowns, all climaxing long drives against the normally strong Providence defense. The Roller settled down after that and shut out the Yellow Jackets the rest of the way while putting up 10 points of their own. Dutch Connor kicked a second-quarter field goal and Bulger Lowe returned a fumble in the fourth quarter for a touchdown to account for the Providence points. The final score was a respectable 21–10 defeat.

The following day, the Steam Roller returned to playing independent and semipro teams and easily handled the Newark Field Club, 25–0, behind touchdown runs by Laird, Connor and Howard Clarke with an Oden-to-Pinky Lester pass mixed in. The New London Submarine Base fell to the Steam Roller 17–0 a week later as Providence prepared for three straight games against NFL opponents.

The Rochester Jeffersons came to Kinsley Park on November 9 with an NFL record of 0–5 (they would finish the season in last place at 0–7). The game was a real dogfight and for three quarters neither team could score. But in the final period, the Steam Roller put together its best drive of the day and moved deep into Jeffersons territory. Providence was stopped short of the goal line, but Connor booted a 30-yard field goal with four minutes remaining and the Roller defense held Rochester at bay for the remainder of the contest. Providence had its first win over an NFL team, a hard-fought 3–0 verdict.

The next week, the Steam Roller hosted the winless Minneapolis Marines (0–6), and this game was no contest. Providence built a 9–0 first-half lead behind Connor's field goal and Oden's touchdown pass to Lowe. The Steam Roller exploded in the third quarter, putting up a team record of 34 points. It scored five touchdowns in a seven-minute span. Lester returned a fumble for a score to start the outburst. Then in rapid succession Bunny Corcoran scored on a short run, Oden tossed a touchdown pass to Laird, Connor followed suit with a beautiful pass to Laird and Oden finished the onslaught with his specialty, a 55-yard punt return. Lester added a fourth-quarter touchdown run to conclude the scoring in a stunning 49–0 victory. "That third period yesterday will ever remain vivid in the memories of the thousands who sat in on the game. Nothing like it has ever been witnessed at Kinsley Park and it is extremely doubtful if as much real live football action has ever been crowded into such short space of time in any previous game in this city," the *Providence Journal* reported.[9]

The following week, in front of a capacity crowd of 7,500, the Steam Roller played a rematch with Frankford at Kinsley Park. The Yellow Jackets, who would finish the NFL season in third place with an 11–2–1 record, fell behind the feisty Steam Roller 3–0 in the second quarter and went to the half trailing the underdogs 3–2. But Providence could not fully contain the Yellow Jackets in the second half. Star fullback Tex Hamer scored two touchdowns, one on a short plunge and the other on a 35-yard run, as Frankford pulled away for a 16–3 victory. Providence might have lost to Frankford, but it had beaten two NFL teams in consecutive weeks and proved it could play in the best league in football.

On Thanksgiving Day, Providence lost a tough game to a touring team from Cleveland by a 6–5 count. The Steam Roller led throughout the game, thanks to a second-quarter field goal by Connor and a safety on a bad snap. But the Panthers scored on a long pass late in the game to take the lead. Providence responded with a drive into field goal range, but Connor missed the kick and the Roller was defeated.

Three days later, the Steam Roller hosted its final NFL opponent of 1924 with a game against the Dayton Triangles. Providence started slowly but Dayton kicker Russ Hathaway missed two field goals. The Steam Roller righted the ship in the second quarter and Connor hit a 20-yard field goal to give the home team a 3–0 lead. Dayton put together a drive deep into Providence territory, but Lester intercepted a Gus Redman pass at the Roller's 23-yard line and raced 77 yards for a score. With Connor's extra point, the Steam Roller led 10–0. Late in the game, Triangles end Frank Bacon hauled in a 35-yard touchdown pass from Ken Huffine to cut the Providence lead to 10–7. With less than five minutes remaining, Dayton was on the move again, but its final scoring opportunity was thwarted as Laird intercepted a Triangle pass. The Steam Roller ran out the clock to secure the hard-fought victory.

Providence finished the NFL portion of its schedule with an impressive 3–2–1 record. Now the team needed to finish the season with victories over Pere Marquette and the Waterbury Blues, both regional powers, to claim the Northeast championship.

On a cold, crisp December day, more than 9,000 fans packed Kinsley Park as the Steam Roller hosted Pere Marquette. The home team delighted the fans early with a first-quarter scoring drive. Former NFLer Bunny Corcoran finished the drive with a short run for the touchdown and a 7–0

Roller lead. Later in the quarter, a Pere Marquette player scooped up a Laird fumble and rambled 14 yards for a touchdown. The point-after failed and the Roller held a slim 7–6 lead. That score held until the final quarter, when the Steam Roller's offense scored on an Oden short run. Then a few plays later, Golembeski intercepted a Pere pass and returned it 60 yards for the clinching touchdown. Providence claimed a 20–6 victory at game's end.

One week later, with 6,000 braving the freezing cold at Kinsley Park, a defensive struggle against the Waterbury Blues took place. The Steam Roller's defense scored the game's only touchdown, as Lester fell on a blocked punt in the end zone to give Providence a 6–0 lead in the second quarter. The Blues penetrated deep into Providence territory on multiple occasions but were turned back each time, either by fumbling or by the Steam Roller's stout defensive line play. Connor added an insurance field goal in the fourth quarter as Providence defeated Waterbury 9–0.

Providence finished with a 12–3–1 overall record with its 3–2–1 NFL slate included and was the undisputed Northeast champions.

During the offseason, the Steam Roller hired current player, former Holy Cross standout and Providence College head coach Archie Golembeski to be its head coach on February 17, 1925, as the team prepared to enter the NFL, though it had not yet been officially granted a franchise.

It was clear that Providence had become one of the best squads in the Northeast and a regional power. "The team's success was enough to make Steam Roller management and fans start thinking about a bigger championship—the championship of the NFL, for instance. And sure enough, Providence joined the big league for the 1925 season," wrote football historian Bob Gill.[10]

On August 1, the official word came from the league meeting in Chicago that four new teams were to be added to the NFL for the 1925 season. In addition to Providence, the cities of Detroit, New York and Pottsville (PA) were granted franchises. Detroit became the Panthers, the New York team took the name of the Giants and Pottsville became the Maroons. The four new teams brought the number of clubs in the NFL to 20. The growing city of Providence had its first major professional sports team in one of the big four American sports leagues.

The Cycledrome

Meanwhile, to effectively compete in the NFL, Providence needed a larger venue than Kinsley Park, and Laudati made sure that would not be a problem. Laudati had already begun to build a new stadium that would be

One. Before the NFL Came to Providence

The Providence Cycledrome, home of the Providence Steam Roller from 1925 to 1931 (courtesy Pro Football Hall of Fame).

ready in the spring of 1925. Though its primary use would be for the popular sport of bicycle racing, the Steam Roller's co-owner knew it could be adapted for the football team if the city was granted an NFL franchise. Once Providence's application was approved, the venue was ready to accommodate the team.

The Steam Roller called the Cycledrome on North Main Street in Providence its home stadium for all seven years of its time in the NFL. The Steam Roller played 57 NFL games and 18 other games in the Cycledrome. Providence was the first team in NFL history to call a cycling arena its home stadium, and only the Hartford Blues for a single season in 1926 ever played in a similar home arena.

The Cycledrome was built in the winter and spring of 1925. At the time of its construction, it was the largest and fastest bicycle track in the country. The track was five laps to the mile with the distance around the track on the pole at 1,056 feet, while the circumference at the top of the bowl was 1,400 feet. The stands had a seating capacity of 12,000. The stadium was built on the Providence/Pawtucket city line. That made the stadium easily accessible for fans, as both city's transit lines ran close to the new facility.

The oval inside the riding surface fit a football field with plenty of room for spectators on the sidelines. However, with the steep banks of the track, one of the end zones was only five yards deep. During construction, more than 400,000 feet of lumber was used; most of it was high-quality spruce from Saskatchewan, Canada.

The venue was easily accessible by streetcar and had plenty of parking for automobiles, as sales of those vehicles were increasing dramatically during the decade. Once at the site, the entrance into the stadium featured long, wide promenades with an occasional flight of stairs to the ticket office. The entrance to the track inside was on a level with the top of the bowl. The fans entered their seats by walking around a broad promenade until they found their section. This new method eliminated a great deal of congestion that had been found in prior stadium designs. The scoreboard was simple, and the facility had a no-frills press box.

The stadium was ideally suited for fans with easy entry and exit, and all the seats in the arena were close to the field and provided excellent sightlines. The Steam Roller ownership even provided halftime entertainment that included Happy Stanley, known as "Mr. Banjo," who at the time was billed as the "No. 1 entertainer in the state."[11]

The stadium hosted the best bicycle racing in the country that brought the top cyclists from all over the United States. The facility also was used for high school football games, professional soccer matches of the Providence Clam Diggers, boxing matches, concerts and several other forms of entertainment. It was the place to go in Providence during this time period.

Charles Turville managed the venue's construction for Laudati. It cost $100,000 to build. He also became the Cycledrome's manager after it was completed and did all the planning and booking of events that helped make it successful. Turville brought a lot of experience from his time managing the Cranston, Rhode Island, cycledrome before it closed in 1924.

The stadium was originally scheduled to open Memorial Day weekend, but some poor weather had caused construction delays and a heavy rainstorm postponed the opening until June 2. A bicycle race to open the stadium drew more than 9,000 on that Tuesday night. The featured race was a 30-miler won by Belgian superstar Charles Verkeyn. The opening was an eagerly anticipated event. The atmosphere was described by the *Providence Journal* this way:

> It was a big night on North Main Street last night—the biggest that thoroughfare has seen in years. The Cycledrome opened, and there was bicycle racing, passing of floral tributes, band concert, singing and excitement galore. More than 9,000 persons from Massachusetts, Connecticut, and these plantations gathered to give "the largest bicycle track in America" a rousing send-off. It was a grand and glorious opening and everybody was happy because the racing was of high quality, marked with close finishes and fairly sizzling with brushes. The night passed all too quickly, and the classic of the evening, the motor-paced race, was over before the crowd realized that a great card of sport had consumed three hours.[12]

One. Before the NFL Came to Providence

The following night a boxing card featuring four fights brought an excellent crowd to the new arena. Babe Herman of California won an unpopular decision over Tommy (Kid) Murphy of Trenton in the feature fight. Following the decision, a stunned Murphy ran after the referee and punched him in the back of the head. With the crowd threatening further violence, the referee was safely whisked out of the arena by friends. The evening continued with Round House Wilson of New Bedford, Young Tiernan of Providence and Frankie Spicer of Newport each winning the other fights on the card.

Bicycle races were conducted regularly at the "Drome" on Tuesday and Friday nights with tickets priced cheaply at 50 cents for general admission and $1.10 for grandstand seats.

The first Steam Roller game played at the Cycledrome was on September 20, 1925, a preseason contest against the West Point Field Artillery. In a stunning display of offense, the Steam Roller piled up a 127–0 victory behind the quarterback play of one of Notre Dame's legendary "Four Horsemen," Harry Stuhldreher, and the running of diminutive speedster Cy Wentworth.

The Steam Roller hosted the first NFL game at the park on October 11, against the New York Giants, before 8,000 excited fans. Ticket prices for Roller games ranged from $.50 to $2.00. Bleacher seats were $.50 or $1.00 and grandstand seats were $1.50 or $2.00, depending on the location. All the seats had good sightlines and the stadium had an intimate feel.

The Cycledrome became a significant home-field advantage for the Steam Roller. The team consistently drew excellent crowds until the Depression took its toll years later, and the fans sat very close to the action. During games, temporary seating was installed on the straightaway portion of the track, which was so close to the field that players often found themselves in the stands after being tackled.

The stadium did not have a public address system in 1925. "An announcer walked the sideline shouting the score, substitutions, and down-and-distance details through a megaphone," John Eisenberg described in his book *The League*.[13] Also, the locker rooms were not ideal. The home locker room was built for cyclists and not for 200-plus-pound football players. Players had to take turns dressing, as the space equaled the size of two phone booths. There were no visiting locker rooms, which meant opposing teams had to dress at their hotel and arrive at the stadium ready to play. That certainly was an advantage for the home team.

With solid ownership, a great place to play, a head coach hired, a solid team of holdover players ready for play and an NFL franchise granted, Providence was ready to step into the big leagues of American sports.

Chapter Two

The Early Years (1925–1927)

1925—The Inaugural Season

Soon after the announcement came that Providence had a team in the National Football League for 1925, the schedule of the Steam Roller's games was released. The *Providence Journal* hailed it with these words: "The Steam Roller club of Providence ... has been given one of the most attractive schedules allotted to any club in the organization."[1] The team's schedule was highlighted with home-and-home series with the Frankford Yellow Jackets (third-place finish in 1924), the Pottsville Maroons (a new team along with Providence) and the New York Giants (another new team), including hosting the Giants in the home opener on October 11. Providence also would host the defending NFL champion Cleveland Bulldogs among their eight games scheduled at the Cycledrome. Providence's initial NFL game was scheduled for October 3 in Frankford, Pennsylvania, against the Yellow Jackets.

The NFL team owners concluded their two-day meeting on August 2 with optimism about the future of the league with 20 teams in the fold. NFL president Joe F. Carr predicted a banner season for the league. "The addition of New York, Providence, Detroit and Pottsville will greatly strengthen our circuit," Carr said. "As in past years, Philadelphia will have a fast team. Great things are promised from New York and I think the Providence Steam Rollers [sic] and Pottsville Maroons will win a lot of games."[2]

With the Steam Roller's NFL schedule finalized, the team added two tune-up games against the West Point Field Artillery on September 20 and against the New London Sub-Base the following week. Both games were scheduled for the Cycledrome.

While the schedule was being completed, Coppen, Golembeski and Johnson were working to add players to the roster to upgrade the squad. In the backfield the Steam Roller added Cy Wentworth and Al McIntosh to go along with returning starters Curly Oden and Jim Laird. Wentworth starred at the University of New Hampshire in 1924,

Two. The Early Years (1925–1927)

finishing third in the country in scoring. McIntosh joined the Steam Roller after lettering at the University of Rhode Island for two seasons.

Providence returned Joe Braney, Joe Kozlowsky, Bert Shurtleff, Jack Spellman and Golembeski on its offensive and defensive lines. But the management trio added five quality players to the mix up front. The front office added Franny Garvey, whom Golembeski recruited from his Holy Cross alma mater; Mike Gulian, a six-foot, 200-pound brawler, and bruising middle guard Dolph Eckstein, both from local Brown University; and Dartmouth star Red Maloney. The team also added Nate Share, from Tufts University, to help on both lines and in the kick return game.

The Steam Roller liked the pedigree of championship wrestlers for its line play. Three of the team's linemen fit that bill and were among the greatest wrestlers in the history of intercollegiate athletics. Spellman was captain of the Brown football and wrestling squads in 1923 and won the US Olympic Trials before heading to Paris to capture the gold medal in 1924. Shurtleff, an All-East center at Brown, won the New England wrestling championship as a junior. Eckstein, whom many consider the greatest center in Brown history, won the intercollegiate wrestling championship twice and made the finals at the Olympic Trials before losing. With the strength and athleticism of these three stalwarts and with the addition of the other new players, Providence was in good shape in the trenches.

Providence Steam Roller vs. New York Giants program from the Steam Roller's first NFL home game played at the Providence Cycledrome on October 11, 1925. The Steam Roller defeated the Giants 14–0 (courtesy Rhode Island Historical Society—RHi X17 4831)

Local Brown University was an important conduit of players to the Steam Roller (18 Brown players would suit up for Providence) during its NFL years. Throughout the 1910s and 1920s, the Bears were a football program of national prominence. Brown appeared in the 1916 Rose Bowl and its Iron Men team of 1926 went undefeated. Head Coach Edward N. Robinson steered the school for 24 years, compiling a 140–82–12 record. He was followed in 1926 by Tuss McLaughry, who led the Bears to the greatest season in school history with the 1926 squad and finished with a 76–68–5 record when he left the program after the 1940 season. Brown drew excellent crowds to Andrews Field from 1899 to 1924, and then the current-day Brown University Field was opened in 1925. The prominence of the Bears football program at that time was helpful in convincing Steam Roller ownership back to 1916 and again in 1925 that pro football in Providence was a viable venture and could tap into some of these players and the football fans of Brown.

Before the 1925 season began, Coppen predicted that Providence was "going to surprise a lot of the squads in Prexy Carr's grid circuit."[3] With all the new additions, the team was ready to take that next step and compete in the NFL. But Coppen had one more major move up his sleeve.

As the Steam Roller was preparing for its preseason game against the West Point Artillery, Coppen brought headline news to his team. On September 18 it was announced that Providence had signed University of Notre Dame star Harry Stuhldreher to a contract worth $5,000, a significant sum at the time. Stuhldreher was one of the famed "Four Horsemen" who had led Notre Dame to an undefeated season in 1924 and the college national championship, while earning first-team All-American honors. That signing gave the Steam Roller instant credibility across the NFL and beyond.

The Cycledrome was buzzing with excitement on September 20 as 6,500 came to see the new version of the Steam Roller. The team did not disappoint. From the opening kickoff it was all Providence. West Point went three and out on its first possession and punted to Wentworth. The speedy back caught the ball at his 45-yard line and weaved his way through the Artillery defense all the way to paydirt. Dutch Connor booted the extra point for a quick 7–0 lead. Connor then intercepted a West Point pass and returned it to the Artillery 25-yard line. A couple of plays later, he romped into the end zone for a touchdown. From there Providence kept scoring and scoring. Chick Burke dashed around right end for a touchdown, Wentworth sprinted 56 yards for a score, Burke again scored on a 43-yard run and Connor bulled in from five yards out. The first period ended with the Steam Roller in command, 41–0.

Though the Artillery was game and played hard, it had no chance and

Two. The Early Years (1925–1927)

offered little resistance. It seemed no matter what the Steam Roller did, it ended up in the end zone. The final score was 127–0 in favor of the home team.

Wentworth led the Providence attack with six touchdowns in his pro debut. "Red" O'Neill, a fullback from the University of Connecticut, scored three touchdowns, with Burke, Connor and Al McIntosh contributing two each. O'Neill was cut before the opening NFL game. Stuhldreher, despite not scoring a touchdown, was lauded for his performance. He directed the offense and mixed some precision passes to complement the powerful running game. As the *Providence Journal* reported, "He showed himself to be one of the finest performers ever to appear on a Providence gridiron."[4] The only negative coming out of the game was that Oden suffered a shoulder injury and was lost to the team for the first four weeks of the regular season.

The joy of the victory faded quickly. Stuhldreher was offered a $7,500 contract by the Waterbury Blues (an independent team) with an additional $500 bonus. After the Artillery game he demanded an increase in pay, saying to Coppen, "From now on it'll be $500 (per game)."[5] Coppen retorted with, "From now on you're out!"[6] The Steam Roller released Stuhldreher on September 21 and off he went, having played only the one exhibition game for Providence. Coppen reacted immediately. He signed Holy Cross captain and three-sport standout Hop Riopel two days later.

Providence's next scheduled game with the New London Sub-Base on September 27 was canceled because of the accidental sinking of submarine S-51. The merchant steamship *City of Rome* collided with the S-51 off Block Island, leading to its tragic sinking. There were 36 onboard and 33 perished. The city of Providence mourned the loss of so many of the crew.

The Steam Roller scheduled a replacement opponent for the next day, September 28. The Stamford All-Collegians were scheduled to play, but five of the team's players were severely shaken and bruised from an automobile accident on the way to the game. None of the players were seriously injured, but they were unable to get to the game in time for it to be played.

The Steam Roller, after the unexpected week off, opened its NFL regular-season schedule on October 3 at Frankford Stadium in Philadelphia, against the Frankford Yellow Jackets. They were a formidable opponent. The Jackets had finished in third place in 1924 with an impressive 11–2–1 record and were led by player-coach Guy Chamberlin and Tex Hamer, a former Penn captain. Hamer was not new to the Steam Roller. He had played a key role in each of the Yellow Jackets' victories over Providence in 1924, with one touchdown pass and two rushing scores.

Providence was missing five starters for the Frankford game because it was played on a Saturday. Each of the five had coaching duties—

Golembeski coached Providence College; Laird was at the University of Norwich; Garvey guided the Holy Cross freshman team; Connor led Farmingdale, Long Island, High School; and Riopel was watching Malden High in Boston. The Saturday game was necessary because of Pennsylvania's blue laws that prohibited professional games, among many other activities, on the Sabbath. But with back-to-back games on Saturday and Sunday (against Pottsville), the five men at least would be fresh for the Pottsville contest.

Here is how the Steam Roller lined up for its first NFL game:

LE—Red Maloney
LT—Jack Spellman
LG—Nate Share
C—Dolph Eckstein
RG—Burt Shurtleff
RT—Joe Kozlowsky
RE—Bulger Lowe
QB—Ching Hammill
RHB—Chick Burke
LHB—Cy Wentworth
FB—Freddy Sweet

The Steam Roller put up a valiant fight, while shorthanded, against the powerful Yellow Jackets before 12,000 boisterous fans. Frankford scored first only five minutes into the game. Providence was forced to punt from inside its 10-yard line. Freddy Sweet attempted the punt, but the pass from center was slow and he bobbled the ball for an instant. That gave Chamberlin enough time to block the kick. The rangy lineman fell on the loose ball in the end zone for a touchdown. Frankford converted the placement and led 7–0.

The Steam Roller had scoring opportunities in the second and third quarters but was turned away by the Frankford defense, with Hamer making several key plays to frustrate the Roller. The Providence defense kept it in the game, consistently thwarting the Yellow Jackets' attack. The Steam Roller's best scoring chance came late in the game while still trailing only 7–0. Wentworth received a Frankford punt at midfield and weaved through the Yellow Jackets' defense all the way to the five-yard line. Hamer made a touchdown-saving tackle on the nifty scatback to keep Providence out of the end zone. The Steam Roller failed to move the ball on its first three downs and faced fourth and goal from the Frankford six-yard line. On fourth down, Wentworth spotted Spellman in the end zone and threw a pass toward the lanky end. But, seemingly out of nowhere came the

Two. The Early Years (1925–1927)

Steam Roller's nemesis, Hamer, to knock the ball away and secure the victory for the Yellow Jackets.

Golembeski's warriors did not have much time to lick their wounds or heal their scars as they traveled by train immediately after the game to Pottsville to battle the Maroons at Minersville Park the next day. The four-hour train ride did not leave much time for the Steam Roller to rest before it hit the gridiron again.

Pottsville, led by hard-charging running back Tony Latone, was fresh off a 28–0 win over the Buffalo All-Americans the week before and was ready for a stiff test against Providence. The game had been hyped as a clash of titans, Latone vs. gold medal wrestling champion Spellman. Spellman had posed "for his pregame publicity shots in his three-point stance with his tongue hanging out like a junkyard dog waiting on a juicy steak bone," David Fleming wrote in his book *Breaker Boys*.[7] Despite the back-to-back games, the Steam Roller defense performed well. Though Pottsville rolled up 15 first downs despite a heavy downpour that turned the field into a swamp, the Roller defense kept the Maroons at bay. Latone contributed many superb runs but Providence kept Pottsville bottled up between the 30s and forced a couple of key turnovers.

The Steam Roller had trouble moving the ball, converting only five first downs, as the mud kept Wentworth from using his speed and elusiveness to full benefit. The first half was scoreless. But Providence broke through on the first play of the third quarter. Pottsville fullback Barney Wentz fumbled the snap from center and the Steam Roller's Red Maloney scooped the football out of the mud and toted it 40 yards for a touchdown. The *Pottsville Republican* described the play: "As the mud-spattered oval bounded over the muck, Maloney scooped up the ball, took a short gallop, and planted it behind the goal post for a touchdown, and that was all there was to it."[8] The point-after kick failed but Providence had a surprising 6–0 lead. The touchdown by Maloney was the first NFL score in franchise history for the Steam Roller.

Riopel made his Providence debut and played well. He had two key interceptions in the fourth quarter to derail Maroon drives and was the team's best offensive weapon. Connor punted extremely well throughout the game as Providence played the field position game. But the contest was won by the defense. Not only did the unit score the game's only points, but it also continually stymied a bigger and stronger Pottsville team with outstanding play from Eckstein, Garvey, Kozlowsky and Spellman. When Golembeski knocked down a pass deep in Steam Roller territory in the final minute and then Riopel intercepted the ball on the next play, Providence had secured its first victory as an NFL franchise, 6–0. The *Republican* reported, "That Pottsville should have won, there is no doubt. The

Maroons outplayed them in almost every department; it was just the one break of the game that gave the Rhode Island guys a victory."[9] Pottsville would lose only one more game for the remainder of the season as it finished with a 10–2 record.

The Steam Roller returned to Providence and hosted the New York Giants in their home opener at the Cycledrome on October 11. It was the first game for Providence at the stadium playing an NFL opponent as a new member of the league. When the Steam Roller fans opened their game program, on the first page they saw the "Policy of the Steam Roller Football Club. Member of the National Football League."[10] At that instance it hit home that Providence was now playing in the biggest league of professional football. It read, "The policy of the Steam Roller Football Club, is to promote clean, healthful sport; to maintain for the City of Providence a football team that will be a leader in this great American out-door sport. This team is composed of American College stars and will have leading football teams of the country as opponents. Our City will gain added publicity in supporting games that will attract nation-wide attention and be recognized as a promoter of clean sports and recreation."[11] And the ownership group lived up to that policy during the seven-year run of the NFL Steam Roller.

The Giants had an impressive array of star players. The backfield included former Carlisle superstar and Olympic gold medalist Jim Thorpe, Dutch Hendrian of Pittsburgh, ex–Syracuse halfback Jack McBride and ex–Penn State fullback Hinkey Haines. The New Yorkers also had five former All-Americans across their frontline. Despite all the Giants' talent that resulted in a 10–1 edge in first downs, Providence created two scoring opportunities that were the difference in the game.

The black-and-orange-clad Roller broke through in the second quarter following two missed field goal attempts by the Giants in the first period. Jack Spellman blocked Thorpe's punt from deep inside Giants' territory and Franny "Stretch" Garvey picked up the loose ball and dived into the end zone for a touchdown. Connor booted the extra point to give Providence a 7–0 lead.

On the ensuing kickoff, with the 8,000 dyed-in-the-wool Steam Roller rooters on their feet and Providence receiving the boot from Thorpe, Wentworth received the ball at his eight-yard line. He proceeded to weave his way through the entire Giants defense on the way to an electrifying 92-yard touchdown. Connor's kick made it 14–0 for the home team and the Steam Roller went into the half in command. Golembeski's troops played conservatively in the second half and turned the game over to the defense. With Spellman, Nate Share, Kozlowsky and Lloyd Young making play after play and Connor's punts pinning the Giants deep in their own territory, Providence cruised to a 14–0 victory for its first official NFL victory at home.

The following week, on October 18, Pottsville was more than ready for its rematch with Providence. The Maroons jumped to a 14–0 second-quarter lead on two misplays by the Roller. Connor fumbled the ball on a running play and Pottsville recovered at the Providence 37. A few plays later, Hoot Flanagan scored the touchdown for the Maroons. Later in the second quarter, Connor had his punt blocked and Pottsville recovered it inside the Providence 10-yard line. One play later, Latone bulled his way in for the touchdown and Pottsville took a 14-point lead to the intermission.

The Steam Roller was unable to penetrate the bigger, stronger front wall of the Pottsville defense and could not score. The Maroons added three fourth-quarter touchdowns to salt the game away. Flanagan and Latone each scored a second touchdown and Wentz, who played brilliantly all day, scored a touchdown as well. Pottsville completely manhandled the smaller Steam Roller by a final score of 34–0. The Associated Press reported, "Baring a powerful line plunging attack with an aerial system that was well-nigh invincible, the Pottsville Maroons gained a sweet revenge over the steam rolling team of this city by trouncing the Juggernauts by a 34–0 score. A crowd of more than 10,000 witnessed the struggle, including a large delegation of Pottsville rooters. The outcome of the game was never in doubt."[12]

The Pottsville game was Dutch Connor's last with Providence. He had other work interests that conflicted with the Steam Roller's practice schedule and he was unable to make it work for the remainder of the season. A week later he signed a contract to play for All-New Britain in New Britain, Connecticut.

Providence was scheduled to play the Columbus Tigers on October 25, but the game

Cartoon inside the Providence Steam Roller vs. New York Giants program from October 11, 1925, touting the first-ever game between the two teams (courtesy Rhode Island Historical Society—RHi X17 4832).

was postponed due to a misunderstanding between the officials at the Cycledrome and the teams. The fans had already arrived and the teams were prepared to play, but to no avail without any officials available. That gave the Steam Roller an extra week to reassess its offense and prepare for the Rochester Jeffersons. Despite winning two of its first four NFL games, Providence was still looking for its first offensive touchdown. The team had scored three touchdowns in those four games, two on blocked punts and one on a kickoff return, but no scores were generated by the offense.

The Steam Roller offense finally broke through on November 1 against Rochester, scoring a touchdown and gaining 15 first downs. But it was the defense that set the tone for the game. The Jeffersons started a drive deep in their own territory at the beginning of the second quarter. Rochester wingback Shag Sheard fumbled a pitchout from Lou Smyth. Sheard fell on the loose ball in his own end zone and several Roller defenders pounced on him to record a safety. On Rochester's next series, the Roller defense held the Jeffersons in check and forced a punt. Sheard attempted the kick from inside his 30-yard line but Young broke through for Providence and blocked it. Spellman picked up the loose ball and raced into the end zone for a touchdown and an 8–0 Providence lead.

In the third quarter, the Steam Roller began a drive at its own 15-yard line. Wentworth broke free for a 40-yard run, and from there Providence quickly moved the ball to the Rochester 19-yard line. On the next play, Curly Oden lateraled the ball to Wentworth and he sprinted down the left side untouched for the first offensive touchdown scored by the Steam Roller. Providence dominated the fourth quarter, racking up eight of its 15 first downs and adding a 15-yard field goal by Freddy Sweet for the 17–0 victory.

The next week, Providence hosted another team from Western New York: the Buffalo Bisons, who were coached by Walter Koppisch. In the pouring rain, Providence defeated the 1-4-2 Bisons by a 10–0 score. All of the Steam Roller's points came in the fourth quarter, following Buffalo miscues. The two teams battled through the first three quarters to a standstill. Neither team could gain much of an advantage over the other.

Early in the fourth quarter with the ball on the Buffalo 10-yard line, Jim Kendrick tried to punt the Bisons out of danger. As he attempted the kick, Kendrick was swarmed under by three Providence defenders and he fumbled the ball. Golembeski alertly jumped on the wet football at the Buffalo eight-yard line. The Steam Roller offense ran Laird on three consecutive plays. He gained two, three and two yards to move the ball down inside the Bisons' one-yard line. Despite being less than a yard away from a touchdown, Golembeski decided to attempt a field goal. Sweet drop-kicked the 12-yard field goal to stake Providence to a 3–0 lead.

Two. The Early Years (1925–1927) 31

Providence Steam Roller vs. Buffalo Bisons game action at the Providence Cycledrome from November 8, 1925. Providence defeated Buffalo 10–0 (*Providence Journal*—USA TODAY NETWORK).

Later in the final quarter, Wentworth punted from his own eight-yard line. Wally Foster tried to field the punt for Buffalo at the Providence 40-yard line but lost his grip on the slippery football. Golembeski scooped it out of the mud and slugged his way for 60 yards and a game-clinching touchdown. Sweet booted the extra point and the Steam Roller went on to the 10–0 victory. The *Providence Journal* reported that the two teams ran 177 plays throughout the game, a tremendous amount at that time. The win raised Providence's NFL record to 4–2 with all the victories by shutout.

The Steam Roller traveled to the New York Polo Grounds on November 15 to take on the Giants. New York entered the game on a four-game winning streak after losing its first three games. A wildly enthusiastic crowd of over 25,000 came to cheer on the Giants. The G-men scored touchdowns in the first and third quarters on a short pass from Jack McBride to Lynn Bomar and a short run by McBride. Providence's Laird booted a 35-yard field goal in the second quarter, but the Steam Roller trailed 13–3 entering the final quarter. Along the way, the Giants also had a big goal-line stand in the second quarter, stopping Providence on fourth down a foot from a touchdown.

Early in the fourth quarter, Laird led the Roller on an impressive 80-yard march and the burly back finished it off with a short touchdown run. His extra point pulled Providence within 13–10. In the closing minutes, Golembeski made a tactical error that cost the Steam Roller the game. Providence had been moving the ball effectively through the air against the Giants defense, but he decided to punt the ball to put New York deep in its own territory. The thinking was that the Roller could obtain excellent field position for a tying field goal or winning touchdown by stopping the Giants' attack and forcing a punt. However, the Giants outsmarted the Providence coach. They took a safety, giving Providence two points but taking the Giants out of danger from having to punt from their own end zone. Instead, New York, punted from its 30-yard line and the Roller ran out of time as the Giants prevailed 13–12 in a highly entertaining game. It was a tough loss for Providence as it had played extremely well. In Golembeski's defense, at that time many times teams punted the ball prior to fourth down to gain a tactical advantage by bottling their opponent in their own end and attempting to gain better field position or forcing a bad play. But in this case the strategy backfired.

The Steam Roller bounced back the following week, on November 22, in front of 14,000 at the Cycledrome with a thrilling 20–7 victory over the Yellow Jackets. Providence got a measure of revenge from the opening-day loss to Frankford. The Roller jumped to a quick first-quarter lead on a touchdown run by Laird. Maloney added a 28-yard field goal in the second quarter that staked Providence to a 10–0 halftime lead. The Steam Roller doubled the lead in the third quarter on a dropkick 17-yard field goal by Maloney, and then Golembeski picked up a Hust Stockton fumble on the Roller's four-yard line and sprinted 96 yards for a touchdown. Frankford scored a fourth-quarter touchdown to avoid a shutout. It was one of the most impressive victories for Providence in its first NFL season and it came in front of the largest crowd in Cycledrome history.

The Steam Roller completed a major personnel move on the day after Thanksgiving. With the Akron Pros' season over, Providence was given permission by the Pros to sign Fritz Pollard for the remainder of the season. Pollard was one of the greatest runners in the game at that time. He had led the Pros to the first league championship in 1920 and was named as a first-team All-Pro. In 1921, Pollard was named co-coach, thus becoming the first Black head coach in the NFL, and led Akron to a 9–3–1 record. The Steam Roller signed Pollard because it had some important games coming up, including tilts against the defending NFL champion Cleveland Bulldogs and the Chicago Bears with superstar Red Grange. When Pollard and Coppen were discussing the star back potentially playing for Providence, Pollard requested to be paid $1,000 per game. Coppen asked, "What makes you think you're worth $1,000 a game?"[13] Pollard's reply was, "Well it's like this. You gentlemen got me made All-American, you're gonna pay me my All-American price!"[14]

On the Sunday following Thanksgiving, Providence tied the defending NFL champion Bulldogs, 7–7, in a fierce battle. Neither team could break through for a score in the first half. Finally in the third quarter Cleveland scored on a beautiful pass from Doc Elliott to first-team All-Pro

Two. The Early Years (1925–1927)

Dave Noble from 19 yards out. The Steam Roller fought back and culminated a 48-yard, fourth-quarter drive with a Laird short run. Maloney kicked the all-important extra point to earn a tie for the Roller. Pollard made his debut with Providence and was lauded for his play by the *Boston Globe*: "The tackling was high for the most part, but there were some good tackles, one especially by Fritz Pollard, the old Brown star who had joined the team after being with Akron."[15]

A couple of days prior to the Steam Roller hosting Curly Lambeau's Green Bay Packers at the Cycledrome for the first time, the details of the Bears versus Providence game were finalized. The game was scheduled for Wednesday, December 9, at Boston Braves Field in Boston. The game was moved to Boston to accommodate a larger crowd than the Cycledrome could manage.

On December 6, the Green Bay Packers beat the Steam Roller 13–10 on a late touchdown by Jim Crowley, another of Notre Dame's fabled "Four Horsemen." Crowley was a thorn in the side of Providence throughout the game and caught a three-yard pass from Charlie Mathys for the game winner. It was the best game of his short professional career. Crowley turned his focus to coaching and is best remembered for leading the "Seven Blocks of Granite" at Fordham.

Providence started strong and took a 7–0 first-quarter lead on a 20-yard touchdown scamper by Wentworth. The score remained the same until the third quarter when Packers defender Eddie Kotal intercepted an ill-advised pass by Pollard and dashed 60 yards for the score. The placement by George Abramson was no good and Providence clung to a 7–6 lead. Early in the fourth quarter, the Roller stretched its lead to 10–6 on a terrific 37-yard field goal by Laird. After the Packers' go-ahead touchdown, Providence had two chances late in the game to score the tying field goal, but it was unable to gain a first down as the game ended.

Immediately following the game, Providence signed Crowley to play in its upcoming game against the Bears. The Steam Roller also signed Crowley's "Four Horsemen" teammate Don Miller for the Chicago game.

The biggest and most anticipated Providence game of the year was played on December 9. It was the first NFL game ever played in the city of Boston. But more important to those in attendance was the fact that the biggest name in all of football was coming to town. Harold "Red" Grange, the superlative running back from the University of Illinois who turned professional in November to launch a barnstorming tour with the Bears, was set to play in Boston for the first time.

Grange had recently completed a spectacular three-year college football career with the Illini. He had been nicknamed the "Galloping Ghost" by Warren Brown of the *Chicago American* for his blinding speed and elusive running ability. Grange scored 34 touchdowns and rushed for 2,071 yards while averaging 5.3 yards per carry while at Illinois. He led the Fighting Illini to the 1923 national championship. He was a three-time consensus All-American and was revered for his performance in the 1924 Michigan game. That game was the grand opening of Illinois's Memorial Stadium. Grange returned the opening kickoff 95 yards for a touchdown. He scored three more touchdowns of 67, 56 and 44 yards before the first quarter was over. Later in the game he added another touchdown run and a touchdown pass in the Illini's 39–14 whipping of the Wolverines. From there Grange's legend grew as he became by far the most popular player the sport had seen.

He signed a professional contract shortly after his college season ended. At first, "The public loudly proclaimed distain over the betrayal of their folk hero (Grange), blaming the pros as well as Grange. ... Fans cursed him for becoming contaminated with an unnatural professionalism."[16] However, the subsequent 10-game barnstorming tour drew enormous publicity for professional football. The tour began on November 26 at Wrigley Field in Chicago and the Providence game was the seventh game of the series. The Bears had won five of the six with a tie in the other game, while drawing 187,000 spectators. But this would be the Bears' seventh game in only 14 days. By the time the team arrived in Boston they were a tired, tattered and bruised bunch. "The Bears

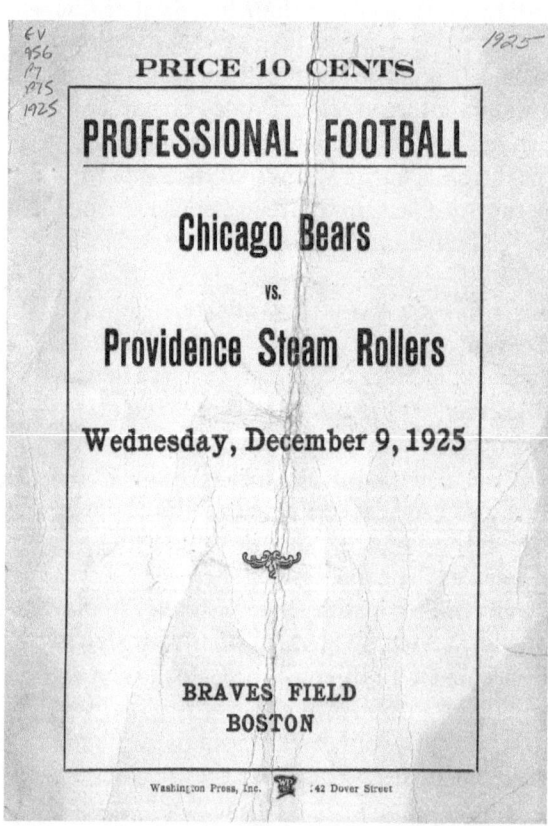

Providence Steam Roller vs. Chicago Bears program from the first NFL game played in Boston, Massachusetts, on December 9, 1925. The Steam Roller defeated the Red Grange-led Bears 9–6 at Braves Field (courtesy Rhode Island Historical Society—RHi X17 4833).

were in a pitiful condition," Grange later recalled, "with many of us bandaged from head to foot. I was in particularly bad shape. I had hurt my left arm in New York and it was badly swollen."[17]

Prior to the game, Steam Roller star running back Cy Wentworth was encouraged to wear No. 77—Grange's number—on his jersey by team owner Coppen. Coppen even had a No. 77 jersey made up for his star player. But the modest and unassuming Wentworth declined to wear it, acknowledging that he was pretty unknown outside of Providence and did not want to draw attention to himself. The jersey was left in the clubhouse before the team's trek to Boston's Braves Field.

The morning of the game, Grange and his teammates arrived in Boston by train. Grange was then whisked off to meet with Joseph P. Kennedy, Sr. Kennedy and Grange had recently signed a $50,000 contract to shoot a movie in the summer of 1927. Kennedy owned a small film company called FBO (Film Booking Offices of America). This was prior to Joe entering politics, and his two boys, John (eight years old) and Robert (three weeks old), were too young to think of what their political futures would become.

While Grange was warming up prior to the game at Braves Field, a big, broad-shouldered man approached him while he stood near the bench area. That man was none other than the "Sultan of Swat," the indomitable Babe Ruth of the New York Yankees. The two men spoke for several minutes and posed for photographs. Grange had become the equal of Ruth in the sporting world. He was that popular and his athletic prowess was considered on par with the greatest baseball player of the generation and beyond.

Despite the frigid conditions and the unusual Wednesday date, 15,000 enthusiastic fans came out to see Grange and the 9-2-3 Bears play the 5-4-1 Steam Roller. Early in the game, Grange flashed his elusive running style with a nifty 15-yard return of a Providence punt. Later in the first quarter, he saved a Steam Roller touchdown when he forced Wentworth to fumble after the speedy back had run 40 yards to the Chicago 21-yard line. But from there the dynamic Grange did very little until he was removed at the end of the third quarter. The fans who cheered him on at first were disappointed in the superstar's performance and expressed their displeasure by cascading boos on him when he carried the ball later in the game. Grange was credited with only 13 yards rushing on five carries, returned the one punt, threw three passes and forced the one fumble.

Meanwhile the Steam Roller played a very solid game, especially defensively, as it not only hemmed in Grange but also slowed the entire Chicago offense. Providence scored first on a blocked punt by Maloney midway through the first quarter. The Steam Roller's end busted through the Bears' line to reach the kick by Hunk Anderson. The ball bounced through the end zone for a safety. In the second quarter, another botched punt attempt by Chicago was costly. As Anderson was ready to kick, the snap from center flew over his head. "Stretch" Garvey picked up the loose ball in full stride and raced 45 yards for the touchdown. Maloney's extra-point kick made the score 9–0.

The Bears finally scored in the final quarter, but only after a fumble by Laird at the Steam Roller's 35-yard line. It was the first time the Bears had even been in Providence territory in the game. Chicago capitalized on the turnover. On second down, Bears quarterback Joey Sternaman tossed a pass to Johnny Bryan, who ran the distance for a 35-yard touchdown. The kick failed and Providence led 9–6. The Roller defense contained Chicago the rest of the game and Dolph Eckstein intercepted a late pass by Earl Britton to clinch the victory for Providence. The next day's *Providence Journal* proclaimed, "Red Grange Team Outplayed by Wide Margin as Providence Squad Smothers Far-Famed Star from Mid-West."[18] Providence's Wentworth acquitted himself well against Grange: "The Roller left half back was the shining star of yesterday's battle, insofar as running with the ball was concerned, and his forward pass was spectacular also."[19]

"It was the big event in Roller history while I was with them," Bert Shurtleff, who never wore a helmet while playing for Providence, said years later. "The Roller recruited every former player who could still work. The ground was frozen hard after being cleated up by Holy Cross and Harvard the previous weekend. The thermometer never got above six below zero that day. Instead of letting themselves be tackled, runners fled for the sidelines. I managed to get in front of Grange once and found that he went down just like any other runner."[20] It was also claimed that for the first time the Galloping Ghost had been caught from behind and tackled, by Joe Kozlowsky.

After the exhilarating victory over Chicago, the Steam Roller ended its season with a disappointing 14–6 loss to the Yellow Jackets on December 12. It was the rubber match in their three-game series with Frankford. Frankford won on opening day and then Providence returned the favor at the Cycledrome in November. The Yellow Jackets turned two lengthy drives into Lou Smyth touchdowns in the first and third quarters for the victory. Despite a great game from Pollard, the Roller was able to garner only two Maloney field goals. The *Boston Globe* commented on Pollard's play, saying, "Fritz Pollard, ex–Brown ace, was the star of the game. Pollard was as brilliant as in his college days and twice threatened to score touchdowns only to be stopped by the last man between himself and the goal. He ran 45 yards through the whole Jacket team on a return from a punt and again squirmed through seven of his opponents for a 25-yard gain to the 20-yard mark."[21]

Two. The Early Years (1925–1927)   37

The Providence Steam Roller and Chicago Bears in front of the Braves Field stands following the first-ever NFL game played in Boston, on December 9, 1925. Providence won 9–6 (courtesy Rhode Island Historical Society—RHi X17 4511).

Originally the Steam Roller was scheduled to play Pottsville on December 12 but the game was altered to have Frankford as the opponent. Providence was not allowed to play Pottsville because it was outlawed by the league. If the Steam Roller played that squad, it would have lost its NFL franchise. Pottsville had played a game against Notre Dame and its "Four Horsemen" at Shibe Park in Philadelphia on December 11. The location of the game infringed on the territorial rights of Frankford and thus Pottsville was stripped of its league standing. After the controversy subsided, Pottsville was allowed to "return" to the NFL for the 1926 season, but it was stripped of the 1925 NFL title and the Chicago Cardinals were awarded the championship with an 11–2–1 record. Charlie Berry of Pottsville led the league in scoring with 74 points and Paddy Driscoll of the Cardinals was second with 67. Latone led the league with eight touchdowns.

Providence finished its inaugural NFL season in 10th place in the 20-team circuit with a 6–5–1 league record. It was 4–3–1 at the Cycledrome and averaged more than 9,500 fans per game, an outstanding result in its first year. Laird led the team in scoring with 29 points that included three touchdowns, three field goals and two extra points. Wentworth tied Laird for the most touchdowns with three. The Steam Roller had three players named to the All-NFL second team—Eckstein, Maloney and Wentworth. Overall, it was a successful first season for the franchise.

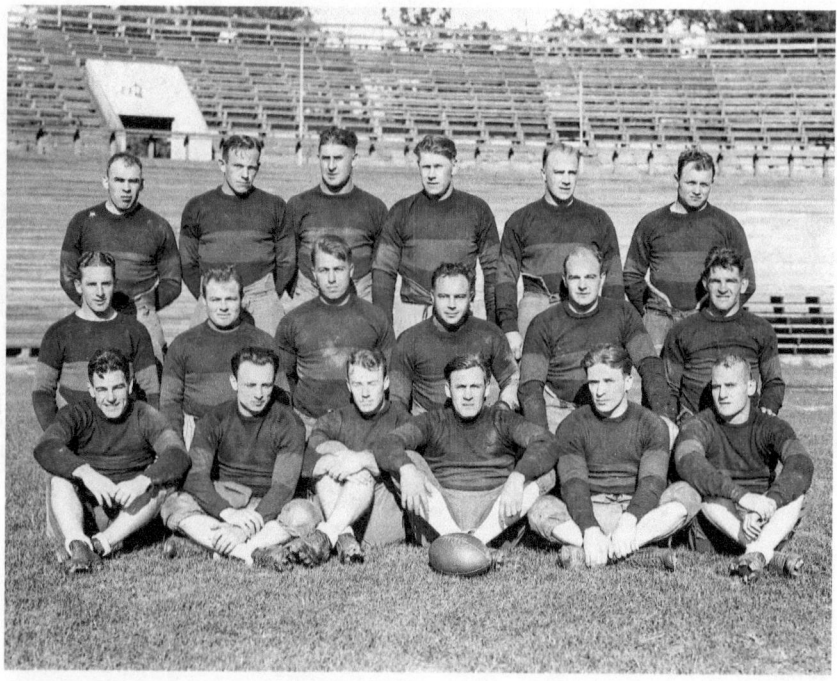

The 1925 Providence Steam Roller, the city's first NFL team, with the wooden track of the Providence Cycledrome in the background (courtesy Rhode Island Historical Society—RHi X3 6826).

1926—Excitement Turns to Disappointment

In recognition of the Steam Roller's first successful NFL season, a testimonial dinner was held at the Metacomet Golf Club in East Providence on February 20. More than 150 football fans were on hand, including the mayor, an assistant attorney general of the United States, the Rhode Island speaker of the House, a former Rhode Island governor and an honored judge. Coppen and Dooley represented the ownership group, and almost the entire Steam Roller roster of players came to be honored. Dooley told the audience, "The pleasure I have derived from the Roller has been immeasurable. You have given us admirable support, and that is why we have gone on from year to year, joined the league, and offered you the best possible professional football. We shall go on, and if you continue to give us your support we shall continue to give you the best that there is in the game."[22]

Now it was time to begin preparations for the 1926 season. Laird was named the new Steam Roller head coach on June 29. He left his head coaching job at Norwich University in Vermont after three seasons to add the title of head coach to his spot on the roster as a Providence player. Laird had formerly played for the Rochester Jeffersons, Buffalo All-Americans and Canton Bulldogs, so he knew his way around the league. Former coach Golembeski remained with the Roller in a playing capacity but could not continue as head coach with his commitment to lead the Providence College team.

The league had 17 cities return for the 1926 season while three dropped out—the Cleveland Bulldogs, Rochester Jeffersons and the Rock Island Independents. Five new cities were added—the Brooklyn Lions, Hartford Blues, Los Angeles Buccaneers, Louisville Colonels and the Racine Tornadoes—to expand the NFL to 22 teams. It was the largest number of teams in the history of the league until the merger of the AFL and NFL in 1966. A competing American Football League also was formed in 1926 that consisted of nine teams. Many new owners were trying to take advantage of the windfall in interest created by Grange's arrival in pro football.

The league owners met on July 11 and released the 1926 schedule. Providence's slate consisted of 14 games with 10 of them in the Cyclodrome, highlighted by home-and-home series with rivals Pottsville, Frankford and the New York Giants and a new potential area rivalry against a new Hartford franchise. The Steam Roller was scheduled to open the season

Providence Steam Roller at Pottsville Maroons program from November 25, 1926. The Steam Roller lost to the Maroons 8-0 on Thanksgiving Day at Minersville Park in a budding rivalry that would continue through 1930 (courtesy Rhode Island Historical Society—RHi X17 4834).

at home against Brooklyn on September 26 and would be hosting the Jim Thorpe–led Canton Bulldogs on November 11.

Other business at the NFL owners' meeting included adoption of a revised league constitution and a set of bylaws, and the expansion of the executive committee from three to five members with Steam Roller part-owner James Dooley being added to the committee. In addition, Coppen was added to a new committee to work with the colleges to improve the relationship between the two sides and clear up some misunderstandings from the previous couple of years.

There was optimism surrounding the Providence squad with the hiring of Laird. Those positive vibes increased as the Steam Roller added some new players to an already strong roster. Lineman Jack Donahue, captain of the Boston College football team in 1925, signed a contract with Providence on August 9. Bob Scott and Bull Wesley, both from the University of Alabama, were added to bolster the line. Brown running back Jack Keefer, a third-team All-American; Jim Manning, a standout fullback at Fordham; Waddy MacPhee, a three-sport star at Princeton; and Joe McGlone, former Harvard star quarterback, joined the Steam Roller backfield.

Pollard did not return as he went back to Akron to fulfill his contract with the Pros. The Roller also lost key contributors from 1925 including Chick Burke, All-Pro Red Maloney, Pard Pearce, Hop Riopel and Bert Shurtleff. Burke did not recover well from his previous season's injury; Riopel and Shurtleff were released. Maloney jumped to the AFL's New York Yankees for reportedly double the money he was making with Providence. By jumping to the rival league, an automatic five-year suspension was imposed on the player. The American Football Coaches Association passed a rule in December 1925 that players associated with professional football would be barred from coaching high school teams effective September 1, 1926. This likely weighed into the decision why Pearce did not return to the Roller for the 1926 season. Pearce joined Providence's Classical High School as an assistant football coach and pursued a teaching career. Shurtleff also became an assistant football coach at Durfee High School.

Despite the loss of some of these key players, the fans were excited for the second season of Steam Roller NFL football to commence. The Providence players reported for their first practice on September 8 with an opening preseason game scheduled for September 12 against Williams of New Haven, Connecticut.

The game with Williams was played on a hot, sunny day, and the combination of the heat and the rustiness of the Steam Roller, after only four days of practice, showed on the field. Providence could score on only a 32-yard Laird field goal in the first half, and the overall performance of both teams lacked sound execution.

The Steam Roller played much better in the second half, rolling to three touchdowns. Manning made his presence felt almost immediately. He had a nice 31-yard run in the first quarter to earn the Roller's initial first down. He then put together two runs totaling 30 yards in the third quarter to score the game's first touchdown that capped off an 81-yard drive.

On the first play of the fourth quarter, returning starter Curly Oden darted through a hole on the right side, reversed his course and then sprinted to the goal for a stirring 51-yard touchdown run. Keefer made his second extra point and Providence led 17–0. Later in the fourth, facing a fourth down and goal at the Williams' three, the Steam Roller did a little trickery and Cy Wentworth ended up with the ball as he scooted around the end for the final touchdown in a 24–0 warm-up victory.

The Steam Roller had one more preseason encounter before their first NFL contest of 1926. On September 19, Laird's bunch looked much sharper in a 41–0 trouncing of the New London Submarine Base squad. It took the Roller a little time to get going as it scored only one first-half touchdown, courtesy of a 36-yard fumble return by Spellman. The big bulky lineman scooped up the ball and rumbled and stumbled his way for the score.

In the second half, Providence looked like the team from 1925. The Steam Roller controlled both lines of scrimmage and the fans saw the darting and dashing runs that they had come to expect from the likes of Oden and Wentworth. Providence exploded in the third quarter. Keefer returned a Sub Base punt 55 yards for a touchdown to get the period underway. Less than two minutes later, Wentworth intercepted a Harrington pass and returned it 42 yards to the London 18-yard line. Two plays later, he ran over for a Steam Roller touchdown. Then Oden finished off a Providence drive with an 18-yard sprint to the end zone. Providence did not stop there. Manning added a fourth touchdown in the quarter on a 55-yard lateral pass from Joe McGlone. And then just to add a little spice to the victory, head coach Laird entered the game in the fourth quarter and scored the game's final touchdown. He carried the ball on each play of a drive that started at the Providence 38-yard line and each of his runs exceeded 10 yards as he earned his nickname, "Ten Yard" Laird.

Laird announced the starting team for the opener against the Brooklyn Lions on September 24 and said how pleased he was with the team he was sending into action.

Here is how the Steam Roller lined up for its 1926 opener:

LE—Lloyd Young
LT—Jack Spellman

LG—Joe Braney
C—Dolph Eckstein
RG—Bull Wesley
RT—Mike Gulian
RE—Pinky Lester
QB—Joe McGlone
RHB—Jim Manning
LHB—Cy Wentworth
FB—Freddy Sweet

Only Spellman, Eckstein, Wentworth and Sweet had started the 1925 season opener.

Providence hosted the first-year, yet highly touted, Lions on September 26 in front of 7,000 Cycledrome spectators. Brooklyn was led by fullback George Snell and wingback Rex Thomas. The Steam Roller started strong by forcing and recovering two first-quarter fumbles caused by Eckstein and Spellman. However, the Roller's offense was unable to score off those turnovers. Providence broke through in the second quarter on a 54-yard drive that was fueled by outstanding runs by Oden, Wentworth and Keefer that set the ball at the Lions' eight. Three runs by Laird put the ball at the Brooklyn one-yard line as the Roller faced fourth down. To the surprise of Brooklyn, Oden took a pitchout from Eckstein and circled around left end to score the touchdown and give Providence a 6–0 lead.

Though Providence dominated the action, outplaying Brooklyn by chalking up 13 first downs to only four for the visitors, the Roller did not put the game away until the fourth quarter. Following a terrific 23-yard run by Keefer that moved the ball to the Brooklyn 21-yard line, Oden surprised his opponent again, this time racing around right end and cruising for a touchdown. Keefer drop-kicked the extra point and Providence had a 13–0 lead that it held until the final gun sounded. The club was off to a good start.

Jim Stifler, 1925 Brown University captain, was signed by the Steam Roller on September 29 to provide backfield depth in time for the upcoming game against the Giants, which took place on October 3 at the Cycledrome. Stifler couldn't prevent a heartbreaking 7–6 loss. The bigger and stronger New Yorkers outplayed the Roller. Providence could muster only three first downs throughout the contest while the Giants seemingly moved the ball up and down the field in registering 13 first downs. Even so, the Providence defense continually held them out of the end zone.

New York scored its only touchdown of the game on a sustained 60-yard march in the second quarter that ended with a beautiful touchdown pass from Hinkey Haines to a wide-open Lynn Bomar. Former

Syracuse standout Jack McBride converted the all-important extra point and the Giants led 7–0. Oden, the brilliant Swede, fielded Paul Hogan's third-quarter punt at the Roller's 20-yard line and raced 70 yards down the sideline to the New York 10 before he was shoved out of bounds. Three plays later, Keefer, under heavy pressure, lofted a 15-yard touchdown pass to a leaping Golembeski that put Providence within a point, 7–6. On the ensuing extra-point attempt to tie the game, McBride broke through the Providence blockers and deflected Keefer's dropkick that secured the Giants' victory.

New York's multilayered attack was too much for the Roller on this day. Haines led the Giants with 75 yards rushing and McBride contributed 50 yards to go along with his big plays in the kicking game. New York also completed 10 passes for an additional 70 yards.

The Steam Roller bounced back on October 10 against the Columbus Tigers. Columbus was not a formidable team and was 1–2 coming into the game. After a scoreless first period, Providence got rolling early in the second quarter. With the ball at the 50-yard line, the Steam Roller moved quickly on the aid of two passes that moved the pigskin to the Tigers' nine-yard line. Oden ran the ball into the end zone from there for a touchdown on a bobbing, weaving run while he dodged several would-be Columbus tacklers. Keefer's kick was good and Providence led 7–0.

The second half became Oden's kick-return show. He took the second-half kickoff at his own 22-yard line and sprinted past the entire Columbus defense, shaking off a final tackle attempt by Bob Rapp, on his way to a spectacular 78-yard touchdown return. On the ensuing kickoff, he almost did it again, returning the kick 27 yards to midfield before he was finally brought down. A few minutes later, Oden returned a punt 25 yards that set up the Roller at the Columbus 35-yard line. Then Keefer, the gem from Dayton, Ohio, darted through a hole at left tackle and cut back across the field on his way to a thrilling touchdown run. That score gave the Roller a 19–0 lead. Though Columbus outplayed Providence in the final period, it was kept out of the end zone. The shutout victory gave the Steam Roller renewed confidence in its offense with the three exciting touchdowns.

A distracting backdrop to the game was that word had leaked out about private negotiations that were going on between Steam Roller management and a group of St. Louis sportsmen who wanted to buy the team and move it to the Midwestern city. The current Steam Roller management was willing to sell because it had losses that had mounted up with lower-than-expected attendance, and the team was carrying more players on the roster than the league limit of 18. The NFL did not police the roster limit and teams that could afford more than the 18 players often did. The rumored sale created considerable comments from fans who wanted the team to remain in Providence. With that in mind, Steam Roller management set a pretty high price for the franchise in the negotiations.

By October 13, the deal had fallen through. The sportsmen would not meet the terms of Providence management. In addition, the St. Louis group had planned to sell the contracts to New York of five players who weren't able to move west with the team. Those players each had commitments that kept them in New England—Eckstein was a medical student at Harvard, Golembeski coached at Providence College, Gulian and Wentworth had business dealings in Boston and Kozlowsky was coaching in Boston. While the team was safe, some on the roster weren't so lucky. The front office reduced the roster to 18 players and cut other expenses to keep the team solvent. It was also announced that Seneca Samson, who shared quarterback duties with Oden, was out for the year with an injury he suffered in the Columbus game.

Curly Oden, All-Pro running back for the Providence Steam Roller, catching a pass while preparing to run with the football (*Providence Journal*—USA TODAY NETWORK).

Connecticut fans were highly anticipating the October 17 game of their Hartford Blues against New England rival Providence. More than 10,000 were expected, and several carloads of Steam Roller supporters made the trip to the Connecticut capital for the game. However, with a steady rainstorm throughout the day, Hartford management called the game off due to poor field conditions only 30 minutes before the scheduled kickoff. Many fans already in the stands were frustrated by the late decision and both teams were disappointed. The game was expected to be rescheduled but it never occurred.

Up next for Providence were the powerful Pottsville Maroons on

Two. The Early Years (1925–1927)

October 24. Pottsville came into the game with a 4–0 record and had allowed only a total of six points. The Maroons were led by fullback Barney Wentz, running back extraordinaire Tony Latone and the league's 1925 leading scorer, end Charlie Berry. Since the franchise began in 1925, Pottsville had an overall 14–2 NFL record coming into the game. One of those two losses was a 6–0 defeat at the hands of the Steam Roller in 1925.

A disappointing crowd of only 4,500 came to see the game in a driving rainstorm at the Cycledrome, but it was worth it for those brave souls. The Steam Roller played outstanding football in a 14–0 victory over Pottsville. The Maroons had only two scoring chances throughout the hard-fought game, reaching the Providence 20-yard line in the first quarter and again in the second, but both times were turned away. The Roller defense played extremely well and also set up the game's first touchdown in the second quarter. Mike Gulian blocked a Maroon punt and Providence took over at the Pottsville 12-yard line. Oden scored on the next play as he sprinted around right end for the touchdown. Keefer's dropkick was good and the Roller went to the half with a 7–0 lead.

The teams battled through a scoreless third quarter. Providence added to its lead in the fourth. With the ball at the Steam Roller's 43-yard line, Oden took the handoff and weaved his way through the Pottsville defense as well as the puddles and ankle-deep mud. He sludged his way 57 scintillating yards to paydirt. The drenched crowd rose to its feet in amazement as the swift Swede put the Roller in control. Keefer passed to Golembeski for the extra point and a 14–0 Providence lead.

Pottsville tried everything in its arsenal to mount a comeback, even passing on almost every play late in the game, but the Roller defense led by Franny Garvey produced the key plays when needed to keep the Maroons from scoring.

It was an incredible victory for the Steam Roller. The *Providence Journal* reported it this way: "It was Curly Oden, the galloping Swede of the professional sport and the idol of every Providence fan, who gave the Orange and Black the greatest and most satisfactory victory that has ever been the lot of the local eleven."[23] The win was even more remarkable when at the conclusion of the season the Maroons had allowed a total of 29 points for the entire year in 14 games and finished with a 10–2–2 record.

The following week, the Steam Roller went from the frying pan to the fire as the team faced its second consecutive undefeated team, the Frankford Yellow Jackets, on October 30 with a rematch scheduled for the next day. The Yellow Jackets—led by player-coach Guy Chamberlin, tailback Hap Moran, wingback Tex Hamer, fullback Hust Stockton and All-Pro tackle Johnny Budd—were loaded with talent. They came into the game with a 6–0–1 record and had outscored their opponents 88–6.

More than 8,000 jammed Frankford Stadium on an Indian summer day to see the battle for first place. The Yellow Jackets on their first drive of the game moved into Providence territory, but the Roller stopped them and forced a field goal attempt. The 40-yard kick by Budd went awry. Later in the quarter, Frankford again moved deep into Providence territory but was stopped at the 16-yard line. Again, Budd attempted a field goal and again it missed. The quarter ended with a 0–0 tie.

Providence moved into scoring position three times in the second quarter. The first drive was stopped by an errant pass from Oden that was intercepted by Doc Bruder. On the Steam Roller's second opportunity, following a blocked punt that gave Providence the ball at the Yellow Jackets' seven-yard line, Keefer fumbled and Stockton recovered for Frankford. Just before halftime, the Roller was on the move again. It advanced into Frankford territory, but Oden's attempt at a 45-yard field goal was well short. The two combatants went to the half with no score.

Providence missed another long field goal attempt early in the third quarter. After Bull Wesley returned the second-half kickoff all the way to the Frankford 38-yard line, the offense could not move the ball. Wesley attempted a 50-yard kick that was well short. Finally, on the Steam Roller's next possession, it broke through. Following a Frankford punt, Keefer made a sensational 51-yard run through the staunch Yellow Jackets defense for a touchdown. Keefer then hit Garvey with a pass for the extra point and a 7–0 Providence lead.

The teams battled back and forth into the final quarter. Providence stopped the Yellow Jackets on a fourth and two at the five-yard line midway through the quarter. But on Frankford's next possession, a pass interference penalty against the Steam Roller set it up at the Providence 10. Three plays netted nine yards and on fourth and goal from the one Ben Jones bulled his way over the goal line for a touchdown. The all-important extra-point kick to tie the game by Budd hit the right goalpost and bounced away. A few plays later the game was over and Providence had upset the mighty Yellow Jackets 7–6 and found itself in first place in the NFL with a 4–1 record.

The two teams took an overnight train to Providence for a rematch on Halloween in the Cycledrome. The Steam Roller was without two of its best offensive players for the game. Keefer was out with a bone bruise and Laird could not play with a twisted knee. The teams were met with a deluge of rain when they took the field that continued throughout the contest, making the field almost unplayable.

Early in the game, Oden set up Providence in great field position. He fielded a Hamer punt at his 41-yard line and scooted 45 yards to the Yellow Jackets' 14-yard line. After two running plays that netted a loss of a yard, Providence decided to kick. Wentworth, with a bad angle and the muddy conditions, somehow made the 26-yard field goal and the Steam Roller jumped ahead 3–0.

Both teams struggled to move the football on the rain-soaked field, and as the game continued the conditions just worsened with more mud and puddles appearing. Frankford caught a big break in the second quarter. Following a Hamer punt that rolled dead at the Providence five-yard line, the Steam Roller tried an end run with Wentworth. As Cy attempted to get around the end, the ball slipped out of his hands and bounded back into the end zone. Yellow Jackets defensive tackle Daddy Potts pounced on the ball for a touchdown. Hamer's extra-point kick was blocked by Golembeski, but Frankford led 6–3.

As the condition of the field worsened after halftime, the game became a punting contest between Hamer and Wentworth. Providence twice had field goal opportunities in the second half, from 20 yards and 40 yards, but both were unsuccessful. The Steam Roller was able to gain only two first downs throughout the game and the Yellow Jackets had three. It was a defensive struggle with Spellman, Jack Donahue and Lloyd Young playing especially well for the Steam Roller. The Wentworth fumble proved costly as Frankford hung on for the 6–3 victory. Providence's hold on first place lasted exactly one day.

The largest crowd of the season turned out at the Cycledrome on November 7 to see the Steam Roller play host to the Los Angeles Buccaneers. The 2-1-1 Bucs were led by first-team All-Pro end and co-coach Brick Muller, co-coach and first-team All-Pro halfback Tut Imlay and fullback Tuffy Maul. Muller was a two-time All-American at California and was the Most Valuable Player in the 1921 Rose Bowl. Muller and Imlay, teammates at California, were known for Imlay tossing a football to Muller from the top of a 415-foot-high building in San Francisco.

On this day the two teammates would not have to resort to something that dramatic, but they did enough to eke out a victory for Los Angeles. The Buccaneers jumped to an early lead. Midway through the first quarter, Los Angeles took the ball at the Steam Roller 40-yard line following a punt. Muller threw a 21-yard pass to Imlay to the Providence 19-yard line. From there, Maul took over and mauled the Providence defense. On the fifth consecutive running play, he crossed the goal line for a touchdown. Maul's extra point gave the Bucs a 7–0 lead.

The Steam Roller was playing shorthanded with Keefer still nursing his injury and Kozlowsky also sidelined. Providence lost two additional players during the game. Laird reinjured his knee and Wesley fractured his ribs. Also, the Roller was counting on new acquisition Dave Noble to play, but he was ruled ineligible by NFL president Joe Carr just before the game. Carr cited "alleged team jumping activities earlier in the season."[24]

Noble, nicknamed the "Big Moose," was a powerful fullback from the University of Nebraska and was a first-team All-Pro in 1925 for the Cleveland Bulldogs. Noble had been playing for the Cleveland Panthers of the American Football League, but they disbanded after playing five games and he signed with the Steam Roller on November 4. He could have helped Providence in this very physical encounter with LA. Noble never played for the Steam Roller and his pro football career was over.

Muller left the game following the touchdown with a badly lacerated nose but returned in the third quarter. His absence stymied the Buccaneers' attack, but the Roller was not able to take advantage and the teams went to the half with LA still leading 7–0.

At halftime, Los Angeles manager Jack McDonough was honored by the crowd and given a gold watch. McDonough was the captain and coach of the first Steam Roller independent pro team in 1916 and helped get the pro game started in Providence. He was an outstanding college player at Syracuse University before playing for the Steam Roller in its infancy.

Early in the second half, Providence moved into Buccaneers territory, but Oden was intercepted by Pete Schaffnit at the LA 34-yard line. On the next play, Muller fired a pass that Oden snared out of the air and returned 21 yards deep into Bucs territory. Four plays later, Providence faced a fourth down and goal at the Los Angeles two-yard line. The Steam Roller set up for a dropkick by Wentworth. Instead of kicking, he threw a pass to Oden in the flat. Though surrounded by LA players, the elusive running back slipped through the would-be tacklers into the end zone for a touchdown. Wentworth's extra point missed wide by a couple of inches and the Bucs now led only 7–6.

After the Steam Roller's score, both teams emptied the playbook in trying to generate offense. Footballs were flying through the air at a frantic rate, but for every good play each team made, it was nullified by a negative play. Late in the game, Providence had one final golden opportunity. The Steam Roller began at its own 20-yard line. Oden passed six yards to Keefer. On second down the combination clicked again, as Keefer caught the ball at the Roller 35 with only Maul between him and the goal. Keefer also had help with offensive guard Bob Scott out in front of him. Scott went to block Maul, but the burly Buccaneer sidestepped the Steam Roller guard and lunged at Keefer. Maul's lunge tripped up the speedy ball carrier and brought him to the ground. Had Scott made that block, it was a sure touchdown. Providence had one more play, another completed pass from Oden to Keefer, but it ended well short of the goal line as the horn sounded to end the game. It was a disappointing 7–6 loss to the team from the City

Two. The Early Years (1925–1927)

of Angels. With the loss, Providence dropped to 4–3 and any dreams of an NFL championship were thwarted.

The famous Thorpe-led Canton Bulldogs came to the Cycledrome on November 11 to battle the Steam Roller. The Bulldogs were twice NFL champions (1922, 1923) but not the same team as the one from those years. Canton was sporting a 1–5–2 record. Providence was smarting from its loss to Los Angeles and displayed a strong resilience as it bounced back with a solid performance.

Oden continued his outstanding season with three more touchdowns, to give him 10 for the campaign, in leading the Steam Roller to a 21–2 victory. Providence got on the board first with help from a howling, chilly wind. Canton was forced to punt from deep in its own end and the kick went less than 10 yards to the Canton 13. Providence took over and four plays later Oden was in the end zone. The galloping Swede faded back to pass and then spotted an opening. He scooted through the hole for the score. Wentworth's kick was good and the Roller was ahead 7–0.

On the first play of the second quarter, Canton's Pete Calac punted to Oden. Curly fielded the ball at his own 35, and with a wall of blockers he raced untouched 65 yards for a touchdown. Wentworth crossed up the Bulldogs defense and ran around left end for the extra point. Later in the quarter, Canton moved the ball to the Providence one-yard line and had a first and goal. But the Roller defense turned in its best goal-line stand of the season as the unit repelled the Bulldogs four straight times. Donahue, Gulian and Spellman held firm and would not let them cross the Roller goal line. After the brilliant stand, rather than trying to punt out of trouble, Wentworth downed the ball in the end zone for a safety. Providence went to the half with a 14–2 lead.

Early in the third quarter Eckstein intercepted Stan Robb's pass and returned it to the Bulldogs' 44-yard line. Following an Oden-to-Wentworth 13-yard pass and an 11-yard run by Dutch Forst, Oden finished the scoring with a 20-yard dash off right tackle. Wentworth's point-after made it 21–2 for the home team. That ended the scoring for the day. It was a nice bounce-back win for the Roller, but it came at a cost. More players were added to the injury list, including Golembeski, Sweet and Garvey. They joined Laird, Kozlowsky and Wesley on the sidelines.

A weary Steam Roller squad, playing its third game in seven days on November 14 and decimated by injuries, was no match for the Kansas City Cowboys. Providence dropped a 22–0 decision to the Midwesterners. Kansas City scored in every quarter in its thoroughly dominant victory.

Al Bloodgood, a former Nebraska quarterback, played an outstanding game for the Cowboys. He set up the game's first touchdown with a nifty 29-yard run that took the ball to the Providence 10-yard line in the first quarter. On the next play, Charley Hill ran across the goal line, and with Bloodgood's extra point it was 7–0 KC. In the second quarter, Bloodgood ran 24 yards for a score, but the extra point failed and the Cowboys went to the halftime break with a 13–0 lead.

Bloodgood made two field goals of 32 and 44 yards in the third quarter. The 44-yarder was the longest in Cycledrome history to that point. He added a 30-yard field goal in the fourth quarter to close out the scoring. Bloodgood scored 16 of the 22 points in the game. Providence lost Keefer to injury in the first quarter and Oden in the fourth quarter. The Steam Roller's deepest offensive penetration in the game was to the Kansas City 30-yard line. This defeat sent the Steam Roller reeling and it never recovered.

Providence traveled to the Polo Grounds for its matchup with the New York Giants on November 21. The Steam Roller, extremely shorthanded for this game, put up a good fight but ran out of gas in the fourth quarter. The Roller held the Giants to one touchdown until the fateful concluding minutes. Hinkey Haines scored on an eight-yard run late in the first quarter to stake New York to a 7–0 lead. The Steam Roller battled valiantly but could not put any points on the board against the tough New York defense led by Al Nesser and Walt Koppisch. Oden, back from his injury, had some nice runs and a few good passes, but not enough to dent the scoreboard.

The Giants pulled away in the final period with two touchdowns. Haines scored on a beautiful 22-yard scamper and McBride finished the scoring with a one-yard plunge to wrap up the win.

The Steam Roller stayed on the road, traveling to Pottsville for a Thanksgiving Day clash with the Maroons. Again, the Providence offense could not dent the scoreboard, as they were shut out for the third consecutive game. The big plays from Keefer, Wentworth and Oden from earlier in the season were gone from the arsenal and they were just not a plodding "three yards at a time" team. Without the explosive plays, the offense went dormant.

The two teams battled to a scoreless first half. Pottsville had the better of the action, spending much of the half in Providence territory. But the Steam Roller defense, led by Gulian, Donahue and Lloyd Young, did not let them penetrate the goal line. Finally, a third-quarter interception by Pottsville defensive guard Frank Youngfleish set up the Maroons to get on the scoreboard. Following a few running plays, the Providence defense stiffened at its 10-yard line and Jim Welsh came on for Pottsville and booted a 20-yard field goal. From there, Pottsville continued to advance the ball into Providence territory. In the fourth quarter, they were stopped on downs and settled for another Welsh field goal.

Two. The Early Years (1925–1927)

The Maroons closed out the scoring by forcing a safety by Laird, when he surrendered in the end zone rather than having his punt blocked. Pottsville went on to an 8–0 victory to avenge its earlier loss to Providence. Despite the setback, the Providence defense was praised for its efforts. "Its impregnable defense was one of the most remarkable exhibitions of courageous football seen here in many a day," reported the *Providence Journal*.[25] With the loss, Providence's NFL record dropped below .500 to 5–6.

The Steam Roller returned home for a November 28 match with the Duluth Eskimos. The Eskimos, led by superstars Ernie Nevers and Johnny Blood, were a formidable opponent and came into the game with a 6–4–2 record. They were primarily a traveling team, having played only one game in Duluth, Minnesota. Nevers, the former Stanford star, was one of the NFL's leading scorers with eight touchdowns to go along with his kicking prowess that included 11 extra points and four field goals. Later that season he would be named first-team All-Pro, an honor he would earn four more times in his career.

This game was defined by the play of the Providence defense. It shut down the Eskimos' attack except for Nevers but was able to contain the standout offensive performer and held the Eskimos out of the end zone. Nevers had several good runs and completed 9 of 17 passes as Duluth garnered 12 first downs to the paltry three for Providence.

The Eskimos moved the ball into Providence territory on several occasions but Nevers, usually a reliable kicker, missed four field goal attempts. He missed from 21, 31, 35 and 50 yards to keep the game scoreless. The punchless Providence attack never threatened the Duluth defense. The Eskimos had one final chance late in the fourth quarter. They drove inside the Providence 25-yard line. Nevers attempted a 28-yard field goal. It sailed high over the uprights, but the officials ruled the kick was not good. The Eskimos vigorously argued the call, but to no avail. The game ended in a scoreless tie. The defensive standouts for the shorthanded Steam Roller were Mike Gulian, Swede Hummel, Vern Hagenbuckle, Jim Stifler and Pinky Lester.

Providence was scheduled to play the Hartford Blues on December 5, this time at the Cycledrome. However, weather again got in the way as a driving snowstorm hit New England and the game was canceled. Hartford's only season in the league ended with a 3–7 record, and the Blues and Steam Roller never did play a game against each other as the previously scheduled game had also been canceled.

The following Saturday, on December 11, the Steam Roller's season mercifully ended with a 24–0 loss at Frankford Stadium against the Yellow Jackets. Providence was able to gain only one first down on the snowy field against the powerful Frankford squad. The Yellow Jackets scored in each quarter while amassing 12 first downs. The Frankford touchdowns were scored by Stockton on a one-yard plunge, Swede Youngstrom on a blocked punt recovery in the end zone and "Two Bits" Homan on a four-yard run with an Ed Weir field goal mixed in. The Steam Roller's next game with Frankford, which was scheduled for Providence for the following day, was canceled. The team was in no condition to play it.

Providence finished the season with a disappointing 5–7–1 record after starting 4–1. It was a discouraging end to what looked like a very promising season. Following its back-to-back upset wins over Pottsville and Frankford, two of the league's best teams, the Roller stood in first place on October 30. But the injury bug took its toll, costing the Roller six of its starting 11 players for various games as the team staggered to a 1–6–1 finish. Providence was shut out in its last five games and Coppen and the Steam Roller front office knew they had work to do in the offseason to improve the offense.

Frankford went on to win the NFL championship with a 14–1–2 record. Its only loss was to the Steam Roller. The Chicago Bears were second with a 12–1–3 record and Pottsville finished third at 10–2–2. Providence was the only team in the league to defeat both Frankford and Pottsville. The Steam Roller's record put them in 11th place among the 22 teams. Providence had a 4–4–1 record at the Cycledrome as attendance dropped by more than 2,000 per game from the successful 1925 season. It was reported that Coppen and the ownership group lost $10,000 from the 1926 season. The Roller's total was hurt by several harsh-weather games.

Curly Oden, the former Brown star, tied for the league lead in touchdowns with 10 and was named second-team All-Pro, the only Roller honored. Oden's 60 points were third best in the league behind only Paddy Driscoll with 86 points and Nevers with 71.

1927—Conzelman Arrives and Fortunes Change

Many NFL teams lost money in 1926, and with the rise and fall of the AFL, gone after only one season, the league needed to reevaluate its franchise structure. It was a serious situation. "Professional football has breathed its last," commented Jack McDonough, head of the NFL's Los Angeles team. "It has failed to strike the popular fancy."[26]

A special meeting of the NFL owners occurred in April and several franchises were either shut down or suspended, including original league members Akron (first league champion), Canton (two-time NFL champion), Columbus and Hammond. By the start of the 1927 season, 12 teams had dropped out, including Los Angeles, with two new teams added to the league: the New York Yankees, sole survivors of the AFL, and the Cleveland Bulldogs. Many of the smaller Midwest cities were beginning to realize that the economics of professional football were changing and they were not able to draw enough attendance to be financially competitive with franchises from bigger cities. And that was the primary source of revenue for the teams. The loss of founding cities was discouraging, but a league with 12 strong franchises was in better shape for the long term.

The owners met again on July 17 and the Steam Roller's 1927 schedule was announced. The team was scheduled to play 13 NFL games with nine at home, highlighted by visits from the famous Chicago Bears, the defending league champion Yellow Jackets, the Bulldogs and the Nevers-led Duluth Eskimos. The season opener was scheduled for September 25 against the Dayton Triangles and the Steam Roller would be making its first trip to Cubs Park on November 6 to tangle with the Bears. The other important news coming from the conference was that Providence would host the 1928 summer owners' meeting.

With all the franchise turmoil and many players seeking new homes, the Steam Roller took advantage and landed its franchise quarterback along with several other key players who would change the trajectory of the team, at least for a few years.

Jimmy Conzelman, who was the owner, man-

Providence Steam Roller vs. Dayton Triangles program from October 23, 1927. The Steam Roller defeated Dayton 7-0 at the Cycledrome with Bill Pritchard scoring the only touchdown of the game (author's collection).

ager, coach and star player of the Detroit Panthers, made the difficult decision to turn the franchise back to the league in early August. The Panthers had attempted to sign University of Michigan star player Benny Friedman to bolster attendance. When that fell through with Friedman signing with the Bulldogs, Conzelman made the decision to forfeit the franchise. He had purchased the team for a reported $500 in 1925, and his play helped the Panthers to an 8–2–2 record that season. The following season was not as successful as the team dropped to 4–6–2 and attendance hovered around 3,000 per game. He realized the franchise was not sustainable without a significant increase in average attendance that he thought Friedman could help provide. Conzelman was paid a reported $1,200 by the NFL when he forfeited the franchise.

Shortly after that was completed, Conzelman signed a contract with the Steam Roller on August 13 to be the manager, head coach and quarterback. He was to be paid $292 per game, which was very lucrative. Conzelman brought several players with him from the Panthers including All-Pro tackle Gus Sonnenberg, the former Dartmouth star; All-Pro end Ed Lynch; guard Jack Fleischmann from Purdue; and Al Hadden, from Washington & Jefferson. All five players, including Conzelman, had multiple years of NFL experience.

Jimmy Conzelman (author's collection).

Two. The Early Years (1925–1927)

In addition, the Roller added some other outstanding players to the roster. Orland Smith, part of the undefeated Brown "Iron Men" and a consensus All-American lineman, was signed on August 23. (The 1926 Brown University football team earned that nickname because of the significant playing time the starting 11 saw in most of the games.) The Boston College Cronin brothers—Bill and Jack—signed with Providence after a training camp stint. BC teammate Grattan O'Connell, an All-East end for the Eagles, also joined the Roller squad. Bill Pritchard, Penn State fullback, and Al Pierotti, lineman from Washington & Lee and veteran NFL player, both inked deals with the Steam Roller. And Bulger Lowe returned to the squad after a year away. William Wise, Holy Cross captain, signed with the Black and Orange on September 9 and would compete for playing time in a crowded backfield. But less than a week later, he took a coaching position in Springfield and with the new Steam Roller training requirements he would not be able to play.

The roster makeover was almost complete when big news broke on September 8. George "Wildcat" Wilson, the superstar back from the University of Washington and 1926 AFL star, had signed with Providence. Wilson was considered one of the greatest backs in the country. He had been pursued by at least six other NFL teams but chose Providence. It was a coup for the Steam Roller to secure a player many considered on par with Red Grange. Prior to coming to Providence, he had played for his own team in the AFL in 1926, the Los Angeles Wildcats. The Wildcats, named after Wilson, went 6–6–2. He also had done some barnstorming. Wilson participated in a series of West Coast exhibition games against Grange and the Chicago Bears in January 1926 and more than held his own against America's best-known football player. While in college at Washington, Wilson broke the school record with 37 touchdowns. His contract paid him $375 per game and he instantly became one of the highest-paid players in the NFL. His brother Abe also joined the Roller.

Laird, despite losing the head coaching job, remained with the Steam Roller. He was moved to guard and was a key contributor throughout the 1927 season. Several other regulars from the 1926 Providence team did not return in 1927, including Jack Donahue, Eckstein, Garvey, Golembeski, Keefer and Wentworth. Keefer went back home to Dayton. He took a job teaching at Steele High School as head of athletic instruction, a job that included coaching baseball, basketball and football.

Providence had a lot of work to do to get the newly constructed team ready for the NFL opener on September 25. Conzelman was a single-wing quarterback, which meant he would call the plays but was more likely to block or catch a pass than to throw one. Wilson, the tailback, would be the player passing the football, more often than not, and would be one of the most frequent ball carriers. It was also expected that Pritchard and Oden would get the bulk of the remaining carries. The team reported for training on September 11 with the first practice on the following day. Providence had only one warm-up game scheduled. The Steam Roller played the New London Submarine Base squad on September 18 and pounded the soldiers 44–0. Conzelman, with only a week of practice under his belt, steered the Roller to scores in every quarter while amassing 24 first downs with an array of running plays mixed with some adept passes that overwhelmed New London.

Lloyd Young scored the first touchdown around left end while dragging six would-be tacklers into the end zone for the score. In the second quarter, Al Hadden scored on a six-yard run that was set up by a 32-yard Conzelman-to-Ed Lynch pass. Providence went to halftime with a 13–0 lead.

Newcomer Wilson, known to be both electrifying and temperamental, lived up to his hype. Wilson did not play until the second half, with his limited practice time, but on his first run from scrimmage he darted off left tackle for 13 yards. Later in the drive, Wilson, wearing jersey No. 88, knifed over from the one-yard line for his first touchdown as a Steam Roller. On the ensuing drive, a Wilson pass to Conzelman set the Steam Roller up for another score and Pritchard smashed over from the six-yard line to put Providence in command 26–0. The Roller scored three more touchdowns in the final period, highlighted by a thrilling 25-yard interception return by Conzelman.

The offense that looked so potent against New London was completely stymied by the New York Giants on opening day, September 25, at the Cycledrome with 7,500 looking on. The Giants missed three field goals throughout the game, one in the first quarter and two in the fourth, but thanks to a blocked punt in the second quarter, New York was able to muster a touchdown. With a drive starting at the Roller's two-yard line, it took all four downs to go those two hard-fought yards. Finally on fourth down, Jack McBride bulled his way into the end zone and the Giants led 6–0. On the next series, Providence was hemmed in its own end, and Bill Cronin was tackled by Cal Hubbard before he could get a punt away from his own end zone. The safety put New York ahead 8–0 and its defense made that stand up for the victory.

Providence was outplayed by the Giants as the New Yorkers earned 10 first downs to only five for the home team. The Steam Roller was hurt by the poor play of Wilson, who had come down with a stomach ailment that threw off his game. The doctor had advised him not to play, but Wilson gave it a brave effort to help his new team. Without Wilson's strong play, the Steam Roller had no sustained offense against the big and strong

New York defense with the likes of Al Nesser, Steve Owen and Pete Henry, along with McBride and Hubbard.

Despite the loss, the game was a financial success, and that was important coming off a season where the team had lost money. The gate receipts from ticket sales were $9,661, and when concessions were included, the total revenue increased to $9,912. The game's total expenses were slightly less than $6,000 that included 1 percent of the gate receipts that was paid to the NFL ($97), the Cycledrome's 15 percent ($1,449), player salaries ($1,972) and the visiting team's share ($2,475). The salaries of the other players besides Wilson and Conzelman were mostly $100 per game with a few exceptions, like Sonnenberg at $200, Oden at $150, Hanny at $145, Orland Smith at $125 and Spellman at $110. Overall, the team earned a tidy profit of almost $4,000.

Another Providence newcomer, Gus Sonnenberg, was the hero of the Steam Roller's 5–0 win over Buffalo on October 2. After a scoreless first quarter, Sonnenberg—the former Detroit Panther—downed a 63-yard Wilson punt at the Buffalo one-yard line. On the next play, the Bisons tried to punt out of danger, but newcomers Ed Lynch and Al Pierotti crashed through the line and pushed Buffalo fullback Ken Houser into the punter. The kicked ball ricocheted off the burly Houser and went through the back of the end zone for a safety.

From there, Providence moved the ball into scoring position on runs by Conzelman, Wilson and Pritchard along with a shovel pass from Conzelman to Wilson. With the ball on the Buffalo 10-yard line, Sonnenberg was called upon to kick and his placement was perfect. The Steam Roller led 5–0.

Both teams had scoring opportunities in the third quarter that went awry. The sweltering heat on this day was taking its toll on the players. Buffalo's Ed Doyle scooped up a Sonnenberg fumble early in the quarter and returned it 34 yards to the Providence six. Conzelman made a touchdown-saving tackle on Doyle, dragging him down from behind. On the next play, Bisons quarterback Charlie Van Horn muffed the snap from center, and Jack Cronin was Johnny-on-the-spot. He picked up the loose ball and raced to the Buffalo 36-yard line. Harlan Carr made a great tackle to keep Cronin from breaking the run for a score. The 58-yard gain was the longest of the game. But the Roller threat was snuffed out on an interception by Ben Rederick of Conzelman's pass at the Bisons' 24-yard line.

Conzelman and Bill Cronin intercepted Buffalo passes in the fourth quarter to keep the Bisons from scoring as the Steam Roller finished the shutout. Laird was lauded for his play at guard and Jack Cronin's punting was key to the Providence victory, as reported by the *Providence Journal*.

The Chicago Bears, led by Paddy Driscoll, Joey "Dutch" Sternaman and George Halas, were scheduled to make their first appearance in Providence on October 9. However, Mother Nature did not cooperate. A heavy rain hit the city on Sunday and continued throughout the day, making the field unplayable, and the game was postponed. It was not rescheduled. For making the trip, the Bears were guaranteed payment from the Steam Roller of $2,220, even though the game was never played. Providence purchased an insurance policy for each game at a cost of $270 that paid the team $2,500 for instances such as this.

Dinger Doane, former Tufts star and previously a member of the independent pro Steam Roller team in 1917–1918 and a six-year NFL veteran, was signed by the team on October 14. He also had previously played with Conzelman in Detroit. Doane had requested his release from his contract with Pottsville so that he could join Conzelman in Providence.

Next on the schedule for Providence was its archrival Pottsville at the Cycledrome on October 16. The outcome of the game ended in controversy. Providence played a strong game throughout and led 3–0 late in the fourth quarter. Sonnenberg made an 18-yard field goal early in the second quarter that put the Steam Roller in the lead. The kick was set up by a brilliant 57-yard run by Oden.

Providence had the better of play for most of the game. Sonnenberg missed three other field goal attempts that could have lengthened the score in the Steam Roller's favor. But, besides his missed kicks, he was spectacular. He downed a Providence punt at the Pottsville two, he booted a 63-yard punt that died at the Pottsville four and he tackled several Pottsville ball carriers for losses throughout the game. He left the game in the fourth quarter with an injury. He was knocked out when he tackled Frank Kirkleski for a five-yard loss on the Pottsville 34-yard line. When Sonnenberg was revived, though woozy, he demanded to stay in the game, but he was taken off the field by force.

And then controversy took over. Pottsville running back Dinty Moore caught a pass and ran five steps before he was clobbered by the Roller's Pritchard. The hit was so hard that the ball sprang loose and Lynch fell on it for Providence. Referee J.T. Hennessey ruled that the ball had touched the ground when Moore caught the ball and therefore it was an incomplete pass. The other officials disagreed with him and thought it was clearly a fumble. But Hennessey stuck to his call. The Steam Roller crowd was furious.

On that same play multiple Pottsville players were caught slugging several Steam Roller players and a 15-yard penalty was assessed ... but the Maroons maintained possession. Pottsville quarterback Kirkleski, sensing an opportunity, took over the game. He completed two beautiful passes, one covering over 40 yards and the other over 30, to move the ball to the

Roller's six-yard line as time was winding down. On the next play, Tony Latone bulled his way to within a foot of the goal line but fumbled the ball. Teammate Kirkleski recovered in the end zone. It was ruled a touchdown, but one official disagreed with the legality of the score. Again, the referee stuck to his call. It made for a heartbreaking 6–3 loss for Providence in a game the Roller felt it deserved to win. Despite the bad calls, the Steam Roller still could have won the game, but its pass defense failed when it mattered most. In addition, Sonnenberg was missed on the last series. The *Boston Globe* described the game as "one of the most stubbornly fought professional contests ever waged in Rhode Island."[27]

Providence played its fourth consecutive home game at the Cycledrome on October 23 against the Dayton Triangles. The Triangles were an original franchise back to 1920 and were one of the last of the small Midwestern cities still playing. They had a 1-3-1 record coming into the game and were led by Earl Britton, former Illinois quarterback, and tailback Fay Abbott, who was a star at Syracuse University.

The Steam Roller, led by an opportunistic defense, defeated Dayton 7–0. The Roller, smarting from the loss to Pottsville because of a poor pass defense, intercepted six Triangle aerials, with Laird snaring three of them. Wilson, Conzelman and Bull Wesley contributed one each.

Early in the second half, Providence put together the only scoring drive of the game. With the ball at midfield, Oden threw a pass to Wilson at Dayton's 30 and he carried it to the 23-yard line. Three runs and an Oden pass to Pritchard set the ball at the Dayton three-yard line, but the Triangle defense was not going to surrender easily. Three more running plays netted only two yards, but on fourth and goal the powerful Pritchard smashed through the Dayton line and into the end zone for the score. Pritchard also converted the extra point for the 7–0 score. From there it was the combination of a solid Providence rushing attack and the opportunistic defense that kept Dayton from denting the scoreboard and helping the Steam Roller improve its NFL record to 2-2.

The Steam Roller traveled to Frankford, Pennsylvania, on October 29 for the first game of a home-and-home weekend series with the defending NFL champion Yellow Jackets. This was not quite the same prolific team of 1926, but it was still formidable. Frankford had lost several key players from the previous year's squad, including Chamberlin, Stockton, Doc Bruder, Johnny Budd and leading scorer Ben Jones.

A boisterous crowd of 15,000 at Frankford Stadium helped the Yellow Jackets to a strong first quarter. After a missed Sonnenberg field goal for the Steam Roller that had been set up by a Yellow Jackets fumble, Frankford controlled the opening quarter. Starting at their own 40-yard line, the Yellow Jackets deftly moved down the field behind the passing of Lou

Mollinet mixed with line plunges by George Tully to reach the Providence 10-yard line. Ken Mercer then bolted off right tackle and into the end zone for the touchdown. He also kicked the extra point and Frankford was on top 7–0.

The second quarter turned out to be what Providence fans had been waiting to see since the acquisition of Conzelman and Wilson. The Steam Roller offense came to life behind its two stars. Providence marched 65 yards at the start of the second quarter with brilliant passes from Wilson and effective runs by Pritchard that moved the ball to the Frankford 18. Wilson then hurriedly tossed a pass to Conzelman while the Yellow Jackets appeared confused, and the clever ball carrier dived into the end zone for a touchdown. Pritchard's kick was good and the game was knotted at seven.

Wilson set up the next Steam Roller touchdown with an interception of a Yellow Jackets pass that he returned to the Frankford 42-yard line. He then threw passes to Lynch (for 25 yards) and Oden, who lugged the ball to the five-yard line. Providence was unable to convert the sparkling pass plays into a touchdown and settled for a Sonnenberg field goal. However, the Yellow Jackets were offsides on the kick. Providence accepted the penalty, taking the points off the scoreboard, and went for the touchdown. Wilson made the decision look ingenious as he dashed 10 yards through the Jackets' defense for the touchdown. Sonnenberg's kick was good and Providence went to the halftime break with a 14–7 lead.

Midway through the third quarter, Providence was at it again. Starting at the 42-yard line, Oden passed to Conzelman for five yards, Wilson tossed a 15-yarder to Oden, Pritchard had two strong runs and another Wilson pass went to Oden as the Roller moved to the Yellow Jackets' 15-yard line. A few plays later, Oden scooted around right end for a beautiful touchdown run to cap off the sterling drive as Providence went on to a very impressive 20–7 victory.

After traveling overnight via train from Frankford to Providence, the two teams met again, this time at the Cycledrome. The rematch was eerily similar to the previous day's contest. Again, Wilson and Conzelman were the stars in a 14–0 Providence victory in front of 9,000.

Wilson scored the first touchdown of the game on an eight-yard slashing run in the second quarter that finished off a 41-yard Steam Roller march. In the third quarter, Conzelman, playing with an illness he had been battling since Thursday, caught a pass from Wilson at the Jackets' 15-yard line and swerved and darted his way through several would-be tacklers for the score. Conzelman also caught passes from Wilson of 26 and 29 yards during the game to keep the Jackets' defense off-balance. Frankford drove deep into Providence territory only once, and that

Two. The Early Years (1925–1927)

occurred in the first quarter. After that, the Steam Roller defense dominated its opponent on the way to the 14–0 victory. Providence's record improved to 4–2 with the three-game winning streak.

Providence continued to have success financially as well. Through the first six games, the team had increased its bank account from $5,070 following the Giants game to more than $8,800 at the end of October. The team was averaging 6,800 fans per game.

The Steam Roller took to the road and traveled to Wrigley Field in Chicago, home of the Chicago Cubs baseball team, for a November 6 matchup with the first-place and unbeaten Bears. Conzelman was not at full strength. He had been stricken with ptomaine poison, which is a type of food poisoning. Despite his illness, he continued to play.

The Steam Roller defense played a remarkable game. It played a bend/don't-break brand of defense. The Roller allowed 23 first downs to the potent Chicago attack and the Bears penetrated inside the Providence 20-yard line on seven different occasions. The Roller defense twice intercepted Chicago passes to thwart drives, forced two fumbles, stopped the Bears once on downs and twice forced Chicago into missed field goal attempts. In addition, Chicago's Paddy Driscoll missed three other field goal attempts from beyond 20 yards. In all, the Bears had 10 prime opportunities to score and each time they failed.

Providence managed only three first downs as the Bears completely dominated the game, yet the Roller defense would not yield. The highlight for the Roller, beyond the play of its defense, was the punting of Wilson. His kicks continually pinned the Bears deep in their territory and forced them to drive long distances to get into scoring position. Incredibly, Providence achieved a 0–0 tie.

The Steam Roller continued its road trip as the team traveled to New York City for an odd Tuesday game against the Giants. New York was in second place with a 6–1–1 record and had beaten the Steam Roller to begin the season. In front of 38,000 at the Polo Grounds, this game was no contest. Providence was a physically and mentally tired team after a short rest and a long train ride, and it clearly impacted the Roller.

New York scored a touchdown in each quarter in its 25–0 conquest of Providence. The game's first score came from the Giants defense, when defensive back Mule Wilson swiped a pass by Providence's Wilson and returned it 55 yards for a touchdown. New York's second touchdown was set up by another Wilson interception, this time by Mickey Murtaugh. The Giants scored on a razzle-dazzle triple-pass play from McBride to Doug Wycoff to Jack Hagerty for the touchdown and a 13–0 Giants halftime lead.

In the third quarter, Hagerty returned a Wilson punt 50 yards for a touchdown, and in the fourth quarter McBride passed to Haines for the final score of the Giants' rout. The Steam Roller was beaten up physically as Kozlowsky, Laird and Conzelman were all forced out of the game due to injuries and did not return. And Sonnenberg briefly was knocked unconscious but refused to leave the game and played until the end.

The Steam Roller returned home for an encounter with the Duluth Eskimos on November 13. The players were happy to see 7,500 cheering them on as they took the field. It was a tightly contested game that was not decided until the fourth quarter. The Eskimos scored first as Nevers, "the greatest triple-threat ever to don a cleated shoe on a Rhode Island gridiron," reported the *Providence Journal*,[28] streaked 36 yards for a first-quarter touchdown and his extra-point kick was good. Providence evened the score after Spellman picked up a Johnny Blood fumble at midfield and rambled to the Eskimos' nine-yard line. Wilson ran the ball for four yards and then Billy Cronin caught a pass in the left flat from Oden and ran in for the score. Sonnenberg's extra-point kick was good and the game was tied at 7–7.

Nevers played a magnificent game. He rushed for 111 yards, intercepted a pass that he returned for 34 yards and completed nine passes for 106 yards. It is the first recorded game that a single player rushed and passed for over 100 yards. The Eskimos had four other chances to score, but each time the Steam Roller defense turned them aside. Three times the Eskimos were stopped by the Providence defense on downs and Nevers missed a field goal try on a fourth possession. Both teams played extremely well, but Nevers was the best player on the field. It appeared the game was going to end in a tie, but Curly Oden changed all that on one play. Midway through the fourth quarter, the elusive Swede fielded a Nevers punt on his 26-yard line. Oden soon reached the open field but he still had to get past Nevers in order to score. Orland Smith came to the rescue as he cleared out Nevers with a perfectly timed block a couple of yards from the goal line, allowing Oden to finish off his spectacular run of 74 yards. The point-after failed, but Providence was in the lead 13–7. The Eskimos had the ball twice more before the gun sounded but the Steam Roller defense did not allow them to score. It was a nice bounce-back victory after the debacle at the Polo Grounds.

The largest crowd of the season at the Cycledrome, about 12,000, came out to see the 5–3–1 Steam Roller battle with the Cleveland Bulldogs on November 20. The Bulldogs were a good draw as they were led by first-team All-Pro Benny Friedman along with other star players including running back Al Bloodgood, fullback Jim Simmons and receiver Carl Bacchus.

The two teams battled through a scoreless first half as the Providence defense was able to stymie Friedman and the Bulldogs' offense. The Steam Roller held the star quarterback to only 4 of 12 passing. Friedman drove Cleveland deep into Providence territory only one time, reaching the Steam Roller's five-yard line, but the defense held on downs. At halftime Cleveland switched quarterbacks and put in Bloodgood, who had led Kansas City to a 22-0 bludgeoning of the Steam Roller in 1926. In the second half of this game, he matched what he accomplished in the previous game against Providence. He again scored 16 total points, this time on two touchdowns, an extra point and a field goal, to lead Cleveland to an identical 22-0 victory.

Bloodgood booted a 35-yard field goal to start the scoring in the third quarter. Shortly after that, Proc Randels blocked a Steam Roller punt deep in Providence territory and recovered the ball in the end zone for a touchdown. Bloodgood's placement was good and Cleveland led 10-0. Later in the quarter, Wilson threw an interception and on the play was knocked out of the game. That turnover led to the first of Bloodgood's touchdowns on a short run early in the fourth quarter. Dave Mishel, the former Brown star, replaced Wilson and saw his first action as a Steam Roller. He was unable to move Providence to the end zone for the remainder of the game. He completed 4 of 10 passes for 57 yards. Later in the final quarter, Bloodgood scored his second touchdown on another short run to complete the scoring.

Despite the beating the Steam Roller took, it was another successful day at the gate. The receipts from ticket sales were $12,374, the highest of the season. Cleveland was paid more than $4,500 for helping to attract the large crowd, but Providence pocketed a nifty profit in excess of $3,500.

Four days after the loss to Cleveland, the Steam Roller traveled to Pottsville for a Thanksgiving Day matchup with the Maroons. Both teams entered the game with disappointing records. Providence sported a 5-4-1 slate and Pottsville was only 4-7.

Pottsville's defense again proved difficult for the Steam Roller to solve. With rain falling heavily throughout the game and the field a sea of mud, Providence still chalked up 320 yards of offense but could not get across the Maroons' goal line. Pottsville had trouble moving the football but put together one excellent drive of 77 yards in the middle of the first half that was aided by a controversial pass interference penalty against Laird. Following the penalty, the 11 Roller defensive players vehemently argued the call, but to no avail. Pottsville took advantage and moved the ball to the Roller 21. On the next play, Frank Kirkleski fired a touchdown pass to George Kenneally. Wilson blocked the extra-point attempt, but Pottsville led 6-0.

Later in the quarter, Providence had its best chance to score. The

Steam Roller drove the ball to the Pottsville eight-yard line. On fourth down, Wilson threw a perfect pass to Conzelman for an apparent first down at the Maroons' three. But the officials ruled that Wilson was not five yards behind the scrimmage line at the time of the pass and nullified the first down. The Steam Roller threatened to score only one other time, late in the game. Wilson completed a beautiful 22-yard pass to Conzelman, who was streaking for a score with seemingly only one man to beat, Eddie Scharer, when Kenneally unexpectedly came up from behind and tackled him short of the goal line as the clock ran out. Pottsville had held on for the 6–0 victory. Providence was hurt by penalties. The team was called for offside four times, had three illegal use of hands penalties for 15 yards each and two illegal shift infractions. It all added up to a disheartening loss for the Steam Roller.

Providence played its third game in seven days on November 27 when it hosted Grange and the New York Yankees at the Cycledrome. Despite rain and drizzle, 10,000 came out to see the action and they were not disappointed. Grange, nursing a sore leg, played only the first half and did not carry the pigskin. However, he made some brilliant passes, completing four of six for 85 yards and catching one pass for 23 yards. But the Roller defense stiffened each time and kept the Yankees off the scoreboard. Wilson's first-half

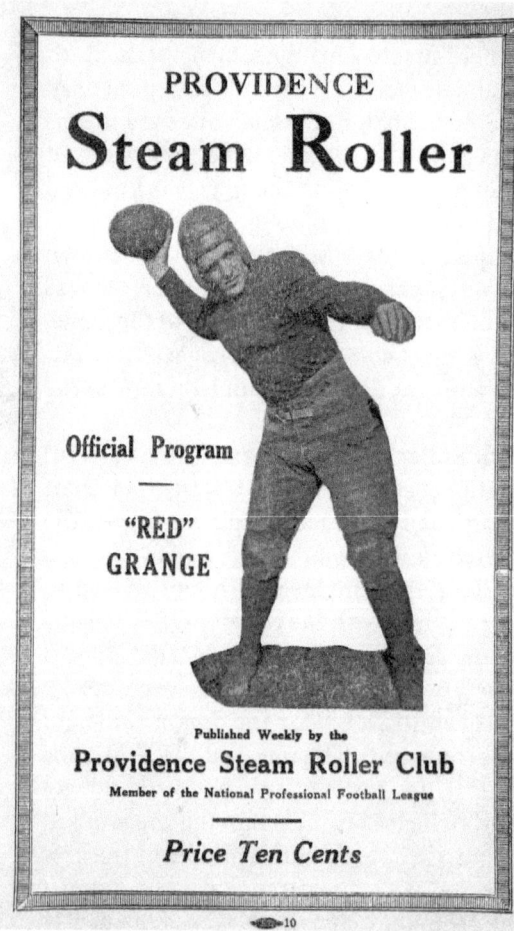

Providence Steam Roller vs. New York Yankees program featuring Red Grange on the cover from the Steam Roller's 14–7 victory on November 27, 1927, at the Providence Cycledrome (author's collection).

punting also helped the Roller keep the Yankees at bay. He averaged more than 60 yards a punt. The game was scoreless at intermission.

Early in the third quarter, Providence put together its best drive of the day. With Wilson completing five passes to Conzelman and Lynch, the latter snatching four of them, the Steam Roller marched 75 yards in 11 plays. The drive was capped by a splendid touchdown pass from Wilson to Lynch. The placement by Sonnenberg was good and Providence led 7–0. Providence chose to receive the ensuing kickoff. Shortly after the kick, Providence was driving again, but a Yankees interception abruptly ended that possession. On the Steam Roller's next series, it was forced to punt. The Yankees' Mike Michalske fumbled Wilson's kick and the ever-alert Sonnenberg pounced on the loose ball at the New York 16-yard line. On third down, Conzelman tossed a lateral to Oden, who scurried around right end and was brought down inches short of the goal line. Conzelman dived into the end zone on the next play, and with Sonnenberg's placement good, Providence led 14–0 early in the fourth quarter.

The Yankees did not concede. On their next possession, Eddie Tryon caught a 20-yard pass from Wes Fry and the former Colgate star raced the final 25 yards for an electrifying touchdown on the game's most exciting play. Tryon's placement was good and New York was back in the game, trailing only 14–7. The Yankees had two more chances to tie the game, but Bull Wesley and Jack Cronin ended each of those offensive thrusts with interceptions as the Steam Roller held on for its sixth win of the season.

A rematch of the same two teams was played less than a week later. The Steam Roller and Yankees traveled to Syracuse University and played the first-ever professional football game at Archbold Stadium on December 3 in front of 5,000 curious spectators.

Archbold Stadium was built in the center of the university campus and opened on September 25, 1907, when Syracuse defeated Hobart 28–0. The stadium was named for John D. Archbold (a vice president at Standard Oil), who was the major benefactor, donating $600,000 for its construction. The all-concrete stadium, the first of its kind in America, became known for its vaunted arched entryway. When it opened, it was called "the greatest athletic arena in America" by some in the national press.[29] The Syracuse University football team called the stadium its home from 1907 through the 1978 season and won the schools' only national championship in 1959 behind the first-ever Black Heisman Trophy winner, Ernie Davis.

The Providence vs. New York game was played for the benefit of the Manlius School building fund. The teams were welcomed to Syracuse with an early winter snowstorm. The field had to be cleared of the white stuff prior to the start of the game. Once it did, it appeared like the Steam Roller enjoyed the snow as it played an outstanding game and thoroughly outplayed the Yankees.

Providence scored first on a second-quarter 12-yard field goal by Sonnenberg that had been set up by a 40-yard pass and run from Wilson to Conzelman. Shortly after the kickoff, the Yankees were forced to punt. Jack Cronin caught Verne Lewellen's kick at the Providence 45-yard line and weaved his way through the entire Yankee defense on his way to a touchdown. "The stands rose en mass and cheered one of the finest bits of broken field running ever seen in the stadium," reported the *Providence Journal*.[30] Sonnenberg's placement failed, but the Roller was now in seeming command, 9–0. Another electrifying play happened only a few seconds later when Wilson picked off a Yankee aerial and returned it 22 yards to the Yankees' 35-yard line. However, a few plays later time ran out in the first half.

The third quarter was evenly played with neither team threatening to score. In the final quarter, each team had a scoring opportunity go awry with the slippery field conditions, and then a Wilson interception ended the Yankees' final threat and Providence secured the 9–0 win. It was the Steam Roller's third victory over a Grange-led team without a loss in the past two seasons.

The Providence squad traveled back from Syracuse to play its final game of the season the next day against Pottsville. Finally,

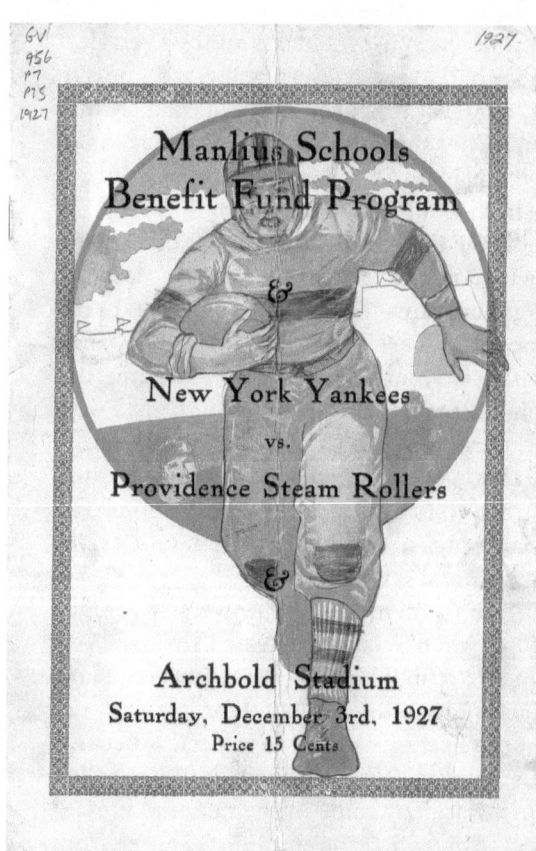

Providence Steam Roller vs. New York Yankees program at Archbold Stadium from December 3, 1927. It was the first NFL game played at Archbold Stadium, Syracuse, New York, and the third consecutive win by the Steam Roller over a Red Grange–led team (courtesy Rhode Island Historical Society—RHi X17 4835).

in the third meeting between the two teams, the Steam Roller found the charm. A small crowd of only 1,500 braved a sleet storm as Providence rolled over the Maroons 20–0. Pottsville's only scoring threat occurred in the first quarter when it marched to the Providence 12-yard line after a Kirkleski-to-Latone 36-yard pass-and-run play. The Steam Roller defense stiffened and kept the Maroons off the scoreboard.

It took Providence more than half the game to get its offense going. Early in the third quarter, the Steam Roller marched 38 yards and Wilson ran the final few yards for the game's first touchdown. Sonnenberg's kick was good and Providence led 7–0. A brief time later, the Steam Roller was on the move again. From midfield, Wilson completed a 10-yard pass to Lynch, which was soon followed by the play of the game. Wilson threw a short pass to Conzelman and the gifted quarterback dodged and weaved his way through six would-be tacklers for a spectacular touchdown. The Steam Roller finished off the scoring late in the fourth quarter. Following an interception by Hadden at the Pottsville 36 and his return to the 23-yard-line, Wilson passed 10 yards to Conzelman. Three Wilson runs, the last for five yards, resulted in a touchdown and a 20–0 Providence shellacking of their archrival from coal country. It was sweet revenge for the Steam Roller to end its season on a high note.

However, the last two games were losers financially. The crowd in Syracuse was disappointing. The shared piece of the gate receipts for the neutral-site game that Providence received did not cover the cost of the train travel of $642 and the players' salaries. The poor weather significantly dampened the expected crowd against Pottsville and the gate receipts of $2,191 were the lowest of the season and did not cover the players' salaries—much less the other expenses. The games highlighted the importance of paid attendance for financial success of an NFL franchise in 1927. Fortunately for the Steam Roller and their fans, the team had some money in the bank from earlier in the season, and the Roller would be back in 1928.

The Steam Roller finished the season on a three-game win streak and ended with an 8–5–1 record, the franchise's best NFL record to that point. That was good for fifth place in the 12-team league. Two of their five losses were against the NFL champion Giants, who finished 11–1–1.

Conzelman and Wilson led the team with four touchdowns each, but it was the defense that made the difference. Led by first team All-Pros Jack Fleischmann, Sonnenberg, Kozlowsky and Oden, the Steam Roller allowed only two teams to score more than a single touchdown and it had six shutouts. Also, Wilson and Lynch were named second-team All-Pros. Providence finished 6–3 at home in the Cycledrome and averaged slightly more than 7,200 per game.

Chapter Three

The NFL Champions (1928)

1928—The Top of the Mountain

With their team coming off a three-game winning streak to end the 1927 season and finishing with the best record in franchise history to that point (8-5-1), expectations of the Providence fans were sky high as the Steam Roller began preparations for the 1928 season.

There was roster turnover as Coppen, Johnson and the rest of the ownership group continued to try to strengthen the team. Several solid contributors in 1927 did not return for the 1928 season. Bulger Lowe retired. Bill Pritchard and Al Hadden were traded. Dinger Doane, Joe Kozlowsky, Ed Lynch, Dave Mishel, Al Pierotti and Bull Wesley did not return.

The Steam Roller dealt Hadden to the Chicago Bears for five-year NFL veteran and four-time second-team All-Pro end Duke Hanny. Pritchard was traded to the New York Yankees for three-year veteran Norm Harvey, a third-team All-Pro lineman. Harvey, who had played in Detroit with Conzelman, was happy to be back with the head coach and quarterback after spending the 1927 season with the Yankees.

Conzelman returned as player-coach and Wildcat Wilson, Jack Fleishmann, Curly Oden and Gus Sonnenberg also returned. In addition, the Cronin brothers (Bill and Jack), Jim Laird, Jack Spellman, Orland Smith and Abe Wilson were back.

Perry Jackson, who Conzelman had heard was an outstanding lineman at Southwestern State Teachers College in Oklahoma, where he was All-Conference twice, was cabled a tryout offer from the Steam Roller. However, at the time Jackson was suffering from paratyphoid fever after working on the Mexican border. Jackson was in no condition to play football. He suggested to his friend and offensive line teammate at Southwestern State, Arnold Shockley, to go in his place. Shockley agreed and headed to Providence. Upon arrival and unbeknownst to Conzelman or any of Roller management, Shockley told the team that he was Jackson. He subsequently signed a contract under the assumed name, made the team and contributed nicely for Providence in 1928. Shockley/Jackson appeared in 10 games and started seven. Playing under an assumed name was somewhat commonplace in the 1920s. Many college players did it to make some extra dollars but maintain their college eligibility. However, this is the only known case where a player assumed another person's identity.

At the February 11–12 owners' meeting, President Joe Carr said the league had its most successful season as it played to more than 500,000 spectators the previous year. However, underlying that were some struggling franchises that were not financially able to play in the 1928 season. The NFL shrunk to 11 teams as the Buffalo Bisons, Cleveland Bulldogs and Duluth Eskimos folded. Ernie Nevers chose to play baseball instead of football, and without its star player the Eskimos decided there was no reason to continue. Detroit reentered the league, this time as the Wolverines. Grange and Eddie Tryon, star backs for the Yankees, did not play in 1928. Grange was out with an injured knee and Tryon played for an independent team. Los Angeles was scheduled to have a team but dropped out at the last minute after having trouble scheduling opponents, leaving the league at 10 franchises.

Providence hosted the owners' annual schedule release meeting at the Biltmore Hotel on July 7–8. However, because there were some franchises still in flux at the meeting and applications for new teams to be acted upon, the finalization of the schedule was delayed until a meeting on August 11 in Detroit. A revised passing rule was adopted and the state of the league was discussed among the owners. Judge Dooley represented the Steam Roller. Carr came out of the meeting predicting that "the coming season will be one of the greatest the league will ever have enjoyed with the individual teams in a sounder state than heretofore and increasing enthusiasm over the game in all parts of the country."[1]

Coming out of the Detroit league meeting there was speculation whether the NFL could exist past the 1928 season. A headline in the *Providence Journal* stated, "National Football League Believed Near Dissolution."[2] The league was down to only 10 teams and several of those were struggling financially. The Grange tour from 1925, though it brought publicity to the game, caused players to demand higher salaries. Gate receipts were not keeping up with the cost of running a franchise.

The preseason favorites were the defending champion New York Giants, the Chicago Bears coached by George Halas with star players Joey Sternaman and Paddy Driscoll, and the Green Bay Packers, coached by Curly Lambeau and boasting stars Lavvie Dilweg and Verne Lewellen.

Providence took advantage of the demise of the Cleveland franchise and signed All-Pro center Clyde Smith and All-Pro guard Milt Rehnquist.

Those moves significantly strengthened the front line. Smith was an All-Pro in 1927, and in addition to being an outstanding center, he was a mobile, powerful-hitting linebacker. Fullback Jim Simmons, the Bulldogs' second-leading scorer in 1927 with five touchdowns, was also acquired from Cleveland. Art "Pop" Williams, the third-leading scorer in Eastern college football in 1927 with 90 points in only eight games, withdrew from the University of Connecticut. Shortly after his withdrawal, he signed with Providence. Williams would turn out to be a great complement to Wilson.

The team stuck to the NFL roster limit of 18 that season, a number it had consistently exceeded in previous seasons. In all, only 19 players played for the 1928 version of the Steam Roller.

Providence's revised league schedule was released on September 12. The Roller sported a 12-game slate with nine home games. The highlights of the home schedule included the first-ever visit by Los Angeles (which did not occur because the team folded), the Detroit Wolverines with Benny Friedman and the Green Bay Packers. Providence had the usual home-and-home series with Pottsville and Frankford and added a similar series with the Yankees. The team was scheduled to open its fourth season in the NFL at home against the Yankees on September 30. Providence also had one warm-up game scheduled against the Long Island Warlow A.C. on September 23.

STEAM ROLLER FOOTBALL SCHEDULE - 1928

Date	Opponent	Location	S. R.	Opp.
September 23	EXHIBITION GAME	At Providence		
September 30	NEW YORK YANKEES	At Providence		
October 7	PHILA. YELLOW JACKETS	At Providence		
October 14	DAYTON, OHIO	At Providence		
October 21	NEW YORK YANKEES	At New York		
October 28	POTTSVILLE, PA.	At Providence		
November 4	DETROIT	At Providence		
November 11	COLUMBUS, OHIO	At Providence		
November 17	YELLOW JACKETS	At Philadelphia		
November 18	YELLOW JACKETS	At Providence		
November 25	NEW YORK GIANTS	At Providence		
November 29	POTTSVILLE, PA.	At Pottsville		
December 2	GREEN BAY, WIS.	At Providence		

YELLOW CAB COMPANY — OFFICIAL CABS FOR STEAM ROLLERS — **GAspee 8800**

Providence Steam Roller 1928 pocket schedule from their NFL championship season (courtesy Rhode Island Historical Society—RHi X17 4571).

Three. The NFL Champions (1928)

The team practiced for the first time together on September 17. Conzelman drilled his troops each day from 11:00 a.m. to 1:00 p.m. to get them ready for the only preseason game prior to the start of the 1928 NFL season that was coming in less than a week. Conzelman expected the Steam Roller to be better than the 1927 edition, primarily because of the improvement across the line with the addition of Smith, Rehnquist, Harvey and Hanny. The size and strength of the line matched up well with any other team in the NFL. Harvey at 220 pounds and Hanny at 210 manned the ends and were more known for their defensive skills and blocking ability than as pass receivers. The interior men, Orland Smith at 215, 185-pound Jack Fleischmann, newcomers Rehnquist (at 230 pounds, the largest man on the team), Jackson (200) and the rangy and quick Clyde Smith (180) were not going to be pushed around by anyone. Then add in returnees Sonnenberg and Spellman, both championship wrestlers who didn't even wear helmets, and the team was stacked with strength and toughness up front.

The backfield, with returnees Wilson and the Cronin brothers, was improved with the additions of Jim Simmons and "Pop" Williams, both power backs with speed who provided Conzelman with more offensive flexibility and firepower.

With more players from outside the New England region on the Steam Roller's roster, several of them needed places to live during the season. Pearce Johnson, assistant general manager of the team, had just the solution. They could rent rooms from him and his mother for $25 a month and she would cook meals for them. Conzelman, Clyde Smith, Rehnquist, Jackson and Simmons were among those who took him up on the offer. Mrs. Johnson quickly became a quasi-mother to several of the players and took a personal interest in their comfort and success. "She became an actual mother to all of those boys. They said that they told her that they were her mother away from home. She did their sewing. She did their ironing. She did their washing. She fed them, and she was a nurse to those who were injured," Johnson said in a 1991 NFL Films interview.[3] Also, Peter Laudati's wife, Madeline, would often cook meals for the players.

Another group of players stayed at the Crowne Hotel in downtown Providence. They were known as more of the carousing bunch. Johnson shared a story in his 1991 interview with NFL Films: "One of the players was a real carouser, Gus Sonnenberg, who was the world's wrestling champ at the time he played for us. I didn't see it but the boys who lived there told me that on one of the evenings they were down there, that he took the radiator right off the floor and threw it out the window. Speak of rowdyism, that is rowdyism to me."[4]

One important rule change went into effect for the 1928 season. The placement of the goalposts was moved to the backline of the end zone, making field goals more difficult and thus somewhat rare in 1928.

Providence looked in midseason form in its exhibition game against Long Island Warlow A.C. Wilson threw the ball all over the field as the Steam Roller introduced a very potent passing attack. Conzelman and Simmons were the recipients of most of Wilson's passes. It was an early indication that the passing game would become more popular in 1928 and would be an important weapon for Providence. It opened the game up but it also led to more interceptions than the league had ever seen.

The Steam Roller scored its first touchdown on a short run by Jack Cronin that capped off a 60-yard march in the first quarter. The bigger, stronger Providence squad imposed its will on the smaller Warlow team and put up three scores in the second quarter that increased its lead to 27–0 as the half drew to a close. Simmons scored all three Steam Roller touchdowns in the quarter. His first was on a 20-yard end run, and then he caught two of Wilson's passes—one of 40 yards and the other from 30 yards.

Simmons continued his outstanding play in the second half, scoring his fourth touchdown of the day on a five-yard run early in the fourth quarter. The play followed a 30-yard scamper of his that brought the ball into scoring position. Providence tallied two additional fourth-quarter touchdowns, a 15-yard run by Williams and a 42-yard pass-and-run from Conzelman to Wilson. Providence's defense did the rest in shutting out the undermanned Warlow A.C. with a final result of 48–0.

The highly anticipated NFL opener against the New York Yankees at the Cycledrome arrived on September 30. It was a drizzly overcast Sunday with temperatures a very autumn-like 50 degrees. The Steam Roller came onto the field in its black-and-orange jerseys and leather helmets; each player was issued one uniform for the season and was responsible for the rest of their equipment that they carried in duffel bags to the games. The equipment for the players, as described by Johnson, consisted of "leather shin guards that were half the shape of the front of your leg. Then you had canvas, really it was. Canvas or khaki pants. No padding. But they did have what they called kidney pads, which were located around the kidneys, and they slipped into pockets inside the pants. Then they had an opening in the front of the thigh into which they put another leather piece. The head gears, I don't see how you could get any protection out of them because, frankly, they were no more than cotton in between two layers of leather. But they did protect the ears and side of the face. They supplied their own shoes. That was the equipment in those days."[5]

The Yankees were without the services of Grange, who was out for the season rehabbing his knee, but they had signed Gibby Welch, who was fresh off an All-American career at the University of Pittsburgh.

Three. The NFL Champions (1928)

Providence displayed a dominating defense, holding the Yankees to a mere four first downs for the entire game while holding them to 39 yards rushing and 2 of 15 passing for 22 yards. The Steam Roller scored first on a two-yard plunge by Williams that had been set up by a 30-yard pass from Wilson to Simmons.

The Yankees stunned Providence later in the first quarter when Welch stepped in front of a pass intended for Conzelman and raced 62 yards for a score. The extra-point kick was good and the quarter ended in a 7–7 tie. The Steam Roller flexed its superiority in the second period. Williams finished off another Providence drive as he galloped 10 yards through a gaping hole that had been opened by superior blocks from Sonnenberg and Clyde Smith. Sonnenberg's kick was good and the Steam Roller was back in front, 14–7. Later in the period, Oden finished off a Providence march with a five-yard scoring run around end and the Roller was in command, 20–7.

Providence had a great chance for another touchdown in the third quarter. Conzelman threw a pass to a wide-open Simmons, who had a clear path to the end zone. But in his haste, he took his eye off the ball and it slithered through his fingertips for an incompletion. Still, the Roller continued to dominate and New York could not dent the Steam Roller defense. Providence completed the impressive 20–7 victory with 234 yards of offense—98 passing and 136 rushing. The 5,000 in attendance were also entertained by the Steam Roller band, a 30-piece ensemble that played the national anthem before the game and also performed at halftime. And Providence part-owner Peter Laudati also got in on the action as he held the pole for the first-down marker, something he would do at every home game.

Williams was lauded for his play by the *Providence Journal*: "It was one of the finest exhibitions of plunging a Roller back has staged in years and while it was William's first professional league football game, there was no question that the burly 210 pounder has arrived."[6] The newspaper also praised the play of Sonnenberg, saying, "Gus Sonnenberg had another one of his field days. It took the Yankee quarterback some time to discover that running plays at Sonnenberg were wasted effort."[7]

The day following the game, one of the most iconic buildings built in Providence history opened. The 428-foot tall Industrial Trust Company skyscraper, the tallest building in Rhode Island, was one of the earliest major art deco buildings constructed in the United States. It eventually received the nickname the "Superman Building" with its similarities to the headquarters of the *Daily Planet* in the fictional Superman comic books and the 1950s television show. (The TV series used Los Angeles City Hall to stand in for the newspaper building.) That October the building was featured on the cover of *Architectural Forum*, and *Providence Magazine* wrote, "The completed structure is a striking demonstration of the company's confidence in the growth and enduring soundness of the City, State and Country."[8] It was a tribute to the prosperity of Providence at that time.

The Frankford Yellow Jackets invaded the Renaissance City on October 7 for a 2:30 p.m. kickoff. The Yellow Jackets were coming off two impressive season-opening victories over Green Bay and Dayton by a combined score of 25–9. Frankford was led by player-coach Ed Weir and a trio of backs—Ken Mercer, Hust Stockton and first-team All-Pro Wally Diehl. The Providence fans attending the game had been promised that the public address announcer would provide periodic updates throughout the game on the World Series clash between the New York Yankees and St. Louis Cardinals that was being played at the same time. (The Yankees won 7–3 with two home runs from Lou Gehrig.)

The two combatants battled through a scoreless first quarter with Providence having the edge, holding Frankford to only one first down. At the end of the quarter, the Steam Roller had moved all the way to the Yellow Jackets' eight-yard line with the help of a Wilson-to-Simmons pass for 22 yards and some nice running by Williams and Simmons. On the second play of the second quarter, Providence set up for a Sonnenberg placekick, but they surprised everyone by faking it. Wilson tossed a strike to a wide-open Conzelman for a touchdown, as the Yellow Jackets' defense looked on in disbelief. Sonnenberg's kick failed but the Steam Roller led 6–0 and that is how the half ended, though the Yellow Jackets' offense had begun to move the ball.

The third quarter belonged to Frankford. The Yellow Jackets compiled eight first downs, but the Roller defense kept denying them. Three times Frankford moved deep into Providence territory but was stymied. The turning point of the game came late in the third quarter on a Providence turnover. Yellow Jackets defensive back Arnie Oehlrich intercepted a Wilson pass on the Frankford 36-yard line. The interception began a 56-yard march that resulted in a go-ahead touchdown for the Yellow Jackets. The backfield trio of Stockton, Mercer and Diehl combined to move the ball on the ground to the Providence five-yard line as they took turns slashing through the Steam Roller line. The Yellow Jackets then crossed up the Providence defense as Mercer tossed a five-yard pass to Diehl for the touchdown. Johnny Roepke booted the extra point to give Frankford the lead, 7–6.

Providence responded with three drives into Yellow Jackets territory in the fourth quarter but Sonnenberg missed two field goal attempts. The Roller's third drive was thwarted by a Roepke interception of Wilson. The Yellow Jackets made Providence pay for that turnover as they drove into field goal range and Roepke nailed a 20-yarder to give Frankford a 10–6 lead. The Steam Roller had one final chance. Wilson made a spectacular run on a punt return from his own end zone. He raced 36 yards and was almost in the clear when a flying tackler hit his legs and upended him to end the game and preserve the hard-fought victory for Frankford.

Providence made a roster move prior to its next game to further strengthen the team. The Roller brought back Al Hadden, who had been traded to the Bears prior to the start of the season.

The Dayton Triangles, a charter member of the NFL, traveled to Providence to take on the Steam Roller on October 14. Dayton was no match for this Steam Roller squad. Providence unleashed a potent offense and scored a touchdown in each quarter while amassing 18 first downs. Wilson was the star of the game. He completed nine passes for 152 yards, rushed 11 times for 81 yards and scored two touchdowns. Wilson also had a team-record 87-yard punt that rolled to the Dayton one-yard line. It was one of the best all-around games by a player in Steam Roller history.

Wilson's first touchdown was a 33-yard run through a big hole off left tackle and then he stiff-armed two would-be tacklers on his way to the end zone. The Steam Roller's second touchdown was set up by a 33-yard pass from Wilson to Conzelman. Williams capped off the 75-yard march by plunging over for the score. A Wilson pass moved the Roller in position for its third-quarter touchdown. From his 45-yard line, Wilson threw a pass to Jack Cronin, who lugged the ball to the Triangles' 17. Two plays later, Wilson ran 13 yards to the Dayton two-yard line for a first down, and then on the next play he dived into the end zone for the touchdown and a 21–0 Providence lead.

Sonnenberg, who had been itching to play in the backfield, got his chance in the fourth quarter. With the crowd of 7,000 in a frenzy, the 5–6, 200-pound dynamo put on a show. He crashed through the line multiple times and rumbled and stumbled for gains from two to 15 yards, threw a 30-yard touchdown pass to Conzelman, ran around right end for an extra point, kicked another extra point and displayed a powerful stiff arm. The crowd loved it. Sonnenberg was becoming a crowd favorite and the Steam Roller polished off a dominant 28–0 victory. Johnson years later relayed Gus telling him how he dominated opponents. "The first time he bothers me, I hit him just as hard as I can with the heel of my hand and I do that three times. After that I don't have any more trouble with him."[9]

The only disappointment from the game was the team lost the services of Simmons to an injured shoulder. He would miss the next three games.

A few days after that win, Sonnenberg and Spellman put on a wrestling show at the Arcadia Ballroom in downtown Providence, as they won

Providence Steam Roller ball carrier in action at the Cycledrome during 1928 in front of a packed stadium (author's collection).

their matches. Both men wrestled in the offseason to earn extra money. For the upcoming Steam Roller game in New York, the Arcadia and the Empire Theater in Providence were set up with access to the Western Union wire that would allow them to receive a play-by-play account of the game. The two locations were charging 50 cents for fans to hear the almost immediate game account read over a loudspeaker. Several hundred fans attended.

For the Steam Roller, it was its first road game of the season as the team traveled to the hallowed grounds of Yankee Stadium for the October 21 battle with the football Yankees. The six-year-old stadium was home to Babe Ruth, Lou Gehrig and the two-time World Series champion New York Yankees. Ruth had set the major league home run record of 60 just the year before in 1927.

Several Providence fans, waving Steam Roller pennants, accompanied the team on the Saturday night Fall River Line cruise ship to New York to attend the Sunday game. However, only 8,000 showed up in the bright sunshine, most supporting the home team, in what felt like a small crowd in the cavernous stadium. The Roller sported bright orange helmets and they showed brightly in the sun. The game turned into a passing dual between Wilson and Gibby Welch as one tried to outdo the other, but both quarterbacks were off the mark throughout. In the first half, each time one team would move deep into enemy territory, a pass would go awry and be picked off. The game went to the half scoreless. The Yankees finally broke through late in the third quarter on a 20-yard touchdown pass from Welch to Sam Salemi.

Providence bounced back and, behind a big play by Wilson, moved into scoring range. The strong-armed quarterback heaved a pass 50 yards to Norm Harvey, who despite being double-teamed, cradled the football and carried it to the Yankees' three-yard line. On the next play, Wilson dashed through a hole for the score. The placement failed and the two teams were tied at six.

With the clock winding down and the Yankees desperately trying to score to pull out a victory, Welch tossed an ill-advised pass that Harvey intercepted at the Providence 30-yard line. The hulking end, with nobody between him and the goal line, carried the ball 70 yards for the winning touchdown. It was not one of the Steam Roller's best games, but the team was happy to get out of New York with the 12–6 victory. Conzelman injured his knee in the game and was lost for the season as a player, although he would continue to coach the team. Orland and Clyde Smith, along with Abe Wilson, Spellman and Hadden, were applauded for their fine play by the local media.

The injury to Conzelman was significant as he was much more than their quarterback and coach. He was an outstanding player, a clutch pass receiver and among the hardest hitters in the league on defense. Conzelman was the heart and soul of the team. His tactical ability, judgment and decision-making were important to the team and the players. Despite his injury, on the steamer ride back to Providence, Conzelman urged his players to get rest for the upcoming game with Pottsville and stayed out on deck until all the players had retired to their rooms.

At 2:00 a.m. everyone on the steamer was awakened with a yell of "man overboard." Apparently one of the Steam Roller players, who had been at the bar most of the evening, had either fallen or jumped into Long Island Sound. The steamer was forced to turn around and find the distressed player. Luckily, he was rescued and became a historical footnote as the only passenger ever to go overboard and be rescued during the New York–to–Providence run. The name of the guilty party was not released. Once the steamer docked, Conzelman was off to Rhode Island Hospital for surgery on his ailing knee.

The Steam Roller returned to the Cycledrome on October 28 to face one of its biggest rivals, the Pottsville Maroons. Pottsville came into the game with a 1–1 record, with its win coming over the Yankees, 9–7. This was not one of the Maroons' strongest teams (they would finish the season with a 2–8 record and it would be their last year in Pottsville), but because it was a rivalry game, the Steam Roller expected to get the Maroons' best shot.

Providence started fast in front of 8,000 at the Cycledrome despite missing Simmons and Conzelman. Acting coach Wildcat Wilson led a six-play, 73-yard drive following the opening kickoff, and he finished it off with a four-yard run for the touchdown. Wilson completed two terrific passes to Oden of 29 and 27 yards to set up the score less than two minutes into the opening quarter. Wilson was at it again near the end of the first half, only this time with his feet. He darted off right tackle and dodged his way through almost the entire Pottsville defense until he was shoved out of bounds at the Maroons' 10-yard line. On the next play, Wilson threw a dart to Oden, who was on the dead run when he hauled in the pass and dived over the goal line for a touchdown. Wilson, after dropping the ball on the extra-point attempt, tossed a desperation pass to Oden, who caught it for the point and a 13–0 Providence halftime lead.

Pottsville, shut down all day by the Providence defense, mounted a rally late in the game. Maroons defensive end Frank Racis broke through the Roller line and blocked Sonnenberg's punt with Pottsville recovering at the Providence 40-yard line. Standout Tony Latone directed the Maroons on a touchdown drive, hitting Will Norman with a two-yard pass for the score. Spellman deflected Johnny Budd's point-after and Providence led 13–6 with time running down.

On Providence's next possession, Wilson was intercepted by Norman, who returned the errant throw 17 yards to the Pottsville 47. Latone, with some brilliant passes, drove the Maroons to the Providence one-yard line. On fourth down and goal, Latone attempted a pass to Jack Ernst, but at the last second Wilson knocked the ball away and the Roller held on for the heart-stopping victory. Hadden was commended in the *Providence Journal* for his excellent play in the game. "It was his ability to diagnose the Pottsville attack which was a big factor in stopping the Maroon line crackers."[10] Clyde Smith, Rehnquist and Spellman "were likewise prominent in smearing the Maroon forwards."[11] As acting head coach, Wilson had done a good job with adjustments to the offense to combat the key injuries. He had Oden play quarterback, with Williams and himself as the halfbacks and Hadden at fullback.

The Steam Roller's next game was a highly anticipated matchup with the Detroit Wolverines, led by the incomparable Friedman. The Wolverines came into the game with a 3–0 record that included impressive shut-out wins over the Giants and Bears. Along with Friedman, Detroit had a strong backfield with fullback Tiny Feather, halfback Ossie Wiberg and wingback Rex Thomas, plus a fine end in Carl Bacchus.

With the excitement surrounding the game, Providence owner Coppen added 500 temporary seats. They weren't needed as the weather did not cooperate. It was a rainy, muddy day as 8,500 diehard Roller fans still turned out for the contest. Conzelman had been released from the hospital on the Thursday before the game and, though he was on crutches, he returned to coach the team.

The two teams slogged through the muddy field for most of the game, unable to create many scoring opportunities. Neither team was able to gain more than seven yards on a single running play. The Steam Roller unleashed a vaunted pass rush on Friedman, led by Perry Jackson, Jack Fleischmann and Orland Smith, and limited the star quarterback to only seven completions while also shutting down the Wolverines' rushing attack. Detroit's only scoring opportunity came in the second quarter, following an Oden fumble, but was stopped by a Hadden interception.

Providence threatened four times as it controlled the game. The Steam Roller was stopped on downs at the Detroit 22-yard line in the first quarter, and Sonnenberg missed an 18-yard field goal attempt in the second quarter. Early in the third period, Providence drove 48 yards from midfield to the Detroit two-yard line, highlighted by a 23-yard pass from Wilson to Oden. But the drive ended on Hadden's fumble that was recovered by the Wolverines at the goal line. The Steam Roller got the ball right back at the Wolverines' 45-yard line following a punt.

Finally, Providence broke through on a stunning catch by Pop Williams. On the play, Williams raced toward the goal line awaiting a pass from Wilson but was double-covered by Friedman and Dosey Howard. Wilson's long pass just eluded the outstretched fingertips of Friedman as Williams leaped high in the air and snared the aerial and then fell into the end zone for the incredible touchdown. Friedman argued with the referee that he was pushed by Williams, but to no avail. Oden converted the extra point and Providence led 7–0. The Steam Roller went on to the shutout victory and tied the Frankford Yellow Jackets for first place to the delight of the rain-soaked crowd.

Following the game, Friedman rated the Steam Roller defense the best he had played against. He also said that Fleischmann was the best pass rusher he had faced. Friedman went so far as to say that he did not think the Roller would lose another game.

After being released from the hospital, Conzelman faced another challenge upon returning to his second-story apartment. His limited mobility made it difficult for the quarterback to navigate the stairs. Mrs. Johnson, of course, came to the rescue. She converted her parlor on the first floor of her home into a bedroom so that Conzelman could reside there. He was thrilled with his new accommodations, especially when he discovered that each morning Mrs. Johnson had a bowl of bananas, corn flakes and milk awaiting him and the other players. With the success of the team, more and more local residents were either calling the Johnson residence or stopping by to try to obtain autographs from the players and meet them. Mrs. Johnson was accommodating and Conzelman was particularly gracious with the children; he and his players obligingly answered questions and provided autographs. Many of them relished the attention.

The following weekend, Providence ventured outside the NFL to play back-to-back games against Pere Marquette, a high-quality independent team from Boston, and the series was deemed for the championship of New England. On November 10, the Steam Roller traveled to Braves Field in Boston for the first game. Wilson lofted a 32-yard pass to Bill Cronin, who raced the final 28 yards for the game-winning touchdown in the final three minutes to give Providence a tough 14–7 victory. The Steam Roller's other touchdown was scored on a two-yard run by Hadden in the first quarter.

The two competitors met again the next day in Providence at the Cycledrome with 6,000 on hand. The Steam Roller dominated the rematch with a resounding 20–0 victory. Providence held Pere to a single first down for the game. Wilson completed six consecutive passes in the second quarter that led the Roller to its first two touchdowns. He passed 46 yards to Hanny, and four plays later Wilson tossed a short pass to Jack Cronin for the touchdown. Later in the second quarter, Wilson threw a 35-yard strike to Oden that set up a short touchdown run by Cronin. The final touchdown by the Steam Roller came in the fourth quarter, following a 65-yard march, with Cronin scoring his third touchdown of the game on a three-yard run. Throughout the game the Steam Roller played many backups or shock troops, as they were known.

Providence was crowned New England champions with the pair of victories. Pere finished its season with a 7–3 record, with its only other loss coming against the Yellow Jackets from Frankford. Williams was injured during the weekend games and was lost to the Steam Roller for the next four games.

The biggest weekend in team history was up next. The first-place 7–1–1 Yellow Jackets, coming off two weekend victories over Pottsville, and the second-place 5–1 Steam Roller were set to play back-to-back games on November 17 and 18 with first place and the inside track to the NFL championship on the line.

Providence traveled to Philadelphia on Friday afternoon, November 16, and stayed at the Adelphia Hotel. On Saturday morning, the team took a short train to Frankford. Frankford Stadium was filled to capacity and then some as they shoehorned 15,000 into the arena. Both teams had strong lines and stingy defenses. It was a bitterly waged battle and neither team scored in the first half, though the Yellow Jackets had the better of the play.

Frankford broke through in the third quarter on a blocked punt. Bull Behman powered his way through the Providence forward wall to deflect Wilson's kick. The ball rolled to the Steam Roller five-yard line, where Ed Weir scooped it up and reached the end zone for the touchdown. It was the only punt all season that Providence had blocked. The extra-point kick failed as Spellman crashed through the Yellow Jackets' forward wall and smothered Weir before he could kick the placement, leaving Frankford with a precarious 6–0 lead.

With time running out, Wilson took the game into his own hands and would not let the Steam Roller be defeated. He carried the ball on seven of eight plays, gouging the Frankford defense. Wilson finished the march with a smashing three-yard run for the touchdown, carrying the right side of the Yellow Jackets defense with him into the end zone. Oden's extra-point dropkick barely missed, going wide by less than a foot. The arduous game ended in an unsatisfying 6–6 result. Wilson was the star of the game for the Roller, but Spellman—with blood flowing down his face from a cut over his eye—along with Hanny, Fleischmann, Laird and Perry Jackson performed extremely well to hold down the Yellow Jackets' vaunted offense.

The two bitter rivals were at it again the next day at the Cycledrome in Providence. Each team boarded a midnight sleeping car train for the ride to the Renaissance City with first place squarely at stake. Both teams were tired when they arrived but knew the importance of the game. However, Providence had a long list of walking wounded and would be without Conzelman and Williams. Meanwhile, Hadden, whose knee had stiffened overnight, and Simmons were limited and would see little action. The Roller would have to do it with a backfield of Wilson, Oden and the Cronin brothers. "It's claimed you play best when you feel mean," Milt Rehnquist said. "After no sleep and being full of aches and pains, we sure felt mean."[12]

Maybe he was right. The "Providence Steam Roller scored the most notable victory in their colorful career when they defeated their greatest rivals, the powerful Frankford Yellow Jackets, 6–0, at the Cycledrome yesterday afternoon, to take undisputed possession of first place in the National Professional Football League for the first time since they entered the circuit in 1925," proclaimed the *Providence Journal* in its lead story on November 19.[13]

How did they do it? Oden caught a short pass from Wilson in the first quarter on the Frankford 40-yard line. He dodged and weaved his way past four Yellow Jackets defenders to the four-yard line, where Sonnenberg obliterated Hust Stockton with a block that sprang Oden for the touchdown. The extra point failed, but Providence had an all-important 6–0 lead that it would not relinquish. With 12,000 fans cheering the team on, the defense was impenetrable throughout. Frankford threatened only near the end of the game and the clock ran out as it reached the Roller 32-yard line, its deepest penetration of the contest. Providence held Stockton and the Yellow Jacket offense to only three first downs, while Providence amassed nine. The Steam Roller also outgained Frankford 149 yards to only 70 in the 6–0 victory.

The *Providence Journal* reported, "From first to last it was a long-to-be-remembered contest. Packed full of sensational performances, it produced football of the finest variety. It was a hard, bruising battle every bit of the way and a Roller victory was not assured until the final whistle."[14] It was a monumental victory for Providence and squarely placed it in the driver's seat toward a potential NFL championship with a 6–1–1 record.

The team had adopted a song earlier in the season for the fans and they enjoyed singing it during this epic football game in Roller history.

> ---- **STEAM ROLLER SONG** ----
> Words and Music by Don Jackson
>
> Steam Roller............... Roll, Roll, Roll
> (Slowly) (Faster)
>
> Across their............ Goal, Goal, Goal,
> For while the band is playin', Stands are swayin'
> Fans are sayin' "ROLL, STEAM ROLLER"
> (Retard.........)
>
> Through their line,
> (Faster...........)
> Around the end! That's fine!
> And, now to swell the score, one touchdown more
> So.............. Roll, Roll, Roll!
> (Hold...........)

At the cash register, the game was also a booming success. The total cash receipts on the day of $12,126.53 resulted in a $3,891.71 profit from the game.

Frankford was not happy with the officiating from Saturday's tie game and filed an official protest with NFL president Carr on November 21. The complaint stated, "Ivan Annenberg, the umpire, ruled that Arnold Oehlrich of Frankford had run out of bounds at the 25-yard line while running for what would have been the winning touchdown. The Frankford management also is protesting an alleged shortening of the periods by the officials."[15] It was the first protest against NFL officials in league history. The league quickly ruled against Frankford and the result stood.

One of the largest Cycledrome crowds in Steam Roller history, 13,000, squeezed into the bicycle track the following Sunday, November 25, with the Giants in town for an all-important contest for the home team.

Three. The NFL Champions (1928)

The Giants were the defending NFL champions, though they sported only a 4–3–2 record. New York was still a very dangerous team. Its roster had the likes of lineman Cal Hubbard, Century Milstead, Steve Owen and Al Nesser. The backfield still had Hinkey Haines, Jack McBride and Al Bloodgood, all accomplished pros.

The freezing temperatures and snow flurries that arrived in time for the opening kickoff did not douse the energy and enthusiasm of the overflow crowd. The Steam Roller had lost four consecutive games to the Giants, not having beaten them since 1925. But this day was different. Providence played like an NFL champion.

After a scoreless first quarter, though Oden had dropped a 50-yard pass from Wilson that would have been a touchdown, the Steam Roller got on the board in the second period. Providence put together an impressive 41-yard drive in seven plays, outmuscling the Giants' forward wall, with Jack Cronin bucking over from the two-yard line for a touchdown. On the Steam Roller's next possession, Sonnenberg booted an 18-yard field goal to put Providence in control, 9–0.

The third period was scoreless and then Providence salted the game away in the fourth quarter. After forcing consecutive fumbles created by big hits from Sonnenberg and Spellman, the Roller took advantage of the second one. Providence started at the Giants' 16-yard line. Jack Cronin ran through a big hole in the New York line and carried the ball to the one-yard line. On the next play, he scored the clinching touchdown and, with Sonnenberg's dropkick, the Roller completed the scoring in a 16–0 victory. It was a key win for Providence as this was thought to be the most difficult game that remained on its schedule. "When you consider everything ... the Giants ... the crowd ... the game ... what happened," Pearce Johnson said years later, "that was one of the team's best days ever."[16]

Prior to the game, Bruce Caldwell, an Ashton, Rhode Island, boy and 1927 Yale superstar was honored and presented with a traveling bag. Despite his playing for the opposition, Caldwell was given a standing ovation from the crowd. He was released by the Giants later in the season and his pro football career ended with having played in only 10 games.

It was another stellar game at the box office. The gate receipts of $15,250.17 were the largest in team history and resulted in a $4,647.79 profit. All was going well in Steam Roller country. And now the 7–1–1 team had only two mediocre opponents between it and an almost unimagined NFL championship.

The Steam Roller traveled to coal country to battle Pottsville on Thanksgiving. Despite threatening weather, 10,000 Maroon fans came out to see the first-place Roller clash with its beloved hometown team. Providence dominated the game in the early going. The Steam Roller put together drives of 60 and 50 yards, only to be turned away each time, the second on a missed field goal by Sonnenberg. The third drive was the charm. Wilson passed 15 yards to Oden, and then another 15 yarder to Hanny with a few running plays mixed in put the Roller on the Pottsville 10-yard line. Jack Cronin raced around right end with tremendous blocking to cross the goal line untouched for a touchdown. Sonnenberg's dropkick was good and Providence led 7–0.

Pottsville's Latone, playing despite the death of his daughter on Monday, moved the ball inside the Steam Roller 10-yard line late in the first half on a 20-yard run. Frank Racis added a 28-yard dash. But the drive was halted on an incomplete pass into the end zone. The Maroons got the ball back and again moved to the Providence 10-yard line on a 40-yard aerial from Hap Moran to Racis, but before Pottsville could get off another play the half ended.

The third period was back and forth with both teams wasting scoring opportunities. The Maroons twice drove deep into Providence territory but first were stopped by a Hadden interception and then halted on downs at the Roller's three-yard line. Providence missed out on its scoring opportunities by a Jack Cronin fumble and then an incomplete pass in the end zone. Neither team threatened to score in the final period, though passes were being thrown all over the field. The Providence defense stood tall as the Roller escaped with a hard-fought 7–0 victory. The Steam Roller outplayed Pottsville, collecting 18 first downs to the home team's 11. Cronin was the star of the game for Providence, but he left the contest in the fourth quarter with a broken nose.

This game ended an intense four-year rivalry between the two teams. It was Pottsville's last game as the Maroons. The franchise moved to Boston for the start of the 1929 season and became the Bulldogs. It still played two games in Pottsville in 1929, but the city was without its own NFL franchise for good. The rivalry ended with Providence holding a 5–4 edge in games won and a 63–60 scoring advantage.

The Steam Roller stopped at a Philadelphia hotel after the game to celebrate its victory and have Thanksgiving dinner before hopping on the train for the ride back to Providence. The Steam Roller arrived at Union Station around midnight and were greeted by more than 200 fans welcoming the team home. The greeting lifted the spirits of the tired and weary ballplayers. Mrs. Johnson was waiting for her players and treated them to a meal of turkey sandwiches, pickles, olives, cranberry and pumpkin pie.

The Steam Roller had only two days to prepare for its next encounter, on December 2, at the Cycledrome against the Green Bay Packers. It was only the second visit by the Packers to Providence and the Roller had an NFL championship riding on the outcome. The Curly Lambeau–led

Three. The NFL Champions (1928)

Green Bay squad came to Rhode Island with a 5–4–2 record. Tailback Verne Lewellen was having an All-Pro season with nine touchdowns and 54 points to lead the green and gold. He also had just been elected district attorney for Brown County, of which Green Bay was a part. In addition to Lambeau and end Lavvie Dilweg, the Packers sported offensive weapons with fullback Harry O'Boyle and wingback Eddie Kotal. Green Bay was a formidable opponent.

Providence needed a victory or a tie over Green Bay in front of the hometown faithful to secure the NFL championship. Frankford stood at 9–2–2 with three games remaining on its schedule but needed a victory by Green Bay to give it a chance to overtake the Steam Roller.

The day following Providence's victory over Pottsville began like many days in the Johnson household in North Providence. Caroline Johnson, mother of the assistant general manager of the Roller, told her son she was going to the grocery store to pick up some bananas and cornflakes for her "boys." Her "boys" were the seven Steam Roller players who rented rooms from the Johnsons during the football season. "She knew the players liked bananas with their cereal for breakfast. And since this was such an important game coming up, she wanted everything to be just right," said Pearce.[17]

Pearce went off to work and telephoned home around lunch time, but one of the players answered and told him that his mother was not home. To Johnson that seemed strange. Later in the day, with an uneasy feeling, he called again around 4:00 p.m. and this time there was no answer. Johnson left work early and met his father on the trolley ride home. When they arrived at the house, it was dark and nobody was there. When they entered, the phone was ringing. Pearce answered it and the neighbor on the other end of the phone told him to look at the front page of that evening's paper. On the front page was a story of an unknown woman who had been killed by a trolley car in front of a grocery store that morning around 7:00 a.m. One of the players drove Pearce and his father to the morgue. "At the morgue we identified my mother. It was a gruesome sight to view her badly battered body on a marble slab like you would pull out a drawer in a steel file," Johnson said.[18] Pearce, his father and her "boys" were quite shaken about the death of Mrs. Johnson. But a game had to be played in a short two days.

Both teams were tired and worn down from the long season and also from having played on Thanksgiving. The Packers had been on an extended East Coast trip. They had beaten the Giants at the Polo Grounds, 7–0, on November 18, had been thrashed by Pottsville 26–0 on November 25 and had lost a defensive struggle to Frankford, 2–0, on Thanksgiving.

Despite his broken nose, Cronin was preparing to play for the Steam

Roller. He was able to get the Brown University trainer, Jack MacKinnon, to make a primitive facemask that resembled a horse's blinders to protect his nose. The Roller had a light workout on Saturday in preparation for the game with Green Bay. When Oden arrived for practice, he was surprised to see Cronin in uniform. "When he told me he was going to play, I thought he was crazy," Oden recalled. "But then he showed me the nose guard and asked me to put it on for him. I did, and I said: 'Jack, you're a handsome guy but with that mask, you'd scare Satan.'"[19] The Providence team also brought heavy hearts into the game with the shocking death of Mrs. Johnson so fresh in the players' minds. It would be as much a mental struggle as a physical skirmish against the Packers.

The game, played on a raw, chilly late New England fall day, was a seesaw battle throughout the first half. The Packers had the best scoring opportunity as they marched inside the Providence one-yard line midway through the second quarter. Green Bay back Larry Marks tried to plunge it over from there, "but Sonnenberg hit him like an elephant and the ball slipped out of his grasp. There was a wild scramble and when the referee pulled the players apart (Clyde) Smith had the ball and it went for a touchback," the *Providence Journal* reported.[20] The Steam Roller committed three first half turn-

Providence Steam Roller vs. Green Bay Packers program from December 2, 1928. Providence clinched the NFL championship with a 7-7 tie against the Packers. Curly Oden scored the game-tying touchdown on a 23-yard pass from George "Wildcat" Wilson and Gus Sonnenberg booted the game-tying extra point (courtesy Rhode Island Historical Society—RHi X17 4830).

overs, one interception and two fumbles, that kept it from scoring. Oden had a spectacular 53-yard punt return to the Packers' five-yard line, but Wilson's interception two plays later ended that scoring chance. The teams went to halftime knotted at zero.

The Packers struck early in the third quarter following a Dutch Webber interception of Wilson at the Steam Roller 35-yard line. Five plays later, from the Roller 20, Lewellen fired a strike to a slanting Marks. The former Indiana University star grabbed the pass at the three-yard line and bobbled it multiple times before finally hauling it in as he stumbled into the end zone for a touchdown. Harry O'Boyle, former Notre Damer under Knute Rockne, booted the extra point and Green Bay was ahead 7–0. "After the Packers scored and we're lining up for the kickoff, Fleish (Jack Fleischmann) made a queer remark," recalled Rehnquist. "Just like he was talking out loud to himself, he said 'Wonder if she knows' (she being Mrs. Johnson). Strange, but I sort of wondered the same thing. I didn't answer him. We just went to work on them."[21]

With the home crowd of more than 10,500 now growing anxious, the Steam Roller put together the most important scoring march of the season. On the ensuing kickoff, Wilson returned the ball from the Providence 10-yard line to the 28. Wilson and Hadden alternated carrying the football on the next seven plays and gained 37 yards while netting three first downs to move the ball into Packers territory. A 13-yard pass from Wilson to Oden put the ball at the Green Bay 25. After a two-yard run by Hadden, Wilson threw a bullet to Oden at the two-yard line and the slithery back caught the pass and lunged into the end zone for a touchdown. Sonnenberg's all-important placement kick split the uprights and the game was tied as the fans breathed a big sigh of relief, though more football was to be played. The noise in the Cycledrome was deafening. "It is a fine tribute to the gameness of the club that it was able to rally after a Green Bay touchdown which would have demoralized most teams with so much at stake," reported John R. Hess, Jr., of the *Providence Journal*.[22]

The Roller had another chance to score later in the third quarter, but Sonnenberg's field goal was blocked by O'Boyle. The ex–Notre Damer scooped up the loose football and raced to midfield, but was caught from behind by the swift Oden, preventing a Packers touchdown. Neither team had a scoring chance in the final period until late in the game when the Packers moved deep into Steam Roller territory. But the Providence defense stiffened and Spellman batted down a final pass attempt at the goal line.

When the gun sounded, the Providence Steam Roller was the National Football League champion! "Although showing the wear and tear of recent hard games, the Roller heroes—Wilson, Oden, Spellman, Clyde Smith and in fact, every one of them—continued their brilliant display of the finest kind of football on their season's last appearance," reported the *Providence Journal*.[23]

The players celebrated like schoolboys, hooting and hollering as they congregated on the warn-out Cycledrome turf. They tossed their helmets in the air, hugged and shook each other's hands as they acknowledged their remarkable accomplishment. Conzelman, despite his crutches, was lifted onto the shoulders of two players and carried over to the stands, where the exhilarated crowd was cheering loudly. Neither the players nor the fans were in any hurry to leave the Cycledrome. They all wanted to bask in the glory of Providence being the champions of the pro football world. "The Steam Roller is an unusual club, however. Few squads, in or out of college, have had finer camaraderie or keener desire to win their games. It has been a team, first, last and all the time that counted with these Roller players and this fine spirit has given Providence the most powerful team in the history of football," wrote Hess, Jr.[24]

The Steam Roller finished its season with an 8-1-2 record and .889 winning percentage. The Yellow Jackets lost one of their three remaining games and finished in second place at 11-3-2 and a .786 winning percentage with Detroit a close third at .778. Providence became the first New

The 1928 NFL Champion Providence Steam Roller (courtesy Pro Football Hall of Fame).

England team to win the NFL championship and the only one until the New England Patriots secured the NFL title on February 3, 2002, by winning Super Bowl XXXVI over St. Louis, 20–17.

Providence completed the season allowing only 42 points with five shutouts and almost unbelievably did not allow a rushing touchdown. Clyde Smith and Wilson were named first-team All-Pros. The Steam Roller also had three second-team All-Pros—Oden, Rehnquist and Sonnenberg. The team finished 6–1–1 in the Cycledrome while averaging 9,000 fans per game, its most since 1925.

The following day, December 3, the funeral was held for Caroline Johnson. "I didn't see the (Packers game); I was at the funeral parlor," Johnson said years later, "and the next day the entire team went to my mother's funeral. We were a football team but we were also a family."[25] Her seven "boys" were the pallbearers for Caroline's casket. "It was good to have the funeral from her home," Conzelman said later. "As we saw her for the last time, we must have all thought of the wonderful hospitality we had there. She made it just like home."[26] Later that day she was laid to rest. "We were young fellows and Mrs. Johnson was wonderful to us, just like a mother away from home," Rehnquist recollected. "She would listen with real interest to us talk football and we all felt part of the family. So what happened was a terrible shock to all of us."[27]

The team continued

The Providence Biltmore Hotel, where the Steam Roller celebrated its 1928 NFL championship on December 4, 1928 (author's collection).

the wild swing of emotions. The next day, the Steam Roller celebrated its NFL championship with a victory banquet at the Biltmore Hotel in the city. More than 200 loyal fans, along with the players, coaches, front office personnel and local dignitaries, took part in the celebration. There was one notable absence: Pearce Johnson, who was mourning his mother's death.

At the banquet, the players spoke about the camaraderie among the team. "There had not been a cross word between any two of the players in three months on or off the field," said Conzelman, despite the pressure and challenges the team faced.[28] Wilson chimed in with, "Never have I played on a football team inside or outside of college that has shown so much spirit, such a desire to win and such friendship for one another. Neither college nor high school football has given me half as much enjoyment as playing under Jimmy Conzelman."[29] And Sonnenberg added that he

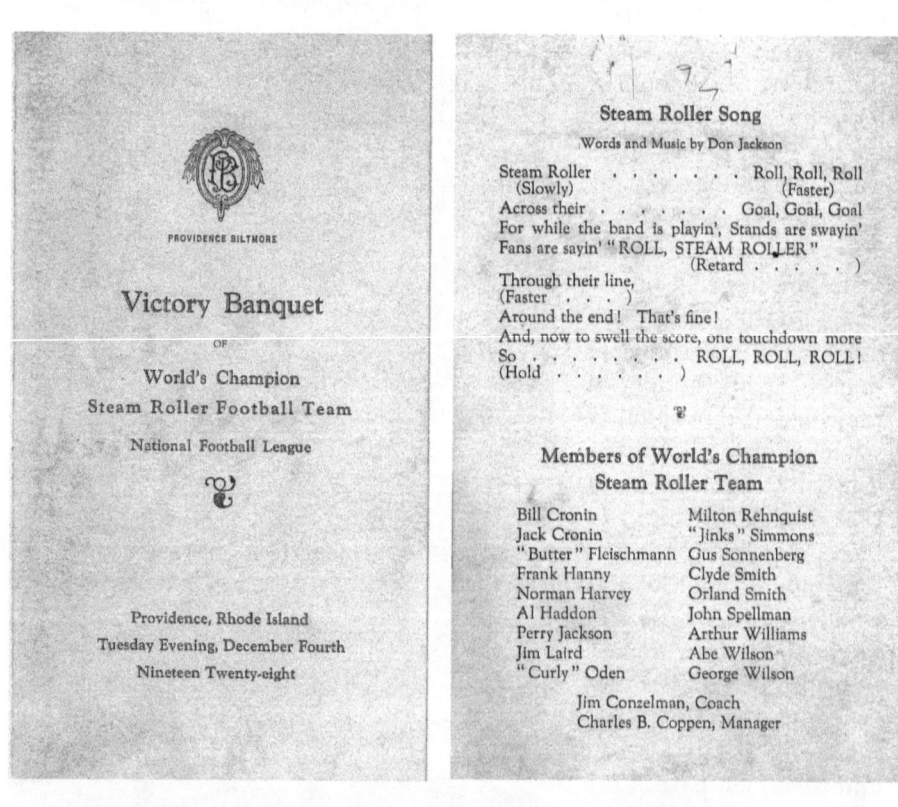

Providence Steam Roller's NFL World Champions Victory Banquet program front and back cover from the team celebration on December 4, 1928, at the Providence Biltmore Hotel (courtesy Rhode Island Historical Society—RHiX174572A and RHiX174572B).

hoped to bring another world championship to the city, by beating Strangler Ed Lewis on the wrestling mat.

Each of the players was awarded a beautiful gold watch to commemorate the championship. The players voted Conzelman as the team's Most Valuable Player, despite his missing many games with his knee injury, and he was given a sterling silver cup. "The Cat (Wilson) and all the rest of us voted for Jim," recalled Oden. "The MVP couldn't have been anyone else because we couldn't have done it without him. On and off the field, Jim was great. In tough times—and we had our share of those—we stayed together because he kept us together. No arguments, no fights, no dissension. He was quiet and friendly, but a top tactician. He never abused or embarrassed a player. If you made a mistake, he'd take you aside and talk privately. He was a real gentleman. We called him Gentleman Jim and we played our hearts out for him."[30] Charles Coppen was given a timepiece to honor him for bringing the Steam Roller to the city and positioning the franchise to win the title. Then the championship banner was unveiled, to the rousing applause of all in attendance. Today that historic relic lives in the Pro Football Hall of Fame in Canton, Ohio.

The mayor of Providence, James E. Dunne, and Lieutenant Governor-elect James G. Connolly lauded the team for its clean brand of football and its well-earned victories. But it was attorney general Charles P. Sisson, a former Brown University player, who had the most noteworthy remarks:

NFL 1928 World Championship Watch presented to each Steam Roller player (author's collection).

"I've seen the Roller play and talked with other football men who have seen them in action, and I want to say to you in all seriousness, in my opinion professional football as played by the Steam Roller is really better football than we see on our college gridirons. I'm using the word better for two reasons. I think it is harder football and I think it is cleaner football. Every man on the Roller is a college man. He knows what a sportsmanlike game is and he carried into professional football all the fine ethical principles that he might have gathered in college and with it he has gained the maturity that come to older men. The type of football you play may act as a stimulus to college and younger team's football. I think the day is coming when pro football if it follows the example set by the Roller, will take its place with baseball as the great national professional sport."[31]

For someone to make that claim in 1928 would have been considered preposterous by some, as the college game was noted to be far superior. But perhaps the pro version was starting to win over some disciples.

Following the celebration, the players scattered, returning home and pursuing employment opportunities while many prepared to return in 1929 to attempt to defend the NFL championship. It was not only a successful season on the field, but owners Coppen, Peter Laudati and James Dooley were also pleased with the fan enthusiasm and the associated profits the team brought in, especially during the stretch run of the season in November when the team consistently drew more than 10,000 fans to each game.

The Steam Roller payroll for its championship season looked like this in per-game salary:

- Wildcat Wilson: $375
- Jimmy Conzelman: $292
- Gus Sonnenberg: $200
- Curly Oden: $150
- Clyde Smith: $150
- Duke Hanny: $145
- Orland Smith: $125
- Jack Spellman: $125
- Jack Fleischmann: $110
- Al Hadden: $110
- Bill Cronin: $100
- Jack Cronin: $100
- Norm Harvey: $100
- Jim Laird: $100
- Milt Rehnquist: $100
- Jim Simmons: $100
- Abe Wilson: $100
- Perry Jackson: $100
- Pop Williams: $88

The 1928 NFL MVP Trophy awarded to Jimmy Conzelman (courtesy Pro Football Hall of Fame).

Providence Steam Roller 1928 NFL World Championship Pennant (courtesy Pro Football Hall of Fame).

Though there appeared to be some discrepancies in fair pay based on overall performance (no different from in today's NFL), there was no dissension among the players. "Players never seemed to talk about salaries," Pearce Johnson said many years later. "Some of them had regular jobs but they were all making more playing football. ... We had no fights or feuds. They were paid players but they wanted above all else to win the NFL championship. It probably sounds odd today but salaries were secondary considerations. ... Everybody was eager to play and the difficulty was to keep out guys who insisted on going in even when hurt."[32]

The team had traveled by train to its away game from its inception. That policy continued until after that 1929 stock market crash when they curtailed budgets and began traveling by bus. Players also received a food allowance of $3.50 a meal and hotel accommodations were among the best. The Roller traveled better than almost any of the other NFL teams.

Sonnenberg, who had taken up wrestling in 1928, had quickly become a phenom on the grappling circuit. He was very entertaining with both his flying tackle move, which was new to the sport, and his braggadocio. He was nicknamed "The Flying Dutchman" because his patented move was to leap at his opponent, wrap his arms around his legs and slam him to the mat, similar to how he would tackle a player on the football field. He also was referred to as "Dynamite Gus" because of his explosive and powerful body despite his 5'6" height. He won his first big match in May 1928 over former champion Wayne "Big" Munn despite being 70 pounds lighter. The *Boston Globe* described the match: "There was nothing stylish about Sonnenberg's wrestling, nothing skillful. It was raw savagery. ... Sonnenberg directed the fury of his attack at his (Munn's) body and long legs. At times, in the whirlwind of action, it seemed that the squat little Sonnenberg intended to make a fight out of the wrestling bout. At other times, it looked like a rough and tumble football game, with Munn representing a live tackling dummy. Only when he had flopped Munn to the floor with his flying tackles did Sonnenberg resort to an orthodox wrestling hold."[33]

Sonnenberg lost his first match against heavyweight champion "Strangler" Ed Lewis, but he had a rematch with the champion on January 4, 1929. Sonnenberg won the championship in decisive fashion, fulfilling his remarks made at the victory banquet a month earlier. He got the first fall on a flying tackle and then repeatedly pounded him into the canvas and smashed him through the ropes seven times as Lewis looked for an escape. Finally, the referee disqualified Lewis and Sonnenberg was the new champion. More than 20,000 fans in the Boston Garden cheered the result. Sonnenberg ultimately retired from the Steam Roller prior to the start of the 1929 season because he would make a lot more money wrestling. Sonnenberg remained heavyweight champion until December 1930 but continued his wrestling well into the late 1930s and reportedly earned more than $1 million. He would be missed by the Steam Roller as the team began preparations for 1929.

Chapter Four

Aftermath and Demise (1929–1931)

1929—The Championship Hangover

Providence was giddy about its newly minted championship sports heroes, but now it was time to prepare to defend that title. Only the 1922–1923 Canton Bulldogs with Guy Chamberlin, Wilbur Pete Henry and William "Link" Lyman had repeated as champions in the NFL's relatively brief history. It was up to Providence to see if it could match that feat.

The loss of Sonnenberg to wrestling was not a good start to that quest. He brought a toughness, brashness and all-out style of play to the Steam Roller that would be difficult to replicate. He was also the team's place-kicker and was quite effective at it.

In late June, a story broke about Sonnenberg that even if he wanted to return to the NFL he might not be wanted. An exposé appeared in the *Boston Herald* about the crookedness of the wrestling game and that several of Sonnenberg's matches had outcomes that were predetermined. "If the people get the impression that Sonnenberg is a crooked wrestler," said a man in close touch with the football councils, "then they are likely to assume that he is also a crooked football player. They will go even farther. They are likely to assume that if the National Football League will harbor one crooked player, it will harbor a dozen."[1] Nothing ever came of the allegations. Sonnenberg continued to be a top draw on the wrestling circuit, and the NFL took no action.

Conzelman returned as head coach for Providence and also as a player, but he never fully recovered from the knee injury he had suffered, though he still appeared in nine games.

The NFL expanded to 12 teams for the 1929 season, but there were no teams west of Minneapolis, Minnesota. The new franchises were in Minneapolis (Red Jackets), Staten Island, New York (Stapletons) and East Orange, New Jersey (the Orange Tornadoes). The New York Yankees franchise was relocated to Buffalo and the Queen City was back in the NFL with the Bisons' nickname. The Pottsville Maroons moved to Boston and became the Bulldogs, and the Detroit Wolverines dropped out of the league.

New England for the first time had two teams, with Boston joining Providence. Sonnenberg was a financial backer of the Boston franchise, investing some of his wrestling winnings back into the NFL.

As had become the norm at the time of the release of the NFL schedule, league president Carr proclaimed that the upcoming season "will be a bigger and better year for pro football than any season since the paid brigade started operations."[2] At the owners' meeting in July, Providence had lobbied to host a night game for the first time in NFL history against any team that would be willing to play it. The Chicago Cardinals volunteered. When the schedule was released, the Steam Roller was granted that opportunity. The game, scheduled for November 3, was the highlight of the Steam Roller's 1929 schedule. Other notable games included opening the season against the Dayton Triangles on September 29, along with home-and-home series versus the New York Giants, Frankford Yellow Jackets and the new Boston Bulldogs. The Steam Roller also would host the new Minneapolis franchise and was scheduled to close the season against the Green Bay Packers at the Cycledrome.

Providence Steam Roller vs. Chicago Cardinals program from the first night game played in NFL history at Kinsley Park, Providence, Rhode Island, on November 6, 1929. Ernie Nevers scored all 16 points for the Cardinals in their 16-0 victory over the Steam Roller (author's collection).

Four. Aftermath and Demise (1929–1931)

There was some controversy getting the Packers game scheduled as Curly Lambeau wanted the Steam Roller to also make a visit to Green Bay. He complained that both the Giants and the Steam Roller "demand such a high guarantee that it would mean a big financial loss to bring them here."[3] Providence did not play in Green Bay in 1929 and Lambeau claimed it had an easier schedule because most of its games were at home.

Lambeau was one of the founders of the Packers in 1919, serving as team captain. He became player-coach in 1920, the position he still held in 1929. Lambeau retired as a player following the 1929 season but remained as head coach and added the title of general manager through the 1949 season. Green Bay's home field is named in his honor.

Providence added one preseason contest that was scheduled for September 22 against the West Weymouth Union Athletic Club at the Cycledrome.

The Steam Roller lost some important performers from the 1928 team beyond Sonnenberg. Oden quit to take a job with an insurance company in Boston. Clyde Smith, the first-team All-Pro, stayed in his hometown in Missouri as a coach, Simmons retired and Laird (who played in the fourth-most games in team history) did not return. But the ownership group did not sit still and brought in some talent in an attempt to bolster the roster from those losses.

Archie Golembeski, still coaching at Providence College, returned to the playing field after being away for two seasons. Veteran lineman Art "Hec" Garvey was signed away from the New York Giants. The six-year vet was an All-Pro with the Chicago Bears in 1923 and had started 17 games for the Giants during the previous two seasons. He was added for insurance because an injury to Milt Rehnquist would keep the star lineman sidelined for the first four games of the 1929 season. Providence also snatched Jack McBride from the Giants. The four-year veteran played halfback, linebacker and kicker for New York and was one of the Giants' leading scorers during his career there. He was a solid addition to the team and replaced Sonnenberg in the kicking game. Providence also signed Boston College All-American tackle Warren McGuirk upon his graduation.

Providence made headlines on September 11 with the signing of former New York Yankee star and University of Pittsburgh All-American quarterback Gibby Welch. He had played for the Yankees in 1928, but when the team disbanded and moved to Buffalo, he was placed with the Frankford Yellow Jackets. That team was not willing to pay the salary that Welch was demanding. The Steam Roller was willing to pay the high price for the star quarterback.

There were published reports in early September that Sonnenberg was considering a return to play in the NFL, but he needed to decide whether to play for Boston or Providence. As it turned out, he did not return to play in 1929; instead he continued to pursue his wrestling exploits.

The saga of the two Perry Jacksons took another unique twist. Arnold Shockley turned up in training camp and continued to use Jackson's name. But the real Perry Jackson also came to training camp with Providence, now recovered from his illness. The twist is that he used Shockley's name. So, the two men continued with the use of each other's name instead of coming clean and using their own names. The players were probably afraid they would both be banned from the league. They continued that practice until after both men retired from football. Jackson (the real Shockley) made the team and played seven games, but Shockley (the real Perry Jackson) was cut. Shockley caught on with the Boston Bulldogs and played six games for the new Boston team before his NFL career ended.

The Steam Roller players reported for their first practice on September 14, and despite the loss of some key players, the team was ready to defend its NFL title.

Providence hosted West Weymouth Union A.C. in its exhibition game on September 22 before a crowd of 6,000. The Steam Roller showed its championship form with a 37–0 victory. Newcomer Welch scored the first touchdown in the first quarter on an 18-yard pass reception from Wildcat Wilson. On Providence's next possession, Wilson ran 47 yards off left tackle and was brought down inside the opponents' 10-yard line. He then broke free on the next play for the touchdown and a 13–0 Providence lead.

Jack Cronin's brother Bill got in on the action and scored Steam Roller touchdowns in both the second and third quarters, and then Al Hadden scored the final touchdown for Providence in the fourth period. Newcomer Lou Jennings, a Cherokee Indian and former Centenary College star, had quite a debut. He drop-kicked a 38-yard field goal, converted three extra points and, late in the game, barely missed a 49-yard field goal attempt.

Steam Roller owner Coppen said "his Providence champions are more powerful than last season ... and states his eleven will be the most colorful on any gridiron unless Gus Sonnenberg decides to put aside the moleskins and continue his acts on the mat," as reported by Frank Korch of *Collyer's Eye*.[4]

The defending champion Steam Roller played host to the Triangles on September 29 with a celebratory crowd of 8,500 on hand. The championship banner was raised to the raucous applause from the crowd, and Providence mayor James E. Dunne finished off the festivities by completing a pass to Conzelman as the fans roared.

Providence looked every bit what Coppen expected as his team

Four. Aftermath and Demise (1929–1931)

manhandled Dayton, 41–0. Welch had a record-setting day with four touchdowns—three on pass receptions from three different quarterbacks (Wilson, Hust Stockton and McBride) and a rushing touchdown. Pop Williams opened the scoring with a short first-quarter touchdown run. Welch caught a seven-yard pass from Wilson and then raced through the Dayton defense on the way to a 32-yard touchdown and a 13–0 first-quarter lead.

Welch was the story in the second quarter, scoring three touchdowns. The first was on a 15-yard run off right guard, and then the lanky quarterback galloped 50 yards on a pass from Stockton for an electrifying 64-yard score. He completed his hat trick with an eight-yard pass reception from McBride, and the Roller went to halftime in complete control, 34–0. In the second half, Coach Conzelman substituted liberally, with the team adding only a short run by Wilson in the fourth quarter for the final touchdown in a record-setting day for the franchise.

The Providence victory was so dominant that Dayton never was able to convert a first down and did not cross midfield for the entire game. The Steam Roller set several team records—the largest margin of victory against an NFL opponent (41), the most touchdowns scored by a player (Welch—four), the most extra points made in a single game (Jennings—four), the fewest first downs allowed in a game (zero) and the largest opening-day crowd (8,500).

Stockton, the former Yellow Jackets halfback who was signed in the offseason and was a backup, left the team after the one game. He joined the Boston Bulldogs, where he became a starter.

The following week, before the largest home crowd in Steam Roller history (14,000), Providence was outmuscled and outplayed by a strong New York Giants team. The Giants set the tone early. New York surprised the Steam Roller as Benny Friedman, playing for his third team in three years, completed three passes in four plays with the final aerial a 10-yarder to Len Sedbrook for the touchdown. Friedman's placement was good and the Giants had a 7–0 first-quarter lead. From there the Giants used a slashing running attack to consistently keep the Steam Roller off-balance.

New York had two other chances to score in the second and fourth quarters but the Providence defense stopped the Giants on downs inches from the goal line. On the fourth-quarter drive, the stout Steam Roller defense stuffed New York on four consecutive plays from the one-yard line to keep the team in the game. The Roller offense, so potent the week before, did not find its rhythm against the physical Giants defense. Providence gained 10 first downs and had two chances to tie the game. The first was stopped at the New York 21-yard line on a fourth-down play that the Giants line drilled Jack Cronin for a loss. The other chance, late in the game, ended with Tiny Feather's interception of Welch on the New

York 35. With Providence unable to score, New York came away with a 7–0 victory.

"The game was the roughest ever played between the pros here. Clipping, roughing and holding were all in evidence with the Giants breaking most of the rules and escaping without penalties," the *Providence Journal* reported.[5] Fleischmann and Spellman played especially well in defeat for Providence.

The Steam Roller licked its wounds and bounced back with a victory over the Orange Tornadoes on October 13. Another good crowd, this time 10,000, at the Cycledrome came to cheer on its beloved champions. After a scoreless first quarter, Conzelman inserted himself at quarterback. Early in the second stanza the one-legged quarterback led Providence on a 10-play, 43-yard touchdown drive. Welch scored on an eight-yard run around right end and McBride, who replaced the departed Jennings, booted the extra point for a 7–0 Roller lead.

The Providence defense again stood tall. Orange quarterback Frank Kirkleski drove the Tornadoes to the Steam Roller's four-yard line following the second-half kickoff. On fourth down, Wilson tackled running back Steven Hamas a foot short of the goal line to stop the Orange march. Following a Steam Roller punt, Orange was at it again. Kirkleski threw a 22-yard pass to Phil Scott that put the ball inside the Providence 10. Four line smashes by the Tornadoes, the last one by Hamas, were again halted just short of the goal line. Golembeski and Spellman made splendid plays to deny the Tornadoes. The game was a defensive struggle in the fourth quarter, as neither team was able to drive into scoring position as the Steam Roller held on for an important 7–0 victory.

For the second week in a row, there was a lot of dismay about the officiating. The game was marred by penalties, and some unruly fans hurled bottles in the direction of the officials when they took exception with their decisions.

The Buffalo Bisons made their first visit to the Cycledrome in more than two years when they came to Providence on October 20. The Bisons, who did not play in 1928, came into the game looking for their first victory of the season. The 0–4 Bisons were coached by Al Jolley and led by wingback Swede Hagberg and quarterback Cassy Ryan, both from the University of West Virginia. Buffalo had the youngest team in the league.

The Steam Roller started strong but committed three turnovers that deprived the team from scoring in the first quarter. Early in the opening quarter, Providence recovered a Buffalo fumble on the Bisons' 18-yard line. But Wilson threw an interception to Hagberg that ended that scoring threat. On the Roller's next possession, Wilson marched the team 37 yards to the Bisons' five-yard line. On the ensuing play, Wilson was knocked out and fumbled with Hagberg recovering. Wilson was badly dazed and did not return until late in the game. The next Providence drive also ended with a fumble, this time by Jack Cronin at the Buffalo 32-yard line.

With the game still scoreless late in the second quarter, Providence was on the move again. Welch passed 23 yards to McBride to the Bisons' 19-yard line. From there the Cronin brothers alternated running the football, and six plays later Jack crashed over from the two-yard line for the score. McBride's placement was good and Providence led 7–0 at halftime.

The upstart Bisons, with Hagberg playing a starring role, tied the game at 7–7 midway through the third quarter. The Phi Beta Kappa student from West Virginia caught a pass from Jim Woodruff and raced the final eight yards for the 44-yard touchdown. Chuck Weimer nailed the extra point.

Early in the fourth quarter, Welch caught a 21-yard pass from McBride and carried it to the Bisons' 20-yard line. However, on the play Hagberg twisted Welch's ankle after making the tackle. The Roller quarterback took exception to the tackle, and after jumping to his feet, punched the Bison defender. Welch was immediately ejected from the game and Providence incurred a penalty of half the distance to the goal, which was a 40-yard infraction. That ended that scoring threat.

Providence had one final chance with the clock ticking down. Wilson threw a 20-yard pass to Jack Cronin and the former Boston College star raced an additional 23 yards before he was shoved out of bounds at the Bisons' nine-yard line. On the game's final play, Providence ran a draw play to Cronin and at first he had some daylight. However, two Buffalo defenders were able to wrestle the big back to the ground short of the goal line as time expired. Despite the Steam Roller's outplaying the Bisons, the game ended in a 7–7 draw.

On October 27, a beautiful sunny fall day, the 2-1-1 Steam Roller traveled to the Polo Grounds for a rematch with the 3-0-1 Giants. Unlike the first game, this was no contest. New York dominated from start to finish in a 19–0 shutout victory. Freidman led the Giants on an 83-yard drive to start the game and never looked back. "The New York line outcharged and outfought the Roller forwards, opening-gaping holes for Friedman, Tony Plansky and Sedbrook on their touchdown drive in the first period," reported Hess, Jr., of the *Providence Journal*.[6] Plansky, the former Georgetown star, ran the final yard for the touchdown with much of the Providence defense hanging on to him. Friedman kicked the extra point. The Giants added to their lead at the start of the second half following a fumble by Welch on the kickoff. New York recovered the football at the Roller's 10-yard line. A few plays later, Plansky crashed over from the one-yard line and the Giants led 13–0. The New Yorkers closed the scoring after

Plansky intercepted a Wilson pass and returned it 24 yards to the Providence 11-yard line. Sedbrook darted through a hole in the demoralized Steam Roller line and scored. With the loss, any thought of a repeat championship for the Steam Roller essentially died on the Polo Grounds turf. Providence couldn't afford to be swept by the powerful Giants and expect to keep up with them in the standings.

The next day, the *Brooklyn Eagle* reported, "Friedman's passing knows no bounds. Benny called on it with the game only a few minutes old and got the ball to midfield, from when unvaried line bucks and plunges smote the vaunted Providence line asunder until Plansky slithered off the right side for the score from the 1-yard line."[7] The story pointed out that pro football was changing. The passing game was becoming a force and was even effective at setting up the run.

The disheartening loss to the Giants was followed a day later by one of the most cataclysmic days in American economic history, the stock market crash. The Dow Jones Industrial Average plummeted by 13 percent on Black Monday, October 28, and an additional 12 percent a day later. By mid-November the market was down almost 50 percent and the US economy was thrust into a recession that would quickly turn to a depression. It would take years for the country to recover. Many families lost their life savings and the downturn left thousands of Americans out of work.

While this financial meltdown was going on, the NFL played on. The Steam Roller embarked on something that had not been done before and has not been accomplished since. Providence played four NFL games in only six days in four different stadiums.

Originally, the first night game in NFL history against the Chicago Cardinals was scheduled for November 3, but heavy rains made the Cycledrome unplayable. The game was moved to Wednesday night, November 6, which caused the scheduling gauntlet for Providence. The Steam Roller did not want to lose a game with a high probability for a nice payday, so the historic night game was hastily rescheduled. Before the team could play that game, the Steam Roller ferried to Staten Island, New York, to play the Stapletons on November 5.

Staten Island's home field was Thompson Stadium, and a good crowd of 10,000 was on hand to see the defending champions. In the opening quarter, Providence put together a 57-yard touchdown march that was highlighted by a 32-yard run by Wilson. Pop Williams finished off the march with a dash through the right side of the line for the touchdown. McBride's placement was good and Providence had an early 7–0 lead.

The Stapletons tied the game in the second quarter, but not without controversy. Ken Strong, the former NYU star, fielded Jack Cronin's punt at his own 48-yard line and proceeded to lumber down the sideline. At the

Four. Aftermath and Demise (1929–1931)

Providence 38-yard line, Hadden appeared to knock him down. However, Strong jumped to his feet and continued down the sideline and crossed the goal line as the Providence defenders looked on in disbelief. The officials ruled it a touchdown. The Roller's coaches and players vigorously argued the decision, but to no avail. Strong added the placement and the game was tied.

From there the game was full of missed opportunities by Providence. Four times the Steam Roller drove deep into Staten Island territory and three ended with fumbles. The last-gasp attempt at victory ended when Wilson's pass to Williams rolled off Pop's fingertips for an interception. The Stapletons, with only four first downs, had one other scoring opportunity, but it went awry with a missed field goal by Strong in the third quarter. The game ended in a 7–7 tie. Rehnquist was finally back in the lineup and the line play showed improvement. McGuirk, Fleishmann and Spellman were recognized for their strong play by the *Providence Journal*.

The Ernie Nevers–led Cardinals were waiting in Providence as the Steam Roller hurried home to battle the next evening. Nevers, a four-sport star at Stanford University and two-time All-Pro (1926 and 1927), was a triple-threat player. He was an excellent passer, runner and kicker and was considered one of the best players in the NFL in 1929. Nevers would go on to be named to the College and Pro Football Halls of Fame after his retirement.

The game was moved to Kinsley Park because the Cycledrome field was still too wet to play the game. Floodlights were installed for the occasion and it was thought that they were just as good as daylight for the players.

The Steam Roller had not played at Kinsley Park since the team's independent pro days of 1924. More than 6,000 jammed into the smaller park to witness the first game under the lights in NFL history. Playing with a white football that was easier to see than the standard version, Nevers stole the show. The "Big Dog," as he was known by many, rushed 23 times for 102 yards with a touchdown. He also completed 10 of 15 passes for 144 yards and a touchdown and kicked a field goal and an extra point to account for all the scoring in the 16–0 Cardinals victory. His touchdown pass was a 46-yard beauty to Chuck Kassel that opened the scoring in the second quarter.

The *Providence Journal* called Nevers's performance "one of the greatest exhibitions of football ever turned in by an individual player."[8] The paper went on to report, "Nevers handled the ball on three out of every four plays. He ran off the tackles, sporting a deceptive hip shift, and twisted his way for yards and yards. When tackled he ploughed ahead, once dragging the 200-pound Spellman, one of the heaviest and strongest players on the Roller team, four yards. It usually took three men to bring him down and he was tireless."[9]

Providence threatened to score three times in the second half, but its drive in the third quarter was stopped on downs by the Cardinals' aggressive defense, and the other two chances in the fourth quarter were halted by Wilson fumbles.

The game was considered a success because of the attendance figure, especially considering the economic times of that moment. With the white ball, a newspaper joked, "It looked like an egg and that there was a panicky feeling that the player who made the catch would be splattered with yellow yolk."[10] That did not happen, but the Steam Roller management was well ahead of its time in seeing the opportunity that night football could bring to the league. Providence installed permanent lighting at the Cycledrome in 1930 and hosted several more evening games. But night football was not popularized in professional football until the advent of *Monday Night Football* in 1970, 40 years later.

The beat-up and exhausted Steam Roller squad had two days to regroup before its trip to Frankford for back-to-back games with the rival Yellow Jackets. Saturday arrived quickly and the Roller was back on the field at Frankford Stadium in front of 6,000. The first quarter was a punting dual between Wilson and Frankford's Wally Diehl. The game turned on a second-quarter drive by Providence. The Roller marched to the Yellow Jackets' nine-yard line via Wilson's passing. However, Providence could not further dent the Frankford line and was stopped on downs. Less than five minutes later, Mike Wilson intercepted a Providence pass and returned it to Frankford's 35-yard line. The Yellow Jackets rode the momentum created by their defense and moved 65 yards for a touchdown. Diehl scooted eight yards for the score and Ed Halicki added the extra point.

Frankford dominated the game from that point forward. The Yellow Jackets moved inside the Providence 25-yard line seven separate times, but the Steam Roller defense did not yield any points. But the Providence offense, after losing Wilson to an injury in the second quarter, could not move the ball into scoring position to tie the game as the Yellow Jackets pulled off a mild upset, 7–0.

The two teams hopped a midnight train to Providence for the rematch the next day at the finally dried-out Cycledrome. The Steam Roller jumped on the Yellow Jackets right from the start. Four plays after the opening kickoff, Providence was in the end zone. Wilson, back after missing much of the previous day's game, returned the opening kick 35 yards. He then connected on a 40-yard pass to Jack Cronin. Two plays later, Wilson tossed a perfect 22-yard touchdown pass to Conzelman for a 6–0 lead. Despite

Providence Steam Roller vs. the archrival Frankford Yellow Jackets in game action on November 9, 1929. The Steam Roller lost 7–0 (courtesy Pro Football Hall of Fame).

the quick start, the Roller had only two other scoring chances throughout the contest, both set up by interceptions. Conzelman snared an errant throw late in the third quarter, but the drive was stopped on downs after reaching the Yellow Jackets' 32-yard line. McBride intercepted a Frankford pass in the fourth quarter, but after the drive stalled, he missed a field goal attempt from the Yellow Jackets' 25-yard line.

The Roller lost the services of Wilson in the first quarter and he returned for only a last-minute desperation play at the end of the game. Conzelman went out with an injury at the end of the third quarter and did not return. As the game moved into the fourth quarter, the Steam Roller players were exhausted from their fourth game in six days. The Yellow Jackets took advantage. Frankford took over the ball at its 26-yard line, still trailing only 6–0, midway through the final quarter. Yellow Jackets quarterback Wild Bill Kelly started the drive with a four-yard run. On the next play, Mike Wilson tossed a pass to Kelly that was tipped by a Steam Roller defender—however, Kelly grabbed the ball and raced another 24 yards to the Providence 25-yard line. A Two-Bits Homan run of 11 and a run by Halicki to the three put Frankford in position for the game-tying touchdown. On the next play, Halicki ran through a gaping hole for the score. Halicki drop-kicked the placement but the ball caromed off the goalpost. After a short convening of the officials, the striped shirts ruled that the ball had gone over the crossbar and the kick was good.

Wilson reentered the game but his third desperation pass attempt was intercepted by Homan and the Yellow Jackets secured the 7–6 victory. Providence finished 0-3-1 in its record-setting stretch of games. The battered and bruised team needed some rest and was glad to get a week before its next game.

The Steam Roller ended its six-game winless streak (0-4-2) with a seesaw victory over the expansion Minneapolis Red Jackets on November 17. This one was not decided until the final minutes. The Red Jackets—coached by Herb Joesting—started fast. After taking the opening kickoff, Minneapolis marched 74 yards for a touchdown on a 10-yard pass from Joesting to Ken Haycraft. Providence matched that score almost immediately. Wilson completed a 41-yard pass to Bill Cronin to move the Roller deep into Red Jacket territory. Pop Williams then lugged the football the final three yards for the tally and a 7-7 tie after one quarter. The Red Jackets did the only scoring in the second quarter on a 15-yard field goal by Hal Erickson.

Providence took the lead in the third quarter on the team's longest drive of the season. The Steam Roller marched 94 yards in 14 plays, with Williams scooting around left end for a seven-yard touchdown. Wilson accounted for 65 yards rushing on the long march. Joesting, the former University of Minnesota All-American, quickly moved the Red Jackets down the field and hit Haycraft with a 22-yard touchdown pass, early in the fourth quarter, and Minneapolis was back in front, 16–13.

The back-and-forth contest continued but the Steam Roller would not be outdone. After a 24-yard kickoff return by Conzelman put the ball at the Providence 38, Wilson tossed a 24-yard pass to the coach. A few plays later, Welch ran the football 30 yards deep into Red Jackets territory. Williams took it from there and crashed over the goal line, carrying half of the Minneapolis defense with him. The point-after failed and the Steam Roller clung to a precarious 19–16 lead.

Erickson, Joesting and Mally Nydall took turns making plays against the Providence defense and moved the ball all the way to the Providence one-yard line. On fourth down, Erickson was brought down by Jack Cronin one foot shy of the goal line—and Providence hung on for the heart-stopping victory.

"The game was the most spectacular professional football contest ever staged in Rhode Island," the *Providence Journal* reported. "Five touchdowns. All of them the result of pulse-stirring runs or passes, a placement which struck the cross bar of the goal posts and bounced over for three

Four. Aftermath and Demise (1929–1931)

points, and two offenses which manufactured a total of 35 first downs had approximately 8,500 fans in a furor from the opening kickoff until the final whistle."[11] It was a great way for the Steam Roller to end the winless streak.

The team rode the momentum into its first-ever game with the Boston Bulldogs on November 24 at the Cycledrome. The 4–3 Bulldogs still had several players from when they were the Pottsville Maroons, including Tony Latone and Frank Racis. Boston also had added several former Steam Roller players to upgrade its roster—Joe Kozlowsky, Red Maloney, Ed McCrillis, Al Pierotti, Burt Shurtleff, Hust Stockton and Cy Wentworth.

Providence scored first on a 75-yard drive in the first quarter that Williams finished off with a brilliant 14-yard run around end. The Steam Roller added to its lead after a fumble on a punt snap that Maloney recovered at his own 15-yard line, putting the Roller in great field position. McBride tossed a pass to Welch at the 18-yard line and he carried the ball into the end zone for a 33-yard touchdown. After McBride's extra point, Providence went to the half with a 14–0 lead.

Boston attempted a comeback and had two scoring chances in the third quarter, but each was thwarted by the stingy Roller defense. Providence put the game away midway through the fourth quarter. Welch returned a Bulldogs punt 36 yards to the Boston 37-yard line. McBride ran for five yards and then Wilson threw a perfect pass to Williams for a 32-yard touchdown and a 20–0 Steam Roller lead. The Bulldogs got on the scoreboard late in the game on Latone's short touchdown run to make the final score 20–6. Wentworth played the best of the former Steam Roller players. He caught two passes in Boston's lone scoring drive that set up the Latone touchdown.

The two teams were scheduled to play again on Thanksgiving Day in Boston, but it was decided to cancel the contest. This was the last NFL game the Bulldogs played as they did not return to the NFL in 1930. The team finished its only NFL season with a 4–4 record.

Before the Steam Roller's final game of the season against Green Bay, it was announced that Conzelman had signed a three-year contract to coach the Providence team. He decided to stop playing and would focus his energy on coaching and trying to bring the Steam Roller back to championship heights.

The Packers traveled to Providence with the shoe on the other foot from 1928. This year it was the Packers needing a result over the Steam Roller to win the NFL championship, while a Providence win would ruin those title aspirations. Green Bay came into the game with a 10–0–1 record and Providence was a disappointing 4–5–2. The Roller made a game of it into the fourth quarter. The Packers scored midway through the first quarter on a 37-yard run by Verne Lewellen. The Steam Roller had the football in Green Bay territory twice in the second quarter with a chance to tie the score. Both times the Green Bay defense held on downs, as the Providence runners could not dent the forward wall of the Packers and Wilson's pass attempts went awry. Green Bay added to its lead in the third quarter on a 29-yard pass from Red Dunn to Johnny Blood.

The Packers added a third touchdown on Cully Lidberg's one-yard run, and with Dunn's extra point Green Bay led 19–0. The highlight play of the game was still to come. With about five minutes remaining, Jack Cronin punted to Green Bay and they had two returners (Dunn and Blood) in tandem to receive the kick. Dunn caught the angling punt at his 30-yard line. Two Providence men converged on Dunn, but before they could tackle him, Dunn threw a lateral pass to Blood across the field. What transpired next Blood later called his "Greatest Thrill in Pro Football,"[12] as reported in the Green Bay Packers' 1933 game-day program.

Here is his description: "The play was perfect (when I caught the ball) not a man was within thirty yards of me, but there were nine Providence men and nine Packers between me and the goal. I tucked the prolate spheroid under my arm and set off with celerity and great animation for the goal line, then seventy yards, as the crow flies, away. Being no crow I had to make several detours. The blocking by my Packer brothers was masterful, timely and at points brutal. If an opponent loomed in my path, I had but to slacken my pace and a blue-shirted projectile would appear and mow the hazard from my path. My way was made straight and my road easy. No enemy laid a hand upon me and I crossed the goal line unharmed and happy. The game was on ice and I was a hero for sixty seconds."[13] Blood was named second-team All-Pro at the conclusion of the season.

The Packers completed the 25–0 victory and won their first NFL championship. The Steam Roller was left to pick up the pieces from a very disappointing season and to look to retool for 1930.

Providence finished in seventh place in the 12-team NFL with a 4–6–2 record, the second sub-.500 record in Steam Roller history. Despite the stock market crash, the team drew excellent crowds to the Cycledrome, with all but three home games drawing 8,500 or more. The team was 4–3–1 at the Cycledrome and 0–1 at Kinsley Park.

Rehnquist, despite missing four games, was named a first-team All-Pro. Welch was named a second-team All-Pro. Williams led the Steam Roller in scoring with seven touchdowns for 42 points and Welch was second with six scores for 36 points. Wilson's overall play fell off and that really hurt the team as he contributed only one touchdown.

The Great Depression that began in the fall of 1929 had a limited immediate impact on the team, but that would change in the coming years.

1930—The Steam Roller Contends but Attendance Falls Off Sharply

New York Telegram reporter Charles E. Parker named an all-time Brown University football team that was announced on February 22, 1930. It contained several players who had played for the Steam Roller, including Mike Gulian, Jack Keefer, Fritz Pollard, Orland Smith and Jack Spellman.

Providence's offseason, leading into the 1930 season, was unprecedented in team history for player turnover. Of the 21 players who participated in a game in 1929, 14 left the Steam Roller for one reason or another. The biggest loss was superstar Wildcat Wilson, who had directed the Providence offense for the previous three years. He ended his career as the third-leading scorer in team history and the leader in touchdown passes. Wilson announced his retirement on September 5, and his brother Abe went into retirement with him. Wilson's dynamic play was severely missed. He started a wrestling career, following in the footsteps of Sonnenberg and Spellman.

Gibby Welch was sold to the Staten Island Stapletons, and with Conzelman only coaching, the team lost three of its backfield mainstays. In addition, Bill Cronin retired and Jack McBride was sold to the Brooklyn Dodgers, further depleting the Steam Roller's backfield. Other noteworthy losses were linemen Jack Fleishmann, Art Garvey, Duke Hanny and Orland Smith. Only seven players remained from the 1928 championship team just two short years later.

With so much player turnover, Coppen and Johnson had their hands full to bring in new players to fill the many holes on the roster, while also managing the team's finances. But the two men began signing players in rapid succession. Providence was seen as a good destination for players and a great place to play, so that was in its favor.

Forrest Douds, a former Washington & Jefferson captain and three-time All-American lineman, signed a one-year contract with the Steam Roller on April 15. With the demise of the Dayton Triangles, Al Graham, who had played for the Triangles for five seasons and was a two-time second-team All-Pro, was sold to Providence. In late July, the Steam Roller rebuilt its backfield with the signings of former Illinois quarterback Frosty Peters, former Brown halfback and captain Bud Edwards and Tony Holm, a former All-American fullback from Alabama. Also, Curly Oden returned to the Steam Roller after a one-year hiatus, and Joe Kozlowsky resigned after being away from the team for two years.

The Steam Roller was also working to upgrade the Cycledrome with the addition of permanent floodlights. The Cycledrome was the first stadium in the country with permanent lighting for night games. This was done to position the team to increase its number of night games in 1930 and beyond, but it also allowed Laudati to schedule other events in the evening at the venue.

Providence continued to add players as August rolled into September. Ted Kucharski, a three-year letter winner at Holy Cross; former University of Detroit end Herm Young; and NFL veteran Frank Racis all signed with the team. Herb Meeker, a small but dynamic quarterback from Washington State, came east to play for Providence. And then as Coppen seemed to do every year, he had a big signing up his sleeve with the announcement on September 12 that former Pottsville star Tony Latone would join the team.

Latone signed an interesting contract. It called for him to be paid $125 for all NFL day games and 60 percent of that sum ($75) for games played at night. When Johnson was questioned as to why, he said that the pay reduction was arranged to help pay the installation costs of the floodlights.

While all the player activity was going on, the NFL was preparing to launch its 11th season. In July it announced the move of the original Dayton Triangles franchise to Brooklyn to become the Dodgers, though most of the players were sold off or left the game. The Boston and Buffalo franchises were shut down, with the lack of playing facilities cited as the reason. Portsmouth, Ohio, was granted an expansion franchise, the Portsmouth Spartans. The NFL was an 11-team league for 1930, down one franchise from 1929.

The most significant announcement made at the July 13 league meeting was that NFL teams would play 15 night games on Wednesdays during the upcoming season. The league had played a single trial night game in Providence in 1929 and with the perceived success of that game, the NFL was making a big bet on night games for the 1930 season. League president Carr again predicted a banner season for the league, despite the economic hardships facing many Americans.

Providence was scheduled to kick off its sixth NFL season at home against the New York Giants on September 28 and its first night game would follow on October 1 against Frankford. Providence was not scheduled to play defending league champion Green Bay as Lambeau was still fuming over the guarantees required by the Steam Roller. A couple of other highlights of the schedule were the visit by the Chicago Cardinals on October 12 and the newly christened Brooklyn Dodgers on October 8.

To start the 1930 season, Providence scheduled three preseason games in eight days and would finish the season against New England powerhouse, but nonleague member, Pere Marquette on November 30.

The defending champion Packers returned almost their entire team and looked poised to repeat. The Giants appeared to be the Packers' great-

Four. Aftermath and Demise (1929–1931)

STEAM ROLLER SCHEDULE -- 1930			
EXHIBITION GAMES		S.R	Opp
Sept. 14 — West Weymouth, Mass.	At home		
Sept. 17 — Quincy Trojans	At home		
Sept. 21 — Brooklyn Professionals	At home		
NATIONAL LEAGUE GAMES			
Sept. 28 — New York Giants	At home		
Oct. 1 — Philadelphia Yellow Jackets (Floodlight)	At home		
Oct. 5 — Newark	At home		
Oct. 8 — Brooklyn (Floodlight)	At home		
Oct. 12 — Chicago Cardinals	At home		
Oct. 15 — Providence	At Newark		
Oct. 19 — Stapleton	At home		
Oct. 22 — Newark (Floodlight)	At home		
Oct. 26 — Providence	At New York		
Nov. 2 — Brooklyn	At home		
Nov. 8 — Providence	At Philadelphia		
Nov. 9 — Philadelphia	At home		
Nov. 16 — Portsmouth	At home		
Nov. 23 — Minneapolis	At home		
Nov. 27 — Providence	At Brooklyn		
Nov. 30 — Stapleton	At home		

WEYBOSSET MINIATURE GOLF COURSE
37 WEYBOSSET STREET — FIRST FLOOR
NINE HOLES   FEE - 25¢
WILL OPEN ON OR ABOUT OCTOBER 1, 1930   (Over)

Providence Steam Roller 1930 pocket schedule displaying its exhibition games and the three floodlight night games to be played at the Cycledrome (courtesy Rhode Island Historical Society—RHiX174732).

est threat with Benny Friedman at the helm. New York's only loss in 1929 came against undefeated Green Bay. The Chicago Bears, with Red Grange, added legendary All-American Bronco Nagurski, and the team co-owned by George Halas and Ed Sternaman looked to be significantly improved. It was hard to know if Providence would be better with all the player turnover, but Coppen, Johnson and the team's fans were cautiously optimistic.

Providence opened its preseason schedule with a 59–0 shellacking of a completely undermanned West Weymouth team in front of 4,014 spectators at the Cycledrome. It was not really a test for the new version of the Steam Roller, but the fans and Coach Conzelman got to see many of the newcomers in action. Meeker, the 5'3", 145-pound dynamo, was impressive in his first appearance. He scored one touchdown and converted three extra points while also making some sparkling runs and leading the team with a confidence that was infectious. Frosty Peters also showed off his talents. The former Illinois star displayed excellent passing and leadership skills while scoring a touchdown and booting three extra points and a field goal. Running back Latone reminded Steam Roller fans of his capabilities that he had displayed when he was with Pottsville. Latone scored three touchdowns for his new team, "giving a splendid exhibition of plunging," wrote John R. Aborn from the *Providence Journal*.[14] Latone was every bit what the fans had hoped.

Three days later, the Steam Roller played its second of three exhibition encounters. This one was special because it was under the newly installed lights at the Cycledrome. The Quincy Trojans were the opponent and provided a much stiffer test. With the beaming new lights, described by the *Providence Journal* as "33 projectors on poles 53 feet high, and nine poles on top of the grandstand, which even daylight could not improve," the Steam Roller started fast.[15] Latone scored the game's first touchdown on a five-yard run. He also contributed two first-quarter interceptions, with the second one setting up a Tony Holm short touchdown run for a 14–0 Providence first-quarter lead.

Meeker entered the game in the second quarter and led the Steam Roller on two touchdown drives in the third quarter and Providence went on to a 28–0 shutout victory. Meeker was becoming a crowd favorite with his daring play. A somewhat disappointing Wednesday night crowd of 3,100 came out for the game.

Providence's final tune-up for the regular season was on September 21 against the Brooklyn Professionals at the Cycledrome. In front of 4,800, the Steam Roller routed Brooklyn 63–0. Meeker, though not starting, was the best player on the field. "He intercepted passes, caught passes, swept the ends for long gains, ran back punts, like a dart through a host of Brooklyn tacklers and formed valuable interference for his fellow-backs in a manner that cannot be denied," Aborn wrote.[16] Meeker scored two touchdowns and made two placements.

Providence led 22–0 at halftime but Conzelman was not at all pleased with the play of his team. After a stern lecture by the coach, the Roller exploded for 41 points in the second half. Both of Meeker's touchdowns came in the second-half onslaught. Latone scored two also and Jack Cronin and Ted Kucharski each contributed one. It appeared the Steam Roller was ready for the NFL season after outscoring its three preseason opponents by a score of 150–0.

Now the real challenges of the season started for the Steam Roller right out of the gate. Providence opened the regular season at home against one of the league's finest in the New York Giants. A capacity crowd of 12,000 came to see the new-look Steam Roller, and the fans left feeling disappointed.

Friedman led New York to a 27–7 victory by mixing his effective passes with a strong ground game that featured no fewer than seven different running backs—Dale Burnett, Tiny Feather, Jack Hagerty, Hap Moran, Led Sedbrook, Ossie Wiberg and Mule Wilson. Three of them scored touchdowns. The Giants scored in each quarter and took control of the

Four. Aftermath and Demise (1929–1931)

game late in the first quarter and never relinquished it. The gifted quarterback Friedman drove New York 37 yards following a Peters punt and Sedbrook carried the ball the final 12 yards for the first touchdown. Friedman kicked the extra point and the Giants were in front 7–0. In the second quarter, Les Caywood intercepted an errant Peters pass and returned it 16 yards for a score and a 14–0 New York halftime lead.

The Giants extended their lead to 20–0 on Burnett's nine-yard jaunt that had been set up by a 50-yard run by Moran to the Roller 14. Providence finally got on the scoreboard in the fourth quarter. Meeker returned a New York punt 26 yards to the Giants' 26-yard line. Several running plays and a 15-yard penalty helped the Steam Roller move the ball to the New York one-yard line. On fourth down, Peters threw a four-yard touchdown pass to Herm Young and Peters's extra-point kick cut the Giants' lead to 20–7. Any thought of a Providence comeback was quickly doused as Friedman threw a 25-yard touchdown pass to Mule Wilson and New York went on to the convincing victory.

Following the game, the Roller reduced the roster by two. The team cut Bud Edwards, who sat out the Giants contest, and Dutch Webber, who had played against New York. Providence had hoped that the six-year veteran Webber would help the team, but it gave up on him after only one game.

The Steam Roller did not have much time to lick its wounds. Archrival Frankford came to town for a Wednesday night game on October 1 and a very disappointing crowd of only 3,500 turned out. The Yellow Jackets were not the star-studded team from only a few years before, but they were still a big rival of the Roller.

The combination of a powerful running game led by Latone and a stout defense propelled the Steam Roller to a 14–0 victory. Holm fumbled early in the game on the Providence 25-yard line, and the Yellow Jackets recovered. However, the Steam Roller defense stonewalled Frankford and Providence took over on downs. That was as close as the Yellow Jackets would get into Providence territory the entire game.

The Roller put the first points on the board in the second quarter. Veteran Pop Williams completed a 28-yard march when he burst over right tackle from two yards out for the touchdown. A short while later, Peters intercepted a Jack Ernst aerial and returned it 40 yards to paydirt. Peters converted both extra points and Providence went to the half with a 14–0 lead. The Steam Roller defense, with the help of some timely punting by Jack Cronin, dominated the second half, and though Frankford netted eight first downs for the game, the Yellow Jackets never came close to scoring. Oden had been inserted as the starting quarterback for Providence and his steady hand plus the outstanding running of Latone helped enable the Steam Roller to control the game after taking the 14–0 lead. There was no additional scoring in a nice bounce-back win for the team.

Playing its third game in eight days, the weary Steam Roller hosted the Newark Tornadoes on October 5. Williams replaced Holm in the backfield for the game, due to an ankle injury, and Young and Kucharski were inserted on the line to supply some fresh legs. Another disappointing crowd, this time numbering 4,500, watched Providence notch its second consecutive 14–0 victory. It was starting to become apparent that the state of the local and national economy was impacting attendance.

Latone was again outstanding as he rushed for 116 yards with a 6.4-per-carry average while scoring the clinching touchdown in the fourth quarter. The star back also intercepted two passes. Providence controlled the game throughout. The Roller backs pounded out 252 yards rushing and mixed in 30 passing yards on three completions while gaining 13 first downs. The Providence defense held Newark to only three first downs and 27 rushing yards.

The Steam Roller scored the first touchdown of the game in the second quarter. Peters intercepted Tornadoes quarterback Frank Kirkleski on the Newark 39-yard line. Providence pounded the Tornadoes' line of scrimmage with several runs to move to the 17. Peters then hit Meeker with a short

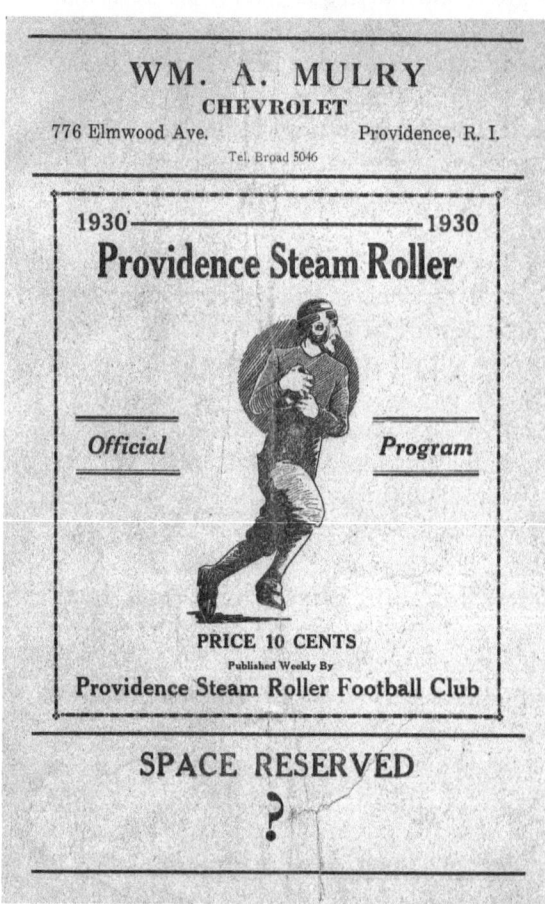

Providence Steam Roller vs. Frankford Yellow Jackets program from November 9, 1930. The two teams played to a 7–7 tie with the Steam Roller touchdown coming on a 95-yard kickoff return by Herb Meeker (courtesy Rhode Island Historical Society—RHi X17 4836).

pass, and the diminutive dynamo scooted through the Newark defense on the way to a 17-yard touchdown. Peters's dropkick was good and the Roller led 7–0. It held that lead until the fourth quarter, when Latone set up his touchdown with an interception.

Newark had two golden opportunities in the third quarter to score but both times the Providence defense stopped the advance. The first time was on downs, and on the second one Perry Jackson recovered a fumble. After the game, Jackson, Ray Smith, Al Graham, Warren McGuirk, Al Rose and Forrest Douds were lauded for their play by the *Providence Journal*. Two more Roller players were released—Jack McArthur and Herm Young—further trimming the roster to reduce expenses.

The gauntlet of a schedule continued on Wednesday night, October 8, for the Roller's third night game of the season. However, Mother Nature did Providence a favor. For two consecutive nights, heavy rains postponed the scheduled affair with Brooklyn. After the second postponement, the game was rescheduled for November 2, giving the Steam Roller a much-needed respite.

The up-and-coming Chicago Cardinals came to town on October 12, and though superstar Ernie Nevers was nursing an injured knee and would not play, the Cardinals would be a good test for the Steam Roller. Close to 13,000 fans poured into the Cycledrome for that Sunday afternoon clash.

It was a bruising battle from the opening kickoff. Cardinal returner Bunny Belden ran 53 yards with the kick, only to be drilled by Hadden. The tackle forced a fumble that was recovered by Rehnquist of Providence. The first points of the game came midway through the second quarter. Providence pounded out three consecutive first downs on effective runs by Latone and Peters to move to the Cardinals' 23-yard line. But the drive stalled and Peters booted a 22-yard field goal for a 3–0 Steam Roller lead. The game stayed that way until well into the third quarter. Cardinal quarterback Mack Flenniken attempted a pass that was deflected by Perry Jackson into the waiting arms of Frank Racis. The lumbering defensive end, with the help of a terrific block from Jackson, rumbled his way 40 yards for the touchdown and a 9–0 Providence lead.

The Steam Roller defense continued to play exceptionally well, with Douds, Rehnquist, Ray Smith and Spellman crashing into the Cardinal backfield to spoil many plays. Chicago desperately tried to score as the game wound down. Finally, with the ball at the Steam Roller's 40-yard line, Flenniken hit two key passes that took the ball to the Roller's six. Two plays later, Flenniken ran it over from four yards for the score, and the placement by George Bogue was good.

Now the Providence lead was a precarious two points with time running down. Meeker made the play to secure the victory. He intercepted a desperation pass by Flenniken at midfield and then the Roller ran out the clock. "Not in two seasons have pro football followers seen a game such as this one at the local 'Drome' and it was the work of the lines which stood out," reported Hess, Jr., of the *Providence Journal*.[17] Both teams struggled mightily to move the ball, but thanks to Peters's dropkick and Racis's interception, the Roller came out victorious.

Providence further reduced its roster by releasing Bud Edwards, again. It was becoming apparent that a weakness in the Steam Roller arsenal was the punting game. In the previous two games, the opponents gained significant yardage on punt exchanges. The Roller was scheduled for a night game in Newark on Thursday, October 16, but the game was canceled.

On October 19, Providence hosted Staten Island. It was the fifth consecutive home game for the Steam Roller. To the surprise of many, Sonnenberg returned to the team. The Stapletons were led by future Hall of Famer Ken Strong and fullback and head coach Doug Wycoff. Providence kept its winning streak going with a tough 7–6 victory in front of 5,000 fans.

Staten Island's two stars each fumbled in the first quarter, providing excellent scoring opportunities for Providence. The Steam Roller capitalized on the second fumble. Meeker, who replaced Oden, ran the ball 13 yards to the Stapletons' seven-yard line. From there, Latone carried the ball on three successive plays and crashed over the goal line from the four to put Providence on the board. Peters booted the extra point for a 7–0 Steam Roller lead at the end of the first quarter.

Both teams struggled to move the ball against the stalwart defenses. Providence rushed 58 times throughout the game for only 156 yards, a paltry 2.6 yards per carry. And the Roller passing game was even worse as it failed to complete a pass in 11 attempts. But the Providence defense held Staten Island to only 123 rushing yards. It was the Stapletons' passing game that almost pulled out a victory. In the fourth quarter, following a missed field goal attempt by Peters, the Stapletons marched 80 yards for a score. Wycoff completed two long passes with some effective runs mixed in to move the team down the field. One of those passes was to Strong, who carried it 37 yards for the touchdown. Strong missed the all-important extra point and Providence held a slim one-point lead. Wycoff continued to put the ball in the air in an attempt to complete the comeback, but to no avail. His three interceptions, highlighted by Peters's 46-yard return of an errant throw in the fourth quarter, sealed the victory for Providence.

Sonnenberg, with a huge ovation from the crowd, played only the second quarter and was a shell of the All-Pro from 1928. It was his only game with the Roller, as he left the team and returned to wrestling full-time. The tinkering with the roster continued. Holm, disappointing in his three

Four. Aftermath and Demise (1929–1931) 117

games, and Weldon Gentry were both released. Bud Edwards was brought back. The Steam Roller defense had rounded into form, having allowed only two touchdowns during the four-game win streak.

The win moved Providence into third place with a 4–1 record and set up a showdown with the second-place Giants (5–1) in a rematch of opening day. (The Packers were leading the NFL with a 5–0 record.) The Polo Grounds was the setting for the teams' second meeting, and 10,000 fans supplied vocal support for the Giants.

Providence battled New York on almost even terms until late in the third quarter. The Steam Roller defense, which was no match for the Giants' running game in the first encounter, held them in check this time. The first quarter was scoreless but Providence had the upper hand with much of the play in New York territory. The Giants broke through in the second quarter for the first touchdown of the game. Friedman threw a 23-yard pass to Glenn Campbell to the Roller two-yard line. One play later, Dale Burnett scored.

With the Giants leading 6–0 in the third quarter, a controversial officials call changed the momentum of the game and the season for Providence. The Steam Roller was knocking at the Giants' door. The ball was at the New York seven-yard line when Latone entered the game. On first down, he smashed through the Giants' line for a five-yard gain to the two. A touchdown seemed imminent. However, referee Tommy Hughitt called a penalty, claiming that Latone did not report into the game, resulting in a five-yard infraction. After the penalty was assessed, a desperate Oden threw a pass into the end zone that was intercepted by Burnett.

New York then became more aggressive in the passing game, since the running attack had been stymied, and it paid off. Late in the third quarter, Friedman threw a 50-yard scoring strike to Mule Wilson to put the Giants in control, 13–0. The gifted quarterback kept passing and threw two more touchdown passes in the final quarter—15 yards to Red Badgro and 25 yards to Burnett. The Giants went on to a 25–0 victory in a game that was much closer than the final score indicated. The third quarter penalty and subsequent interception seemed to take the momentum away from Providence and it did not recover. Friedman had become a Roller killer. He completed 10 of 15 passes for 174 yards and three touchdowns and was the difference in the game. The Steam Roller's title hopes took a major hit with the second loss to New York.

The rescheduled game with Brooklyn was up next on November 2. Brooklyn came into the game riding a four-game winning streak and had moved into third place. The Dodgers were missing halfback Rex Thomas, one of the team's leading scorers, with a knee injury. The Steam Roller and Dodgers battled on even terms throughout the contest, with the defenses dominating the action. Providence rushed 43 times for a measly 56 yards and Brooklyn did not do much better with 46 runs for 90 yards. The Steam Roller had three scoring opportunities in the game but failed on the first two. Shortly before halftime, Providence moved the ball to the Brooklyn four-yard line but was held on downs. In the third quarter, Peters missed a field goal. Later in the quarter, the Steam Roller moved into scoring territory one more time. This time Peters was successful on a 27-yard field goal and the home team was in the lead 3–0.

Brooklyn threatened only once. The Dodgers drove 85 yards to the Providence five-yard line early in the final quarter. "It was here that the locals gave as fine an exhibition of defensive football as they have this season. Douds, McGuirk, Smith, Spellman and Edwards were brilliant in the extreme throughout the game, and each of that quintet had a part in the four goal-line plays," reported F.C. Matzek of the *Providence Journal*.[18] On fourth down, former Steam Roller Jack McBride threw an incomplete pass into the end zone and Providence took over and went on to a 3–0 victory.

Following the game, Kozlowsky was released. He was re-signed a few days later, after injuries to Edwards, Rehnquist and Graham that could keep them from playing against the Yellow Jackets.

The Steam Roller traveled to Philadelphia via the New York steamer boat on November 7 to tangle in a home-and-home series with the woeful Yellow Jackets that started the next day. Frankford came into the back-to-back games with a dismal 2–10 record and on a 10-game losing streak. However, NFL president Carr, in an attempt to prop up the franchise, gave the Yellow Jackets permission to use players from the Minneapolis Red Jackets. "Because of the demoralized condition into which the Jackets had fallen as a result of a string of disasters," was the reason given by Carr as reported by the *Providence Journal*.[19] The best players from the Red Jackets, including All-American Herb Joestling, joined the Frankford roster, and the combination made a much more formidable opponent. Eight of the starting 11 players were new to the team for this game.

The newly strengthened Yellow Jackets stunned Providence with two second-quarter touchdowns. With Joestling providing direction and leadership and Art Pharmer punting the Yellow Jackets into favorable field position, the former Red Jackets gave Frankford confidence and momentum. On the first play of the second quarter, Clyde Crabtree darted off left tackle for a five-yard touchdown, completing a short Frankford drive. A short while later, following a missed Pharmer field goal, Peters threw an ill-advised pass that was intercepted by Bob Tanner. The speedy defender sprinted 30 yards for a touchdown and a surprising 13–0 Yellow Jackets halftime lead.

Neither team scored in the third quarter and another Peters inter-

Four. Aftermath and Demise (1929–1931)

ception set up a 21-yard game-clinching touchdown run by Joestling with five minutes left in the game. Providence scored a meaningless touchdown by Peters late in the game as the Steam Roller trudged off the field with an extremely disappointing 20–7 defeat. Frankford outplayed the visitors, compiling 227 yards of offense compared with only 94 by the Steam Roller, and the two interceptions thrown by Peters led directly to 13 points. Any thoughts of another NFL championship for Providence were erased with the upset loss.

Both teams jumped on an overnight train for the trip to Providence and a rematch the next day at the Cycledrome.

The game started with a bang. Diminutive speedster Butch Meeker took the opening kickoff and raced 95 yards, shaking off two would-be tacklers, for a thrilling touchdown. Meeker, the second-fastest player on the team, added the extra point and the Roller was in front 7–0. Providence had a chance to extend the lead late in the first quarter but Peters missed a 20-yard field goal attempt. Frankford tied the game in the second quarter after a short Providence punt. Quarterback Kelly Rodriquez threw a 12-yard pass to Tony Kostos, his only completion of the day in 16 attempts, to the Providence five-yard line. Ed Halicki knifed through the Providence defense for the touchdown, and his placement was good to tie the game.

In the fourth quarter, Providence had two more chances to take the lead, but each time Peters missed the attempted field goal. The game ended in a 7–7 tie. The Steam Roller outplayed Frankford, amassing nine first downs to only four for the Yellow Jackets, but the three missed field goals cost them a victory.

A week later, the Steam Roller was scheduled to play the expansion Portsmouth Spartans, but the game was canceled due to heavy rain. It was rescheduled for two nights later, but the weather did not cooperate and the game was canceled again. It was not rescheduled.

Providence's last home game of the 1930 season was held on November 23 against the 1-5-1 Minneapolis Red Jackets. Joestling, Pharmer and the other Red Jackets who had been loaned out to Frankford were back with the team, and several reinforcements from Frankford joined Minneapolis for this game. It was, to be polite, a curious arrangement.

The Steam Roller got some revenge for its earlier debacle in Philadelphia. It was Butch Meeker Day at the Cycledrome. Prior to the game, he was honored by several Providence friends and presented with a traveling bag. He then let his play do the talking. Meeker returned punts for 119 yards, had 40 yards rushing, caught two passes for 15 yards, intercepted a pass that he ran back 17 yards and kicked a field goal. It was his three-pointer in the first quarter that gave Providence the lead for good.

The score stayed at 3–0 until the fourth quarter with the Providence defense dominating the game. It completely shut down Joestling and the Red Jackets' running game that hurt them so much when those players played for Frankford. Minneapolis had only one scoring opportunity in the game and Al Rose ended that drive with a timely interception of a Mally Nydall pass at the Providence 17-yard line in the second quarter.

The Steam Roller padded its lead in the fourth quarter. After Meeker returned a punt 19 yards, Oden threw two passes to Spellman that set the Roller up at the Red Jackets' three-yard line. It took Latone three line smashes, but on the third one he tumbled into the end zone for the touchdown. Oden booted the extra point and Providence extended its lead to 10–0. Cronin picked off a Nydall pass and that ended any hint of a threat from the visitors. The Steam Roller finished its home schedule with a satisfying 10–0 victory. Minneapolis played one more game that season and exited the NFL.

Providence traveled to Ebbets Field for a Thanksgiving Day clash with Brooklyn and the team's final NFL game of the season. The Dodgers, with 8,000 cheering them on, blasted the Roller 33–12 and gained revenge for their 3–0 loss earlier in the season. Providence was playing without Peters, who had been sold to the Portsmouth Spartans, as well as Graham, Douds and Ray Smith, but it did not matter. Brooklyn outplayed the Roller from the outset. Stumpy Thomason, a former Georgia Tech star, scored the first touchdown of the game on a seven-yard run in the first quarter. McBride ran in from five yards out in the second quarter to stake Brooklyn to a 13–0 lead. Providence scored before the end of the first half to stay in the game. Edwards caught a pass from Oden and raced into the end zone for the touchdown, his first and only as a Steam Roller. The half ended with Brooklyn ahead 13–6.

The Dodgers took control of the game in the third quarter by scoring two touchdowns, a 40-yard pass from Wild Bill Kelly to Mike Stramiello and a three-yard run by Thomason. Those two scores pushed the Dodgers' lead to 26–6. Each team scored fourth-quarter touchdowns to close out the scoring; Williams tallied for Providence. The loss dropped the Steam Roller's NFL record to 6–4–1. Providence finished fifth in the NFL standings, with two of the losses coming at the hands of the second-place Giants. Green Bay repeated as NFL champions with a 10–3–1 record.

The final game of the Roller's season came only three days later, November 30, with a tilt against Pere Marquette at Braves Field in Boston. It was the first game against Pere since 1928. The semipro outfit from Boston gave a good showing and kept the game scoreless until the final quarter. It appeared the game would end in a 0–0 tie, until Williams broke a 25-yard touchdown run. The Steam Roller garnered 11 first downs to only five for Pere but was unable to score until Williams's brilliant run. Providence had several chances, but two were halted by interceptions and one by an incomplete pass in the end zone. The final score was a 6–0 victory for Providence.

Peters led the Roller in scoring for the season with 25 points that included two touchdowns, seven extra points and two field goals. Latone led the team with three touchdowns but overall was a disappointment. Spellman was named the team MVP and was awarded a gold watch. No Providence players were selected to the league's official All-Pro teams. Despite having two crowds of more than 12,000, the average attendance at the Cycledrome fell below 6,500 per game. After a solid 4–1 start to the season, the team had a disappointing 2–3–1 record to close out the NFL schedule.

The economic conditions in the United States continued to worsen. Unemployment had risen to 8.7 percent, and by the end of 1931 it would increase to 15.9 percent. The number continued to rise from there. The New York Giants agreed to play a game on December 14 against an All-Star team of Notre Dame graduates coached by Knute Rockne at the Polo Grounds. All the proceeds from the game went to the New York Unemployment Fund. It was a great opportunity for pro football to show that its game was the equivalent or an even better brand of football than the more popular college game. Most fans expected a Notre Dame victory. With a crowd of 55,000 looking on, Friedman led New York to a convincing 22–0 victory. The profile of the Giants and the NFL improved significantly from the game, while the Unemployment Fund received more than $100,000 from the game's receipts.

Despite the worsening economic conditions, Coppen and his partners were committed to press on, and preparations for the 1931 season commenced almost immediately.

1931—More Games, Fewer Fans, the End Is Near

The first substantial change for the Steam Roller for the 1931 season was that Conzelman decided to retire from football coaching and would not be returning to the team. It was the first time in four years that the outstanding coach would not be roaming the Steam Roller sideline. He ended his Providence career with a 26–16–4 record, a .604 winning percentage. Conzelman could no longer play and did not see the future success of the league. "When I didn't see the league progressing very far, I decided to go back to St. Louis where I had been born, where I played my high school and college ball and, more important, where my family was," he said years later.[20]

Ed Robinson, an accomplished college football head coach who was well-known in Providence, was hired to replace Conzelman. It was Robinson's first foray into the professional game but he was a highly regarded hire. Robinson had been a very successful coach at Brown for 24 seasons, compiling a 140–82–12 record, including a Rose Bowl berth in 1915. Before joining the Steam Roller, he was the head coach at Boston University for four seasons. He was the first big-time college coach to take over a professional team. "Robinson was noted for his resourcefulness and his ability to design plays and formations which are well in advance of the times," reported the *Providence Journal*.[21]

The player losses, though less than in 1930, were still significant. Jack Cronin (third in games played in team history) and Latone were gone from the backfield and Peters had been sold at the end of last season, so the backfield needed reinforcements. Cronin had come to training camp with the intention of playing. But on August 14, he requested his release, citing his commitment to LaSalle Academy that would not allow him to regularly attend practice. Across the front line, Forest Douds, Perry Jackson, Ted Kucharski, Warren McGuirk and Frank Racis all left the team.

Coppen was not as aggressive with salaries in 1931 in his player recruitment, given the economic challenges facing the team, but he was still able to bring in several quality players. To reinforce the backfield, Coppen and the team went to many lengths to find players. The Steam Roller signed a pair of newly graduated college players: Syracuse All-East quarterback Herb Titmas and Purdue halfback Lew Pope. Coppen found former Villanova tailback Sky August playing with a semipro team in northern Pennsylvania and plucked Lee Woodruff, a former Mississippi starter, off a semipro team in Memphis, Tennessee. The co-owner also signed players with previous NFL experience—running back Royce Goodbread, formerly of Frankford; and halfback Oran Pape from the NFL champion Packers. It was reported by the *Iowa City Press-Citizen* that "it is worth noting that the Steam Rollers have a 'find' in Oran Pape of Iowa. He is one of the finest looking backs to show here in a long time. He is the shiftiest running halfback that the Rollers have had. Pape's speed is deceptive … he has a baffling change of pace which throws tacklers off their stride."[22]

Providence solidified the line with the signing of three recent college players—Tex Irvin, Joe Schein and Alec Sofish. Irvin played tackle and fullback for four seasons at Davis & Elkins and earned All-American honors in 1929. Schein was an All-American tackle at Brown during his three seasons. Sofish played collegiately at Grove City, where he started on the line for three years. The team also re-signed Weldon Gentry.

In addition, Coppen pursued Washington State center Mel Hein. The college All-American had signed a contract to play for Providence and put it in the mail to the team. In the meantime, New York Giants assistant coach Ray Flaherty spoke with Hein and told him that he would offer a better contract. Hein decided he wanted to play for New York and contacted the local post office to try to retrieve the signed Providence contract. Hein was instructed to complete a form for the return of the letter. After he signed the form, the postmaster at Washington State sent a telegram to Providence and asked the postmaster there to intercept the letter. The post office was able to find the contract before it was delivered to Steam Roller management.

Hein went on to play for the Giants and became a Hall of Famer. He was enshrined with the first Pro Football Hall of Fame class in Canton in 1963. Had the postmaster not found the letter, he would have played for Providence. "At the time Jimmy Conzelman was the coach of the Steamrollers and for years after that whenever we met he would kid me about my sudden change of mind," Hein recalled.[23]

At the NFL owners meeting in July, President Carr was reelected. Judge Dooley, representing the Steam Roller franchise, was again named to serve on the league's executive committee. The owners added Cleveland as a new franchise and the Minneapolis and Newark franchises disbanded. The now 10-team league announced its 1931 schedule. The owners also expanded team rosters from 18 to 23 players with the thought that the larger roster would improve overall play. With the continued worsening economic conditions, Coppen held out deciding on whether to play in 1931 or suspend operations. He was persuaded by fellow owners at the meeting to continue when provided a favorable schedule that included seven home games.

Providence was scheduled to open the season on September 27 against the Giants at the Cycledrome, two weeks after the league officially was scheduled to open its 12th season with a game between Brooklyn and Portsmouth. A few highlights of the Steam Roller's schedule were a home-and-home series with Frankford and with defending champion Green Bay along with two home games against the newly christened Cleveland Indians.

The Roller also scheduled three exhibition games in September as they had in 1930. In addition, the team sprinkled the schedule with non-league opponents, and they would add more as the season progressed. The Providence owners continued to add more games in an attempt to increase revenue to help keep the franchise viable.

Green Bay was the overwhelming favorite to become the first team to three-peat as champions. The Packers returned their star-studded lineup of Verne Lewallen, Curly Lambeau, Johnny Blood, Lavvie Dilweg, Red Dunn, Cal Hubbard and Mike Michalske. Lambeau added some rookies and a couple of veteran linemen to the mix. The New York Giants, the Packers' primary threat in the previous two seasons, lost Benny Friedman to retirement; they were expected to fall back. Then shortly before the season began, Friedman returned to New York and hopes for the 1931 season rebounded. The Chicago Bears and Portsmouth Spartans were expected to be improved, especially since the Spartans had hired Potsy Clark as head coach and had added quality players including George Christensen, Dutch Clark, Ox Emerson and Glenn Presnell. Providence was expected to finish in the middle of the pack.

The Steam Roller gathered for their first practice on August 31, their earliest gathering in team history. With new coach Robinson, there was a lot of work to do to prepare for the new season.

Providence opened the preseason against the Boston Collegians, a makeshift group who all had played collegiate football, on September 6 at the Cycledrome. After a scoreless first quarter, Pape scored on a seven-yard touchdown run. Fred DeGata, who had played his college football at Providence, kicked the extra point and the Steam Roller was in front 7–0. Providence recovered a fumble on the ensuing kickoff and five plays later Pape was in the end zone again, increasing the Roller lead to 13–0.

Providence added another touchdown on an 85-yard march at the start of the second half. Meeker concluded the drive with a 14-yard jaunt for the score. Providence went on to win 20–0. Other first-year players for Providence who played well included Pawtucket product Titmas, Pope, Woodruff, Goodbread and Irvin.

The Quincy Trojans came to town on September 13 and went home with a 34–7 defeat at the hands of the Steam Roller. Providence scored two touchdowns in the first quarter as Pope rambled 20 yards and Pape went 17 yards for the scores. Goodbread scored in the second quarter, capping a 49-yard drive with a 14-yard run. The Roller went to the half with a 20–0 lead. Bud Edwards, in his first stint at quarterback in his Providence career, drove the Roller to a score in the third quarter that Pape finished off. Sky August scored on a two-yard run late in the game that offset a 90-yard Quincy interception return for its only score.

The final tune-up for the Steam Roller prior to the start of the regular season was a 66–0 rout of West Weymouth on September 20. The Weymouth squad, as in the previous meeting in 1930, provided very little resistance. Goodbread returned from an injury, from the week before, and rushed for 128 yards and four touchdowns. Providence ran a remarkable 43 plays in the first quarter on its way to 26 points behind the quarterbacking of Titmas. August, Pop Williams, Meeker and Irvin were each lauded for their play. It was now decision time for head coach Robinson. How was he going to use the plethora of backfield options in the arsenal, who was going to direct the team and what backs would carry the load on the ground?

The Giants came to town to open the Steam Roller's seventh NFL season on September 27. A somewhat disappointing crowd of 8,000 came out to see the latest edition of its NFL team. Robinson went with an all-new backfield. Titmas started at quarterback with Pape and Pope at halfbacks and Woodruff at fullback. The Steam Roller moved the ball against the strong defense of the Giants, outgaining its opponent 190 yards to 147 and compiling nine first downs to six. However, the Roller was unable to generate an offensive touchdown.

Providence's only score came on Al Graham's blocked punt and an end zone recovery by Rose in the second quarter. The Giants sandwiched the Providence score with two of their own. Glenn Campbell hauled in a 30-yard pass from former Chicago Cardinals quarterback Mack Flenniken to start the scoring and Dutch Kitzmiller was good with the point-after. Following Rose's touchdown, Flenniken completed multiple passes, and a big 15-yard roughness penalty against DeGata set the Giants up at the one-yard line. Flenniken dived into the end zone for the touchdown, and the extra point gave New York a 14–6 halftime lead. Neither team threatened in the second half, and though the Roller played evenly with the favored Giants, they came away with an opening-day loss. Newcomers Schein and Irvin, along with hold-

Providence Steam Roller vs. Weymouth program from the Roller's 66–0 victory on September 20, 1931 (courtesy Rhode Island Historical Society—RHi X17 4837).

overs Spellman, Graham, Gentry and Ray Smith, were outstanding in containing the New York rushing attack. DeGata was released after the game—his only NFL appearance.

Frankford came to Providence on October 4. The two teams battled valiantly, but mistakes cost each a chance at scoring as the game ended in a 0–0 tie. The Yellow Jackets had the best chance of the day in the first quarter when they drove to the Providence seven-yard line. Art Pharmer was flattened for a seven-yard loss by Spellman. Then Pharmer was hit and fumbled, with Ray Smith recovering for Providence to end the threat. The Steam Roller had chances to score in each of the final three quarters, but a penalty cost them on the second-quarter opportunity and passes went awry on its other two scoring chances. It was a very evenly played game, with Providence gaining 193 yards and Frankford 191. The Jackets had 13 first downs and the Roller finished with 12. Woodruff, with the nickname "Cowboy," was praised for his performance in the game by Hess, Jr., of the *Providence Journal*. "Cowboy Woodruff, Roller fullback, was the standout for the Providence warriors, Woodruff hit the Jackets' line hard and did some excellent work defensively."[24]

During the week leading up to the rematch with the Yellow Jackets in Frankford, the Steam Roller signed former University of Texas star running back Dexter Shelley. He was All-Conference for Texas in 1928 and 1930 while leading the Longhorns to the Southwest Conference title in both years. Shelley had been surprisingly released by the Portsmouth Spartans. It was speculated that he was let go because of his good-sized contract. The Steam Roller hoped that he could add some life to the offense.

The two teams were back at it on October 10 at the Baker Bowl in Frankford. Only 3,000 fans, the lowest attendance in the history of the rivalry, came to see the game. Part of the problem was the contest was competing with Game 7 of the World Series with the Philadelphia Athletics playing the St. Louis Cardinals. To the chagrin of Philadelphia fans, the Cardinals won 4–2 to capture the championship.

The Providence-versus Frankford game was almost a repeat of the previous week's contest. The two teams battled well into the fourth quarter in another scoreless duel. The Yellow Jackets had the upper hand with scoring opportunities, twice losing fumbles inside the Providence 20-yard line, and Mort Kaer missed a 16-yard field goal attempt late in the game.

The Steam Roller offense struggled throughout the day until it came to life with no time to spare. With the clock running out, Oden began throwing passes. He found Pape open in the Frankford secondary and the fleet running back carried the ball to the Yellow Jackets' 18-yard line for a 37-yard completion. On the next play, Oden tossed a pass to Rose on the goal line. The husky end leaped in the air to pull the ball down and crossed the goal line just when he was hit by multiple Frankford tacklers. Even though Oden missed the extra point, the clock ran out. Providence had pulled out a thrilling 6–0 victory. The two teams played nearly 120 minutes of scoreless football until Oden's heroics. "There have been spectacular finishes to football games, but it is doubtful that there will be any more sensational than the one here today," Hess, Jr., wrote.[25]

The next day, the Steam Roller was back at it with a nonleague matchup against the Bridgeport All Stars from Bridgeport, Connecticut. Recently signed Dexter Shelley made his Providence debut and he was terrific in the Steam Roller's 67–7 rout. Shelley completed 10 of 12 passes for 171 yards and three touchdowns. He also scored two touchdowns, kicked two extra points, rushed for 27 yards on six carries and caught a pass for another 17 yards. Williams contributed three touchdowns, two on passes from Shelley and the other on a 29-yard run. Pape had the longest run of the day with a 47-yard touchdown gallop. Spellman, who had always wanted to get a chance in the backfield, carried the ball in the final two minutes of the game to the delight of the crowd. Several Steam Roller players sat out the game nursing injuries, including Oden, Woodruff, Gentry and Irvin.

October 18 was "Ed Robinson" Day at the Cycledrome in honor of his many years coaching Brown and Boston University. Robinson was presented with a wristwatch by his former Brown player Curly Oden, with 6,000 fans cheering. Providence hosted the new Cleveland Indians, who came into the game with a 1–3 record and were said to have the heaviest line in the NFL with an average weight of more than 235 pounds. The Indians also featured Dave Mishel, a former Steam Roller and a star quarterback at Brown, and another former Brown star, fullback Al Cornsweet.

The Indians surprised Providence on the first drive of the game following Mishel's 45-yard return of the opening kickoff. Mishel completed two screen passes that netted 45 yards for the visitors. Algy Clark caught another short pass from Mishel and ran the final two yards for the touchdown. Mishel's placement was good and Cleveland was quickly ahead 7–0.

The game remained 7–0 into the fourth quarter, with Providence missing two scoring opportunities that ended with a Pape fumble and an Oden intercepted pass. Cleveland struck again early in the fourth quarter when Otto Vokaty scored from three yards out to take a 13–0 lead. Shelley began passing with great success—23 yards to Spellman, 13 to Oden, 15 to Pape—and a penalty moved the ball to the Indians' one-yard line. Woodruff on his second attempt bulled over for the score, although the extra point failed.

With time running out, Shelley moved the Roller again through the air. Two more completed passes covered 34 yards and put the ball at the Cleveland 15-yard line. Shelley then lofted a pass to Oden in the end zone, but the ball sailed just over his fingertips. Under the rules of the day, this was a touchback and Cleveland gained possession. Two plays later the game was over.

However, there was some postgame controversy. Providence claimed that the referee mistimed the second half and that it was much shorter than the first half. The Steam Roller argued that more time should be left to play. The referee, Larry Spellman from Reading, Massachusetts, ruled the game over. In looking at the statistics, it appears the Roller's complaint was legitimate. In the first half, the two teams ran 83 plays, while in the second half only 51 plays were run despite having more pass attempts in the latter half. At the time, a typical 15-minute quarter would feature about 40 plays.

The Steam Roller's players were frustrated. They outplayed Cleveland yet lost what they believed was a shortened game that they could have won. Providence outgained the Indians 310 to 137 and had 13 first downs to Cleveland's eight.

Shelley was compared in the media to former Steam Roller superstar Wildcat Wilson because of his similar versatility and success in both passing and running that he had displayed through his first few games with Providence.

The Steam Roller traveled to Green Bay on October 25 to take on the undefeated Packers (6–0). The Lambeau-led team had outscored its opponents 133–20.

Green Bay played like the two-time defending NFL champions. Before Providence could catch its breath, the Steam Roller trailed 21–0. Providence fumbled on the first play of the game at its 25-yard line. A few plays later, Wuert Englemann, a second-year man from South Dakota State, caught a touchdown pass from Red Dunn. Green Bay stymied the Roller offense and Englemann hauled in a 32-yard scoring pass from Dunn. On the ensuing kickoff, Englemann raced 85 yards with the football for another touchdown and the Packers were in command. The return was described by the *Providence Journal* as "one of the most remarkable exploits since the Green Bay team became a real factor in big time football."[26] In less than six minutes, the Packers had scored three touchdowns.

Despite trailing by such a large margin so quickly, the Steam Roller battled back. Oden led a 65-yard touchdown drive in eight plays that was capped off by Pape's one-yard run to get Providence on the board. Pape had been cut by the Packers at the end of the 1930 season, so he was looking for some revenge. Green Bay answered that score before the half with one of its own. Dilweg caught a touchdown throw from Roger Grove and the Packers went to the half with a 28–7 lead.

Providence came out with vengeance in the second half. Shelley led the Roller to a pair of third-quarter touchdowns. Pape and Shelley hooked up on two scoring passes, 10 yards and then six yards, and the deficit was cut to 28–20. Then a poor officiating call cost the Steam Roller a touchdown and the game. Packer ball carrier Mule Wilson was running down the sideline when it appeared that he was shoved out of bounds by a Providence defender. However, Wilson kept running and when he crossed the goal line the officials ruled a touchdown. The Roller sideline was in an uproar, but to no avail. The score stood and the momentum of the game swung in the Packers' favor. Green Bay added two more scores as it pulled away for a 48–20 victory. Pape had an outstanding game for Providence with three touchdowns as he showed the Packers that maybe they had made a mistake by letting him go. But the poor play of the defense and the big plays were costly for the Roller.

On the train trip back to Providence from Wisconsin, the Steam Roller stopped in Buffalo for an exhibition game with the Buffalo Bears. Frank J. Offermann, president and owner of the independent team, had announced the game the previous week. This was the second exhibition game against an NFL opponent to be played in Bison Stadium in Buffalo since the Bisons folded in 1929. Buffalo had lost an 8–7 tussle earlier in the season to Cleveland. By the way, Bison Stadium later was named after Offermann, who owned a minor league baseball team in Buffalo from 1928 to 1935.

Providence arrived just in time for kickoff after traveling 800 miles by rail from Green Bay. It showed in the first half, as the Steam Roller failed to score and went to the half in a 0–0 tie. Pape fielded the second-half kickoff at his five-yard line and darted and dashed his way 95 yards untouched for a touchdown. "Coaches and officials at the game declared it was the fastest piece of open field running ever witnessed here," reported the *Buffalo Evening News*.[27]

Providence compiled 13 first downs and more than 300 yards of offense to the Bears' two first downs. Jack Dubienny, a former Canisius back, helped keep Buffalo in the game with his terrific punting. The Steam Roller had three other chances to score, penetrating the Buffalo five-yard line each time, but errant passes in the end zone resulted in touchbacks that ended each drive. Providence was happy to leave Buffalo with the 6–0 victory.

The traveling warriors from Providence headed to Staten Island, New York, to meet the Stapletons at Thompson Stadium on November 1. Staten Island struck first. Fullback Ken Strong, a former New York University All-American, broke through the Steam Roller line and raced 45 yards for a first-quarter touchdown. He added an extra point for a 7–0 lead. Providence drove to the Stapletons' one-yard line in the second quarter, courtesy of passes from Shelley to Titmas and then to Pape that covered 50 yards. But on fourth down, Pape slipped and was tackled short of the goal line. Later in the quarter, Providence had another chance to score, thanks to a 55-yard return by Pape of Strong's punt. But Shelley's passes were knocked down by the ever-present Strong and the Steam Roller was denied.

Providence had another chance in the third quarter as they again drove to the Stapletons' one-yard line, but Shelley's pass into the end zone was incomplete and Staten Island took over at the 20-yard line. All seemed lost until a fourth-quarter booming punt by Strong to Oden at the Providence 30-yard line. The swift Swede caught the ball on a dead run and raced by three would-be tacklers as he accelerated to the 50-yard line. Spellman took out another potential tackler with a savage block. Oden sped to the end zone, breaking free of Strong's grasp as he scored. Meeker made the all-important extra point. The game ended in a 7–7 tie.

The Steam Roller returned home to host the Brooklyn Dodgers on November 8. The 33–12 loss that Brooklyn had administered on Providence at the end of the 1930 season still stung for some of the players. This game was different. Brooklyn threatened to score on its first drive of the game, but the Providence defense held the Dodgers on downs at the three-yard line. It was Brooklyn's only offensive threat of the game. The Steam Roller defense held the Dodgers to only 67 yards rushing. The Providence offense came to life and was in a position to score seven different times as the team amassed 16 first downs and 287 yards of offense. The Roller scored only once, but it was enough to gain the victory.

The score came in the second quarter on a beautifully executed pass play from the two Texans on the team, Shelley to Rose. They teamed for a 35-yard catch-and-run touchdown. Rose caught a 16-yard pass from Shelley and then stiff-armed his way another 19 yards for the score. Shelley made the placement and Providence went on to a 7–0 victory.

A week later, Providence hosted Staten Island in a rematch and this time the Steam Roller came out on top 6–0, but only 2,000 fans braved the cold and damp weather. Defense dominated the game as the two teams combined to punt 25 times. Providence finally broke through in the fourth quarter on a one-yard plunge by Woodruff. The touchdown was set up by a 50-yard pass from Shelley to Edwards to the Stapletons' 11-yard line. Four running plays by Shelley and Edwards earned a first down at the one, where Woodruff carried it over for the game's only score.

The Indians made their second visit to the Cycledrome on November 21, with Providence seeking revenge for its controversial defeat by Cleveland in October. Neither of the former Brown stars, Dave Mishel or Al Cornsweet, played for Cleveland in this game, as they had left the team since the first matchup of the squads. Hoge Workman, a former All-American quarterback at Ohio State and former Major League Baseball player with the Boston Red Sox, was the Indians' quarterback. Workman led Cleveland on a first-quarter scoring drive following a Pape fumble at the Providence 24-yard line. Otto Vokaty finished the march with a one-yard run for the score. Oden's 28-yard punt return in the second quarter to the Indians' 42-yard line paved the way for a Providence score. Shelley completed two passes to Pape of 14 and 21 yards, with the second one putting the ball on the Cleveland one. Woodruff ran for the score, but Meeker's point-after was no good and the Indians went to halftime with a 7–6 lead.

Late in the third quarter, Gentry recovered a Cleveland fumble at the Indians' 46-yard line. A 10-yard pass from Shelley to Rose, a five-yard run by Shelley and then a 15-yard penalty against the Indians put the ball at the Cleveland 16-yard line. Two plays later, Providence perfectly executed a delayed triple pass with Shelley to Rose to Titmas gaining the final 16 yards and a touchdown. Woodruff caught a pass for the extra point and Providence led 13–7.

With time running down, Cleveland made one final thrust to win. Workman passed 15 yards to Red Joseph to the Steam Roller 45-yard line. Workman then completed a 44-yard pass thanks to a terrific catch by Chuck Weimer, who carried the ball to the one-yard line, where Spellman brought him down. Workman called a timeout, but Cleveland had none remaining and was penalized five yards. Workman, from the six-yard line, threw two incomplete passes and then a running play was stopped as the clock expired. Providence, with the 13–7 triumph, had notched its third consecutive NFL victory to raise its league record to 4–3–2. It would be the Steam Roller's last NFL victory in franchise history.

The following day, in one of the most unusual events in football history, the Steam Roller hosted four different semipro teams on the same day at the Cycledrome. Each team competed against the Roller for a 15-minute mini-game. There were 2,000 fans in attendance and almost all of them had to be friends and family of the semipro players to watch them play against the pros. The four teams—the Watchemoket All Stars, the Speedways of Cranston, the Natick Sacred Hearts and the East Providence Townies—were among the best semipro teams in the area.

Even with no rest, the Steam Roller showed the difference between semipro football and the NFL. Providence outscored its four opponents by a total of 78–0. Natick was the most competitive as it lost only by 7–0 on a late touchdown. The Watchemokets were beaten 27–0 in the opening quarter and the Speedways were routed 32–0 in the second period. The final quarter saw the Steam Roller defeat the Townies 12–0. None of the four teams was able to net a first down or complete a pass and in total gained 13 offensive yards.

Sky August led the pros with four touchdowns, with Meeker and Pop Williams adding two each. Four other Providence players—Edwards, Pape, Pope and Rose—scored touchdowns. Meeker had the highlight play of the day with a 75-yard punt return touchdown against Speedway. The game format certainly was unique and has not been tried again by any team in NFL history.

In the final home game of the season, and the last home game in team history, Providence hosted the Packers on Thanksgiving Day, November 26. Just like the first game, Green Bay started fast but this time it never looked back. The Packers scored twice in the first quarter and three more times in the second behind a dazzling passing display. Four of the Green Bay touchdowns were scored through the air, with Blood hauling in three and Dilweg the fourth. The quarterback combination of Paul Fitzgibbon and Bo Molenda amassed 209 passing yards for the game. After the first half onslaught, the Packers returned to their reliable running game that produced one more score in the fourth quarter. Providence's only touchdown of the game came on a second-quarter two-yard run by Woodruff in the 38–7 defeat. A disappointing holiday crowd of 5,000 watched the Packers' onslaught.

Three days later, a battered Providence squad traveled to New York to play the Giants at the Polo Grounds. With 18,000 on hand, in cold and shivering conditions, the two teams played to a scoreless tie. The Steam Roller held nemesis Friedman in check as the defense led by Ray Smith played one of its best games of the season. Only twice did the Giants have serious scoring threats. The first was halted by a missed 25-yard kick by Dutch Kitzmiller, and a fourth-quarter chance was thwarted on downs by the aggressive Providence defense. The Roller made two advances into scoring territory but each time was denied, once on downs and the other on an interception at the New York five-yard line. The Giants had 17 first downs to the Steam Roller's five.

It was the last time Friedman played against Providence. He played eight games against the Roller with a 6–1–1 record with five of those games in Providence. "When we went up to play the Providence Steamrollers—they used to pay off the newspaper people at that time for the publicity they gave them by using them as officials in the games—you can imagine the kind of officiating we had," the star quarterback said years later.[28] Friedman went into the Pro Football Hall of Fame in 2005.

The Steam Roller's NFL schedule was complete but the team had two nonleague games still to play. On December 5, Providence traveled to Worcester, Massachusetts, for a game against the Waterbury Bearcats at

Fitton Field on the campus of Holy Cross College. The game was played to benefit the unemployed as the Steam Roller annihilated the Bearcats 64–0. Providence scored 10 touchdowns and bolted to a 51–0 halftime lead in front of 3,000. August led the brigade with three scores and Williams added two, while five others scored one. "Most of the spectators forgot the chilling blasts as they watched the greatest pro machine ever seen in action in this college arena," reported the *Providence Journal*.[29]

Providence traveled to Memphis, Tennessee, for its final game of the season against the undefeated Memphis Tigers at Hodges Field on December 13. On a drizzly, damp day that made the field a mud pit, Providence scored twice in the first quarter and then held off a fourth-quarter Tigers rally to win 12–6. The Steam Roller's touchdowns came on passes from Shelley to Meeker and Shelley to Rose. Memphis scored on a three-yard run by Bucky Moore, a former three-time All–Southern Conference star at Loyola–New Orleans. Late in the game, the Tigers drove deep into Providence territory but a fumble at the three-yard line was recovered by the Steam Roller to preserve the victory. It was the last game in Providence Steam Roller history, so Rose has the honor of scoring the team's last touchdown.

Providence finished with a 4-4-3 NFL record, good for sixth place in the 10-team league. Green Bay won its third straight NFL championship with a 12-2 record, with Portsmouth finishing second at 11-3. Two Providence players were selected as All-Pros. Al Graham was chosen to the second team and Al Rose to the third team. Woodruff led the Steam Roller in scoring with 25 points while Pape and Rose had 18 points each. Two of Rose's three touchdowns were game winners.

The Steam Roller defense had a very good season except against Green Bay. The unit gave up 86 points in the two Packer games, but for the other nine games the defense allowed a total of 41 with five shutouts.

Attendance fell off precipitously because of the continuing effects of the Great Depression. The average fell to less than 5,000 per NFL game, down from a high of more than 9,000 only three years earlier. Coppen and the other two owners faced a monumental decision whether to continue to compete in the NFL or not. There were no signs at the beginning of 1932 that economic conditions were going to improve. In fact, 1932 saw the unemployment rate rise to 23.6 percent nationally, and Rhode Island was especially hard hit with unemployment at 32 percent.

With that as the backdrop and with dwindling attendance, the Steam Roller ownership decided to opt out of playing in the NFL in 1932. They officially withdrew from the league at that summer's NFL owners meeting, but for only one year. The franchise was given a year's reprieve to either rejoin the NFL in 1933 or find a buyer for the franchise. There were only eight teams in the NFL in 1932. Cleveland and Frankford also dropped out. Boston reentered the league as the Braves. The league split its teams into East and West Conferences for the first time, with four teams in each.

The ownership was hopeful that the economy would improve and that it could rejoin the league or find an interested buyer. Dooley remained on the league's executive committee, which meant that Providence had every intention of returning to the NFL a year later.

Epilogue: The End and the Steam Roller Legacy

After withdrawing from the NFL for the 1932 season, Pearce Johnson convinced the Steam Roller's owners to field a much less expensive independent pro football team with the idea that Providence would reenter the NFL in 1933. The schedule included multiple games with Pere Marquette along with the Connecticut Yankees, the Boston Fittons and the New London Boys Club, all solid independent outfits. Providence also scheduled two NFL squads, the Boston Braves and Chicago Cardinals, at the Cycledrome.

Most of the players from the 1931 Providence team had either retired or moved on to other NFL rosters. However, a few continued playing for the independent Steam Roller, including Jack Spellman, Ray Smith, Joe Schein, Pop Williams and Lew Pope.

The Steam Roller opened its season on September 25 against the Boston Braves at the Cycledrome. The Braves, coached by Lud Wray, had joined the NFL in 1932 and replaced Providence as the New England team in the circuit. This was the Braves' final preseason tune-up before the team played its first official NFL game on October 2. The Steam Roller stunned the new NFL entry with a 9–6 upset victory.

Boston scored first when Kermit Schmidt blocked Pope's first-quarter punt that gave the Braves the ball on the Providence 10-yard line. On the next play, Reggie Rust scooted through a hole on the left side of the Steam Roller line and scored. The point-after failed. Boston held the 6–0 lead until the third quarter. Rust attempted a pass to Ernie Pinckert that Tommy Dowler, an ex–Colgate star, intercepted and raced 50 yards for a touchdown. The extra point was good and the Steam Roller led 7–6. Providence added to its lead in the fourth quarter when Pinckert was tackled for a safety by "Dixie" Mathews. The Braves had a final 60-yard drive that took Boston to the Steam Roller 20-yard line. But Providence's defense stiffened and held on downs for the surprising victory. Boston went on to finish its first NFL season with a 4-4-2 record. The Braves were renamed the Redskins in 1933 and in 1937 moved to Washington.

The Steam Roller defeated the Connecticut Yankees 28-0 and lost to Pere Marquette 14-0 prior to hosting the NFL's Chicago Cardinals on October 23. Providence stayed right with the big-league team but a costly turnover proved to be the difference in the game. The Cardinals' Milan Creighton intercepted a Steam Roller lateral pass and ran 48 yards for a first-quarter touchdown. Despite Providence penetrating the Chicago 20-yard line on eight separate occasions, the Cardinals held on for a 7-0 victory. It was the last game featuring an NFL opponent to be played at the Cycledrome.

The Steam Roller won four of its last five games, highlighted by a 3-0 win over Pere Marquette and a 52-0 rout of the Philadelphia Yellow Jackets. Providence finished its independent season with an overall 6-3 record, with seven of the nine games played at the Cycledrome.

The American economy continued to struggle, with national unemployment reaching an all-time high of 24.75 percent. Coppen and the rest of the Providence ownership group were not inclined to continue to fund the franchise. They searched for a buyer but when nobody came forward with an interest to purchase the team prior to the 1933 NFL season, the franchise was given back to the league. NFL football in Providence was no longer.

The Steam Roller did not even field an independent team in 1933. A reincarnation of the team as an independent pro outfit named the Providence Huskies, owned by North Attleboro sportsman Sam Rushton, played one season in 1933, but football in Providence with connections to the NFL was gone forever.

The Steam Roller finished with an overall NFL record of 41-32-11, a .554 winning percentage, with one NFL championship in its seven-year run. Including nonleague games, the franchise's overall record was 64-32-11, a .650 winning percentage. Providence's overall record at the "Drome" was 51-18-6, a .720 winning percentage, and the team was 33-18-6 in NFL games at the bicycle track. Many nights the fans went home happy from this one-of-a-kind NFL stadium.

The Cycledrome continued to host cycling and football until it was condemned on November 8, 1934. Laudati tried to sell the venue, but when no deal came forward he had another idea. The stadium was razed, with the depression having taken its toll. It was replaced in 1937 by the E.M. Lowe's Theatre, only the third drive-in movie theater in America. It was very popular and remained in business for 40 years, until 1977, when it was replaced by a shopping center that still inhabits the site.

The Steam Roller left a lasting legacy with several NFL firsts and records including:

Epilogue: The End and the Steam Roller Legacy

- The first NFL team in New England.
- The first NFL team with a singular nickname—Steam Roller.
- Providence was the first and one of only two NFL teams to ever play its home games in a bicycle track arena—the Cycledrome.
- The Steam Roller played the first NFL game in Boston on December 9, 1925, in a 9–6 win over Red Grange and the Chicago Bears. The game was played at Braves Field, home of baseball's National League Boston Braves.
- Providence was the first team to defeat Grange and the Bears on the famous 1925 Tour in that December 9 game.
- The Steam Roller played the New York Yankees on December 3, 1927, in the first NFL game ever played at Archbold Stadium in Syracuse, New York. Providence won 9–0.
- The Frankford Yellow Jackets filed the first protest against game officials in NFL history on November 21, 1928, in a game played against the Steam Roller on November 17. The protest was denied by the league.
- The Steam Roller tied the Green Bay Packers 7–7 on December 2, 1928, and claimed the NFL championship with an 8–1–2 record. Providence was the first New England team to win an NFL championship.
- On November 6, 1929, the Steam Roller hosted the first night game in NFL history at Kinsley Park in a 16–0 loss to the Chicago Cardinals.
- Between November 5 and November 10, 1929, the Steam Roller played four NFL games in those six days. It is the only NFL team to ever play four league games in the span of six days.
- In 1930, Providence became the first team to install permanent floodlighting equipment for night games and hosted four that season at the Cycledrome.
- Providence is the only team to play four opponents on the same day in a single 60-minute game with each quarter broken into separate games. The Steam Roller defeated all four teams by a combined 78–0 score.
- The Steam Roller was the first team to hire a big-time college coach (Ed Robinson) to coach in the NFL.
- The Providence Steam Roller is the last defunct team—that is to say, the franchise no longer exists—to win the NFL championship.
- The Roller was the only New England team to win the NFL championship until Tom Brady led the New England Patriots to the Super Bowl title on February 3, 2002.

Jimmy Conzelman was named to the NFL All-Decade team of the 1920s, the only Steam Roller so honored.

Pro Football Illustrated in 1947 named an All-Time All-NFL Team that encompassed the first 25 years of the league. Five Steam Roller players were selected to the 51-man team—Duke Hanny, end; Curly Oden, halfback; Clyde Smith, center; Gus Sonnenberg, tackle; and Wildcat Wilson, quarterback. All five played on the 1928 NFL championship team.

Many times over the years Johnson had been asked who the greatest players in Steam Roller history were. In an interview with the *Providence Journal* in 1962, he said: "At the top of the list comes Olaf 'Curly' Oden. He was the most colorful backfield performer in breakaway field reverses, punt returns and end arounds. To my mind George 'Wildcat' Wilson was outstanding on both offense and defense. From a wealth of good linemen, my vote goes to John Spellman and Gus Sonnenberg. All of those players were on the 1928 World Champion team."[1] His complete all-time Steam Roller team is in the appendix.

The Gridiron Club of Providence staged a 50th-anniversary salute on October 11, 1978, at Caruso's Restaurant to honor the 1928 NFL championship team. At the celebration were the remaining living players—Jack Cronin, Arthur "Pop" Williams, Abe Wilson, Clyde Smith and Jack Fleischmann—along with Assistant General Manager Pearce Johnson. Cronin and Williams each addressed the attendees and shared many stories from their playing days with the Steam Roller, including mentioning many of their teammates.

A few of the more prominent Steam Roller players had distinguished careers after their NFL playing days were over. Only Conzelman had an extended career in pro football. He returned to the NFL in 1940 to coach the Chicago Cardinals and led the franchise to the NFL championship in 1947. Conzelman was enshrined in the Pro Football Hall of Fame in 1964. Jack Cronin coached the LaSalle Academy football team for 45 years, from 1927 to 1972, and compiled a 274–120–19 record. Oden was a Rhode Island state investigator for many years and Pinky Lester was the East Providence police chief for 11 years. Orland Smith became a renowned Providence physician, and Dolph Eckstein was a prominent Providence surgeon. Warren McGuirk was the athletic director at the University of Massachusetts for almost 25 years, and the school's football stadium is named in his honor.

Though Fritz Pollard and Tony Latone each played a limited time in Providence, their NFL careers were outstanding. Pollard is enshrined in the Pro Football Hall of Fame and Latone was selected to the Hall of Very Good. Several Steam Roller players pursued professional wrestling careers, including Archie Golembeski, Lou Jennings, Al Pierotti, Bert

Shurtleff, Sonnenberg, Spellman and Wildcat Wilson. Sonnenberg won several championships and was enshrined in the Professional Wrestling Hall of Fame and Museum. Johnson claimed in his NFL Films interview that 16 opponent players who played in the Cycledrome against the Steam Roller are now in the Pro Football Hall of Fame, including Ernie Nevers, Guy Chamberlin and Red Grange.

Several Steam Roller players who played at Brown are in the school's Athletic Hall of Fame, including Eckstein, Bud Edwards, Mike Gulian, Jack Keefer, Dave Mishel, Oden, Pollard, Shurtleff, Orland Smith and Spellman. And three were named to the Bears' 125th anniversary team in 2003—Keefer, Pollard and Smith.

An 18-inch-by-24-inch plaque was unveiled on November 28, 1982, at the Providence Civic Center to honor the 1928 championship team. It was part of Providence's 150th anniversary celebration. Former player Jack Cronin was on hand for the festivities. Mayor Vincent A. Cianci, Jr., said the Steam Roller had "real football players who did everything because of their love of the game of football."[2] And the mayor issued a proclamation declaring it "Providence Steam Roller Day" in the city.

Cronin was the oldest living player and Pearce Johnson the only living management person when a plaque commemorating the 1928 championship at Super Shaw's market (where the Cycledrome once stood) in 1990 was unveiled; however, it no longer is at the site. Cronin died on January 18, 1993—less than four months shy of his 90th birthday. Pearce outlived everyone associated with that 1928 championship team. He died on July 20, 1996, less than three months shy of his 98th birthday. He had continued to live in the same house in North Providence that he had inhabited when the Steam Roller won the championship.

The NFL played a few exhibition games in Providence in the late 1930s and one in 1941. The Boston Redskins defeated an independent Steam Roller–named team in 1936 by a score of 26–0. In 1938 and 1939, the Chicago Bears and New York Giants each came to Providence to play charity games against a college all-star team to benefit Shrine Crippled Children's Hospital. With 20,000 in attendance at Brown University Field on September 1, 1938, the Bears won 26–14. Future Supreme Court Justice Byron "Whizzer" White played for the collegians and scored a touchdown. The following year, the Giants won 31–0 with 10,000 on hand at Cranston Stadium. The Philadelphia Eagles routed another independent pro Steam Roller outfit to benefit the Shrine Hospital, 61–6, in 1941 with a disappointing crowd of only 3,500.

The Boston Patriots, a founding franchise in the American Football League (AFL), brought three preseason exhibition games to Providence, in 1960, '61 and '62. The first two games were played at Mount Pleasant

High School, with the Patriots defeating Denver 43–6 and the Buffalo Bills 28–10, respectively. In 1962, the game was played at Brown University Field and the Oakland Raiders squeaked out a 21–20 victory.

On September 4, 1965, NFL football returned to Providence for the first time since 1941. The Pittsburgh Steelers held their training camp at the University of Rhode Island from 1964 to 1966 and decided to play a preseason game in the state. The Steelers hosted the San Francisco 49ers at Brown University Stadium. The game was broadcast coast to coast by CBS, and with 12,020 fans on hand, the 49ers defeated Pittsburgh 23–9. The game was sponsored by the Rhode Island Heart Association and with the national coverage, it was a great advertisement for Rhode Island. It is the last NFL game that has been played in Providence.

No fewer than six teams have used the Steam Roller nickname through the years, though it has had the "s" added to the end in most cases. That kept the legacy of the NFL team in the memory of Rhode Islanders. Johnson did his best to keep a team playing independent pro football from 1934 through 1948, participating in various leagues including the New England Circuit, the Professional Football Association and the New England Pro Football Conference, until it folded for good. The Steam Roller won New England Pro Football Conference championships in 1947 and 1948. Other teams came along, and the most prominent actually played a completely different sport.

Providence had an original franchise in the Basketball Association of America (BAA) named the Steam Rollers for three seasons from 1946 to 1949 with limited success. The BAA merged with the National Basketball League (NBL) in 1949 to form today's NBA. The team is noted for having one of the worst seasons in pro basketball history with a 6–42 record and .125 winning percentage in 1947–48. The most noteworthy player was local Pawtucket product Ernie Calverley, who was named All-BAA in 1946–47 and holds almost all the of the Steam Rollers' scoring records. This franchise was the only other major professional sports team in Rhode Island history.

The most notable of the various independent and minor league football teams with the Steam Roller(s) nickname was the 1962–1964 Atlantic Coast Football League (ACFL) team. Providence joined the new ACFL and by finishing the regular season in second place with an 8–1–1 record played the Paterson Miners on December 16, 1962, for the inaugural league championship. The game was played indoors at Atlantic City's Convention Hall. The two teams were tied 14–14 late in the fourth quarter and the Steam Rollers had a chance to capture the championship. However, Bob Kessler missed the potential game-winning field goal from the 27-yard line. Paterson kicker Neal Buckman, 11 minutes into the second overtime, kicked a 33-yard field goal to end the longest game in pro football history at that time and deliver the championship to Paterson, 17–14. The Steam Rollers played for two more seasons before running into financial problems and shutting down the franchise early in 1965. The team finished with a 22–12–2 record and two playoff appearances.

The last Providence-based team to utilize the moniker was the New England Steam Rollers of the Arena Football League. The team played one season at the Providence Civic Center in 1988 and finished with a 3–9 record.

With the New England Patriots playing since 1971 in Foxboro, Massachusetts—a location that is closer to Providence than Boston—the Patriots have become Providence's adopted NFL team. Therefore, the Capital City will never again have its own NFL franchise with the city name. Despite that, the unique and exciting history of the Steam Roller will live on in Providence lore for eternity.

And its lasting legacy just might be what Rhode Island attorney general Charles P. Sisson said at the 1928 championship banquet: "The type of football you play may act as a stimulus to college and younger team's football. I think the day is coming when pro football if it follows the example set by the Roller, will take its place with baseball as the great national professional sport."[3]

A Steam Roller Who's Who

August, Edward W. "Sky"

Position: OH-DH; Height: 5'10"; Weight: 180; High School: Mahanoy Area (Mahanoy City, PA); College: Villanova; Born: 8/5/1904, Mahanoy City, PA; Died: 10/15/1993, Mahanoy City, PA; 1931 Providence Steam Roller: 7 Games, 1 Started.

Sky played a single season with the Steam Roller in 1931, appearing in seven games. Prior to coming to Providence, he played semipro football for the Hazleton Mountaineers in the Twin-County Football League. Known for his jumping ability, August played tailback and wingback at Villanova before his single season in the NFL. Sky lettered in all four seasons he played for the Wildcats. He served in the US Army in the South Pacific during World War II.

He is enshrined in the North East Football Hall of Fame and the Jerry Wolman Sports Hall of Fame (for Pennsylvania). As a high schooler, August played on a state basketball championship team at Mahanoy City High School. Following his football career, he operated August Beverage in Mahanoy City.

Braney, Joseph Patrick "Speed"

Position: DG-OG-OT-DT; Height: 6'0"; Weight: 188; High School: Dean Academy (Franklin, MA); College: Syracuse, Fordham; Born: 6/29/1893, Ireland; Died: 12/01/1949, Providence, RI; 1925 Providence Steam Roller: 6 Games, 0 Started; 1926 Providence Steam Roller: 7 Games, 4 Started.

Originally named Joseph Breheney, he later changed the spelling to Braney. He played for the Steam Roller from 1919 through 1924, before it joined the NFL. Braney was captain of the team from 1920 to 1924 and was the coach of the 1924 squad that won the mythical undisputed championship of the Northeast. Braney was replaced as coach by Archie Golembeski prior to the start of the 1925 NFL season. Braney played two more seasons with the Steam Roller after it joined the NFL, appearing in a total of 13 games.

Braney played football and basketball at Dean Academy. He played one varsity season of college football at both Syracuse and Fordham, lettering for each team. He joined the Fordham Ambulance Unit in 1917 and sailed to France to join the war effort. Braney served 30 months and was awarded the Croix de Guere by the French Army for conspicuous bravery.

Braney also played professional basketball in 1921 for the Steam Roller Five, when the team captain was Lou Pieri (future owner of the Rhode Island Auditorium, and owner and general manager of the Providence Reds AHL hockey team and the Providence Steamrollers Basketball Association of America team that operated from 1946 to 1949). Braney also coached the baseball and football teams at LaSalle Academy, 1921–1926, and became the first basketball coach at the school in 1925.

Burke, Charles Francis "Chick"

Position: WB-DH; Height: 5'9"; Weight: 166; High School: Natick (Natick, MA); College: Dartmouth; Born: 9/30/1901, Natick, MA; Died: 5/20/1973, Keene, NH; 1925 Providence Steam Roller: 5 Games, 2 Started.

Chick played one season of pro football in 1925 for the Steam Roller, appearing in five games. He starred for Dartmouth, playing four seasons from 1919 to 1922. He was enshrined in the Dartmouth "Wearers of the Green" Athletics Hall of Fame in 2004. Chick played for the Steam Roller prior to its entry in the NFL. He played for Providence in 1923 and was part of the 1924 squad that won the mythical Northeast championship before the team joined the NFL.

Connor, Stafford Joseph "Dutch"

Position: FB-LB; Height: 6'0"; Weight: 190; High School: Exeter (Exeter, NH); College: New Hampshire; Born: 4/16/1895, Poland; Died: 11/24/1978, Alamo Heights, TX; 1925 Providence Steam Roller: 3 Games, 3 Started, 2 Extra Points Made, 2 Total Points.

Dutch played one season with the Providence Steam Roller and kicked two extra points, appearing in three games. He left the team partway through the 1925 season as his other business interests did not allow him to practice enough with the team. He then signed with All-Britain in

New Britain, Connecticut. Connor also had played for Providence prior to the team joining the NFL. He was on the team in 1923 and was part of the 1924 Northeast championship squad. Connor played one game for the Brooklyn Lions in 1926. He served as head football coach at Norwich University in 1931. Connor was also the head men's basketball coach at Brooklyn College for the 1935–36 season.

Connor played college football at New Hampshire College in Durham, New Hampshire, from 1918 through 1921. He was captain for the 1921 season. He was enshrined in the inaugural class of the New Hampshire University Hall of Fame in 1982. Connor served in the United States Navy during World War II. He was a teacher and coach at Spaulding High School, Rochester, New Hampshire; Athol High School, Athol, Massachusetts; and Odessa High School, Odessa, Texas.

Non-Providence Stats

1926—Brooklyn Lions: 1 Game, 0 Started.

Conzelman, James Good "Jimmy"

Position: BB-TB-HB-E-WB-DH-LB-S-DE-OE-QB-FB; Height: 6'0"; Weight: 175; High School: McKinley (St. Louis, MO); College: Washington University (St. Louis, MO); Born: 3/06/1898, St. Louis, MO; Died: 7/31/1970, St. Louis, MO; 1927 Providence Steam Roller: 14 Games, 6 Started, 4 Touchdowns, 24 Total Points, and Head Coach, 8–5–1; 1928 Providence Steam Roller: 4 Games, 3 Started, 2 Touchdowns, 1 Extra Point, 13 Total Points, and Head Coach, 8–1–2; 1929 Providence Steam Roller: 9 Games, 2 Started, 1 Touchdown, 6 Total Points, and Head Coach 4–6–2; 1930 Providence Steam Roller: Head Coach, 6–4–1.

Conzelman played three seasons with the Steam Roller and coached a fourth, though two were impacted after he suffered a significant injury in 1928. He scored four touchdowns in 1927, tied for the team lead. Three of his scores were touchdown receptions from Wildcat Wilson and all came in Steam Roller victories. In 1928, Jimmy scored two touchdowns on pass receptions and converted one extra point before he was injured. Conzelman was a player-coach his first three seasons with Providence and was only the head coach in his final season. His overall head coaching record with Providence was 26–16–6 and his seven career touchdowns are fourth on the all-time Steam Roller touchdown list.

Conzelman was enshrined in the Pro Football Hall of Fame in 1964, and his Hall of Fame biography said about him, "While Jimmy Conzelman was a success at most of his endeavors, which included stints as a newspaper publisher, playwright, author, orator, and actor, it was primarily as a football player and coach that he excelled."[1]

Conzelman was a halfback at Washington University in St. Louis and he began his post-college football career as a member of the Great Lakes Navy team that won the 1919 Rose Bowl. One of his Great Lakes teammates was George Halas, who recruited him for his 1920 Decatur Staleys team in the newly formed American Professional Football Association, which later changed its name to the National Football League.

Jimmy played one season with the Staleys and then moved on to the Rock Island Independents, where Conzelman began his career as a player-coach. He stayed with the Independents through seven games of the 1922 season before jumping to the Milwaukee Badgers for the remainder of the season and the 1923 campaign. He was named a first-team All-Pro for the Badgers in 1923 by the *Canton Daily News*. Conzelman was offered a unique opportunity in 1925 to obtain and own an NFL franchise in Detroit for a reported $500 investment. He jumped at the chance and became an NFL owner. The newly christened Panthers had an excellent first season with an 8-2-2 record and Conzelman was named a second-team All-Pro by *Collyer* magazine. The second season did not go as well, with Detroit finishing 4-6-2, and the team never caught on with Motor City fans.

Conzelman returned the franchise to the league and in 1927 and joined the Steam Roller as player-coach. As a quarterback, he suffered a serious knee injury in 1928, but as coach he led the team to an 8-1-2 record and the NFL title. He was named team MVP following the season. Conzelman left Providence in 1930 wanting to try his hand at other careers. He went into the publishing business and also coached his alma mater, Washington University, for eight seasons with three Missouri Valley Conference championships to his credit. But in 1940, the popular Irishman was lured back into the NFL with the Chicago Cardinals. He helped the team stay strong during the challenging World War II years before leaving to work in Major League Baseball. In 1946, Conzelman returned to the Cardinals and the following season his Cards won the NFL title. In 1948, Chicago under his tutelage won a second straight division title.

He retired from football for good at the end of the 1948 season and returned to his hometown of St. Louis. He took a job as vice president with the D'Arcy Advertisement Agency.

Non-Providence Stats

1920—Decatur Staleys: 11 Games, 3 Started.
1921—Rock Island Independents: 7 Games, 6 Started, 2 Touchdowns, 1 Field Goal, 15 Total Points, and Head Coach, 4-1.

1922—Rock Island Independents: 7 Games, 6 Started, 7 Touchdowns, 2 Field Goals, 48 Total Points, and Head Coach, 4-2-1.
1922—Milwaukee Badgers: 3 Games, 3 Started, Head Coach, 0-3.
1923—Milwaukee Badgers: 12 Games, 12 Started, 4 Touchdowns, 2 Extra Points, 26 Total Points, and Head Coach, 7-2-3.
1924—Milwaukee Badgers: 13 Games, 13 Started, 1 Touchdown, 6 Total Points.
1925—Detroit Panthers: 12 Games, 9 Started, 3 Touchdowns, 18 Total Points, and Head Coach, 8-2-2.
1926—Detroit Panthers: 12 Games, 4 Started, 2 Touchdowns, 1 Extra Point, 13 Total Points, and Head Coach, 4-6-2.
1940—Chicago Cardinals: Head Coach, 2-7-2.
1941—Chicago Cardinals: Head Coach, 3-7-1.
1942—Chicago Cardinals: Head Coach, 3-8-0.
1946—Chicago Cardinals: Head Coach, 6-5-0.
1947—Chicago Cardinals: Head Coach, Regular Season, 9-3-0; Postseason, 1-0; NFL Champions.
1948—Chicago Cardinals: Head Coach, Regular Season, 11-1-0; Postseason, 0-1.

Cronin, John Patrick "Jack"

Position: QB-TB-HB-WB-FB-DE-OE-LB-DH-S; Height: 5'11"; Weight: 178; High School: Dean Academy (Franklin, MA); College: Boston College; Born: 5/03/1903, Hingham, MA; Died: 1/18/1993, Jupiter, FL; 1927 Providence Steam Roller: 12 Games, 3 Started, 1 Touchdown, 6 Total Points; 1928 Providence Steam Roller: 8 Games, 5 Started, 3 Touchdowns, 18 Total Points; 1929 Providence Steam Roller: 12 Games, 5 Started, 1 Touchdown, 6 Total Points; 1930 Providence Steam Roller: 10 Games, 3 Started.

Jack played four seasons with the Steam Roller. He is third all time in games played for Providence with 42. Cronin was part of the 1928 NFL championship team. During the 1928 season, he scored two touchdowns on November 25, leading the Steam Roller to a 16-0 win over the New York Giants, and the following week he scored the game's only touchdown in a key 7-0 win over the Pottsville Maroons that put Providence in a position to win the NFL championship the next week. He scored his first touchdown with Providence on a spectacular 55-yard punt return in a 9-0 win over the New York Yankees on December 3, 1927. Cronin forced a fumble at the Providence one-yard line to preserve a tie with the Green Bay Packers on December 2, 1928, that clinched the NFL championship for the Steam Roller.

Cronin played four years of college football at Boston College and was a true "triple threat" as he excelled in passing, running and punting. Jack averaged 60 yards per punt during his senior season, the best in the country. His brother Bill also played for the Steam Roller. While playing with the Steam Roller, Jack also coached and taught at LaSalle Academy and went on to stay at the school for 46 years, where he won 12 football, four baseball and two hockey championships. Cronin was enshrined in the Rhode Island Hall of Fame in 1973 and the Boston College Athletic Hall of Fame in 1980. He was the last surviving member of the Steam Roller.

Cronin, William Richard "Bill"

Position: TB-FB-HB-LB-DE-DH-S-WB-OE; Height: 5'10"; Weight: 182; High School: Hingham (Hingham, MA); College: Boston College; Born: 12/05/1901, Hingham, MA; Died: 3/16/1956, Hingham, MA; 1927 Providence Steam Roller: 9 Games, 3 Started, 1 Touchdown, 6 Total Points; 1928 Providence Steam Roller: 9 Games, 1 Started; 1929 Providence Steam Roller: 10 Games, 7 Started.

Bill played three seasons with the Steam Roller and was part of the 1928 NFL championship squad. He scored his only touchdown in a Providence uniform on November 13, 1927, when he squirted through the line for a five-yard score in a 13–7 win over the Duluth Eskimos. Prior to coming to Providence, he played one season with the Boston Bulldogs of the AFL (1926) and scored the team's only offensive touchdown during its 2–4 season. While playing with the Steam Roller, Bill also coached football at LaSalle Academy.

He played four years of college football at Boston College and was the captain of the baseball team in 1926. He also starred at Hingham High School. Cronin started the hockey program at the high school in the early 1940s and was president of the South Shore Hockey League. He was the hockey and baseball coach at Hingham and was enshrined in the Hingham High School Athletic Hall of Fame in 1999. His brother Jack also played for the Steam Roller.

Crowley, James Harold "Sleepy"

Position: TB-DH; Height: 5'9"; Weight: 165; High School: Green Bay East (Green Bay, WI); College: Notre Dame; Born: 9/10/1902, Chicago, IL; Died: 1/15/1986, Scranton, PA; 1925 Providence Steam Roller: 1 Game, 0 Started.

Crowley played one game for the Steam Roller as he was brought in to play against Red Grange and the Chicago Bears in 1925. Prior to coming to Providence, Crowley played two games for the Green Bay Packers. His lone NFL touchdown came on a three-yard pass reception from Charlie Mathys that ironically was the winning score in the Packers' 13–10 victory over the Steam Roller on December 6. Three days later, Crowley suited up for Providence against Grange. Crowley's game with the Steam Roller was his last NFL game.

He is best known as one of Notre Dame's famed "Four Horsemen." After his brief pro football career, Crowley turned to coaching. He served as the head football coach at Michigan State from 1929 to 1932, at Fordham University from 1933 to 1941 and at the North Carolina Pre-Flight School in 1942, compiling a career college football record of 86-23-11. While at Fordham, he coached the "Seven Blocks of Granite" that included Vince Lombardi. Crowley also coached the Chicago Rockets of the All-America Football Conference in 1947. He was the commissioner of the AAFC in 1946, the league's inaugural season.

Crowley was inducted into the College Football Hall of Fame as a player in 1966. He served for the US Navy in World War II. Following his unsuccessful coaching stint with the Rockets, he moved to Pennsylvania and worked as an insurance salesman and in television.

Non-Providence Stats

1925: Green Bay Packers: 2 Games, 0 Started, 1 Touchdown, 6 Total Points.
1947: Chicago Rockets (AAFC): Head Coach, 0–10–0.

DaGata, Frederick Albert "Fred"

Position: FB-LB; Height: 5'10"; Weight: 187; High School: Durfee (Fall River, MA); College: Boston College, Providence; Born: 4/4/1908, Fall River, MA; Died: 5/13/1980, Fall River, MA; 1931 Providence Steam Roller: 1 Game, 0 Started.

DaGata played only one game for the Steam Roller in 1931. He played his college football at Providence College and is one of only five Friars who have played football in the NFL. Following his football career, he had a lengthy academic career as a teacher and coach in Fall River, Massachusetts, at Durfee High School, at Morton Junior High and Ruggles School (14 years as principal). He also was an assistant and head football coach at Durfee for 30 years, assisting Luke Urban for many of those years.

Doane, Erling Eugene "Dinger"

Position: FB-LB-TB-DH; Height: 5'10"; Weight: 190; High School: Somerville (Somerville, MA); College: Tufts; Born: 10/14/1893, Natick, MA; Died: 6/5/1948, Fall River, MA; 1927 Providence Steam Roller: 5 Games, 2 Started.

Doane played for the Steam Roller for one season, 1927, appearing in five games. He signed with Providence after requesting his release by Pottsville. He had played in two games with the Maroons. Doane had played with Conzelman on the Detroit Panthers prior to the 1927 season for both years they played in the NFL and wanted to play with him in Providence. He contributed eight touchdowns for the Panthers during those two seasons. In addition to the Panthers, Doane also played in the NFL for the Cleveland Tigers, Milwaukee Badgers and the New York Brickley Giants.

Prior to joining the NFL, Doane was a standout at Tufts University. Doane was a player on the 1916 Tufts squad that was the first integrated football team in the school's history, as two Black players were starters for the Jumbos. The team finished with a 5–3 record. Doane previously played with the Steam Roller when it was an independent pro team in 1917 and 1918. He also played a game for the pre-NFL Frankford Yellow Jackets in 1921 against the Union Quakers of Philadelphia. Following his football career, he spent 25 years living in Detroit, Michigan.

Non-Providence Stats

1920—Cleveland Tigers: 4 Games, 3 Started.
1921—New York Brickley Giants: 1 Game, 1 Started.
1922—Milwaukee Badgers: 9 Games, 8 Started, 1 Touchdown, 6 Total Points.
1923—Milwaukee Badgers: 9 Games, 9 Started, 2 Touchdowns, 12 Total Points.
1924—Milwaukee Badgers: 11 Games, 11 Started, 4 Touchdowns, 24 Total Points.
1925—Detroit Panthers: 11 Games, 3 Started, 5 Touchdowns, 30 Total Points.
1926—Detroit Panthers: 12 Games, 2 Started, 3 Touchdowns, 18 Total Points.
1927—Pottsville Maroons: 2 Games, 0 Started.

Donahue, John J. "Jack"

Position: OG-DG-OT-DT; Height: 6'2"; Weight: 230; High School: Peabody (Peabody, MA); College: Boston College; Born: 12/30/1904, USA;

Died: 11/10/1984, Quincy, MA; 1926 Providence Steam Roller: 13 Games, 9 Started.

Donahue played 13 games during the 1926 season for the Steam Roller. He signed with the team on August 9. After leaving the Steam Roller, Donahue played semipro football for the University of Peabody and Pere Marquette.

Donahue played guard on the Peabody High School football team. He played guard and tackle for Boston College from 1922 to 1925 and was captain his senior year. In addition, Donahue was a member of the Boston College Eagles baseball team and a boxer.

In 1928, Donahue joined the faculty of East Bridgewater High School as head football coach and history teacher. In 1932, he became the first-ever football coach at North Quincy High School. He continued to coach the team until his resignation in 1960. Donahue compiled a 128–95–20 record with the school. He also served as NQHS golf coach and guided the team to a state championship in 1948. Donahue retired from teaching in 1971.

Douds, Forrest McCreery

Position: OT-DT; Height: 5'10"; Weight: 216; High School: Rochester (Rochester, PA) and Bellefonte Academy (Bellefonte, PA); College: Washington & Jefferson; Born: 4/21/1905, Rochester, PA; Died: 8/16/1979, Sewickley, PA; 1930 Providence Steam Roller: 9 Games, 7 Started.

Douds played part of the 1930 season with the Steam Roller, appearing in nine games. He also played in the NFL for the Portsmouth Spartans, Chicago Cardinals and the Pittsburgh Pirates. Douds was named to the 1930 NFL All-Pro first team by the *Green Bay Gazette*. In 1933, he became the first coach of the Pittsburgh Steelers, leading the team to a 3–6–2 record before he was replaced in the offseason.

Douds was an All-American football player at Washington and Jefferson College, where he was selected All-American three times and was the first player ever chosen to play in the East-West Shrine Game on two separate seasons.

He worked for 25 years for Alleghany Court as a court tipstaff, an officer of the court, and he also coached football, basketball and gymnastics at Mars High School. He was inducted into the Beaver County Sports Hall of Fame in 1976.

Non-Providence Stats

1930: Portsmouth Spartans: 3 Games, 3 Started.
1931: Portsmouth Spartans: 13 Games, 13 Started.

1932: Chicago Cardinals: 10 Games, 4 Started.
1933: Pittsburgh Pirates: 7 Games, 5 Started, Rushing: 1-2-0, and Head Coach, 3-6-2.
1934: Pittsburgh Pirates: 11 Games, 8 Started.

Eckstein, Adolph William "Dolph"

Position: C-MG; Height: 5'10"; Weight: 185; High School: Battin (Elizabeth, NJ); College: Brown; Born: 5/7/1902, Elizabeth, NJ; Died: 6/28/1963, Providence, RI; 1925 Providence Steam Roller: 12 Games, 12 Started; 1926 Providence Steam Roller: 13 Games, 12 Started.

Eckstein played two seasons for the Steam Roller as the starting center, appearing in 25 games. He was named second-team All-Pro by the *Green Bay Gazette* in 1925. Eckstein is generally regarded as the greatest center ever to play for Brown University. The four-year letter winner was considered one of the three best centers of his era. He was terrific at diagnosing plays, and his quick reactions enabled him to effectively block in both the run and pass game. He was a great tackler and was excellent on punt coverage as well.

Eckstein was a championship wrestler at Brown. He was the intercollegiate heavyweight champion twice. He also competed in the 1924 Olympic Trials and lost in the final. Eckstein was elected to the Brown University Athletic Hall of Fame in 1971. In 1927, George Trevor of the *New York Sun* said about him, "Eckstein was the

Dolph Eckstein, Providence Steam Roller All-Pro center (1925–1926) (John Hay Library, Special Collections, Brown University).

fighting Dutchman if you ever saw one. Smiling and good natured off the field, the freckle-faced kid was vigorous and unrelenting in action. His forte was mobility. No roving center ever had greater range."[2]

Following his football career, Eckstein was a prominent Providence surgeon and was associated with Rhode Island Hospital, Roger Williams Hospital and Chapin Hospital, among others.

Edwards, Charles Halleck "Bud"

Position: OH-DH-FB-LB; Height: 5'11"; Weight: 190; High School: Moses Brown (Providence, RI); College: Brown; Born: 3/21/1908, Chicago, IL; Died: 8/11/1986, Scottsdale, AZ; 1930 Providence Steam Roller: 9 Games, 3 Started, 1 TD, 6 Total Points; 1931 Providence Steam Roller: 9 Games, 4 Started.

Edwards played two seasons with the Steam Roller and scored one touchdown on a pass reception from Curley Oden in a 33–12 loss to Brooklyn on November 27, 1930. He also played one game for the Chicago Bears, and in 1933 he played six games for the Passaic Red Devils of the Interstate Football League.

Edwards played his college football at Brown, where he was a fine all-around halfback and captain of the 1929 squad. He was the first Brown player to play in the East-West Shrine Game. He scored both Bruins touchdowns in Brown's 13–12 win over

Bud Edwards, Providence Steam Roller back (1930–1931) (John Hay Library, Special Collections, Brown University).

Princeton in 1929. Coach Tuss McLaughry selected him to his all-time Brown team as one of the halfbacks. He was noted as a terrific blocker but also was an effective ball carrier. Edwards was elected to the Brown University Athletic Hall of Fame in 1973. Following his football career, he served as president of Edwards Realty Corp. in Fort Wayne, Indiana.

Non-Providence Stats

1931—Chicago Bears: 1 Game, 0 Started.

Eschbach, Herbert Heins "Herb"

Position: C-MG; Height: 6'0"; Weight: 190; High School: Franklin & Marshall Academy (Lancaster, PA); College: Penn State; Born: 4/26/1907, Lancaster, PA; Died: 2/22/1970, Williamsport, PA; 1930 Providence Steam Roller: 7 Games, 4 Started; 1931 Providence Steam Roller: 4 Games, 1 Started.

Eshbach played two seasons with the Steam Roller on the interior line, appearing in 11 games. After leaving the Steam Roller, he played for the semiprofessional Big Green of Maple Grove, Pennsylvania, for several seasons. He starred at Franklin & Marshall Academy and he played college football as a center for Penn State from 1926 to 1929. Eschbach lettered in his final two seasons playing football for the Nittany Lions. He also studied electrical engineering and threw the discus for the track team while at Penn State.

He worked as an engineer and salesman at Bethlehem Steel in Williamsport, Pennsylvania, for many years.

Etelman, Carl Edward

Position: BB-DH; Height: 5'8"; Weight: 160; High School: Fairhaven (Fairhaven, MA); College: Boston University, Tufts, Harvard; Born: 4/2/1900, Fairhaven, MA; Died: 12/18/1963, Boston, MA; 1926 Providence Steam Roller: 1 Game, 1 Started.

Etelman played only a single game for the Steam Roller in 1926. He also played professionally for the Boston Bulldogs of the AFL, appearing in three games and kicking one field goal. Prior to joining the Steam Roller, he played semiprofessional football for the St. Alphonsus Athletic Association for two seasons. Etelman also spent three seasons with the semipro Fitton Athletic Club after playing for the Bulldogs. Etelman coached the Whitman High School football team for 18 years and also coached the semiprofessional Old Town team of Abington for two seasons.

Etelman was the team captain as a senior at Fairhaven High School, playing quarterback and leading the team to several "big wins with his dramatic passing and running," according to the *Standard-Times*.[3] At 5'8", he was nicknamed "midget" by his teammates.

Etelman attended Tufts University, where he starred in football, baseball and basketball. He earned five varsity letters, including three in football. A 1922 article in the *Boston Globe* said, "Coach Casey's best bet at quarterback is Carl Etelman. He is a good general and may be trusted to run the team in an excellent manner and, if need be, reel off many gains himself."[4] Following the 1923 season, he was named All–New England at quarterback and to the All-Eastern team by the *New York Times*. After graduating from Tufts with a bachelor's degree in 1924, Etelman did graduate study work at Harvard University and Boston University.

He worked as a sales manager for Ward Machinery Co. of Brockton, Massachusetts, from 1945 until 1963.

Fleischmann, Godfrey Jacob "Jack"

Position: OT-DT-OG-DG; Height: 5'6"; Weight: 184; High School: East Detroit (Eastpointe, MI); College: Purdue; Born: 8/15/1901, Monroe, MI; Died: 4/27/1988, Monroe, LA; 1927 Providence Steam Roller: 14 Games, 12 Started; 1928 Providence Steam Roller: 11 Games, 6 Started; 1929 Providence Steam Roller: 12 Games, 12 Started.

Fleischmann played three seasons with the Steam Roller, anchoring its interior offensive and defensive lines. He was part of the 1928 NFL championship team. Prior to coming to Providence, he played two seasons with Conzelman and the Detroit Panthers. He signed with the Steam Roller after the demise of the Panthers. Fleischmann was named to the *Green Bay Press-Gazette* and *Chicago Herald* All-Pro teams in 1927. He played his college football at Purdue.

Fleischmann also played a season of minor league baseball in 1920 for the Winston-Salem Twins of the Piedmont League. He pitched and had a 14–11 record with a 3.00 ERA. He also had a batting average of .212 in 99 at-bats.

Fleischmann was a teacher and coach at Mangham High School and then for 30 years was principal at Start High School in Toledo, Ohio.

Non-Providence Stats

1925—Detroit Panthers: 9 Games, 3 Started.
1926—Detroit Panthers: 11 Games, 10 Started.

Forst, Arthur Henry "Dutch"

Position: FB-LB; Height: 5'8"; Weight: 195; High School: Villanova Prep (Villanova, PA); College: Villanova; Born: 2/17/1891, Derby, CT; Died: 10/5/1963, Seymour, CT; 1926 Providence Steam Roller: 2 Games, 2 Started.

Forst appeared in only two games for the 1926 Steam Roller. He then played and coached a semipro team in Seymour, Connecticut, for six years. Before coming to Providence, he was one of the top backs on the 1925 independent Waterbury Blues alongside Ken Simendinger from Holy Cross. In their only game against an NFL opponent, the Blues beat the Rochester Jeffersons 7–6. Prior to that, he played for the All-Bridgeport and Williams of New Haven teams. Forst played four years of college football at Villanova, lettering each season.

Forst served in the army during World War I. He worked 10 years at the Norwalk Chemical Company and then was appointed postmaster in Seymour, Connecticut, and served in that capacity for 18 years. He was the founder of the George L. Hummel Little League in Seymour and was active in the league for many years. He received the Connecticut Sports Writers Alliance Gold Key Award in 1963.

Garvey, Arthur Aloysius "Hec"

Position: OG-DG-OT-DT; Height: 6'1"; Weight: 234; High School: Holyoke (Holyoke, MA); College: Notre Dame; Born: 2/20/1900, St. Louis, MO; Died: 9/22/1973, Chicago, IL; 1929 Providence Steam Roller: 9 Games, 7 Started.

Garvey played only one season with the Steam Roller, appearing in nine games in 1929. He had an eight-year NFL career, including stints with seven teams, highlighted by two seasons each with the Chicago Bears and New York Giants. Garvey was a first-team All-Pro in his second season, 1923, with the Bears. He was a starting guard on the Giants' 1927 NFL championship team. Garvey played center, guard, tackle and end during his NFL career. He also played professionally for two AFL teams in 1926, the New York Yankees and Brooklyn Horsemen.

A graduate of Notre Dame University, where he played two varsity seasons for Knute Rockne, Garvey and his team won 19 of 20 games. He blocked for George Gipp. Garvey also moonlighted for the Green Bay Packers, playing against the Milwaukee American Legion on December 4, 1921, in a 3–3 tie game. He was suspended from all Notre Dame athletic engagements when the deception was discovered. Garvey went professional in 1922 with the Bears. He retired from football in 1931.

Following his football career, he tried his hand at professional boxing, and then professional wrestling.

Non-Providence Stats

1922—Chicago Bears: 12 Games, 12 Started.
1923—Chicago Bears: 12 Games, 12 Started.
1926—Brooklyn Lions: 1 Game, 1 Started.
1926—Hartford Blues: 4 Games, 3 Started.
1927—New York Giants: 8 Games, 8 Started.
1928—New York Giants: 11 Games, 9 Started.
1930—Brooklyn Dodgers: 12 Games, 12 Started.
1931—Staten Island Stapletons: 11 Games, 7 Started.

Garvey, Francis Daniel "Franny"

Position: OE-DE; Height: 6'1"; Weight: 175; High School: Unknown; College: Holy Cross; Born: 5/18/1901, Worcester, MA; Died: 11/18/1972, Chelsea, MA; 1925 Providence Steam Roller: 9 Games, 8 Started, 2 TDs, 12 Total Points; 1926 Providence Steam Roller: 10 Games, 7 Started, 1 Extra Point, 1 Total Point.

Garvey played two seasons of professional football, both with the Steam Roller. He scored two touchdowns in 1925, on a blocked punt return and on a fumble return. He scored an extra point in 1926. Garvey played his college football at Holy Cross and helped the Crusaders to a 7–2–1 record in 1922.

Garvey became a teacher and basketball and football coach in Chelsea, Massachusetts, in 1927. He later became director of athletics, and superintendent of parks, retiring as a teacher in 1962.

Gentry, Weldon Christopher

Position: OG-DG; Height: 5'10"; Weight: 195; High School: Lawton (Lawton, OK); College: Arkansas, Oklahoma; Born: 9/9/1906, Lawton, OK; Died: 3/19/1990, Oklahoma City, OK; 1930 Providence Steam Roller: 4 Games, 0 Started; 1931 Providence Steam Roller: 7 Games, 4 Started.

Gentry played parts of two seasons in the NFL with the Steam Roller, appearing in 11 games. He also played for the independent Memphis Tigers for parts of those seasons.

Gentry played college football at Arkansas for two years and then transferred to Oklahoma and played three additional seasons with the Sooners. He was named an All Big-Six guard in 1929.

Following his playing career, he and Jimmy Humphries founded the first professional football team in Oklahoma City, the Oklahoma City Chiefs. He played for the Chiefs in 1933, and the team finished with a 7-2-2 record. He also coached the Oklahoma University freshman team and later coached high school football at Pryor, Oklahoma. Gentry later worked for the Oklahoma Highway Patrol and then for the Federal Bureau of Investigation, focusing on bank robbery cases.

Golembeski, Anthony Edward "Archie"

Position: C-MG-OG-DG-OE-DE; Height: 5'10"; Weight: 185; High School: Worcester Classical (Worcester, MA); College: Holy Cross; Born: 5/25/1900, Lyon Mountain, NY; Died: 3/9/1976, Worcester, MA; 1925 Providence Steam Roller: 11 Games, 11 Started, 2 TDs, 12 Total Points, Head Coach, 6-5-1; 1926 Providence Steam Roller: 9 Games, 7 Started, 1 TD, 1 Extra Point, 7 Total Points; 1929 Providence Steam Roller: 8 Games, 5 Started.

Golembeski played and coached for the Steam Roller in 1925. The team finished with a 6-5-1 record in its inaugural NFL season. He continued as a player, playing two more seasons with Providence, in 1926 and 1929. Golembeski scored three touchdowns for the Steam Roller, highlighted by a 96-yard fumble return against Frankford on November 22, 1925, to help spark Providence's 20-7 victory. He had also played end for Providence in 1923 and was part of the 1924 squad that won the mythical Northeast championship, before the team joined the NFL.

He played three sports at Holy Cross and became an All-East football star. Golembeski lettered three years in football. He served as the head football coach at Providence College from 1925 to 1933, compiling a record of 27-34-12. He was a professional wrestler in the 1930s. Following his sports career, Golembeski operated a men's wear shop in Shrewsbury, Massachusetts.

Goodbread, Royce Ethelbert

Position: OH-DH-FB-LB; Height: 5'11"; Weight: 207; High School: St. Petersburg (St. Petersburg, FL); College: Florida; Born: 8/23/1907, Crystal River, FL; Died: 5/19/1991, Dallas, TX; 1931 Providence Steam Roller: 4 Games, 2 Started.

Goodbread played part of one season for the Steam Roller, appearing in four games in 1931. Before coming to Providence, he played one other NFL season, splitting time with the Frankford Yellow Jackets and Minneapolis Red Jackets. He scored his only NFL touchdown on a 40-yard pass reception from Wally Diehl on September 24, 1930. It was the winning touchdown in Frankford's 13–6 victory over Newark.

Goodbread played high school football for the St. Petersburg Green Devils, and in 1925 he accounted for 189 points and led the state with 31 touchdowns. He also led his team to the state football championship.

After graduating from St. Petersburg, he attended the University of Florida, where he played from 1927 to 1929. In Goodbread's three varsity seasons, the team posted won-loss records of 7-3, 8-1 and 8-2—a three-year peak for the Gators not exceeded for over six decades. Goodbread was a member of the Gators' "Phantom Four" offensive backfield that included Carl Brumbaugh, Rainey Cawthon and Clyde Crabtree, when the 1928 Gators led the country with 336 points scored and lost only at Tennessee by a single point, 13–12.

Goodbread graduated from the University of Florida with a bachelor's degree in physical education in 1930. During World War II, he served as an intelligence officer in the US Army. After his football career ended, he was an insurance agent in Dallas, Texas.

Non-Providence Stats

1930—Frankford Yellow Jackets: 13 Games, 10 Started, 1 TD, 6 Total Points.
1930—Minneapolis Red Jackets: 1 Game, 0 Started.

Graham, Alfred J. "Al"

Position: OG-DG; Height: 6'0"; Weight: 211; High School: West Carrollton (West Carrollton, OH); College: None; Born: 9/29/1905, West Carrollton, OH; Died: 10/18/1969, Knoxville, TN; 1930 Providence Steam Roller: 9 Games, 9 Started; 1931 Providence Steam Roller: 11 Games, 10 Started.

Al played two seasons of his nine-year NFL career with the Steam Roller. He appeared in 20 games in Providence's final two NFL seasons. Graham spent five seasons with the Dayton Triangles and scored two touchdowns, both off fumble returns, highlighted by a 72-yarder in a 6–3 win over Frankford on September 24, 1927. He was second-team All-Pro three times and third team once. When the Dayton franchise was sold in July 1930 and the team moved to Brooklyn, Graham was sold to the Steam

Roller. He ended his career in Chicago, playing his final two seasons with the Cardinals. Graham was forced to retire due to an intestinal ailment.

He did not play college football.

After his football career ended, Graham joined the Frigidaire Fire Department, West Carrollton, Ohio, and served as a firefighter until his retirement.

Non-Providence Stats

1925—Dayton Triangles: 8 Games, 8 Started.
1926—Dayton Triangles: 6 Games, 6 Started.
1927—Dayton Triangles: 8 Games, 8 Started, 1 TD, 6 Total Points.
1928—Dayton Triangles: 7 Games, 6 Started.
1929—Dayton Triangles: 5 Games, 5 Started, 1 TD, 6 Total Points.
1930—Portsmouth Spartans: 3 Games, 3 Started.
1932—Chicago Cardinals: 8 Games, 5 Started.
1933—Chicago Cardinals: 8 Games, 1 Started.

Graham, Frederick Hartley "Fred"

Position: OE-DE; Height: 6'0"; Weight: 175; High School: Morgantown (Morgantown, WV); College: Indiana State, West Virginia; Born: 12/11/1900, Masontown, WV; Died: 8/29/1952, Fairmont, WV; 1926 Providence Steam Roller: 1 Game, 0 Started.

Fred played one game for the Steam Roller in 1926. His NFL career included only one other game that he played for the Frankford Yellow Jackets. In 1926, Graham also played five games for the AFL's Chicago Bulls.

Prior to his brief NFL career, he played his college football at West Virginia University. At West Virginia, Graham excelled in football and basketball from 1921 to 1925 and earned first-team All-American honors in basketball in 1924. He also earned four letters in football as an end and served as the team's captain in 1924.

He was a member of West Virginia's 1922 undefeated football team, which posted a 10-0-1 record. Graham also helped West Virginia collect its first bowl game victory, a 21-13 decision over Gonzaga in the 1922 San Diego East-West Christmas Classic. During his Mountaineer career, WVU posted a 30-6-3 record. On May 25, 2009, Graham was inducted into the University of West Virginia Athletics Hall of Fame.

After his football career, he was a manufacturer's representative for Graham Products.

Non-Providence Stats

1926—Frankford Yellow Jackets: 1 Game, 1 Started.

Gulian, Milanese J. "Mike"

Position: OT-DT; Height: 6'0"; Weight: 205; High School: Newton (Newton, MA); College: Brown; Born: 7/29/1900, Marash, Armenia; Died: 1/10/1970, Newton, MA; 1925 Providence Steam Roller: 8 Games, 8 Started; 1926 Providence Steam Roller: 13 Games, 12 Started; 1927 Providence Steam Roller: 2 Games, 1 Started.

Gulian played three seasons with the Steam Roller and held a starting tackle position for two of those seasons. Gulian, sometimes known as the Armenian Prince, was an Ottoman Empire–born player. He was the first Armenian-born player in the NFL.

Gulian was born in Marash in Western Armenia, then part of the Ottoman Empire. He immigrated to the United States at a young age and grew up in Newton, Massachusetts. Gulian played his college football at Brown and was captain of Brown's 1922 team. He played a terrific game against Harvard in 1922 and is credited with leading Brown to the 3-0 victory. Gulian was selected as a first-team All-American at the conclusion of that season. He was a four-year letter winner. Gulian was known as "a rough, tough but sportsmanlike"[5] athlete.

Mike Gulian (at right), Providence Steam Roller tackle (1925–1927) (John Hay Library, Special Collections, Brown University).

Gulian, in addition to his three seasons with the Steam Roller, played two NFL seasons prior to coming to Providence. He was named third-team All-Pro in 1924 while playing for Frankford. After his football career, Gulian worked for the Equitable Life Assurance Company in Boston. During World War II, he served in the United States Army and for the American Red Cross.

He was enshrined in the Brown University Athletic Hall of Fame in 1971.

Non-Providence Stats

1923—Buffalo All-Americans: 11 Games, 11 Started.
1924—Frankford Yellow Jackets: 14 Games, 10 Started.

Hadden, Aldous Bernard "Al"

Position: OE-FB-LB-TB-DH-HB-WB-S; Height: 5'8"; Weight: 186; High School: Jesup Wakeman Scott (Toledo, OH); College: Washington & Jefferson; Born: 11/8/1899, Toledo, OH; Died: 2/26/1969, Toledo, OH; 1927 Providence Steam Roller: 10 Games, 7 Started; 1928 Providence Steam Roller: 9 Games, 7 Started; 1929 Providence Steam Roller: 9 Games, 7 Started; 1930 Providence Steam Roller: 9 Games, 4 Started.

Hadden played four seasons with the Steam Roller, appearing in 37 games, and was part of the 1928 NFL championship team. Prior to coming to Providence, he was the third-leading scorer for the 8–2–2 Detroit Panthers of 1925. He scored four touchdowns, three receiving and one rushing, playing with future Steam Roller player/coach Jimmy Conzelman. Hadden scored the first two touchdowns on December 12 in a key 21–0 victory over George Halas and the Chicago Bears. In 1926, he scored one additional touchdown for the Panthers, a 36-yard pass reception in a 25–0 win over Akron. Hadden joined Conzelman and the Steam Roller in 1927 after the Panthers folded following the 1926 season.

Non-Providence Stats

1925—Detroit Panthers: 12 Games, 12 Started, 4 TDs, 24 Total Points.
1926—Detroit Panthers: 12 Games, 8 Started, 1 TD, 6 Total Points.
1928—Chicago Bears: 1 Game, 0 Started.

Hagenbuckle, Vernon Bertram "Vern"

Position: OE-DE; Height: 5'8"; Weight: 185; High School: Mount Vernon (Mount Vernon, NY); College: Dartmouth; Born: 12/6/1901, Mount Vernon, NY; Died: 11/17/1997, Brattleboro, VT; 1926 Providence Steam Roller: 2 Games, 2 Started.

Hagenbuckle played two games with the Steam Roller in 1926. Prior to joining Providence, he played for the Boston Bulldogs of the AFL. However, they went out of business after starting the season 2–4. Hagenbuckle, along with teammate Carl Etelman, signed with the Steam Roller.

Hagenbuckle did not make the Providence team in 1927 and his professional football career ended.

He played his college football at Dartmouth, where he lettered his junior and senior seasons. He graduated from Dartmouth in 1924 and received a master's degree in history and French from Middlebury College in 1934. Hagenbuckle taught and coached at the Hill School and Phillips Andover and was an assistant football coach at Dartmouth. During World War II, he was a US Navy officer and later rose to the rank of commander. Later on he served in civil service and was in the US Army Civil Corps at Fort Belvoir, Virginia.

Non-Providence Stats

1926—Boston Bulldogs (AFL): 1 Game, 1 Started.

Hammill, James E., III "Ching"

Position: BB-S; Height: 5'7"; Weight: 158; High School: Central (Bridgeport, CT), Hebron Academy (Hebron, ME); College: Connecticut; Born: 9/28/1902, Bridgeport, CT; Died: 11/25/1925, Bridgeport, CT; 1925 Providence Steam Roller: 1 Game, 1 Started.

Hamill played only one game for the Steam Roller against the Frankford Yellow Jackets, on October 3, 1925. Later that year, he died in a tragic accident while working for American Tube and Stamping Company.

He played four years of varsity high school football, three at Bridgeport High School and his final season at Hebron Academy. While at Bridgeport, he was twice named to the all-state team and as a junior he was captain at Bridgeport. Hamill initially committed to play his college football at Georgetown University but changed his mind and instead enrolled at the University of Connecticut. He performed well for the Aggies and was named all-New England as a quarterback. He left Connecticut after just one season and turned professional.

Hamill signed a contract with a team in Bridgeport. He scored the game-winning touchdown over a team called "Williams," which helped them head "straight for a state championship."[6] The *Bridgeport Telegram* reported in a 1922 story that his "greatest feat on the gridiron this season was his 53-yard run back of a punt which he scored a touchdown."[7] He played two more seasons with Bridgeport, in 1923 and 1924. Hammill made one of his longest career plays in 1924 against the "West Sides," scoring on a 65-yard rush.

In November 1925, he also played for All–New Britain of New Britain, Connecticut.

Hanny, Frank Matthew "Duke"

Position: OE-DE-OT-DT; Height: 6'0"; Weight: 199; High School: Aurora East (Aurora, IL); College: Indiana; Born: 12/10/1897, Aurora, IL; Died: 9/3/1946, Aurora, IL; 1928 Providence Steam Roller: 11 Games, 10 Started, 1 TD, 6 Total Points; 1929 Providence Steam Roller: 11 Games, 7 Started, 1 Extra Point, 1 Total Point.

Hanny played two seasons with the Steam Roller, appearing in 22 games. He was part of the 1928 NFL championship squad. Hanny scored the winning touchdown on a 50-yard interception return in the Steam Roller's 12–6 victory over the New York Yankees on October 21, 1928. He scored his only other point as a Steam Roller on an extra-point kick in a 41–0 win over Dayton at the start of the 1929 season. Prior to coming to Providence, he played five seasons with the Chicago Bears, and after leaving the Steam Roller he played one final season in 1930 with the Portsmouth Spartans and Green Bay Packers. He also played a few games in 1930 for the independent Milwaukee Nighthawks. Hanny is believed to be the first player ever to be ejected from an NFL game, on November 23, 1924, in a fight with Packer end Tillie Voss in a 3–0 Chicago victory. Hanny scored eight touchdowns in his career, converted one extra point and scored on a safety. Three of his touchdowns were interception returns. He was named to the All-Pro second team four consecutive years from 1923 through 1926 by *Collyer Magazine*.

He played college football at Indiana University. Hanny enrolled at Indiana in 1916 but World War I took him out of school. When he returned, he became a starting end and was captain of the 1922 team that finished the season 1–4–2.

Following his football career, he became the personnel manager at the Aurora Pump Company, a position he held until his death.

Non-Providence Stats

1923—Chicago Bears: 11 Games, 11 Started, 1 TD, 6 Total Points.
1924—Chicago Bears: 11 Games, 11 Started, 1 TD, 6 Total Points.
1925—Chicago Bears: 17 Games, 17 Started, 1 TD, 6 Total Points.
1926—Chicago Bears: 16 Games, 14 Started, 4 TDs, 24 Total Points.
1927—Chicago Bears: 14 Games, 14 Started, 1 Safety, 2 Total Points.
1930—Portsmouth Spartans: 4 Games, 1 Started.
1930—Green Bay Packers: 2 Games, 1 Started.

Harvey, Norman C. "Norm"

Position: C-MG-OT-DT-OG-OE-DE; Height: 6'0"; Weight: 196; High School: Calumet (Calumet, MI); College: Detroit Mercy; Born: 5/19/1899,

MI; Died: 12/24/1941, Detroit, MI; 1928 Providence Steam Roller: 9 Games, 4 Started; 1929 Providence Steam Roller: 8 Games, 2 Started.

Harvey played two seasons with the Steam Roller, appearing in 17 games. He was part of the 1928 NFL championship squad. Prior to coming to Providence, he played three NFL seasons and in 1925 was named a third-team All-Pro. He played with Providence teammate Jimmy Conzelman with Detroit in 1926. He also was a teammate of Red Grange in 1927 while playing with the Yankees.

Harvey played two years of college football at Detroit Mercy, lettering both seasons.

He died at 42 years old following a lengthy illness.

Non-Providence Stats

1925—Buffalo Bisons: 5 Games, 5 Started.
1926—Detroit Panthers: 8 Games, 1 Started.
1927—Buffalo Bisons: 5 Games, 5 Started.
1927—New York Yankees: 9 Games, 7 Started.

Holm, Bernard Patrick "Tony"

Position: OH-DH-FB-LB-TB; Height: 6'1"; Weight: 214; High School: Fairfield (Fairfield, AL); College: Alabama; Born: 5/22/1908, Birmingham, AL; Died: 7/15/1978, Waukegan, IL; 1930 Providence Steam Roller: 3 Games, 2 Started.

Holm played part of one season for the Steam Roller, appearing in three games in 1930. He also played some games with the independent Memphis Tigers in 1930. After 1930, he played three more NFL seasons for three different teams—the Portsmouth Spartans, Chicago Cardinals and Pittsburgh Pirates. He scored his only two career NFL touchdowns in 1931 with Portsmouth, the first on an 18-yard pass reception to help the Spartans defeat the Chicago Cardinals 13–3, and the second on a two-yard rush in a 14–0 win over Frankford on Halloween.

Holm was the Pirates' (today's Pittsburgh Steelers) first quarterback, appearing as the starter in Pittsburgh's September 20, 1933, loss to the New York Giants. His NFL career ended following that season. He became head coach of the Charlotte Bantams of the AFL in 1934, and they finished with a 3-7 record. He also played a few games for the Bantams before retiring from football.

Holm played his college football at Alabama, lettering for three years. As a junior in 1928, he made All-Southern, and in 1929 he was named an

All-American. Those two seasons he was one of Alabama's leading ground gainers and scorers.

He was a salesman for Sears, Roebuck & Co. before retiring in 1973.

Non-Providence Stats

1931—Portsmouth Spartans: 14 Games, 5 Started, 2 TDs, 12 Total Points.
1932—Chicago Cardinals: 8 Games, 5 Started, Rushing: 34–73–0, Receiving: 1–9–0.
1933—Pittsburgh Pirates: 9 Games, 9 Started, Rushing 58–160–0, Receiving: 2–13–0, Passing: 17–52, 406, 2 TDs, 13 Int.

Hummel, Arthur J. "Swede"

Position: BB-DH-FB-DG-OG; Height: Unknown; Weight: 195; High School: Unknown; College: Lombard; Born: 5/30/1902, Belleville, IL; Died: 7/24/1965, Los Angeles County, CA; 1926 Providence Steam Roller: 4 Games, 3 Started.

Hummel played part of the 1926 season for the Steam Roller, appearing in four games. Providence purchased Hummel from the Kansas City Cowboys in November 1926. He played five games for the Cowboys prior to coming to the Steam Roller. Hummel played one more NFL season, with the Chicago Cardinals in 1927.

He played two seasons of college football at Lombard.

Following his retirement from football, he joined his father and brother in operating Hummel Bakery, a position he held for 48 years.

Non-Providence Stats

1926—Kansas City Cowboys: 5 Games, 5 Started.
1927—Chicago Cardinals: 8 Games, 4 Started.

Irvin, Cecil Paul "Tex"

Position: OT-DT-FB-LB-MG-C; Height: 6'0"; Weight: 225; High School: Cisco (Cisco, TX); College: Davis & Elkins; Born: 10/9/1906, DeLeon, TX; Died: 2/11/1978, DeLeon, TX; 1931 Providence Steam Roller: 10 Games, 9 Started.

Irvin played one season for the Steam Roller, its last in the NFL, appearing in 10 games. After the demise of the Providence team, Irvin played four seasons with the New York Giants and he scored one touchdown, on a 15-yard pass reception. He was on the 1933 Giants NFL championship team.

Irvin started his college football career playing one season for the Schreiner Institute, where he helped lead it to an undefeated season. He then transferred to Davis & Elkins (in Elkins, West Virginia), where he played four more seasons as a tackle and fullback. He earned All-American honors in 1929. The highlight of his collegiate career was a 6-0 upset win over Navy, and the headline of a West Virginia paper the next day was "Tex Irvin 6 Navy 0." Irvin tackled a Navy ball carrier on the opening kickoff at the two-yard line. Four plays later, he blocked the Navy punt and recovered the ball for the game's only touchdown.

Irvin returned to De Leon, Texas, to work for the Humble Pipeline Company after retiring from football and spent his career with the company. He served in the United States Navy during World War II and was a coach for several military football teams during the war years. Irvin was inducted into the Texas High School Football Hall of Fame in 1969.

Non-Providence Stats

1932—New York Giants: 10 Games, 6 Started.
1933—New York Giants: 12 Games, 6 Started, Receiving: 1-15-0, Scoring: 1 TD, 6 Total Points.
1934—New York Giants: 12 Games, 6 Started.
1935—New York Giants: 12 Games, 2 Started.

Jackson, Jesse Perry "Perry"

Position: OE-DE-TB-DB-OT-DT; Height: 6'1"; Weight: 202; High School: Mountain View (Mountain View, OK); College: SW Oklahoma State; Born: 4/24/1905, Dryden, OK; Died: 6/22/1973, Houston, TX; 1929 Providence Steam Roller: 0 Games, 0 Started.

Jackson tried out for the Steam Roller in 1929 but was cut in training camp. He originally had a tryout offer from the team in 1927. Per *The Steam Roller Story*, a book by Dick Reynolds, "In 1927, Jimmy Conzelman heard of a lineman, named Perry Jackson, who had acquired a glowing reputation in the west as a superstar at Southwest State University in Oklahoma. When Conzelman cabled a tryout offer, Jackson was much too ill to be thinking of football. But his friend and teammate, Arnold Shockley, reported to Roller camp as Perry Jackson and played three years under the assumed name. In 1929, the real Perry Jackson, now quite recovered, tried out with the Roller under the name of Arnold Shockley. He was cut and played one season under his buddy's name for a Boston team."[8]

Jackson played for Southwest Oklahoma State during the mid-1920s and teamed with Arnie Shockley to help make the Bulldogs one of the most feared teams in the state. Jackson lettered all four years and twice was named to the all-conference team. He was also a wrestler and won conference championships at heavyweight in 1926 and 1927. He was named captain of the 1928 wrestling team. Jackson was elected to the SWOSU Alumni Association Athletic Hall of Fame in 1965.

After his football career, he was a construction engineer in Houston in the pipeline industry.

Non-Providence Stats

1929—Boston Bulldogs: 6 Games, 2 Started.

Jennings, Louie Walter "Lou," "Blue Sun"

Position: C-MG; Height: 6'3"; Weight: 230; High School: Muskogee (Muskogee, OK), St. Mark's (Dallas, TX); College: Haskell Indian, Centenary; Born: 1/12/1904, Muskogee, OK; Died: 10/25/1957, Travis County, OH; 1929 Providence Steam Roller: 2 Games, 2 Started, 4 Extra Points, 4 Total Points.

Jennings was with the Steam Roller at the start of the 1929 season. He set the team record by kicking four extra points in the Steam Roller's 41-0 opening-day victory over the Dayton Triangles on September 29. He played only one more game with Providence. In 1930, he joined the Portsmouth Spartans and played one season before he retired from professional football.

Jennings was recruited to play football for the Terrill School, a Dallas boarding high school that was the forerunner of St. Mark's School of Texas. He graduated from Terrill in 1923. He then attended Haskell Indian College before transferring to Centenary College, where he played on the varsity football team for four years. He helped lead Centenary to two Southern Intercollegiate Athletic Association championships, including a 10-0 season in 1927.

Jennings competed as a professional wrestler from 1931 to 1939, using his Native American name, Blue Sun. He participated in 571 bouts and is credited with 159 wins and 315 losses.

Non-Providence Stats

1930—Portsmouth Spartans: 9 Games, 9 Started.

Keefer, Jackson Milliman "Jack"

Position: WB-DH-BB; Height: 5'9"; Weight: 172; High School: Steele (Dayton, OH); College: Michigan, Brown; Born: 5/1/1900, Olney, IL; Died: 8/3/1966, Dayton, OH; 1926 Providence Steam Roller: 11 Games, 5 Started, 2 TDs, 1 TD Pass, 3 Extra Points, 15 Total Points.

Keefer played one season with the Steam Roller in 1926, appearing in 11 games. He scored two rushing touchdowns, one against the Columbus Tigers and the other the winning touchdown on October 30 in a 7-6 win over Frankford. He also threw a 20-yard touchdown pass in a loss to the New York Giants and converted three extra-point kicks during the season. Keefer played for the Dayton Triangles in 1928. In 1929, he played for the Ashland Armco Yellowjackets of the Ohio Valley League, helping lead the team to a second-place 8-2-1 finish.

Keefer played halfback for the Michigan Wolverines in 1922. He transferred to Brown in the fall of 1923. While playing for Brown, he was selected as a third-team All-American in both 1924 and 1925. He was inducted into the Brown University Athletic Hall of Fame in 1971, and in 2003 he was selected as one of four backs on the 125th Anniversary All-Time Brown Football Team. Keefer scored 250 points in a 10-game schedule during his senior year at Steele High School. He led the school to the Ohio State football championship.

Keefer also played minor league baseball for Springfield (Eastern League) and Haverhill (New England League) in 1927 and 1928. His overall batting average was .285 in 424 at-bats. Keefer coached baseball, basketball and football at his high school alma mater, Steele High School.

He was an army major in World War II, serving in the Pacific Theater. He also served in World War I. He was the head of Keefer-Allen Sporting Goods company in Dayton, Ohio, for many years.

Non-Providence Stats

1928: Dayton Triangles: 3 Games, 2 Started.

Koplow, Louis H. "Lou"

Position: OT-DT; Height: 6'3"; Weight: 235; High School: English (Boston, MA); College: Boston University; Born: 2/1/1904, Malden, MA; Died: 8/12/1988, Boston, MA; 1926 Providence Steam Roller: 1 Game, 1 Started.

Koplow played a single game for the Steam Roller in 1926. He started at tackle.

Koplow played his college football at Boston University.

Kozlowsky, Joseph Alexander "Joe"

Position: OT-DT-OE-DE-OG-DG; Height: 5'10"; Weight: 201; High School: Cambridge Latin (Cambridge, MA); College: Boston College; Born: 8/9/1901, Cambridge, MA; Died: 12/22/1970, Cambridge, MA; 1925 Providence Steam Roller: 11 Games, 11 Started; 1926 Providence Steam Roller: 10 Games, 8 Started; 1927 Providence Steam Roller: 12 Games, 8 Started; 1930 Providence Steam Roller: 8 Games, 2 Started.

Kozlowsky played four seasons with the NFL's Steam Roller. He was named first-team All-Pro in 1927 by the *Chicago Tribune*. His 41 games played with Providence are the fifth-best total in team history. He played for the Steam Roller in 1924, prior to the team joining the NFL, when it was mythical Northeast champions with an overall 12–3–1 record. Kozlowsky also played one season with the Boston Bulldogs of the NFL.

He played his college football at Boston College, where he was a four-year letter winner. Kozlowsky also captained the 1924 squad. He was "rugged, fast and fearless and one of the finest two-way tackles in the history of Boston College football," as described by the Boston College Varsity Club Hall of Fame.[9] He was enshrined in the school's Athletic Hall of Fame in 1971.

Kozlowsky was the city of Cambridge director of physical education in 1953, a position he held into the late 1960s. He was an assistant football coach at Boston College and Fordham under Major Frank Cavanaugh. He also was an assistant basketball coach at Cambridge Latin for 25 years before taking over the head coaching job.

Non-Providence Stats

1929—Boston Bulldogs: 8 Games, 8 Started.

Kucharski, Theodore Michael "Ted"

Position: OE-DE; Height: 6'1"; Weight: 185; High School: Exeter (Exeter, NH), St. Anselm Prep (Manchester, NH); College: Holy Cross; Born: 8/26/1907, Exeter, NH; Died: 10/7/1992, Mesa, AZ; 1930 Providence Steam Roller: 8 Games, 0 Started.

Kucharski played a single season with the Steam Roller in 1930, appearing in eight games. It was his only NFL experience.

He played four years of college football at the College of the Holy Cross, lettering in three of the four years. After his one year of pro football, Kucharski became an assistant football coach in 1931 and a teacher in 1933, and his teaching career lasted through 1965. He was principal at Leominster High School in Leominster, Massachusetts, from 1953 until he retired.

During World War II, he served in the US Army in the Pacific Theater. He also received a master's degree from Fitchburg State College in 1942.

Laird, James Tyler "Jim"

Position: FB-LB-OG-DG-WB-DH; Height: 6'0"; Weight: 194; High School: Holderness (Plymouth, NH); College: Colgate; Born: 9/10/1897, Montpelier, VT; Died: 8/16/1970, Windham, CT; 1925 Providence Steam Roller: 11 Games, 8 Started, 3 TDs, 2 Extra Points and 3 Field Goals, 29 Total Points; 1926 Providence Steam Roller: 9 Games, 6 Started; 1927 Providence Steam Roller: 14 Games, 12 Started; 1928 Providence Steam Roller: 8 Games, 0 Started.

Laird played four seasons with the NFL Steam Roller and was part of the 1928 NFL championship squad. He also coached and played for the 1924 version of the Steam Roller that won the mythical Northeast championship prior to joining the NFL. He was second on the 1924 team in points scored with 25.

In his first year with the NFL version of the Steam Roller, he led the team in scoring with 29 points. Laird scored three touchdowns rushing, highlighted by the first touchdown in the Roller's 20-7 win over Frankford on November 22 and the team's only touchdown in a 7-7 tie with Cleveland the following week. He also kicked for the team and converted two extra points and three field goals during the season. In 1926, Laird became the head coach and also played as the Rollers stumbled to a 5-7-1 record. His 42 NFL games played for Providence places him fourth on the all-time-games-played list in Steam Roller history.

Laird played three NFL seasons (1920-22) prior to coming to Providence with three different clubs—Buffalo, Canton and Rochester—and he finished his career in 1931 with a single season with the Staten Island Stapletons. He was named second-team All-Pro in 1922. In 1921, Laird played for the New York Brickley Giants; however, he is not listed as being on the team as he played for the Giants only when they scheduled nonleague opponents. He also played for the independent Union Quakers of Philadelphia in 1921. Intermingled between his NFL playing career, Laird was the head football coach at Norwich University, a private military college in Vermont, from 1923 to 1925 and again from 1932 to 1934.

He played his college football at Colgate and lettered in 1916. His college career got diverted because of World War I. Laird served in the

Marines for two years (1917 and 1918). He returned to Colgate and lettered in 1919 and was voted team captain for 1920. However, he was barred from playing for the Red Raiders when it was discovered that he had played a professional football game with the Buffalo Prospects in 1919.

Laird was ranked in 2021 by Ainsworth Sports as the fourth-best football player to ever play for Colgate.

Non-Providence Stats

1920—Buffalo All-Americans: 1 Game, 1 Started.
1920—Rochester Jeffersons: 9 Games, 1 Started.
1921—Buffalo All-Americans: 1 Game, 0 Started.
1921—Rochester Jeffersons: 6 Games, 5 Started, 4 TDs, 24 Total Points.
1921—Canton Bulldogs: 1 Game, 1 Started, 2 TDs, 12 Total Points.
1922—Buffalo All-Americans: 10 Games, 9 Started, 4 TDs, 24 Total Points.
1931—Staten Island Stapletons: 9 Games, 3 Started.

Latone, Anthony Joseph "Tony"

Position: FB-LB-OH-DB; Height: 5'11"; Weight: 195; High School: Unknown; College: None; Born: 4/18/1897, Spring Valley, IL; Died: 11/24/1975, Detroit, MI; 1930 Providence Steam Roller: 11 Games, 7 Started, 3 TDs, 18 Total Points.

Latone played one season for the Steam Roller, in 1930, his last season of his six-year NFL career. His touchdowns against the Staten Island Stapletons and Minneapolis Red Jackets sparked the Steam Roller to 7–6 and 10–0 victories, respectively. His two-yard fourth quarter touchdown run against the Newark Tornadoes clinched Providence's 14–0 win.

Latone began working in the coal mines of northeastern Pennsylvania at 11 years old. He excelled at the sandlot football played in the area as a teenager. In 1915, he earned a spot with the Edwardsville Lithuanian Knights, where he made local headlines. Latone joined the navy and served in World War I until 1919. He returned to play for Edwardsville and then played for teams in Pine Brook, Mount Carmel and Wilkes-Barre. In 1924, he played for Anthracite League champion Pottsville and made the All-Star team. The Maroons joined the NFL in 1925 and Latone came along. He led the NFL in touchdowns with eight and unofficially finished second in rushing yardage. He earned first-team All-Pro honors in 1926 and second-team honors in 1928 and an honorable mention in 1929. He had a career high in touchdowns with nine in 1929. David Neft's research made him the half-decade leader in interceptions (20) and the decade leader in yards rushing (2,365). The *Pro Football Chronicle* named him to their 1920s All-Decade Team. Latone was named to the Pro Football Researchers' Hall of Very Good in 2021.

Non-Providence Stats

1925—Pottsville Maroons: 12 Games, 10 Started, 8 TDs, 48 Total Points.
1926—Pottsville Maroons: 12 Games, 5 Started, 4 TDs, 24 Total Points.
1927—Pottsville Maroons: 12 Games, 11 Started.
1928—Pottsville Maroons: 10 Games, 9 Started, 3 TDs, 18 Total Points.
1929—Boston Bulldogs: 8 Games, 8 Started, 9 TDs, 54 Total Points.

Lester, Harold W. "Pinky"

Position: OE-DE-OT-DT; Height: 5'6"; Weight: 160; High School: East Providence (East Providence, RI); College: None; Born: 3/13/1900, New London, CT; Died: 1/1/1972, Providence, RI; 1926 Providence Steam Roller: 8 Games, 5 Started.

Lester played one season with the NFL version of the Steam Roller, appearing in eight games. He did not attend college. He also played for Providence before they joined the NFL. He played for the team in 1923 and was part of the 1924 mythical Northeast championship squad, for which he was the leading scorer with 30 points.

Lester served in both World War I and World War II. During the First World War, he served on transports that ran between Europe and America. He volunteered for a second tour in the navy when World War II began.

He was in the original class of Rhode Island state police trainees in 1925 but left the force in 1931 to begin a 35-year career with the East Providence police, where he served as police chief for his last 11 years on the force.

Lowe, Jr., George Henry "Bulger"

Position: OE-DE; Height: 5'11"; Weight: 180; High School: Arlington (Arlington, MA), Philips Exeter Academy (Exeter, NH); College: Lafayette, Fordham; Born: 6/21/1895, Arlington, MA; Died: 2/18/1939, Boston, MA; 1925 Providence Steam Roller: 2 Games, 1 Started; 1927 Providence Steam Roller: 11 Games, 6 Started.

Lowe played part of the 1925 season with the Steam Roller and then a full season in 1927, when he appeared in 11 games. Prior to playing for Providence, he began his NFL career with the Canton Bulldogs in 1920 and he scored the only points of his NFL career on a safety. The following season while playing for the Cleveland Indians he was named a first-team All-Pro by the *Buffalo News*. In 1923, he played for the independent Frankford Yellow Jackets (prior to them joining the NFL) and in 1924 he was on the Steam Roller squad that won the mythical Northeast championship. He returned to the NFL in 1925 with the Yellow Jackets and played parts of two seasons with the club. He also was an assistant coach for the Boston Bulldogs of the AFL in 1926.

In 1909, Lowe started his football career as a 14-year-old, playing guard for Arlington High School. He played one season for Fordham University in 1917 and was one of the team captains, with the school claiming a 22-3 record. Prior to the NFL being formed in 1920, he played for the Akron Indians, the Cleveland Tigers and the Canton Bulldogs.

Lowe served with the United States Army Ambulance Service in World War I, getting wounded and ending up in a hospital in France.

Lowe was the first player from Fordham to play pro football, when in 1920 he joined the Canton Bulldogs. The Gridiron Club of Greater Boston established the George H. "Bulger" Lowe Award in 1939 to recognize New England's best offensive and defensive players in the NCAA Bowl and Championship divisions, after his unexpected death. The award is the third-oldest collegiate football award in the United States, following the Heisman and Maxwell trophies. The award is sometimes referred to as "New England's Heisman Trophy."

Non-Providence Stats

1920—Canton Bulldogs: 10 Games, 6 Started, 1 Safety, 2 Total Points.
1921—Cleveland Indians: 7 Games, 7 Started.
1925—Frankford Yellow Jackets: 8 Games, 5 Started.
1926—Frankford Yellow Jackets: 2 Games, 2 Started.

Lynch, Edward James

Position: E-T; Height: 6'0"; Weight: 191; High School: St. Michael's (Northampton, MA); College: Catholic; Born: 10/4/1896, Northampton, MA; Died: 8/24/1967, Dearborn, MI; 1927 Providence Steam Roller: 11 Games, 10 Started.

Lynch played one season with Providence, starting 10 games. He scored his only career touchdown on a pass from Wildcat Wilson in the

Steam Roller's 14-7 win over the New York Yankees on November 27, 1927. Lynch came to the team along with Jimmy Conzelman and others when the Detroit Panthers disbanded in August 1927.

He began his NFL career with the Rochester Jeffersons in 1925. Lynch was named a first-team All-Pro at the conclusion of that season. In 1926, he joined the Panthers and was a second-team All-Pro. He also played one game with the Hartford Blues prior to coming to Providence. Lynch finished his pro football career playing five games with the Orange Tornadoes in 1929.

He played five seasons of college football at Catholic University and lettered three times.

Non-Providence Stats

1925—Rochester Jeffersons: 6 Games, 6 Started.
1926—Hartford Blues: 1 Game, 1 Started.
1926—Detroit Panthers: 12 Games, 12 Started.
1929—Orange Tornadoes: 5 Games, 2 Started.

MacPhee, Walter Scott "Waddy"

Position: WB-DH-FB-LB-BB; Height: 5'8"; Weight: 160; High School: Erasmus Hall (Brooklyn, NY); College: Princeton; Born: 12/23/1899, Brooklyn, NY; Died: 1/20/1980, Charlotte, NC; 1926 Providence Steam Roller: 10 Games, 1 Started.

MacPhee played one season with the Steam Roller, primarily as a reserve in the backfield. It was his only NFL season.

He also played professional baseball. After graduating from Princeton in 1922, MacPhee signed with the New York baseball Giants, managed by John McGraw. MacPhee played in two games for the eventual World Series champions during their 1922 season, his only two major league appearances. In his first game on September 27, he recorded a hit and a walk in four at-bats against Philadelphia Phillies pitcher Jimmy Ring at the Polo Grounds. His second and last major league game came three days later at the Polo Grounds, this time against the Boston Braves and pitcher Garland Braxton. MacPhee played third base and went 1-for-4 with a triple and a run scored in the Giants' 5-3 win. In two major league games, MacPhee batted .286 with a walk and two runs scored and committed one error in nine fielding chances.

Following his debut with the Giants, he played six minor league seasons before retiring at the end of the 1928 season. In 1923, MacPhee played for the Denver Bears of the Western League, batting .280 with 182 hits. He spent 1924 and 1925 with the Pittsfield Hillies of the Eastern League, where he had batting averages of .242 and .277, respectively. During his remaining three minor league seasons, MacPhee played for seven different teams, mostly clubs in the Eastern League. He batted .248 in 1927 and .266 in 1928. In 1929 and 1930, he played shortstop for Falmouth in the Cape Cod League, a semiprofessional circuit. He helped lead the team to the league pennant in 1929. At midseason in 1930, he moved to play for Osterville.

MacPhee was a star in high school at Erasmus Hall, where he was class president, played football and was captain of the baseball and ice hockey teams. Upon his high school graduation, he attended Princeton, where he played all three sports, and was captain of the Tigers baseball team as a senior in 1922.

MacPhee served three years in the US Navy during World War II. He taught high school history for 40 years at East Providence High School, Tome School and Manlius School, from which he retired in 1968. He also coached baseball and football at East Providence.

Maloney, Gerald Stack "Red"

Position: OE-DE; Height: 5'11"; Weight: 180; High School: Worcester (Worcester, MA); College: Dartmouth; Born: 9/5/1901, Ware, MA; Died: 5/16/1976, Newton, MA; 1925 Providence Steam Roller: 12 Games, 12 Started, 1 TD, 4 Extra Points, 3 Field Goals, 19 Total Points.

Maloney played one season for the Steam Roller in its inaugural year of 1925. He started all 12 games at end. He was named second-team All-Pro by the *Green Bay Gazette*. Maloney scored the first NFL touchdown in franchise history on a fumble return against the Pottsville Maroons on October 4. His touchdown was the only score in the Steam Roller's 6–0 victory, the first NFL win in team history. He was also the team's kicker and contributed four extra points and three field goals during Providence's first NFL season. His 19 points were second on the team.

In 1926, Maloney played for the AFL's New York Yankees and he scored two touchdowns. Maloney followed the Yankees into the NFL in 1927, playing 12 games for the 7–8–1 squad. He played one final NFL season with the Boston Bulldogs, in 1929. Maloney played his college football at Dartmouth. He was enshrined in the Dartmouth "Wearers of the Green" Athletic Hall of Fame in 2004. In 2021, Ainsworth Sports listed Red Maloney as the 10th-best football player of all time at Dartmouth.

Non-Providence Stats

1927—New York Yankees: 12 Games, 9 Started, 1 TD, 6 Total Points.
1929—Boston Bulldogs: 8 Games, 7 Started.

Manning, James Joseph "Jim"

Position: BB-DH; Height: 5'11"; Weight: 195; High School: Xavier (New York, NY); College: Fordham; Born: 11/20/1900, Holyoke, MA; Died: 8/5/1973, Springfield, MA; 1926 Providence Steam Roller: 1 Game, 1 Started.

Manning played a single game for the Steam Roller in 1926. Prior to coming to Providence, he played six games for the Hartford Blues in 1926. With the Blues he scored three touchdowns, including two rushing scores in Hartford's 16–0 win over Dayton on November 21. Manning played only that one season of NFL football.

He was a four-year letter winner at Fordham in football.

Non-Providence Stats

1926—Hartford Blues: 6 Games, 5 Started, 3 TDs, 18 Total Points.

McArthur, Ira Jackson "Jack"

Position: OG-DG-DE-OE-C-MG-OT-DT; Height: 5'11"; Weight: 211; High School: St. Mary's (Berkeley, CA); College: St Mary's (CA); Born: 5/30/1902, Acampo, CA; Died: Unknown; 1930 Providence Steam Roller: 4 Games, 0 Started; 1931 Providence Steam Roller: 9 Games, 3 Started.

McArthur played 1½ seasons with the Steam Roller at the end of his NFL career. He joined the squad midway through the 1930 season after he was released by Newark. He substituted in four games for the Steam Roller. McArthur was back with Providence in 1931 for the full season, appearing in nine games—three as a starter.

Prior to coming to Providence, McArthur played for six NFL teams, beginning in 1926 with the Los Angeles Buccaneers, highlighted by his two seasons with the New York Yankees, where he started 20 games. After his NFL career ended, he played a single season with the Staten Island Stapletons, in 1933, when they played as an independent team. In 1934, he began a wrestling career that he continued into the early 1960s.

Non-Providence Stats

1926—Los Angeles Buccaneers: 10 Games, 10 Started.
1927—Buffalo Bisons: 5 Games, 5 Started.

1927—New York Yankees: 8 Games, 7 Started.
1928—New York Yankees: 13 Games, 13 Started.
1929—Orange Tornadoes: 10 Games, 2 Started.
1930—Brooklyn Dodgers: 5 Games, 0 Started.
1930—Frankford Yellow Jackets: 2 Games, 2 Started.
1930—Newark Tornadoes: 1 Game, 1 Started.

McBride, John F. "Jack"

Position: FB-LB-OH-DH; Height: 5'11"; Weight: 185; High School: Conshohocken (Conshohocken, PA), Bellefonte Academy (Bellefonte, PA); College: Syracuse; Born: 11/30/1901, Conshohocken, PA; Died: 10/11/1966, Tonopah, NV; 1929 Providence Steam Roller: 12 Games, 6 Started, 2 TD Passes, 6 Extra Points, 6 Total Points.

McBride played one season with the Steam Roller in a lengthy NFL career. In addition to playing in the offensive backfield, at linebacker and at defensive halfback, he also kicked for Providence. McBride threw two touchdown passes and converted six extra points throughout the 1929 season for the Steam Roller.

McBride played nine additional NFL seasons beyond his one year in Providence. He was the leading scorer for the New York Giants in each of their first three seasons (1925-27). In 1927, he led the entire NFL with 57 points. As a passer, McBride ended his career with 3,123 yards passing, 31 touchdown passes and 57 interceptions. As a runner, McBride totaled 2,093 yards and 26 touchdowns, while averaging 4.2 yards a carry.

He was an NFL champion twice with the New York Giants, in 1927 and 1934. He made first-team All-Pro in 1925 and 1927 and was third-team All-Pro in 1926 and 1930.

McBride played his college football at Syracuse University, where he finished second in the nation in scoring in his senior year to Heinie Benkert of Rutgers, a future teammate with the Giants of 1925. McBride scored 90 points on seven touchdowns, 11 field goals and 15 extra points in his senior year.

McBride maintained his connection with pro football after his career in the NFL ended, serving as the player/coach of the Paterson Panthers in 1934 and 1935. He led the team to back-to-back championships in the New Jersey Circuit in 1934 and the Greater New York Circuit in 1935. The 1934 squad finished 7-2-3, with McBride leading the league with seven touchdown passes. In 1935, the Panthers finished with a 9-2-1 record and McBride threw 14 touchdown passes to lead the league. He also scored a touchdown and kicked 11 extra points. McBride became head coach of the

New York Yankees of the second American Football League in 1936 and served two years, compiling a 7-6-3 record. He then coached the New York Yankees of the third AFL in 1940-1941 and compiled a 9-7-1 record.

Non-Providence Stats

1925—New York Giants: 12 Games, 12 Started, 2 TDs, 7 Extra Points, 2 Field Goals, 25 Total Points.
1926—New York Giants: 13 Games, 9 Started, 5 TDs, 15 Extra Points, 1 Field Goal, 48 Total Points.
1927—New York Giants: 12 Games, 12 Started, 6 TDs, 15 Extra Points, 2 Field Goals, 57 Total Points.
1928—New York Giants: 9 Games, 9 Started, 1 TD, 2 Extra Points, 8 Total Points.
1930—Brooklyn Dodgers: 11 Games, 11 Started, 8 TDs, 8 Extra Points, 56 Total Points.
1931—Brooklyn Dodgers: 13 Games, 13 Started, 3 TDs, 1 Extra Point, 19 Total Points.
1932—Brooklyn Dodgers: 3 Games, 0 Started, Rushing: 3-23-0.
1932—New York Giants: 9 Games, 6 Started, Rushing: 84-302-1, Passing: 36-74-6 TDs, 9 Int., 363 Yards, Scoring: 1 TD, 6 Total Points.
1933—New York Giants: 11 Games, 2 Started, Rushing 33-87-0, Passing: 11-24-2 TDs, 2 Int., 138 Yards, Scoring: 7 Extra Points, 7 Total Points.
1934—New York Giants: 1 Game, 0 Started, Rushing: 4-14-0, Passing: 3-3-1 TD, 0 Int., 37 Yards, Scoring: 1 Extra Point, 1 Total Point.

McCrillis, Edgar Vincent Frederick "Ed"

Position: OG-DG; Height: 6'5"; Weight: 205; High School: Classical (Providence, RI); College: Brown; Born: 9/7/1904, New York, NY; Died: 9/1/1940, Warwick, RI; 1926 Providence Steam Roller: 1 Game, 0 Started.

McCrillis played one game for the Steam Roller in 1926. He played one other NFL season with the Boston Bulldogs, in 1929, appearing in eight games.

McCrillis played his college football at Brown, lettering in both 1924 and 1925. He also was an accomplished boxer and wrestler at Brown. McCrillis was named to the Brown All-Decade football team of the 1920s as a guard. He graduated from Harvard Law School in 1929 and was a practicing attorney in Providence until his untimely death in 1940.

Non-Providence Stats

1929—Boston Bulldogs: 7 Games, 5 Started.

McGlone, Joseph Carlton "Joe"

Position: TB-S; Height: 5'7"; Weight: 150; High School: Natick (Natick, MA), Phillips Exeter Academy (Exeter, NH); College: Harvard; Born: 9/12/1896, Natick, MA; Died: 1/25/1963, New York, NY; 1926 Providence Steam Roller: 1 Game, 1 Started.

McGlone played a single NFL game for the Steam Roller in 1926. He had an outstanding preseason game in the team's 41–0 win over New London as he directed three of the Steam Roller's scoring drives. After his short stint with Providence, he played for the Boston Bulldogs of the AFL in 1926, appearing in five games and scoring an extra point.

McGlone played his college football at Harvard. He was on the varsity football squad for three years and lettered in one season. McGlone served as an assistant football coach at Lowell High School.

McGlone also served his country during World War I. He went over with one of the first contingents deployed and he was awarded the Croix de Guerre, Distinguished Service Cross, for his bravery and courage.

McGoldrick, Hugh Francis

Position: OT-DT; Height: 5'10"; Weight: 180; High School: Medford (Medford, MA), Dean Academy (Franklin, MA); College: Lehigh; Born: 11/22/1900, Boston, MA; Died: 10/7/1965, Cotuit, MA; 1925 Providence Steam Roller: 1 Game, 0 Started.

McGoldrick played one game for the Steam Roller as a reserve in 1925. It was his only NFL appearance.

He played his college football at Lehigh.

McGuirk, Warren Pierce S.

Position: OT-DT; Height: 5'11"; Weight: 200; High School: Dorchester (Boston, MA), St. Anselm Prep (Manchester, NH); College: Boston College; Born: 1/2/1906, Boston, MA; Died: 2/19/1981, Boston, MA; 1929 Providence Steam Roller: 12 Games, 10 Started; 1930 Providence Steam Roller: 11 Games, 8 Started.

McGuirk played two seasons with the Steam Roller and was the team's starting right tackle, appearing in 23 games. Those were his only seasons in the NFL. He left the Steam Roller after the 1930 season when he was named the head football coach and director of physical education at Malden High School, a position he served until 1942.

McGuirk played his college football at Boston College as a tackle and was the captain of the Eagles' 1928 undefeated team. He also played on the 1926 undefeated Boston College squad. He was named All-American following his senior season. McGuirk joined the war effort in 1942, leaving his position at Malden High School. He served in the United States Navy, earning the rank of commander before his discharge in 1946.

McGuirk was appointed the athletics director at the University of Massachusetts (Amherst) in 1948, a post he occupied until his retirement on January 1, 1972. During his more than three-decade tenure, he made improvements in facilities, curriculum and intramural programs at the school. He was instrumental in the construction of the Women's Physical Education Building, the Boyden Building and the football stadium. McGuirk was a member of the NCAA Television Committee from 1954 to 1959. At one time he was president of the Eastern College Athletic Conference and the US Olympic Committee. In 1980 he was enshrined in the UMass Hall of Fame.

The Warren McGuirk Alumni Stadium at UMass is named in his honor. The stadium was dedicated on November 3, 1984.

McIntosh, Ira Daniel "Al"

Position: TB-WB-BB-DH; Height: 5'9"; Weight: 180; High School: Technical (Providence, RI); College: Rhode Island; Born: 4/12/1903, Providence, RI; Died: 10/13/1973, CA; 1925 Providence Steam Roller: 9 Games, 7 Started; 1926 Providence Steam Roller: 2 Games, 0 Started.

McIntosh played nine games for the Steam Roller during its inaugural season of 1925 and two games for the franchise in 1926. Those were his only NFL games. He was also with Providence in 1924 and was part of that championship team. McIntosh played college football at the University of Rhode Island and lettered two seasons, 1922 and 1923.

McIntosh served as the head football coach at Lake Forest College from 1929 to 1932, compiling an 11-11-6 overall record. He then coached at Northern Arizona University from 1933 to 1935, with his team winning the Border Conference title in 1933. After leaving Northern Arizona, he became head football coach at Swarthmore in 1936 and his teams finished 4-9-1 over two seasons. His overall coaching record at the three schools was 24-29-11. McIntosh was also the head basketball coach at Lake Forest from 1929 to 1932, tallying a mark of 16-30.

Meeker, Herbert Lawrence "Butch"

Position: QB-S-OH-DH-FB-LB; Height: 5'3"; Weight: 145; High School: Lewis & Clark (Spokane, WA); College: Washington State; Born: 3/19/1905, Washington; Died: 12/28/1960, Seattle, WA; 1930 Providence Steam Roller: 11 Games, 3 Started, 2 TDs, 1 Extra Point, 1 Field Goal, 16 Total Points; 1931 Providence Steam Roller: 9 Games, 3 Started, 1 Extra Point.

Meeker played two seasons with the Steam Roller, appearing in 20 games. He scored two touchdowns in 1930, one on a 17-yard pass reception from Frosty Peters that helped to spark the Steam Roller to a 14–0 victory over Newark, and his second was an electrifying 95-yard kickoff return to open the game against Frankford on November 9 that ended in a 7–7 tie.

Meeker played his college football at Washington State, where he lettered for three seasons. He is most remembered for his outstanding play in leading the Cougars to a 17–12 upset victory over the University of Southern California in 1925. He was named first-team all-conference quarterback later that season. Meeker set season and career records as a dropkicker and was considered an excellent broken-field runner. At the conclusion of his outstanding three-year career at WSU, he was chosen to play in the East-West Shrine Game and he turned in a memorable performance, thrilling the crowd with his kick returns. Meeker graduated from Washington State with a degree in journalism and for many years he worked in the newspaper industry. He was then involved in the retail meat business with his brother, working as a butcher.

In 1927, the Washington State mascot was named in his honor and still carries the name "Butch" to this day. Meeker was enshrined in the Washington State Honor Hall of Fame in 1978.

Miller, Donald Charles "Don"

Position: WB-DH; Height: 5'11"; Weight: 170; High School: Defiance (Defiance, OH); College: Notre Dame; Born: 3/29/1902, Defiance, OH; Died: 7/28/1979, Cleveland, OH; 1925 Providence Steam Roller: 1 Game, 1 Started.

Miller played one game for the Steam Roller in 1925. He joined fellow Notre Dame alumnus Jim Crowley for Providence's game against Red Grange and the Chicago Bears. Providence won the game 9–6 with Miller contributing some important runs during the game. It was his only NFL game. Miller also played part of the 1925 season with the Hartford Blues, who at the time were an independent team.

Miller was one of the famed "Four Horsemen" at the University of Notre Dame under coach Knute Rockne. Miller was a speedy halfback and he played under the tutelage of Rockne from 1922 to 1924. He teamed with quarterback Harry Stuhldreher, halfback Jim Crowley and fullback Elmer Layden to lead Rockne's troops to a 29-2-1 record during that span, which was capped by a 1925 Rose Bowl win over Stanford University to give Notre Dame the college football championship. Their dominant performances on the field as a collective unit inspired sportswriter Grantland Rice to give them their now legendary nickname. Miller was inducted into the College Football Hall of Fame in 1970.

In high school, Miller was a substitute player and nobody foresaw his rise to become a star in college football. Rockne was even surprised that Miller came out for football. "With his fleetness and daring, he quickly sized up as a halfback to cheer the heart of any coach," Rockne later admitted. "Once in the open field, he was the most dangerous of the Four Horsemen. I would have to call him the greatest open-field runner I ever had."[10] Miller's churning, high-knee action made him extremely difficult to bring down. For his three-year college career, Miller averaged 6.8 yards per carry and he rushed for 1,933 yards. He was also the Irish's leading pass receiver each of the three seasons with a total of 31 receptions for 590 yards. Miller was an All-American selection in 1923. He also was a basketball letterman and president of his senior class.

Miller served as an assistant coach at Georgia Tech and then Ohio State. He was also the head coach at St. Xavier High School in Louisville, Kentucky. Miller then left the football world and became a judge in Cleveland, Ohio.

Mishel, David F. "Dave"

Position: HB-TB-DH-WB-S; Height: 5'9"; Weight: 182; High School: Classical (Lynn, MA); College: Brown; Born: 7/6/1905, Lynn, MA; Died: 3/11/1975, Boston, MA; 1927 Providence Steam Roller: 4 Games, 3 Started.

Mishel played part of one season for the Steam Roller, appearing in four games in 1927. He signed with Providence in mid-November and made his debut on November 20 in a 22-0 loss to the Cleveland Bulldogs. Mishel also played for the Cleveland Indians in 1931 and was an assistant coach for the 2-8 team. He played in six games for the Tribe and scored an extra point.

He played his collegiate football at Brown, lettering in two seasons, 1925 and 1926.

Mishel was considered one of the driving forces behind the success of the undefeated Brown Iron Men of 1926. He was a superb player in every department of the game. Mishel ranked with Benny Friedman of Michigan as one of the nation's finest collegiate passers in the decade of the 1920s. He was also a dependable dropkicker, excellent runner (he had 132 yards rushing in the first half against New Hampshire in 1926) and an aggressive defensive man and blocker. He led the Iron Men in scoring with 51 points on four touchdowns, 18 conversions and three field goals. Mishel dominated the offense in the three big victories that year. He completed 5 of 9 passes for 76 yards in the 7-0 upset of Yale; threw a touchdown pass to Red Randall, kicked the extra point and added a field goal as the Bears defeated Dartmouth, 10-0; and had two more touchdown passes as Brown whipped Harvard, 21-0.

He set two school records while at Brown—the longest touchdown pass (66 yards to Capt. Jim Stifler vs. Bates in 1925) and the most passes thrown in one game (22 with 11 completions vs. Dartmouth in 1925). Mishel was a smart, cocky and inspirational-type player. He was named an All-American in 1926.

Following his football career, Mishel was an assistant coach at Brown and Boston University, where he earned a master's degree in education. For 42 years, he was director of Camp Brunonia in Casco, Maine, that he founded. Mishel was enshrined in the Brown University Athletic Hall of Fame in 1972.

Non-Providence Stats

1931—Cleveland Indians: 6 Games, 3 Started.

O'Connell, John Grattan "Grat"

Position: OE-DE; Height: 5'11"; Weight: 185; High School: Bristol Central (Bristol, CT), Dean Academy (Franklin, MA); College: Boston College; Born: 10/27/1902, Thomaston, CT; Died: 3/14/1942, Simsbury, CT; 1927 Providence Steam Roller: 2 Games, 2 Started.

O'Connell started two games for the Steam Roller in 1927, the only games he played for the team. He played most of the 1927 season for the independent Hartford Blues and led them to the football championship of Hartford. Prior to coming to Providence, he played for the NFL version of the Hartford Blues in 1926. He scored his only career touchdown on an interception return that helped spur the Blues to a 16-7 victory over the Canton Bulldogs on November 7.

O'Connell was head coach of the independent Hartford Blues in 1940 and 1941. He led them to an overall 18-4-2 record.

He played his college football at Boston College. While at BC, he started every game of his four-year football career with the Eagles. He once blocked six kicks in a five-game span. He also earned All-American honors during his junior year. In addition to football, he also was a formidable player for the school's basketball team.

O'Connell was a cartoonist and contributed to *The Heights* while at Boston College. Following his professional football career, he was a sportswriter for the *Hartford Courant* for more than 10 years. He also was a football official in his spare time.

While a lifeguard in the summer of 1927, he saved the life of a drowning woman in his hometown of Bristol, Connecticut.

In 1971, he was inducted into the Boston College Varsity Club Athletic Hall of Fame.

Non-Providence Stats

1926—Hartford Blues: 10 Games, 10 Started, 1 TD, 6 Total Points.

Oden, Olof Gustave Hazard "Curly"

Position: TB-BB-WB-S-DH-HB-LB-FB-QB; Height: 5'6"; Weight: 163; High School: Classical (Providence, RI); College: Brown; Born: 5/10/1899, Stockholm, Sweden; Died: 8/31/1978, Cranston, RI; 1925 Providence Steam Roller: 8 Games, 7 Started; 1926 Providence Steam Roller: 13 Games, 12 Started, 10 TDs, 60 Total Points; 1927 Providence Steam Roller: 13 Games, 11 Started, 2 TDs, 12 Total Points; 1928 Providence Steam Roller: 11 Games, 9 Started, 4 TDs, 3 Extra Points, 27 Total Points; 1930 Providence Steam Roller: 10 Games, 6 Started, 1 TD Pass, 1 Extra Point, 1 Total Point; 1931 Providence Steam Roller: 11 Games, 4 Started, 1 TD, 1 TD Pass, 6 Total Points.

Oden played for the Steam Roller from 1925 through the 1931 season, with the exception of 1929. He holds team records for most points with 106 and most touchdowns with 17, and he is second in games played with 66 and seasons played with six. Oden led the team in scoring with 60 points in 1926, including a three-touchdown effort against the Canton Bulldogs. That same season he scored both touchdowns in the Steam Roller's 13–0 opening-day victory over Brooklyn; he scored two touchdowns in a 19–0 win over Columbus; and he scored both touchdowns in a 14–0 win over Pottsville.

Oden was second on the team in scoring in 1928 with 27 points, highlighted by a 46-yard pass-reception touchdown for the only score in a 6–0 win over Frankford, and he scored the tying touchdown on a 23-yard pass reception against Green Bay. That game ended in a 7–7 tie and ensured the Steam Roller would be NFL champions. Oden was named second-team All-Pro in both 1926 and 1928. He played on the Steam Roller's 1928 NFL championship team. He once held the NFL record for most return touchdowns, with four punt returns and one kickoff return for a total of five. He played a single game for the Boston Braves before retiring from the NFL in 1932.

Oden also played for the Steam Roller prior to the team joining the NFL from 1921 to 1924 and was part of the 1924 team that was the mythical Northeast champion. That was the squad that set the stage for Providence to join the NFL in 1925. While playing professional football, he also played baseball for Falmouth of the Cape Cod League from 1926 to 1928. He was an all-league shortstop and also managed the squad in 1927 and 1928. In addition, Oden played professional hockey for the Rhode Island Reds.

Oden attended Classical High School in Providence, where he captained the school's ice hockey team in 1917 and remained a fixture in Rhode Island hockey throughout the 1920s. He played college football, baseball and hockey at Brown University. Oden, who weighed only 160 pounds, was described by Brown University as "a dancing, shifting runner with good speed, Oden electrified the fans ... with his broken field runs. As a senior the Bruin signal caller scored eight touchdowns and passed for five."[11] His 85-yard return of an intercepted pass against Springfield is the fifth longest in Brown history. Oden was also an outstanding college baseball player while at Brown. He was an excellent fielding shortstop and timely hitter. He had a tryout with the Brooklyn Dodgers. Oden also played hockey and was a member of an independent ice polo team that won the championship of New England.

In the 1930s, he served for four years on the Providence City Council. Oden went to work for the state of Rhode Island in 1941 and served 25 years as an investigator in the state attorney general's office.

He graduated from Brown in 1921, was a World War I Army veteran and was inducted into the university's Athletic Hall of Fame in 1971.

Non-Providence Stats
1932—Boston Braves: 1 Game, 0 Started.

Pape, Oran Henry "Nanny"

Position: OH-DH-QB-S; Height: 5'11"; Weight: 180; High School: Dubuque (Dubuque, IA); College: Iowa; Born: 3/10/1904, Waupeton, IA;

Died: 4/30/1936, Muscatine, IA; 1931 Providence Steam Roller: 11 Games, 7 Started, 3 TDs, 18 Total Points.

Pape played one season with the Steam Roller, appearing in 11 games and scoring three touchdowns. All three touchdowns came in a single game that Providence lost, 48–20, to the Green Bay Packers on October 25. Prior to coming to Providence, he played for the Packers and Minneapolis Red Jackets in 1930. Pape was part of Green Bay's 1930 NFL championship team. He scored his first NFL touchdown for the Minneapolis Red Jackets on a 78-yard run in a 7–7 tie with the Chicago Cardinals. After leaving the Steam Roller, he caught on with the Staten Island Stapletons and played with the Boston Braves in 1932 before retiring from the NFL. He scored his final NFL touchdown on a 90-yard kickoff return for the Braves.

After retiring from football, Pape attended the State Police Academy at Camp Dodge and was appointed to the newly formed Iowa Highway Patrol in August 1935. On April 28, 1936, Pape pulled a car over that had reportedly been stolen. As Pape approached the car, the driver, Roscoe Barton, pointed his gun at Pape and ordered him into his car. Barton drove away with Pape as his hostage. The two engaged in a scuffle, and during the melee, Pape was shot in the abdomen and Barton in the head. Barton died instantly. Pape survived for a brief time but died from his wounds the following day. He became the first Iowa State Patrol officer killed in the line of duty.

His badge number, 40, was retired from service and the I-80 bridge over the Cedar River in Cedar County, Iowa, was named in his honor the "Trooper Oran Pape Memorial Bridge."[12]

Non-Providence Stats

1930—Green Bay Packers: 2 Games, 1 Started.
1930—Minneapolis Red Jackets: 6 Games, 3 Started, 2 TDs, 12 Total Points.
1932—Staten Island Stapletons: 2 Games, 0 Started, Rushing: 6–12–0, Passing 1–7–1 TD, 1 Int., 26 yards.
1932—Boston Braves: 5 Games, 0 Started, Rushing: 9–148–0, Passing 1–2–0 TD, 1 Int., 5 Yards Passing, Scoring: 1 TD, 6 Total Points.

Pearce, Walter Irvin "Pard"

Position: BB-S; Height: 5'5"; Weight: 150; High School: Classical (Providence, RI), Morris Heights Prep (Morris Heights, NJ); College: Pennsylvania; Born: 10/23/1896, Providence, RI; Died: 5/24/1974, Newport, RI; 1925 Providence Steam Roller: 8 Games, 1 Started.

Pearce played his final year in the NFL with the Steam Roller during its inaugural 1925 NFL season. He appeared in eight games with Providence. Pearce began his NFL career in 1920 with the Decatur Staleys, who became the Chicago Staleys in 1921 and won the APFA championship. Then they were renamed the Bears in 1922, while the league was christened the NFL. Pearce played a key role for the team through those years, appearing in 32 games and scoring three touchdowns. He played part of one season for the Kenosha Maroons before joining the Steam Roller in 1925.

Pearce played for the independent pro Steam Roller team in its inaugural season of 1916 and appeared in the first-ever game and scored the franchise's second-ever touchdown. He also played for that rendition of the franchise in 1917 and again in 1923. Pard entered the Wharton School at the University of Pennsylvania in the fall of 1917 and played freshman baseball the following spring. He joined the navy on July 27, 1918, as World War I was winding down. Pearce was discharged in January 1919.

That spring, he played baseball for the Rockford Rox of the Three I baseball league, but he played under the name Dwyer to protect his college eligibility. In the fall of 1919, he returned to Penn and played halfback on the varsity football team. However, just before Thanksgiving, it was discovered that Pearce had played baseball for money and he was ruled ineligible to play any sports at Penn. He dropped out of school. Pearce attended the Cubs' spring training camp in 1920 but was cut and rejoined Rockford, playing 129 games. Later that summer, he joined up with George Halas and played on the Decatur Staley factory baseball team.

Pearce then joined the Staley football team with Halas in the fall of 1920. During the next few years, Pearce would balance professional football and baseball. He played sparingly for Reading, Pennsylvania, and Rochester, New York, in the International League in 1921, joined Sacramento of the Pacific Coast League for the 1922 baseball season and then played two years with Salt Lake City in the PCL.

After playing for the Steam Roller, he stayed in Providence and continued to play semipro baseball, officiated sporting events and became a teacher. He served as football and baseball coach at Pawtucket, Rhode Island, East High School in the 1930s, then was a physical education teacher at North Attleboro, Massachusetts, and finally in 1944 was a coach and teacher at Providence Central High School until his retirement in 1965.

Pearce served as president of the Rhode Island Football officials organization and in 1965 was awarded the association's trophy "for service to Rhode Island schoolboy football."[13] He retired from football officiating just after turning 77 years old and collapsed and died while umpiring a high school baseball game on May 24, 1974.

Non-Providence Stats

1920—Decatur Staleys: 13 Games, 8 Started.
1921—Chicago Staleys: 11 Games, 8 Started, 2 TDs, 12 Total Points.
1922—Chicago Bears: 8 Games, 1 Started, 1 TD, 6 Total Points.
1924—Kenosha Maroons: 2 Games, 1 Started.

Peters, Forrest Ingman "Frosty"

Position: QB-S-OH-DH; Height: 5'10"; Weight: 183; High School: Billings (Billings, MT); College: Montana State, Illinois; Born: 4/22/1904, Creston, IA; Died: 4/17/1980, Decatur, IL; 1930 Providence Steam Roller: 12 Games, 8 Started, 2 TDs, 2 TD Passes, 7 Extra Points, 2 Field Goals, 25 Total Points.

Peters played one season with the Steam Roller, in 1930. He led the squad in scoring with 25 points. His two touchdowns were both scored against the Frankford Yellow Jackets in the two games between the teams. The highlight was his 40-yard interception return that helped the Roller win 14–0 on October 1. Peters also threw two touchdown passes while with Providence, one a key 17-yarder to Butch Meeker in a 14–0 win over Newark. He finished the 1930 season by playing three games for Portsmouth. Peters played two more seasons in the NFL. In 1932, he was with the Brooklyn Dodgers and in 1933 with the Chicago Cardinals. In 1932 and 1933, he also played for the independent Memphis Tigers. Peters stayed one more season with Memphis after they joined the AFL, and he was named second-team All-League quarterback in 1934. Peters also contributed 12 points kicking. In 1933 and 1934, he also coached the Tigers and led them to an overall 10-8-3 record.

Peters started his college football career at Montana State in 1924, and he converted 17 dropkicks for field goals in a game between the Bobcats' freshman team and Billings Poly Institute. Peters also made 15 dropkicks in another game. Montana State athletic director Schubert Dyche said, "We agreed that every time we got inside the 30-yard line, Frosty would drop kick one."[14]

Peters transferred to play for the University of Illinois in 1925. He joined the varsity in 1926 and played three seasons, lettering in each. Peters played in the 1930 East-West Shrine football game and he drop-kicked two field goals and an extra point in the East's 19–7 victory. In addition to football, he participated in track and field and he helped lead Illinois to the outdoor track and field national championship as a member of the 1927 team.

In 1931, Peters switched sports and played minor league baseball from 1931 to 1936 for teams in San Antonio, Memphis and St. Louis. Peters attended the George Barr umpire school in Hot Springs, Arkansas, in the mid–1930s and then spent time as a baseball umpire, serving in the Florida State League and the American Association from 1938 to 1946. Peters interrupted his umpiring career to serve in World War II and became a sergeant. After returning from the war, he resumed his umpiring career until he was assaulted in an American Association game in 1946. He resigned following the incident and said, "When an umpire gets socked and they fine the guy only $100 and five days, it's an open invitation for everybody in the league to start punching you around."[15]

Non-Providence Stats
1930—Portsmouth Spartans: 3 Games, 2 Started.
1932—Brooklyn Dodgers: 9 Games, 5 Started, 1 TD Pass, 2 Extra Points, 2 Total Points.
1933—Chicago Cardinals: 1 Game, 1 Started.

Pierotti, Albert Felix "Al"

Position: C-MG-OG-DG-OT-DT; Height: 5'10"; Weight: 204; High School: Everett (Everett, MA); College: Washington & Lee; Born: 10/24/1895, Boston, MA; Died: 2/12/1964, Revere, MA; 1927 Providence Steam Roller: 14 Games, 11 Started.

Pierotti played one season with the Steam Roller, appearing in 14 games during the 1927 season. That was his single-season career high. He began his NFL career in 1920 with Akron, and later that season he was player-coach of the Cleveland Tigers, steering Cleveland to a 2–2–1 record. Pierotti continued his NFL career in 1921 with the New York Brickley Giants, and then he played three seasons with the Milwaukee Badgers from 1922 through 1924. Along the way, he played one game in 1923 for Racine Legion. In 1926, Pierotti played in the AFL for the Boston Bulldogs, and when the league folded he joined the semipro University of Peabody. Pierotti returned to the NFL with Providence, and then after his year with the Steam Roller he played one final NFL season with the Boston Bulldogs in 1929.

Prior to playing professional football, Pierotti played his college football at Washington & Lee, lettering all four years he played at the school. He coached football for one year (1918) at Tufts, where his team had a 2–3 record.

Pierotti also played professional baseball and began his career in 1919 with the minor league Providence Grays of the Eastern League, where he compiled a 2-3 pitching record. The following season, he joined the Boston Braves of the National League and appeared in six games, achieving a 1-1 record and 2.88 ERA. He pitched two more games for the Braves the following season but was 0-1 with a 21.60 ERA and was demoted to Pittsfield in the Eastern League. Pierotti had a stellar season with the Hillies, winning 21 games and losing only 7. After one more baseball season, split between Pittsfield and the Waterbury Brasscos, Pierotti determined his future was in football and returned to that game full-time.

In 1931, Pierotti began a wrestling career. On July 30, 1931, he challenged Jim Londos for the World Heavyweight Championship at the Coney Island Velodrome. Londos defeated Pierotti in 17:05 with an airplane spin. In 1932, Pierotti began refereeing matches at the Boston Arena while continuing to wrestle occasionally. He became an assistant football coach at Chelsea High School in 1935 and the following year he became head coach of the school's baseball team. Pierotti remained at Chelsea High School as a teacher and baseball coach until his death on February 12, 1964.

Non-Providence Stats

1920—Akron Pros: 1 Game, 0 Started.
1920—Cleveland Tigers: 5 Games, 3 Started, Head Coach, 2-2-1.
1921—New York Brickley Giants: 2 Games, 2 Started.
1922—Milwaukee Badgers: 9 Games, 9 Started.
1923—Milwaukee Badgers: 3 Games, 3 Started.
1923—Racine Legion: 1 Game, 0 Started.
1924—Milwaukee Badgers: 4 Games, 2 Started.
1929—Boston Bulldogs: 7 Games, 6 Started.

Pohlman, John Theodore

Position: FB-LB; Height: 5'9"; Weight: 178; High School: New Haven (New Haven, CT); College: Brown; Born: 9/18/1902, New Haven, CT; Died: 5/8/1957, Milford, CT; 1925 Providence Steam Roller: 2 Games, 0 Started.

Pohlman played two games for the Steam Roller's inaugural season of 1925 and that was all for his NFL career.

He lettered for two years in football at Brown, in 1923 and 1924.

Pollard, Frederick Douglass "Fritz"

Position: TB-WB-DH; Height: 5'9"; Weight: 165; High School: Lane Tech (Chicago, IL); College: Bates, Brown; Born: 1/27/1894, Chicago, IL;

Died: 5/11/1986, Silver Spring, MD; 1925 Providence Steam Roller: 4 Games, 0 Started.

Pollard played part of one season with the Steam Roller, appearing in four games in 1925. He joined Providence at the conclusion of the Akron Pros season, which ended on Thanksgiving. The Roller was 1–2–1 in the games Pollard played, which included a 9–6 victory over Red Grange and the Chicago Bears. He also was an assistant coach for the 1917 independent pro Outland Company Steam Roller that finished with a 5–3–1 record.

Pollard began his professional football career in 1919 with the Akron Pros, which joined the new American Professional Football Association in 1920. Two years later, the league was renamed the NFL, making Pollard and Bobby Marshall the first two Black players in the NFL. He helped lead the Pros to an 8–0–3 record in 1920 to capture the first league championship. He was named a first-team All-Pro. In 1921, Pollard was named co-coach and thus became the first Black head coach in the NFL. He led the Pros to a 9–3–1 record while scoring seven touchdowns.

Pollard was an elusive, dynamic running back and was considered among the best in the NFL. Legendary coach Walter Camp said that Pollard is "one of the greatest runners these eyes have ever seen."[16] Pollard played four additional seasons in the NFL with four different teams, including the Steam Roller. Following the 1926 season, the nine Black players playing in the NFL at that time were expelled from the league, never to return. During his NFL years, Pollard also mixed in playing in Pennsylvania coal country. In 1923 and 1924, he played in the Anthracite League with the Gilberton Catamounts, serving as player-coach the first season. He then

Fritz Pollard, Providence Steam Roller back (1925) (author's collection).

returned in 1926, when the Catamounts played in the Eastern League. Pollard then finished his stint in Pennsylvania playing for the Bethlehem Bears in 1927. He was a league All-Star in both 1924 and 1926.

In 1935, Pollard, along with Harlem promoter Herschel "Rip" Day, founded the New York Brown Bombers. Pollard was a player-coach for the team until 1938, when he decided to leave the squad, and that ended his football-playing career.

Pollard, a star halfback at Brown University in 1915, led the Bruins to the first Rose Bowl against Washington State. In 1916, he returned and helped Brown finish with an 8–1 record. He starred in wins over Yale and Harvard on back-to-back weekends. Pollard had 294 all-purpose yards in the 21–6 win over Yale, including 144 rushing, and in the 21–0 win over Harvard, he contributed 243 all-purpose yards, including 148 rushing. His 12 touchdowns in 1916 are still a Brown school record for most in a single season. At the conclusion of the season, he was the first Black player named to the Walter Camp All-American team.

After his football career ended, Pollard worked in a talent agency, did some tax consulting and engaged in film and music production. He produced *Rockin' the Blues* in 1956. Pollard also published the *New York Independent News* from 1935 to 1942, purportedly the first Black-owned tabloid in New York City. He was enshrined in the Brown University Athletic Hall of Fame in 1971. He was also named to the 125th Anniversary Brown University team in 2003.

Non-Providence Stats

1920—Akron Pros: 11 Games, 9 Started.
1921—Akron Pros: 12 Games, 11 Started, 7 TDs, 42 Total Points, Head Coach, 9–3–1.
1922—Milwaukee Badgers: 7 Games, 5 Started, 3 TDs, 2 Extra Points, 20 Total Points.
1923—Hammond Pros: 2 Games, 2 Started, 1 Extra Point, 1 Total Point.
1925—Akron Pros: 8 Games, 5 Started, 2 TDs, 12 Total Points.
1925—Hammond Pros: 1 Game, 0 Started, Head Coach, 0–1.
1926—Akron Pros: 4 Games, 4 Started.

Pope, Lewis Lawrence "Lew"

Position: OH-DH-QB-S; Height: 6'0"; Weight: 196; High School: Frederick (Frederick, OK); College: Purdue; Born: 2/18/1908, West Lafayette, IN; Died: 2/5/1964, Unknown; 1931 Providence Steam Roller: 8 Games, 3 Started.

Pope played the final season of the Steam Roller's run in the NFL, appearing in eight games in 1931. After leaving Providence, he played two seasons with the Cincinnati Reds. The highlight of his NFL career was a 48-yard game-winning touchdown run in a 12-9 win over the Chicago Cardinals on November 12, 1933. He also played for the Tulsa Oilers of the AFL in 1934.

Pope played collegiately at Purdue, where he was a halfback in 1929 and 1930.

He joined his father, Marion, in the grocery business at Pope Mills, New York, following his football career.

Non-Providence Stats

1933—Cincinnati Reds: 10 Games, 10 Started, Rushing: 56-179-1 TD, Receiving: 1-20-0, Passing: 5-21-0 TDs, 2 Int., 115 yards, Scoring: 1 TD, 6 Total Points.

1934—Cincinnati Reds: 8 Games, 5 Started, Rushing: 40-163-0, Receiving: 1-17-0, Passing: 10-42-0 TDs, 10 Int., 115 yards.

Pritchard, William England "Bill"

Position: FB-LB-HB-DH; Height: 5'10"; Weight: 185; High School: South Park (Buffalo, NY); College: Penn State; Born: 12/23/1901, Frostburg, MD; Died: 4/10/1978, Buffalo, NY; 1927 Providence Steam Roller: 12 Games, 9 Started, 1 TD, 3 Extra Points, 9 Total Points.

Pritchard played one season with the Steam Roller, appearing in 12 games. He scored the first Providence touchdown of the 1927 season—a one-yard run against the Dayton Triangles on October 23. He also booted the extra point and scored all seven points in the Steam Roller's 7-0 victory. After leaving Providence, he played one season with the New York Yankees and scored his only touchdown on a 52-yard pass reception from Billy Kelly in a 14-0 win over Frankford on October 13, 1928.

He played his college football at Penn State, lettering in 1925 and 1926. He also played lacrosse for the Nittany Lions. After retiring from the NFL, he returned to his hometown of Buffalo, New York, and played for several semiprofessional clubs in western New York. He also was an assistant football coach at the University of Buffalo and took over as head coach for the 1931 season, leading the Bulls to a 2-6 record.

After his stint as a coach at UB, he became a teacher and principal in the Buffalo Public School system for 35 years. Pritchard taught from 1932 to 1950 before becoming a principal. He was principal of the Fosdick-Masten

Vocational High School from 1956 to 1962 and Seneca Vocational High School from 1962 until his retirement in 1967. Pritchard also officiated football games for high schools, colleges and the All-America Football Conference.

Non-Providence Stats

1928—New York Yankees: 13 Games, 11 Started, 1 TD, 1 Extra Point, 7 Total Points.

Pyne, Jr., George Francis

Position: OT-DT; Height: 5'11"; Weight: 218; High School: Milford (Milford, MA); College: Holy Cross; Born: 10/17/1909, Marlboro, MA; Died: 6/3/1974, Milford, MA; 1931 Providence Steam Roller: 2 Games, 1 Started.

Pyne played two games for the Steam Roller during their final NFL season in 1931. It was Pyne's only NFL experience.

He played collegiately at Holy Cross and lettered for three seasons. His son George III played the 1965 season with the AFL's Boston Patriots and his grandson Jim played seven NFL seasons with Tampa Bay, Detroit, Cleveland and Philadelphia. Jim was the first overall choice of the Browns in the 1999 NFL expansion draft. The Pynes were the first family to have three generations play professional football.

He served in World War II with the army in the Philippines. He was a court officer at Milford, Connecticut, District Court for many years.

Racis, Frank J.

Position: OG-DG; Height: 6'0"; Weight: 200; High School: Shenandoah Valley (Shenandoah, PA); College: None; Born: 11/9/1899, Shenandoah, PA; Died: 8/19/1982, Shenandoah, PA; 1930 Providence Steam Roller: 11 Games, 6 Started, 1 TD, 6 Total Points.

Racis played one season with the Steam Roller, appearing in 11 games in 1930. He scored one touchdown with Providence on a 40-yard interception return that keyed a 9–7 win over the Chicago Cardinals on October 12. Prior to coming to the Steam Roller, Racis played four seasons for the Pottsville Maroons and helped lead them to the NFL title in 1925. However, the championship was stripped from the team due to a disputed violation of the rules and the title was awarded to the Chicago Cardinals. Racis was named a first-team All-Pro in 1926. He played for three other NFL teams and in 1929 was named a second-team All-Pro while playing with the Boston Bulldogs. Prior to playing in the NFL, he played minor league football from 1918 to 1924, highlighted by his time with the Shenandoah Yellow Jackets in the Anthracite League in 1923 and 1924. Following his NFL career, he played for and coached the Shenandoah Presidents, an independent team, from 1932 to 1936, winning several state championships.

He also excelled in baseball in the North Schuylkill League.

Racis was inducted into the Pennsylvania State Hall of Fame and was considered for induction into the Pro Football Hall of Fame with the endorsement of George Halas but was never elected.

Non-Providence Stats

1925—Pottsville Maroons: 12 Games, 11 Started.
1926—Pottsville Maroons: 14 Games, 14 Started, 1 TD, 6 Total Points.
1927—Pottsville Maroons: 13 Games, 13 Started, 1 TD, 6 Total Points.
1928—Pottsville Maroons: 10 Games, 10 Started.
1928—New York Yankees: 1 Game, 1 Started.
1929—Boston Bulldogs: 7 Games, 7 Started.
1931—Frankford Yellow Jackets: 8 Games, 7 Started.

Rehnquist, Milton E. "Milt"

Position: OG-DG-OT-DT-C-MG; Height: 6'0"; Weight: 229; High School: Smoky Valley (Lindsborg, KS); College: Bethany (Kansas); Born: 6/6/1897, Chicago, IL; Died: 2/5/1956, RI; 1928 Providence Steam Roller: 11 Games, 11 Started; 1929 Providence Steam Roller: 8 Games, 7 Started; 1930 Providence Steam Roller: 10 Games, 7 Started; 1931 Providence Steam Roller: 2 Games, 0 Started.

Rehnquist played four seasons with the Steam Roller and anchored the line. He was part of the 1928 NFL championship squad. He was a second-team All-Pro in 1928 and a first-teamer in 1929. His four seasons with the Steam Roller is the third-longest tenure in team history. Prior to coming to Providence, he played for three different NFL teams, highlighted by a second-team All-Pro season with the Cleveland Bulldogs in 1927. Rehnquist finished his NFL career playing with the New York Giants and Boston Braves.

He played his collegiate football at Bethany College in Kansas.

Rehnquist was a prison guard and finished his career as captain of the guards for the Rhode Island State Prison, a position he was serving at the time of his death.

Non-Providence Stats
1924—Kansas City Blues: 3 Games, 0 Started.
1925—Cleveland Bulldogs: 4 Games, 4 Started.
1925—Kansas City Cowboys: 7 Games, 5 Started.
1926—Kansas City Cowboys: 10 Games, 9 Started.
1927—Cleveland Bulldogs: 13 Games, 12 Started.
1931—New York Giants: 8 Games, 1 Started.
1932—Boston Braves: 1 Game, 0 Started.

Riopel, Albert Didace "Hop"

Position: TB-WB-DH; Height: 5'8"; Weight: 165; High School: Worcester Tech (Worcester, MA); College: Holy Cross; Born: 10/11/1900, Worcester, MA; Died: 9/4/1966, Worcester, MA; 1925 Providence Steam Roller: 4 Games, 1 Started.

Riopel played part of the Steam Roller's inaugural season, appearing in four games. It was his only NFL season.

He was a standout athlete at the College of the Holy Cross, playing football, basketball and baseball. He captained the 1923 football team as a running back. Riopel was known as a hustling guard in basketball and a solid hitter and excellent fielder on the diamond. He is the only athlete in Holy Cross history to earn 11 letters. The baseball team won 100 games during his four years, while the football team posted a 25-10-1 mark. His game-saving catch helped snap Boston College's 23-game baseball winning streak in 1923.

He taught at Milford High School from 1924 to 1933, and when he joined the school, Riopel spurned an opportunity to play professional baseball with the New York Giants or Yankees. From 1928 to 1932, he coached basketball at Assumption College. In 1933, he returned to Holy Cross as a freshman baseball, basketball and football coach. Riopel later became the athletic director at his alma mater, a position he held until his retirement in 1966. He also served as head basketball coach for four seasons and head baseball coach for six years. Riopel was enshrined in the Holy Cross Varsity Club Hall of Fame in 1957. Also, the school has a baseball award in his name given each year to the MVP of the Holy Cross baseball team.

Rose, Alfred Grady "Al"

Position: OE-DE; Height: 6'3"; Weight: 205; High School: Highland Park (Dallas, TX); College: Texas; Born: 1/26/1905, Temple, TX; Died:

10/1/1985, DePere, WI; 1930 Providence Steam Roller: 11 Games, 11 Started; 1931 Providence Steam Roller: 11 Games, 11 Started, 3 TDs, 1 TD Pass, 18 Total Points.

Rose played two seasons with the Steam Roller. In his second season with the team, he was named third-team All-Pro by the *Green Bay Gazette*. He was second on the Steam Roller in scoring with 18 points that year. Rose scored the only touchdowns in two of Providence's wins in 1931, an 18-yard pass reception from Curly Oden in a 6-0 win over Frankford and a 35-yard touchdown reception from Deck Shelley in a 7-0 win over Brooklyn. His third touchdown was scored on a blocked punt return. Rose also threw the game-winning touchdown pass of 16 yards to Herb Titmas in the Steam Roller's 13-7 win over Cleveland on November 21. That victory was the last in Steam Roller history.

After the demise of the Providence franchise, Rose caught on with the Green Bay Packers and he stayed with the Pack for the next five years. In his first season with Green Bay, he led the NFL with two non-offensive touchdowns as he scored on a blocked punt return and an interception return. When the Packers released him early in the 1936 season, Rose moved to the AFL's New York Yankees and played eight games for the 5-3-2 club.

Rose played collegiately at the University of Texas and lettered in football for three years.

Rose worked in the financial services industry and was a branch manager of CIT Financial Corporation when he retired in 1964. He was selected to the Texas Legion Hall of Honor in 1985.

Non-Providence Stats

1932—Green Bay Packers: 13 Games, 9 Started, Receiving: 1-20-0, Returns: 2 TDs, Scoring: 2 TDs, 12 Total Points.
1933—Green Bay Packers: 12 Games, 7 Started, Receiving: 6-89-1, Scoring: 1 TD, 12 Total Points.
1934—Green Bay Packers: 9 Games, 5 Started, Receiving: 6-117-2, Scoring: 2 TDs, 12 Total Points.
1935—Green Bay Packers: 12 Games, 7 Started, Receiving: 8-91-0.
1936—Green Bay Packers: 2 Games, 0 Started.

Samson, Seneca Gadsden

Position: TB-WB-S-DH; Height: 5'8"; Weight: 160; High School: Stuyvesant (New York, NY); College: Brown; Born: 11/10/1899, New York, NY; Died: 4/2/1930, Wakefield, RI; 1926 Providence Steam Roller: 2 Games, 1 Started.

Samson played two games for the 1926 edition of the Steam Roller. Those were the only games of Samson's NFL career.

He played his college football at Brown, where he lettered in 1919. Following his football career, he was engaged in the real estate and insurance business in New York before becoming part owner and manager of the Old Orchard Beach Hotel in Maine. Samson died on April 2, 1930, in an automobile accident.

Schein, Joseph "Joe"

Position: OT-DT; Height: 5'10"; Weight: 212; High School: South Side (Newark, NJ); College: Brown; Born: 11/11/1910, New York, NY; Died: 5/27/1969, Providence, RI; 1931 Providence Steam Roller: 11 Games, 11 Started.

Schein played one season with the Steam Roller, manning the right tackle spot for 11 starts in 1931. It was his only NFL season. He played for the Orange Tornadoes in 1934 in the New Jersey Circuit. He also played for the 1937 rendition of the Providence Steam Roller, an independent team that finished with a 1–3–5 record.

Schein played collegiately at Brown, where he lettered from 1928 to 1930 and made several All-American teams. Schein had the nickname "60-minute Joe"[17] because he almost never came out of a game. He also earned letters in basketball and lacrosse.

Schein began a teaching career in 1934 that he continued until his death in 1969. He was the founder of the Providence Teachers' Union and was an outspoken critic of the status quo in the local school system.

Scott, Robert C. "Bob"

Position: C-MG-OG-DG-OT-DT; Height: Unknown; Weight: 195; High School: Phil Campbell (Phil Campbell, AL); College: None; Born: 8/5/1895, Phil Campbell, AL; Died: 8/12/1973, Hamilton, AL; 1926 Providence Steam Roller: 6 Games, 1 Started.

Scott played one season with the Steam Roller, appearing in six games. It was his only NFL season.

He did not play college football.

Seyboth, Frank Cornelius

Position: BB-DH; Height: 5'9"; Weight: 180; High School: Attleboro (Attleboro, MA); College: Vermont; Born: 4/5/1904, Attleboro, MA;

Died: 4/30/1979, Attleboro, MA; 1926 Providence Steam Roller: 1 Game, 0 Started.

Seyboth played one game with the 1926 Steam Roller. It was his only NFL game. He was a coach of the Attleboro, Massachusetts, semipro team during a time in the mid-1920s. He also played for the 1923 version of the Steam Roller.

He played football collegiately at the University of Vermont in 1923. Seyboth also played minor league baseball from 1924 to 1928. He began his minor league career playing for the Parksley Spuds in the Eastern Shore League as an outfielder. During the next few years, he patrolled the outfield for the Durham Bulls in the Piedmont League and the Lynn Papooses and Nashua Millionaires in the New England League.

Seyboth was a longtime Major League Baseball scout after his playing days, working for the Kansas City Athletics, New York Giants and San Francisco Giants. He was the Giants' chief New England scout in the 1960s.

Share, Nathan Lewis "Nate"

Position: OG-DG; Height: 6'1"; Weight: 210; High School: Boston English (Boston, MA); College: Tufts; Born: 1904, New York; Died: 1/15/1950, Unknown; 1925 Providence Steam Roller: 10 Games, 10 Started.

Share was a starting guard for the Steam Roller's inaugural team in 1925. He started 10 games for the team. It was his only season playing in the NFL. In 1926, Nate played in the AFL for the Brooklyn Horsemen, appearing in two games. In 1927 and 1928, he played for the very successful independent Orange A.C. that compiled an 18-6-3 record in that span.

Share played his college football at Tufts University, where he lettered three consecutive years, from 1922 to 1924. He also played basketball at Tufts as a senior and was active in dramatics. After his professional sports career, he settled into a career in civil engineering until his death in 1950.

Sheehan, Frederic William "Fred"

Position: OG-DG; Height: 6'2"; Weight: 210; High School: Abington (Abington, MA); College: Georgetown (DC); Born: 12/21/1902, Abington, MA; Died: 9/2/1984, Boston, MA; 1925 Providence Steam Roller: 1 Game, 1 Started.

Sheehan started and played in only one game for the 1925 Steam Roller. It was his only NFL game.

Sheehan played his college football at Georgetown in Washington, DC, and captained the 1924 team that finished 4-4. He was outstanding in a 3-0 loss to the University of Pennsylvania and in a 20-0 victory over Furman. Sheehan joined the Georgetown football coaching staff in 1925 as line coach.

Following his football career, he became owner of the Granite City Cold Storage Warehouses in Quincy, Massachusetts. He joined the navy on December 8, 1941, a day after the attack on Pearl Harbor, and served in the Atlantic Theater and became a commander.

He was a director and first vice president of the Abington National Bank at the time of his death.

He was enshrined in the Georgetown Athletic Hall of Fame.

Shelley, Robert Pendexter
"Dexter or Deck"

Position: OH-DH-QB-S; Height: 5'11"; Weight: 191; High School: St. Mark's (Dallas, TX); College: Texas; Born: 6/4/1906, San Antonio, TX; Died: 12/17/1968, Temple, TX; 1931 Providence Steam Roller: 8 Games, 5 Started, 3 TD Passes, 4 Extra Points, 4 Total Points.

Shelley played one season with the Steam Roller, appearing in eight games. After coming over from Portsmouth early in the season, Shelley helped the Providence offense. He threw three touchdown passes and converted four extra points for the team. One of his touchdown passes was a 35-yard throw to Al Rose for the only score in the Steam Roller's 7-0 victory over Brooklyn on November 8, 1931. After the demise of the Providence franchise, Shelley played two games for the Chicago Cardinals and Green Bay Packers during the 1932 season. He also spent time with the independent Memphis Tigers in 1932.

He played his college football at the University of Texas and was an all-conference running back in 1928 and 1930 while leading the Longhorns to the Southwest Conference title both years. Shelley was a catalyst in the 1929 Texas vs. Oklahoma rivalry game by recovering an early fumble on defense and later scoring a rushing touchdown in the 21-0 Texas victory. He was the team captain in 1930. Shelley led the Longhorns in scoring in both 1929 and 1930. He played in the 1930 East-West Shrine Game. Shelley was enshrined in the University of Texas Sports Hall of Honor in 1968.

He coached high school football at Orange and Cisco High Schools before entering the insurance business. At the time of his death, he was employed by the Texas Education Agency.

Non-Providence Stats
1931—Portsmouth Spartans: 2 Games, 1 Started.
1932—Chicago Cardinals: 2 Games, 1 Started, Rushing: 5–11–0, Passing: 1–1–0 TDs, 0 Int., 3 yards.
1932—Green Bay Packers: 2 Games, 0 Started, Rushing 5–3–0.

Shockley, Arnold A. "Arnie"

Position: OG-DG-OT-DT; Height: 6'2"; Weight: 220; High School: Mountain View (Mountain View, OK); College: SW Oklahoma State; Born: 8/31/1903, McKinley Township, MO; Died: 4/27/1988, Lawton, OK; 1928 Providence Steam Roller: 10 Games, 7 Started; 1929 Providence Steam Roller: 7 Games, 5 Started; 1930 Providence Steam Roller: 10 Games, 5 Started.

Shockley played three seasons with the Steam Roller. He was part of the 1928 NFL championship team. Per Dick Reynolds's book *The Steam Roller Story*, "In 1927, Jimmy Conzelman heard of a lineman, named Perry Jackson, who had acquired a glowing reputation in the west as a superstar at Southwest State University in Oklahoma. When Conzelman cabled a tryout offer, Jackson was much too ill to be thinking of football. But his friend and teammate, Arnold Shockley, reported to Roller camp as Perry Jackson and played three years under the assumed name. In 1929, the real Perry Jackson, now quite recovered, tried out with the Roller under the name of Arnold Shockley. He was cut and played one season under his buddy's name for a Boston team."[18]

Shockley was an all-conference tackle in 1926 and 1927 for Southwest Oklahoma State. He teamed with Perry Jackson to help make the Bulldogs one of the most feared teams in the state. Following his professional football career, he went on to be a coach and administrator, working for more than 30 years in schools at Jackson, Greer and Kiowa Counties. He spent his last 13 years at Mountain High School before retiring in 1965. Shockley was elected to the SWOSU Alumni Association Athletic Hall of Fame in 1965.

Shurtleff, Bertrand Leslie "Bert"

Position: OG-DG-OT-DT; Height: 5'11"; Weight: 190; High School: East Greenwich Academy (East Greenwich, RI); College: Brown; Born: 8/3/1897, Adamsville, RI; Died: 2/15/1967, Anaheim, CA; 1925 Providence Steam Roller: 11 Games, 3 Started.

Shurtleff played for the Steam Roller during its inaugural season of 1925, appearing in 11 games. He had also played for Providence in 1923 and was part of the 1924 squad that won the mythical Northeast championship, before the team joined the NFL. Shurtleff also played one other season in the NFL, in 1929, with the Boston Bulldogs.

Shurtleff played his college football at Brown. He lettered two years as a tackle and in his senior season he switched to be the starting center, also lettering. He was quick at diagnosing plays and was an aggressive but clean tackler. During his football career, he never wore a helmet. Shurtleff also wrestled for four years at Brown and was the collegiate light-heavyweight champion. He went on to a professional wrestling career under the name "Mad Murdock."

Bert Shurtleff, Providence Steam Roller, center, guard (1925) (John Hay Library, Special Collections, Brown University).

He was the seventh of 10 children and was part of the US Naval Reserve Force stationed in Newport, Rhode Island, during World War I. Shurtleff became a published author and between 1938 and 1963 he published 14 books and wrote over 30 magazine articles. He also taught, coached, wrote poetry, lectured widely and attempted to break into the movies.

Shurtleff was enshrined in the Brown University Athletic Hall of Fame in 1971.

Non-Providence Stats

1929—Boston Bulldogs: 4 Games, 2 Started.

Simmons, James Ellington "Jim"

Position: WB-DH-TB-FB-LB-OT-DT; Height: 6'0"; Weight: 186; High School: Sentinel (Sentinel, OK); College: SW Oklahoma State; Born:

4/3/1903, Sentinel, OK; Died: 1/16/1977, Elmore City, OK; 1928 Providence Steam Roller: 8 Games, 4 Started.

Simmons played one season for the Steam Roller, its NFL championship year of 1928. He joined his college teammate Arnie Shockley on the Providence squad. Prior to coming to Providence, he played one season with the Cleveland Bulldogs. He scored five touchdowns for the 8-4-1 Bulldogs in 1927. Simmons scored the only touchdown on a one-yard plunge in a 6-0 victory over the New York Giants on October 16 and he scored the go-ahead touchdown in 30-19 win over the New York Yankees on November 24. Following his one season with the Steam Roller, he retired from football.

Simmons was known as "Mr. Basketball of Oklahoma" coming out of high school at Sentinel. He attended SW Oklahoma State and starred for the Bulldogs in baseball, basketball, football and track. He is most remembered for making a half-court buzzer-beating shot over rival Phillips to win the conference championship.

Following his pro football career, he coached basketball at Northeastern State University for seven years. He then coached at El Reno High School and won state championships in 1932, 1933, 1946, 1949 and 1953. The 1933 and 1949 teams were undefeated champions.

He was enshrined in the Southwestern Oklahoma State Athletic Hall of Fame in 1963.

Non-Providence Stats

1927—Cleveland Bulldogs: 12 Games, 6 Started, 5 TDs, 30 Total Points.

Smith, Clyde Wise

Position: C-MG; Height: 5'10"; Weight: 184; High School: Sapulpa (Sapulpa, OK); College: Missouri; Born: 7/17/1904, Steelville, MO; Died: 12/30/1982, Lawrenceville, IL; 1928 Providence Steam Roller: 11 Games, 11 Started.

Smith played one season with the Steam Roller. He was the starting center and middle guard on the 1928 NFL championship team and was named first-team All-Pro by the *Green Bay Gazette*. Prior to coming to Providence, Smith played three seasons of NFL football. He was named first-team All-Pro by the *Green Bay Gazette* in both 1926 with the Kansas City Cowboys and 1927 with the Cleveland Bulldogs.

He played collegiately at Missouri, where he lettered in football in 1922, 1923 and 1924 and was named to the 1924 All-American team at center. He was captain for one season, and his head coach, Gwinn Henry, called him "the greatest center Missouri ever had."[19]

Following his professional football career, Smith served as the head football coach at the College of Emporia from 1931 to 1934, compiling a record of 10-19-4. He later coached football at Bridgeport High School in Bridgeport, Illinois. He owned the Lawrenceville Greenhouses, was chairman of the Lawrence County Housing Authority and was a Lawrence County Chamber of Commerce board member. In 1976, Smith received the Civitan of the Year award presented by a service organization, Civitan International. His brother, Ray Smith, played for the Steam Roller in 1930-31.

Non-Providence Stats

1925—Kansas City Cowboys: 1 Game, 1 Started.
1926—Kansas City Cowboys: 9 Games, 7 Started.
1927—Cleveland Bulldogs: 12 Games, 12 Started.

Smith, Orland Francis

Position: OT-DT-OG-DG; Height: 5'11"; Weight: 215; High School: Brockton (Brockton, MA); College: Brown; Born: 11/5/1905, Gorham, MA; Died: 8/14/1977, Providence, RI; 1927 Providence Steam Roller: 13 Games, 9 Started; 1928 Providence Steam Roller: 9 Games, 2 Started; 1929 Providence Steam Roller: 10 Games, 4 Started.

Smith played three seasons with the Steam Roller, including the 1928 NFL championship year. While playing for the Steam Roller, Smith was attending medical school at Boston University. His three years with Providence were his only NFL seasons.

Orland Smith, Providence Steam Roller, tackle, guard (1927-1929) (John Hay Library, Special Collections, Brown University).

He played his college football at Brown, where he lettered in 1924, 1925 and 1926. Smith played offensive guard and defensive tackle on the undefeated Iron Men of 1926. He was selected to Grantland Rice's All-American team in 1926 as well as several wire services teams. He was an extremely competitive player. As his Brown coach, Tuss McLaughry, said about him, "He always went for the jugular."[20]

He was enshrined in the Brown University Athletic Hall of Fame in 1971. In addition, he was named to the 125th Anniversary Brown University team in 2003.

Smith, Raymond Henry "Ray"

Position: C-MG; Height: 5'10"; Weight: 195; High School: Sapulpa (Sapulpa, OK); College: Tulsa, Missouri; Born: 8/27/1908, MO; Died: 5/1984, Tulsa, OK; 1930 Providence Steam Roller: 10 Games, 7 Started; 1931 Providence Steam Roller: 10 Games, 10 Started.

Smith played two seasons with the Steam Roller, including their final season in the NFL in 1931. He played one game for the Philadelphia Eagles in 1933 that ended his NFL career. He held down the center spot for most of those two seasons with Providence. Smith played collegiately at Missouri and lettered in 1928 and 1929 for the Tigers.

His brother, Clyde Smith, was a member of the 1928 NFL champion Steam Roller squad.

Non-Providence Stats

1933—Philadelphia Eagles: 1 Game, 0 Started.

Smyth, Louie Lehman "Hammer," "Lou"

Position: WB-DH; Height: 6'1"; Weight: 200; High School: Sherman (Sherman, TX); College: Texas, Centre; Born: 3/19/1898, Cleburne, TX; Died: 9/11/1964, Long Beach, CA; 1926 Providence Steam Roller: 3 Games, 3 Started.

Smyth played three games for the Steam Roller in 1926, at the end of his seven-year NFL career. Prior to coming to Providence, he played with four NFL teams. He spent four years with the Canton Bulldogs, including the 1922 and 1923 NFL championship teams. He was a bruising runner and an adept passer. Smyth scored his first career touchdown on a one-yard dive on November 24, 1921, in a 14–0 victory over Akron. Three days later, he scored another rushing touchdown and also threw his first touchdown pass, a 10-yarder to Harry Robb in a 15-0 win over the Washington Senators. His best season came in 1923, when he scored seven touchdowns and threw six touchdown passes for the champion Bulldogs. He led the NFL in touchdowns scored and touchdown passes and tied Conzelman's record of most touchdown passes in a season. Smyth was named a first-team All-Pro by the *Canton Daily News*.

In 1924, he played primarily for the Gilberton Catamounts of the Anthracite League and was a teammate of Fritz Pollard. He played only one NFL game that season, with the Rochester Jeffersons. He returned to the Jeffersons for the full season of 1925 and threw three touchdown passes; Rochester scored only four total touchdowns that season. He was part of the 1926 Frankford Yellow Jackets NFL championship team but he played for the squad only early in the season as he also played for the Hartford Blues and finished his season and NFL career with Providence.

He lettered in two seasons of college football.

Non-Providence Stats

1920—Canton Bulldogs: 9 Games, 3 Started.
1921—Canton Bulldogs: 6 Games, 4 Started, 2 TDs, 1 TD Pass, 12 Total Points.
1922—Canton Bulldogs: 5 Games, 4 Started, 1 TD, 1 TD Pass, 6 Total Points.
1923—Canton Bulldogs: 12 Games, 9 Started, 7 TDs, 6 TD Passes, 42 Total Points.
1924—Rochester Jeffersons: 1 Game, 1 Started.
1925—Rochester Jeffersons: 7 Games, 7 Started, 3 TD Passes.
1925—Frankford Yellow Jackets: 3 Games, 2 Started, 2 TDs, 12 Total Points.
1926—Frankford Yellow Jackets: 4 Games, 2 Started.
1926—Hartford Blues: 5 Games, 5 Started, 1 TD, 1 TD Passes, 6 Total Points.

Sofish, Alexander Nicholas "Alec"

Position: OG-DG; Height: 6'2"; Weight: 200; High School: Uniontown (Uniontown, PA); College: Grove City; Born: 12/6/1906, Keisterville, PA; Died: 7/14/1958, East Providence, RI; 1931 Providence Steam Roller: 11 Games, 8 Started.

Sofish played one year with the Steam Roller, its final season in 1931. He held down the right guard position for most of the year, appearing in 11 games. It was his only NFL season.

He played his college football at Grove City, where he started on the line for three seasons. He also participated on the track team as a javelin thrower.

During World War II, he was a special policeman at the Providence Biltmore Hotel. He later owned and ran a gas station in East Providence.

Sonnenberg, Gustave Adolph "Gus"

Position: OT-DT-TB-DH; Height: 5'6"; Weight: 196; High School: Marquette (Marquette, MI); College: Dartmouth, Detroit Mercy; Born: 3/6/1898, Ewen, MI; Died: 9/12/1944, Bethesda, MD; 1927 Providence Steam Roller: 14 Games, 11 Started, 7 Extra Points, 3 Field Goals, 16 Total Points; 1928 Providence Steam Roller: 11 Games, 10 Started, 1 TD Pass, 7 Extra Points, 1 Field Goal, 10 Total Points; 1930 Providence Steam Roller: 1 Game, 0 Started.

Sonnenberg played two full seasons with the Steam Roller and one game in his final season of 1930. He was on the 1928 NFL championship team and contributed 10 points as a kicker. His extra point after Curly Oden's touchdown catch against the Green Bay Packers on December 2 secured a tie for the Steam Roller and ensured it would win the NFL championship. Sonnenberg holds the team record for the most career extra points with 14 and the most career field goals with four. He was named first-team All-Pro by the *Green Bay Press-Gazette* in 1927 and second team in 1928.

Prior to coming to Providence, Sonnenberg began his NFL career in 1923 with the Columbus Tigers. He scored his first and only NFL touchdown on a one-yard run in a 27–3 victory over the Oorang Indians on November 25. Sonnenberg also played one game for the Buffalo Bisons that season. In 1924, he did not play in the NFL but rather with the Pottsville Maroons of the Anthracite Football League. The Maroons won the league title with a 6–0–1 record and Sonnenberg was named an All-Star at guard. He returned to the NFL in 1925 and played two years with the Detroit Panthers, where in addition to playing the line, he was the team's primary kicker. In his two seasons with the Panthers, he converted 14 field goals and 19 extra points and was named first-team All-Pro each year. He came to Providence with former Detroit teammate Jimmy Conzelman.

While Sonnenberg was playing for the Steam Roller, he took up professional wrestling with the encouragement of teammate Jack Spellman. He made his ring debut on January 24, 1928, at the Arcadia Ballroom in Providence and defeated Ivan Ludlow. Despite no previous wrestling experience, Sonnenberg quickly became a sensation in the sport. His patented move, the "flying tackle," changed the style of wrestling. He became a main-event wrestler for Boston-based promoter Paul Bowser. Sonnenberg unsuccessfully challenged world heavyweight champion Ed "Strangler" Lewis on June 30, 1928, at Boston Arena.

After returning to the Steam Roller for its championship season, Sonnenberg again wrestled Lewis for the world title on January 4, 1929, and won the championship, which essentially ended his Steam Roller career. He played only one more game for the franchise in 1930. Sonnenberg held the title for nearly two years before losing it to Ed Don George on December 10, 1930. Sonnenberg was one of the largest draws in pro wrestling in 1929–1930.

In July 1932, Sonnenberg was involved in a fatal car accident in Lawrence, Massachusetts, when the car he was driving hit the car of policeman Richard Morrissey, who was killed. Sonnenberg was charged with drunken driving but was acquitted in March 1933. He had a short stint as an actor, appearing in the 1937 movie *Big City*.

Sonnenberg was again recognized as world wrestling champion in the Boston area in 1939, after defeating The Shadow (Marvin Westenberg) to become the American Wrestling Association titleholder. He held the championship belt for only 13 days before losing to Steve "Crusher" Casey on March 29. He continued to wrestle until joining the navy in 1942.

He was still in the navy when he died of leukemia at the Naval Hospital in Bethesda, Maryland, on September 12, 1944.

He was enshrined in the Professional Wrestling Hall of Fame and Museum in 2007.

Gus Sonnenberg, Providence Steam Roller All-Pro tackle (1927–1928, 1930) (author's collection).

Non-Providence Stats

1923—Buffalo Bisons: 1 Game, 1 Started.
1923—Columbus Tigers: 10 Games, 10 Started, 1 TD, 6 Total Points.
1925—Detroit Panthers: 12 Games, 12 Started, 12 Extra Points, 5 Field Goals, 27 Total Points.
1926—Detroit Panthers: 12 Games, 12 Started, 7 Extra Points, 9 Field Goals, 34 Total Points.

Spellman, John Franklin "Jack"

Position: OT-DT-FB-LB-BB-DH-OE-DE; Height: 5'10"; Weight: 201; High School: Enfield (Enfield, CT); College: Brown; Born: 6/14/1899, Middletown, CT; Died: 8/1/1966, Mangula, Zimbabwe; 1925 Providence Steam Roller: 10 Games, 7 Started, 1 TD, 6 Total Points; 1926 Providence Steam Roller: 12 Games, 8 Started; 1927 Providence Steam Roller: 14 Games, 10 Started; 1928 Providence Steam Roller: 11 Games, 10 Started; 1929 Providence Steam Roller: 12 Games, 11 Started; 1930 Providence Steam Roller: 11 Games, 10 Started, 1931 Providence Steam Roller: 11 Games, 10 Started.

Jack Spellman, Providence Steam Roller end, tackle (1925-1931) (John Hay Library, Special Collections, Brown University).

Spellman was the longest-tenured Steam Roller in team history. He played in all seven seasons that Providence was in the NFL and he appeared in a team-record 81 games. Spellman scored his first and only career touchdown on a blocked punt that he recovered in the end zone in the Steam Roller's 17-0 victory over the Rochester Jeffersons on November 1,

1925. He was a key part of the 1928 NFL championship team, starting in 10 of the Steam Roller's 11 games. He played in both the first NFL game and the last NFL game in franchise history. Jack also played for the 1924 mythical Northeast champion Steam Roller before it joined the NFL. Spellman played one final NFL season with the Boston Braves after the demise of the Steam Roller.

Prior to beginning his NFL career, he competed in the 1924 Olympics in Paris, winning the gold medal as the freestyle light-heavyweight wrestling champion. He won six of his seven bouts to win the title and become the first Brown University athlete to win an Olympic gold medal. While at Brown, he captained both the football and wrestling teams as a senior. Spellman was also a three-time letter winner in football from 1921 to 1923. He was a two-time AAU champion in wrestling. Spellman was outstanding in both sports, and during his senior wrestling season he did not lose a match. He continued his wrestling career as a professional in 1928. He fought for the AWA World Heavyweight title three times and each time he lost to former Steam Roller teammate Gus Sonnenberg. Spellman also wrestled for the NWA championship, losing to Jim Londos. In all, he wrestled 229 matches in his professional career.

In 1936, Spellman went on a world wrestling tour and arrived in Africa in 1938. When World War II broke out, he was unable to return to the United States, and he lived the rest of his life in Africa as a mining engineer.

Spellman was enshrined in the Brown University Athletic Hall of Fame in 1971 and the Rhode Island Heritage Hall of Fame in 1968.

Non-Providence Stats

1932—Boston Braves: 7 Games, 4 Started.

Staff, Edgar Jonathan "Spike"

Position: OG-DG; Height: 6'0"; Weight: 210; High School: Brockton (Brockton, MA); College: Brown; Born: 3/13/1892, Brockton, MA; Died: 2/14/1970, Providence, RI; 1925 Providence Steam Roller: 1 Game, 0 Started.

Staff played one game in the Steam Roller's inaugural 1925 season, his only NFL game. Staff had previously played for the Steam Roller prior to the franchise joining the NFL. He played in the Steam Roller's first-ever game as a franchise on September 30, 1916. Staff was player-coach of the Steam Roller, 1917–1919, and played for the squad again,

1921–1924. He was part of the 1924 mythical Northeast championship team.

He played collegiately at Brown and lettered for three seasons, 1913–1915, where he picked up the nickname "Spike" for his line play. Staff played in the Rose Bowl on January 1, 1916, against Washington State. He returned to Brown as line coach in 1920 for six seasons and then coached the freshman team, a post he held for several years.

Staff was a bacteriologist who headed the Rhode Island state health department laboratories for 28 years.

Spike Staff, Providence Steam Roller guard, center (1925). He was one of only two players to play in the Steam Roller's first game in 1916 and their first NFL game in 1925 (John Hay Library, Special Collections, Brown University).

Stifler, James Madison "Jim"

Position: OG-DG-OE-DE-DH-BB; Height: 5'10"; Weight: 175; High School: Peddie School (Hightstown, NJ); College: Brown; Born: 8/25/1901, Swarthmore, PA; Died: 7/17/1954, Boston, MA; 1926 Providence Steam Roller: 7 Games, 3 Started; 1927 Providence Steam Roller: 2 Games, 1 Started.

Stifler played parts of two seasons with the Steam Roller, appearing in nine games across the 1926 and 1927 seasons. That was his only NFL experience.

Stifler played his college football at Brown, where he was a three-time letter winner, 1923–1925, and a captain of the 1925 squad. He also was a very accomplished swimmer, breaking several Brown records, including the 100-yard breaststroke mark.

Stockton, John Houston "Hust," Jr.

Position: OH-DH; Height: 5'11"; Weight: 193; High School: Parma (Parma, ID), Columbia High School (Portland, OR); College: Gonzaga;

Born: 9/23/1901, Parma, ID; Died: 4/27/1967, Bremerton, WA; 1929 Providence Steam Roller: 1 Game, 0 Started, 1 TD Pass.

Stockton played only one game for the Steam Roller, at the beginning of the 1929 season. He threw a 64-yard touchdown pass to Gibby Welch in Providence's 41-0 win over the Dayton Triangles. After that game, he was off to Boston, where he finished the season and his career with the Bulldogs. Prior to coming to Providence, Stockton played three years with the Frankford Yellow Jackets.

His first career touchdown pass came while playing for Frankford on October 31, 1925, a 20-yarder to Rae Crowther in a 19-0 win over Columbus. One of his most exciting plays came during Frankford's Thanksgiving Day game in 1926. Stockton tossed a 38-yard touchdown pass to Two-Bits Homan in the fourth quarter that delivered a 20-14 victory for the Yellow Jackets over the Green Bay Packers. Stockton repeated the same play to Homan on December 4, this time from 27 yards out, in the fourth quarter as the Yellow Jackets beat the Chicago Cardinals 7-6. Frankford went on to win the NFL championship with a 14-1-2 record that season. Stockton was named second-team All-Pro by the *Green Bay Press-Gazette* at the end of that memorable season.

While playing high school football, Stockton set the Portland, Oregon, city scoring record in 1920 with 104 points that included 14 touchdowns and 20 extra-point conversions in only eight games for Columbia Prep. He attended Gonzaga University, where he played baseball and football. He was a triple-threat halfback. As a junior, Stockton scored 112 of the team's 214 points and threw for 1,011 yards. As a senior, he was named an honorable mention All-American. Stockton was coached by former Notre Dame star Gus Dorais, who helped popularize the passing game as a player at Notre Dame along with Knute Rockne. Stockton threw passes to Ray Flaherty, a future Pro Football Hall of Famer. While Stockton was at Gonzaga, he was compared to the legendary Red Grange.

He was an assistant coach at Gonzaga in 1927. He was briefly a professional wrestler in Spokane and worked for the highway department in Idaho. Stockton was the grandfather of future NBA Hall of Famer John Stockton, who starred for the Utah Jazz from 1984 to 2003.

Non-Providence Stats

1925—Frankford Yellow Jackets: 14 Games, 13 Started, 6 TD Passes.
1926—Frankford Yellow Jackets: 17 Games, 14 Started, 2 TDs, 4 TD Passes, 12 Total Points.
1928—Frankford Yellow Jackets: 13 Games, 6 Started, 4 TDs, 1 TD Pass, 24 Total Points.
1929—Boston Bulldogs: 8 Games, 7 Started, 1 TD, 2 TD Passes, 6 Total Points.

Fred Sweet, Providence Steam Roller back (1925–1926) (John Hay Library, Special Collections, Brown University).

Sweet, Frederick "Fred"

Position: WB-FB-LB-DH-BB-OG-DG; Height: 5'10"; Weight: 165; High School: West Philadelphia (Philadelphia, PA); College: Brown; Born: 8/17/1901, Philadelphia, PA; Died: 10/31/1976, Cape May, NJ; 1925 Providence Steam Roller: 8 Games, 1 Started, 1 Extra Point, 2 Field Goals, 7 Total Points; 1926 Providence Steam Roller: 9 Games, 4 Started.

Sweet played two seasons with the Steam Roller. He was a versatile player who played many positions, including some kicking in 1925. Sweet made his first career field goal on November 1 when he kicked a 15-yarder in a 17–0 win over the Rochester Jeffersons. The following week, he made another field goal and booted an extra point in the Steam Roller's 10–0 win over Buffalo.

Sweet played for the 1924 Steam Roller's mythical Northeast championship team that helped position the franchise to join the NFL in 1925. He played his collegiate football at Brown, where he lettered all four years from 1921 to 1924 and was a team captain in his senior year.

Talbot, John Orechia

Position: OE-DE; Height: 6'2"; Weight: 182; High School: Mercersburg Academy (Mercersburg, PA); College: Brown; Born: 4/27/1900, South Weymouth, MA; Died: 12/5/1981, Keene, NH; 1926 Providence Steam Roller: 2 Games, 0 Started.

Talbot played two games with the Steam Roller in 1926, his only NFL experience.

He played collegiately at Brown and was a three-year letter winner, from 1923 to 1925.

Thomas, John Webster

Position: FB-LB; Height: 6'1"; Weight: 188; High School: Jamestown (Jamestown, ND); College: Jamestown, Chicago; Born: 2/13/1900, Ocheyedan, IA; Died: 8/19/1977, Woodstock, IL; 1925 Providence Steam Roller: 1 Game, 0 Started.

Thomas played one game during the Steam Roller's inaugural season in 1925. Prior to playing for Providence, he played two games in 1924 for the Racine Legion. He played under the alias "John Webster" because his wife, Mildred, had asked him to stop playing football. His one game with the Steam Roller was his last NFL game.

Thomas served in World War I in 1918. After the war, he attended Jamestown College in North Dakota in 1919 and 1920 and was chosen All-State fullback both years. In 1921, he transferred to the University of Chicago. Thomas played for three years under the tutelage of Amos Alonzo Stagg. In 1921, he was picked to the All-Big Ten Conference team. He was lauded for his performance in the Princeton game that season. That particular game was the first Western triumph over an Eastern powerhouse and was a primary stimulus in college football becoming a national game. In 1922, Walter Camp selected Thomas as the first-team fullback on his All-American squad.

In 1923, Thomas had another solid year. He was named All-Big Ten Conference alongside Grange by the *Chicago Tribune*. He was also class president in 1923. In his years with the Maroons, they had an overall 18-3-1 record. The three losses were by a total of 17 points.

Thomas taught physical education and coached at Danville High School in Danville, Illinois, from 1924 through 1927. In his three years as the school's football coach, he directed undefeated squads in both 1924 and 1925. Thomas also coached the basketball and track teams during his tenure at Danville, with his track team winning the state championship in 1925. From 1927 to 1929, he coached at Haskell Indian Institute in Lawrence, Kansas, and directed them to an overall 10-7-1 record. Thomas worked for the American Red Cross and Cummins Business Machine of Chicago and had several other jobs later in life.

Non-Providence Stats

1924—Racine Legion: 2 Games, 1 Started.

Titmas, Herbert James

Position: QB-S-OH-DH; Height: 5'8"; Weight: 165; High School: Manlius Military Academy (Manlius, NY); College: Syracuse; Born: 12/14/1905, Pawtucket, RI; Died: 8/16/1976, Bay Village, OH; 1931 Providence Steam Roller: 11 Games, 5 Started, 1 TD, 6 Total Points.

Titmas played for the Steam Roller throughout its final NFL season in 1931. He scored the winning touchdown in a 13-7 victory over the Cleveland Indians on November 21. Titmas snared a 16-yard pass from Al Rose in the fourth quarter for the game-winner. The win over Cleveland was the Steam Roller's last in franchise history.

He played collegiately at Syracuse University and lettered three straight seasons, from 1928 to 1930. Following his senior season, he was named All-East quarterback. Ainsworth Sports listed him as the 65th-best football player in Syracuse University history in 2021.

He founded a junior football league for the Fairview Park Recreation Commission in 1952.

Titmas was an area sales representative for Pratt & Lambert Inc. from 1932 to 1971.

Triggs, John Stephen "Jack"

Position: FB-LB; Height: 6'0"; Weight: 200; High School: Brockton (Brockton, MA), Little Rock Central (Little Rock, AK); College: Providence; Born: 1/11/1903, Brockton, MA; Died: 2/16/1951, Brockton, MA; 1926 Providence Steam Roller: 3 Games, 0 Started.

Triggs played part of one season for the Steam Roller, appearing in three games in 1926. Triggs had no other NFL experience. He played for the semipro Pere Marquette team as a fullback and kicker.

Triggs played his college football at Providence College and is one of only five Friars to have played football in the NFL. He also played varsity baseball at the school.

Webber, Howard Gilbert "Dutch"

Position: OE-DE; Height: 6'2"; Weight: 190; High School: Unknown; College: Kansas State; Born: 12/15/1901, Oxford, NE; Died: 6/15/1985, Ulysses, KS; 1930 Providence Steam Roller: 1 Game, 1 Started.

Webber played a single game for the Steam Roller in 1930, a very small part of his six-year NFL career. His career spanned from 1924 through

1930 and he played for six other NFL teams. He never played for any team longer than a single season, and in three of his seasons he played for multiple teams. Webber also played parts of two seasons with the Portsmouth Spartans of the Ohio Valley League. He was on the Spartans' championship team of 1929 when they went 12-2-1.

Webber played his college football at Kansas State. He lettered during the 1922 and 1923 seasons for the Wildcats.

He owned and ran Webber Supply Co., Inc. in Salina, KS, for many years.

Non-Providence Stats

1924—Kansas City Blues: 9 Games, 9 Started.
1925—Kansas City Cowboys: 8 Games, 8 Started.
1925—Cleveland Bulldogs: 4 Games, 4 Started.
1926—Hartford Blues: 8 Games, 8 Started.
1926—Kansas City Cowboys: 1 Game, 0 Started.
1926—New York Giants: 2 Games, 1 Started.
1927—Cleveland Bulldogs: 3 Games, 3 Started.
1928—Green Bay Packers: 3 Games, 1 Started.
1930—Newark Tornadoes: 3 Games, 0 Started.

Welch, Gilbert Lawrence "Gibby"

Position: QB-S-OH-DH-FB-LB; Height: 5'11"; Weight: 178; High School: Parkersburg (Parkersburg, WV), Bellefonte Academy (Bellefonte, WV); College: Pittsburgh; Born: 12/24/1904, Parkersburg, WV; Died: 2/10/1984, Pittsburgh, PA; 1929 Providence Steam Roller: 12 Games, 10 Started, 6 TDs, 36 Total Points.

Welch played one season with the Steam Roller, appearing in 12 games and scoring six touchdowns. Welch had a day to remember in his first NFL game with Providence. He set the team record by scoring four touchdowns in the Steam Roller's 41-0 victory over Dayton. He caught three touchdown passes, including a 64-yarder from Hust Stockton and a 32-yarder from Wildcat Wilson. In the Steam Roller's 7-0 win over the Orange Tornadoes on October 13, Welch scored the only touchdown of the game on a nifty run. His 36 career points scored are fifth all time in Steam Roller history.

Prior to coming to Providence, he played one season with the New York Yankees. He led the Yankees in scoring with 48 points in 1927. He had six pass-receiving touchdowns. His 55-yard touchdown catch sparked the

Yankees' 19–13 win over the cross-town rival Giants on December 2. Welch signed with Providence after the Yankees disbanded. Upon his signing, the *Coshocton Tribune* reported, "'Gibby,' who was once known to have been addressed as Gilbert, functions effectively as a punter, pass dispatcher or receiver, line perforator and broken-field runner. It is understood that the Roller management was forced to quote the highest figures ever whispered into a pro football player's ears before Welch affixed his signature to a contract. 'Gibby' was thrown on the open market by the recent dissolution of the New York Yankees."[21]

He played collegiately at the University of Pittsburgh. Welch was a three-year letter winner for the Panthers from 1925 to 1927. He played in the first game ever played at Pitt Stadium. Welch competed on the Pitt track team in 1926, 1927 and 1928. He was one of the country's leading college discus throwers and also competed in the shot put, javelin and broad jump. Welch captained both the football and track teams as a senior. He was the signal-calling left halfback in the single-wing offense run by coach Jock Sutherland in 1926 and 1927.

In 1926, Welch broke the single-season collegiate rushing yardage record set by Red Grange, gaining 1,964 yards in just nine games. Welch was described by the *Decatur Daily Review* as "one of the most dazzling open field sprinters in the collegiate ranks," an athlete whose "sensational runs are aided by his excellent use of twirls and pivots through an open field."[22]

As a senior in 1927, Welch led the Panthers to their first-ever bowl game, the 1928 Rose Bowl against Stanford. Pitt lost 7–6—its only defeat in an 8-1-1 season. Welch had many highlights during his senior season, including a 105-yard kickoff-return touchdown in a 40–0 win over West Virginia, an 84-yard kickoff return touchdown and a 71-yard pass reception for a touchdown in a 21–13 win over Nebraska and a terrific all-around game in a 30–0 win over archrival Penn State. At the conclusion of the season, Welch was a consensus All-American.

After his retirement from pro football, Welch was a football coach at Morris Harvey College in 1931. He later was a leading real estate businessman in Parkersburg, West Virginia. In 1956, the *Charleston Daily Mail* called Welch "one of the most fabulous characters ever produced in West Virginia athletics."[23] Welch's career total of 4,108 total yards and his rushing records at Pitt stood for more than 50 years until they were broken by Tony Dorsett in the 1970s.

Non-Providence Stats

1928—New York Yankees: 13 Games, 12 Games, 8 TDs, 1 TD Pass, 48 Total Points.

Wentworth, Shirley P. "Cy"

Position: TB-WB-DH-LB-BB-FB; Height: 5'8"; Weight: 160; High School: Salem (Salem, MA), Thayer Academy (Braintree, MA); College: New Hampshire; Born: 1/2/1904, Salem, MA; Died: 1/19/1986, Salem, MA; 1925 Providence Steam Roller: 12 Games, 12 Started, 3 TDs, 18 Total Points; 1926 Providence Steam Roller: 8 Games, 7 Started, 1 TD Pass, 3 Extra Points, 1 Field Goal, 6 Total Points.

Wentworth played for the Steam Roller in the first two years of the team's NFL existence. He was an important and versatile player. Cy contributed 24 points over those two seasons. His first touchdown for the Steam Roller was an exciting 92-yard kickoff return in a 14–0 victory over the New York Giants on October 11, 1925. Wentworth was named a second-team All-Pro by the *Green Bay Press-Gazette* at the conclusion of the 1925 season. He played his final NFL season in 1929 with the Boston Bulldogs. His best game with the Bulldogs was a three-touchdown performance in a 41–0 win over the Dayton Triangles. He scored on 27- and 48-yard pass receptions from Hust Stockton and on a 45-yard punt return.

Prior to playing pro football, Wentworth played collegiately at the University of New Hampshire. Wentworth scored 166 career points. He had a career-high 11 touchdowns and 85 points in 1924 and was second in the East in scoring. Wentworth led the team in scoring from 1922 to 1924 and he was New Hampshire's team captain for the 1923 and

Cy Wentworth, Providence Steam Roller All-Pro halfback (1925–1926) (author's collection).

1924 seasons. Wentworth holds the New Hampshire record for the most points scored in a single game, 37, achieved on November 3, 1923, against Lowell Tech. He scored six touchdowns and one extra point. Wentworth also played baseball and basketball and ran track at the school, lettering in each, and was timed in the 100-yard dash in 10 seconds.

Wentworth was an inaugural member of the University of New Hampshire Wildcats Hall of Fame in 1982.

Non-Providence Stats

1929—Boston Bulldogs: 6 Games, 3 Started, 3 TDs, 6 Extra Points, 24 Total Points.

Wesley, Lecil Olen "Bull"

Position: OG-DG-LB-FB-C-MG; Height: 6'1"; Weight: 190; High School: Marion County (Guin, AL); College: Alabama; Born: 9/26/1901, Guin, AL; Died: 1/9/1980, Tuscaloosa, AL; 1926 Providence Steam Roller: 7 Games, 7 Started; 1927 Providence Steam Roller: 10 Games, 4 Started.

Wesley played two seasons with the Steam Roller, appearing in 17 games. He played two more seasons in the NFL with the New York Giants and Portsmouth Spartans.

Wesley played his collegiate football at the University of Alabama, where he lettered in 1922 and 1923. During the 1922 season, the Crimson Tide traveled to Philadelphia to play the Penn Quakers. At the time, Penn was considered one of the best teams in the country. Alabama pulled a stunning 9–7 upset win over the Quakers. Wesley scored the deciding points in the game with a 35-yard field goal.

While playing for Marion County High School, Wesley was once described as "the most powerful man to ever run across a gridiron turf," as stated on the MCHS Football History Facebook page.[24]

Non-Providence Stats

1928—New York Giants: 5 Games, 3 Started.
1929—Portsmouth Spartans: 13 Games, 5 Started.

Williams, Arthur Vincent "Pop"

Position: FB-LB-WB-TB-QB-DH-S; Height: 6'0"; Weight: 205; High School: Killingly (Killingly, CT); College: Connecticut; Born: 5/4/1906, Jewett City, CT; Died: 2/5/1979, Brooklyn, CT; 1928 Providence Steam

Roller: 7 Games, 5 Started, 4 TDs, 24 Total Points; 1929 Providence Steam Roller: 12 Games, 8 Started, 7 TDs, 42 Total Points; 1930 Providence Steam Roller: 11 Games, 8 Started, 2 TDs, 12 Total Points; 1931 Providence Steam Roller: 8 Games, 2 Started.

Williams played four seasons with the NFL Steam Roller, appearing in 38 games. He was a key part of the 1928 NFL championship team, scoring four touchdowns. His two scores in the season-opening game against the New York Yankees spurred the team to a 20-7 victory, and his touchdown against the Detroit Wolverines was the only score in the Steam Roller's 7-0 win on November 4. In 1929, Williams led Providence in scoring with seven touchdowns and 42 points. He scored three times against the Minneapolis Red Jackets on November 17 to key the Steam Roller's 19-16 victory, including the winning touchdown late in the game. The following week, he scored two more touchdowns in Providence's 20-6 victory over the Boston Bulldogs. His 13 career touchdowns and 78 points are second most in Steam Roller history.

After the demise of the Steam Roller, Williams caught on with the Brooklyn Dodgers and played one game with them before his NFL career ended. In 1937, he played in the American Football Association for the Mount Vernon Cardinals.

Williams played his college football at the University of Connecticut, where he lettered for two seasons, 1926-1927, before leaving the school prior to the start of his senior year. Williams as a sophomore was the third-highest scorer in the East with 90 points for the 7-1 Aggies. He was nagged by a knee injury during his junior season. Despite that, UConn coach Sumner Dole said, "'Pop' is the greatest offensive back I have ever seen and would make any college team in the country. He would have been an All-American selection if he had been playing on one of the larger college or university elevens."[25] Williams also played baseball as a first baseman and relief pitcher and basketball as a guard at the school. He was captain of the basketball squad as a junior and was named All-New England for his play. At that time he was considered by many as the best athlete to ever come through Storrs.

Williams was president of his class at Connecticut, president of the athletic association and an officer in the ROTC unit.

He served in World War II and the Korean War and won two Bronze Stars. He was inducted into the Killingly High School Sports Hall of Fame in 2014.

Non-Providence Stats

1932—Brooklyn Dodgers: 1 Game, 0 Started.

Wilson, Abe Yeoman

Position: MG-OG-DG-OT-DT-C; Height: 5'10"; Weight: 192; High School: Everett (Everett, WA); College: Washington; Born: 10/6/1899, AR; Died: 5/13/1981, Seattle, WA; 1927 Providence Steam Roller: 14 Games, 12 Started; 1928 Providence Steam Roller: 9 Games, 5 Started; 1929 Providence Steam Roller: 10 Games, 3 Started.

Wilson played three seasons with the Steam Roller, appearing in 33 games. He was part of the 1928 NFL championship team. He was teammates with his brother George "Wildcat" Wilson. Prior to coming to Providence, he played one season for the Los Angeles Wildcats of the AFL in 1926.

Abe played collegiately at the University of Washington. He lettered at the school in 1923 and 1924 playing alongside his brother. He was also an assistant football coach for the Huskies in 1925.

Wilson, George Schly "Wildcat"

Position: QB-WB-TB-HB-FB-LB-DH; Height: 5'10"; Weight: 200; High School: Everett (Everett, WA); College: Washington; Born: 9/6/1901, Everett, WA; Died: 12/27/1963, San Francisco, CA; 1927 Providence Steam

George "Wildcat" Wilson, Providence Steam Roller All-Pro halfback (1927–1929) (David Eskenzai collection).

Roller: 14 Games, 12 Started, 4 TDs, 4 TD Passes, 24 Total Points; 1928 Providence Steam Roller: 11 Games, 11 Started, 5 TDs, 6 TD Passes, 30 Total Points; 1929 Providence Steam Roller: 12 Games, 12 Started, 1 TD, 3 TD Passes, 6 Total Points.

Wilson played for the Steam Roller for three seasons and was a key contributor throughout his Providence career, including the 1928 NFL championship squad. He scored his first two touchdowns with Providence in 1927 in back-to-back victories over Frankford on October 29 (20-7) and October 30 (14-0). In each win he also threw his first two touchdown passes, one in each game. Wilson scored two touchdowns in the Steam Roller's 20-0 win over the Pottsville Maroons on December 4 that closed out the 1927 season.

In 1928, Wilson led the NFL champions in scoring with five touchdowns and 30 points. He tallied two touchdowns in a 28-0 victory over Dayton and his 12-yard fourth-quarter touchdown run secured an important 6-6 tie with Frankford on the Yellow Jackets' home turf. Wilson also threw six touchdown passes in 1928, none was more important than the 23-yarder he completed to Curly Oden in the third quarter of the season's final game against Green Bay. The play secured a 7-7 tie and clinched the NFL championship for the Steam Roller. He also completed another touchdown pass to Oden on October 28 that broke a 6-6 tie with Pottsville in a 13-6 Steam Roller victory, and his touchdown pass to Pop Williams the following week was the only score in Providence's 7-0 win over Detroit. Wilson was named first-team All-Pro at the conclusion of the 1928 season by the *Chicago Tribune* and the *Green Bay Press-Gazette*.

His final touchdown pass in a Providence uniform came on November 24, 1929, a 32-yard strike to Williams in the Steam Roller's 20-6 victory over Boston. Wilson finished his career in Providence in third place on the team's all-time list in touchdowns (10) and points (60) and was the all-time leader in touchdown passes (13).

Prior to coming to Providence, Wilson participated in a series of West Coast exhibition games against Red Grange and the Chicago Bears in January 1926. His first game was with the Los Angeles Wildcats in the Los Angeles Memorial Coliseum, and he rushed for 123 yards in a 17-7 loss. He then played for the San Francisco Tigers at Kezar Stadium, and Wilson outrushed Grange 87 to 41 and the Tigers won 14-7. Wilson also led all-star teams in Portland and Seattle.

Grange's agent, C.C. Pyle, approached Wilson about signing a contract with him worth $15,000 to play professional football in the fall of 1926. During that summer, Grange and Wilson collaborated on the movie *One Minute to Play*, with Wilson serving as the antagonist to Grange's team. Pyle enticed Wilson to join the first American Football League and named him president of the league's traveling team, the Wildcats. Wilson played for what became the Los Angeles franchise of the AFL, and he scored four touchdowns and threw five touchdown passes for the 6-6-2 Wildcats.

He played his college football at the University of Washington, where he scored a school-record 37 touchdowns. He lettered as a Huskie in 1923, 1924 and 1925, and his No. 33 jersey is one of only three retired in school history. "Wilson was a master of the stiff-arm tactic, pushing would-be tacklers aside with uncanny ease. Most foes found 'Wildcat' to be unpredictable whenever he got his hands on the ball, for one never knew whether he would run, pass or kick—and he did each equally well."[26] He is enshrined in the University of Washington Husky Hall of Fame. He was also elected to the College Football Hall of Fame in 1951, and the Rose Bowl Hall of Fame in 1991. His brother is Abe Wilson and they were teammates in college, in Los Angeles and with the Steam Roller.

Woodruff, Lee Thornton

Position: FB-LB; Height: 6'0"; Weight: 202; High School: Batesville (Batesville, MS); College: Mississippi; Born: 4/4/1910, Batesville, MS; Died: 2/22/1947, Batesville, MS; 1931 Providence Steam Roller: 11 Games, 7 Started, 4 TDs, 1 Extra Point, 25 Total Points.

Woodruff played one season with the Steam Roller, in 1931, the franchise's final season in the NFL. He led the team with four touchdowns and 25 total points. He scored his first touchdown with the Steam Roller on a one-yard plunge in a 13-6 loss to the Cleveland Indians on October 18. On November 15, he scored the only touchdown in the Roller's 6-0 win over Staten Island and the following week he scored again to pull Providence within a point at 7-6 in a game they eventually won 13-7 over the Indians.

After the demise of the franchise, Woodruff signed with the Boston Braves. He played the 1932 season in Boston and then finished his NFL career with the Philadelphia Eagles in 1933. With the Eagles, he scored a rushing touchdown in a 25-6 win over the Pittsburgh Pirates and returned an intercepted pass 55 yards to clinch a 20-3 victory over the Cincinnati Reds.

Prior to coming to Providence, he played for the independent Memphis Tigers in 1930. Following his NFL career, Woodruff again played for Memphis, who were at that point in the American Football League. He played the 1934 season with the Tigers, appearing in 10 games and scoring one touchdown.

He played his college football at the University of Mississippi, where he lettered for three seasons, 1927-1929.

Non-Providence Stats

1932—Boston Braves: 7 Games, 4 Started, Receiving: 2-35-0.
1933—Philadelphia Eagles: 9 Games, 2 Started, Rushing: 22-74-1, Receiving: 3-57-0, Passing: 0-1-0 TDs, 1 Int., Scoring: 2 TDs, 12 Total Points.

Young, Frederick Lloyd "Lloyd"

Position: OG-DG-OT-DT-FB-LB; Height: 6'2"; Weight: 192; High School: Austin (Austin, MN); College: Macalester (ND); Born: 5/27/1903, Austin, MN; Died: 7/10/1978, Austin, MN; 1925 Providence Steam Roller: 11 Games, 4 Started; 1926 Providence Steam Roller: 13 Games, 10 Started; 1927 Providence Steam Roller: 1 Game, 1 Started.

Young played three seasons with the Steam Roller, appearing in 25 games and starting 15. After his career with the Steam Roller, he played two seasons with the Minneapolis Red Jackets.

He played collegiately at Macalester College.

Non-Providence Stats

1929—Minneapolis Red Jackets: 8 Games, 8 Started.
1930—Minneapolis Red Jackets: 2 Games, 1 Started.

Young, Herman DeVerne "Herm"

Position: OE-DE; Height: 5'11"; Weight: 178; High School: Central (Flint, MI); College: Detroit Mercy; Born: 3/21/1906, Flint, MI; Died: 6/16/1985, Bradenton, FL; 1930 Providence Steam Roller: 3 Games, 0 Started, 1 TD, 6 Total Points.

Young, played part of the 1930 season with the Steam Roller, appearing in three games. He scored the first touchdown of the season for Providence on a four-yard pass reception from Frosty Peters, but the Steam Roller lost to the New York Giants 27-7. He played in only two more games for Providence and then his NFL career ended.

He played collegiately at Detroit Mercy and lettered at the school for three seasons, 1927–1929.

He was the Flint, Michigan, City Hall controller for many years.

Appendix: Year-by-Year Results, Team Rosters and Statistics

Providence Steam Roller (NFL)— Overall Won-Lost Records (1925–1931)

Year	NFL W–L–T	Nonleague W–L–T	Overall W–L–T	Overall Win Pct.
1925	6–5–1	1–0–0	7–5–1	.577
1926	5–7–1	2–0–0	7–7–1	.500
1927	8–5–1	1–0–0	9–5–1	.633
1928	8–1–2	3–0–0	11–1–2	.857
1929	4–6–2	1–0–0	5–6–2	.462
1930	6–4–1	4–0–0	10–4–1	.700
1931	4–4–3	11–0–0	15–4–3	.750
Total	41–32–11	23–0–0	64–32–11	.650

Providence Steam Roller (Independent Pro Team)— Overall Won-Lost Record (1916–1924)

Year	Overall W–L–T	Overall Win Pct.
1916	7–2–0	.778
1917	5–3–1	.611
1918	1–1–0	.500
1919	6–2–0	.750
1920	0–2–4	.333
1921	2–3–3	.438
1922	8–2–2	.750
1923	12–1–0	.923

228 Appendix: Year-by-Year Results, Team Rosters and Statistics

Year	Overall W-L-T	Overall Win Pct.
1924	12-3-1	.781
Total	53-19-11	.705

Providence Steam Roller—1925

YEAR: 1925
HEAD COACH: Archie Golembeski (coach/player)
LEAGUE: NFL
HOME STADIUM: Cycledrome
SCHEDULE/RESULTS OF GAMES:
Regular-season NFL record: 6-5-1; 10th-place finish
Overall record: 7-5-1
Points For: 111 (9.3/game)
Points Against: 101 (8.4/game)

1925 Schedule/Results

Date	Opponent	Site	Game Score	H/A	Attendance
09/20	West Point Field Artillery	Cycledrome	W 127-0	H	-------
09/27	New London Sub-Base	Cycledrome	Canceled	H	-------
10/03	at Frankford Yellow Jackets	Frankford Stadium	L 0-7	A	12,000
10/04	at Pottsville Maroons	Minersville Park	W 6-0	A	5,000
10/11	New York Giants	Cycledrome	W 14-0	H	7,500
10/18	Pottsville Maroons	Cycledrome	L 0-34	H	10,000
10/25	Columbus Tigers	Cycledrome	Canceled	H	-------
11/01	Rochester Jeffersons	Cycledrome	W 17-0	H	-------
11/08	Buffalo Bisons	Cycledrome	W 10-0	H	2,200
11/15	at New York Giants	Polo Grounds	L 12-13	A	25,000
11/22	Frankford Yellow Jackets	Cycledrome	W 20-7	H	14,000
11/29	Cleveland Bulldogs	Cycledrome	T 7-7	H	12,000
12/06	Green Bay Packers	Cycledrome	L 10-13	H	7,000
12/09	Chicago Bears	Braves Field	W 9-6	H	15,000
12/13	Frankford Yellow Jackets	Cycledrome	L 6-14	H	-------

Team Roster (30)

Player	Position	GP/GS	WT	HT	College
Joe "Speed" Braney	DG-OG	6/0	188	6-0	Syracuse, Fordham
Charley "Chick" Burke	WB-DH	5/2	166	5-9	Dartmouth

Appendix: Year-by-Year Results, Team Rosters and Statistics

Player	Position	GP/GS	WT	HT	College
Dutch Connor	FB-LB	3/3	190	6-0	New Hampshire
Jim Crowley	TB-DH	1/0	165	5-9	Notre Dame
Dolph Eckstein	C-MG	12/12	185	5-10	Brown
Franny Garvey	OE-DE	9/8	175	6-1	Holy Cross
Archie Golembeski	OG-DG	11/11	185	5-10	Holy Cross
Mike Gulian	DT	8/8	205	6-0	Brown
Ching Hammill	BB-S	1/1	158	5-7	Connecticut, Villanova, Georgetown
Joe Kozlowsky	OT-DT	11/11	201	5-10	Boston College
Jim Laird	WB-LB-OG	11/8	194	6-0	Colgate
Bulger Lowe	OE-DE	2/1	180	5-11	Lafayette, Fordham
Red Maloney	OE-DE	12/12	180	5-11	Dartmouth
Hugh McGoldrick	OT-DT	1/0	180	5-10	Lehigh
Ira "Al" McIntosh	TB-WB-DH	9/7	180	5-9	Rhode Island
Don Miller	WB-DH	1/1	170	5-11	Notre Dame
Curly Oden	BB-S	8/7	163	5-6	Brown
Walt "Pard" Pearce	BB-S	8/1	150	5-5	Pennsylvania
John Pohlman	FB-LB	2/0	178	5-9	Brown
Fritz Pollard	TB-WB-DH	4/0	165	5-9	Bates, Brown
Al "Hop" Riopel	TB-WB-DH	4/1	165	5-8	Holy Cross
Nate Share	OG-DG	10/10	210	6-1	Tufts
Fred Sheehan	OG-DG	1/1	210	6-2	Georgetown
Bert Shurtleff	OG-DG-OT-DT	11/3	190	5-11	Brown
Jack Spellman	OT-DT-FB-LB	10/7	201	5-10	Brown
Spike Staff	OG-DG	1/0	210	6-0	Brown
Fred Sweet	WB-LB-DH	8/1	165	5-10	Brown
Evan "John" Thomas	FB-LB	1/0	188	6-1	Jamestown, Chicago
Cy Wentworth	TB-WB-DH	12/12	160	5-8	New Hampshire
Lloyd Young	OT-DT-OG-DG	11/4	192	6-2	Macalester, North Dakota

Scoring

Player	Rush TD	KR TD	Fbl TD	Oth TD	Tot TD	XP	FG	Safety	TPs
Jim Laird	3				3	2	3		29
Red Maloney		1			1	4	3		19
Cy Wentworth	2	1			3				18
Franny Garvey			1	1	2				12

Appendix: Year-by-Year Results, Team Rosters and Statistics

Player	Rush TD	KR TD	Fbl TD	Oth TD	Tot TD	XP	FG	Safety	TPs
Archie Golembeski			2		2				12
Fred Sweet					0	1	2		7
Jack Spellman				1	1				6
Dutch Connor					0	2			2
Team Totals	5	1	4	2	12	9	8	3	111
Opponent Totals					15	11			101

Score by Quarter	1	2	3	4	Total
Steam Roller	16	38	28	29	111
Opponents	14	21	19	47	101

NFL Standings—1925

Team	W–L–T	W–L%	PF	PA
Chicago Cardinals	11–2–1	.846	230	65
Pottsville Maroons	10–2–0	.833	270	45
Detroit Panthers	8–2–2	.800	129	39
Akron Pros	4–2–2	.667	65	51
New York Giants	8–4–0	.667	122	67
Frankford Yellow Jackets	13–7–0	.650	190	169
Chicago Bears	9–5–3	.643	158	96
Rock Island Independents	5–3–3	.625	99	58
Green Bay Packers	8–5–0	.615	151	110
Providence Steam Roller	6–5–1	.545	111	101
Canton Bulldogs	4–4–0	.500	50	73
Cleveland Bulldogs	5–8–1	.385	75	135
Kansas City Cowboys	2–5–1	.286	65	97
Hammond Pros	1–4–0	.200	23	87
Buffalo Bisons	1–6–2	.143	33	113
Dayton Triangles	0–7–1	.000	3	84
Duluth Kelleys	0–3–0	.000	6	25
Columbus Tigers	0–9–0	.000	28	124
Milwaukee Badgers	0–6–0	.000	7	191
Rochester Jeffersons	0–6–1	.000	26	111

Providence Steam Roller—1926

YEAR: 1926
HEAD COACH: Jim Laird (coach/player)

Appendix: Year-by-Year Results, Team Rosters and Statistics 231

LEAGUE: NFL
HOME STADIUM: Cycledrome
SCHEDULE/RESULTS OF GAMES:
Regular-season NFL record: 5-7-1; 11th-place finish
Overall record: 7-7-1
Points For: 89 (6.8/game)
Points Against: 103 (7.9/game)

1926 Schedule/Results

Date	Opponent	Site	Game Score	H/A	Attendance
09/12	New Haven Williams	Cycledrome	W 24-0	H	4,000
09/19	New London Sub-Base	Cycledrome	W 41-0	H	-------
09/26	Brooklyn Lions	Cycledrome	W 13-0	H	7,000
10/03	New York Giants	Cycledrome	L 6-7	H	8,000
10/10	Columbus Tigers	Cycledrome	W 19-0	H	-------
10/17	Hartford Blues	Velodrome	Canceled	A	-------
10/24	Pottsville Maroons	Cycledrome	W 14-0	H	4,500
10/30	at Frankford Yellow Jackets	Frankford Stadium	W 7-6	A	8,000
10/31	Frankford Yellow Jackets	Cycledrome	L 3-6	H	-------
11/07	Los Angeles Buccaneers	Cycledrome	L 6-7	H	11,000
11/11	Canton Bulldogs	Cycledrome	W 21-2	H	6,000
11/14	Kansas City Cowboys	Cycledrome	L 0-22	H	-------
11/21	at New York Giants	Polo Grounds	L 0-21	A	10,000
11/25	at Pottsville Maroons	Minersville Park	L 0-8	A	-------
11/28	Duluth Eskimos	Cycledrome	T 0-0	H	-------
12/05	Hartford Blues	Cycledrome	Canceled	H	-------
12/11	at Frankford Yellow Jackets	Frankford Stadium	L 0-24	A	4,500
12/12	Frankford Yellow Jackets	Cycledrome	Canceled	H	-------

Team Roster (34)

Player	Position	GP/GS	WT	HT	College
Joe "Speed" Braney	DG-OG-OT	7/4	188	6-0	Syracuse, Fordham
Jack Donahue	OG-DG-DT	13/9	230	6-2	Boston College
Dolph Eckstein	C-MG	13/12	185	5-10	Brown
Carl Etelman	BB-DH	1/1	160	5-8	Boston University, Tufts, Harvard

232   Appendix: Year-by-Year Results, Team Rosters and Statistics

Player	Position	GP/GS	WT	HT	College
Dutch Forst	FB-LB	2/2	195	5-8	Villanova
Franny Garvey	OE-DE	10/7	175	6-1	Holy Cross
Archie Golembeski	OE-DE	9/7	185	5-10	Holy Cross
Fred Graham	OE-DE	1/0	175	6-0	Indiana State, West Virginia
Mike Gulian	OT-DT	13/12	205	6-0	Brown
Vern Hagenbuckle	OE-DE	2/2	185	5-8	Dartmouth
Swede Hummel	BB-DH	4/3	195		Lombard
Jack Keefer	WB-DH-BB	11/5	172	5-9	Michigan, Brown
Lou Koplow	OT-DT	1/1	235	6-3	Boston University
Joe Kozlowsky	OT-DT-OE-DE	10/8	201	5-10	Boston College
Jim Laird	FB-LB	9/6	194	6-0	Colgate
Harold "Pinky" Lester	OE-DE-OT-DT	8/5	160	5-6	None
Waddy MacPhee	DH-FB-LB	1/1	160	5-8	Princeton
Jim Manning	BB-DH	1/1	195	5-11	Fordham
Ed McCrillis	OG-DG	1/0	205	6-5	Brown
Joe McGlone	TB-S	1/1	150	5-7	Harvard
Ira "Al" McIntosh	TB-BB-DH	2/0	180	5-9	Rhode Island
Curly Oden	TB-WB-S-DH	13/12	163	5-6	Brown
Seneca Samson	TB-WB-S-DH	2/1	160	5-8	Brown
Bob Scott	C-MG-OG-DT	6/1	195		None
Frank Seyboth	BB-DH	1/0	180	5-9	Vermont
Lou Smyth	WB-DH	3/3	200	6-1	Texas, Centre
Jack Spellman	OT-DT-FB-LB	12/8	201	5-10	Brown
Jim Stifler	OE-DE-DG	7/3	175	5-10	Brown
Fred Sweet	WB-LB-DH	9/4	165	5-10	Brown
John Talbot	OE-DE	2/0	182	6-2	Brown
Jack Triggs	FB-LB	3/0	200	6-0	Providence
Cy Wentworth	TB-WB-DH	8/7	160	5-8	New Hampshire
Bull Wesley	OG-DG-LB-FB	7/7	190	6-1	Alabama
Lloyd Young	OG-DG-DT	13/10	192	6-2	Macalester, North Dakota

Scoring

Player	Rush TD	Rec TD	PR TD	Tot TD	XP	FG	Safety	TPs
Curly Oden	6	1	3	10				60
Jack Keefer	2			2	3			15

Player	Rush TD	Rec TD	PR TD	Tot TD	XP	FG	Safety	TPs
Archie Golembeski		1		1	1			7
Cy Wentworth				0	3	1		6
Franny Garvey				0	1			1
Team Totals	8	2	3	13	8	1	0	89
Opponent Totals				12	9	6	2	103

Score by Quarter	1	2	3	4	Total
Steam Roller	10	27	38	14	89
Opponents	28	24	16	35	103

NFL Standings—1926

Team	W-L-T	W-L%	PF	PA
Frankford Yellow Jackets	14-1-2	.933	236	49
Chicago Bears	12-1-3	.923	216	63
Pottsville Maroons	10-2-2	.833	155	29
Kansas City Cowboys	8-3-0	.727	76	53
Green Bay Packers	7-3-3	.700	151	61
New York Giants	8-4-1	.667	147	51
Los Angeles Buccaneers	6-3-1	.667	67	57
Duluth Eskimos	6-5-3	.545	113	81
Buffalo Rangers	4-4-2	.500	53	62
Chicago Cardinals	5-6-1	.455	74	98
Providence Steam Roller	5-7-1	.417	89	103
Detroit Panthers	4-6-2	.400	107	60
Hartford Blues	3-7-0	.300	57	99
Brooklyn Lions	3-8-0	.273	60	150
Milwaukee Badgers	2-7-0	.222	41	66
Dayton Triangles	1-4-1	.200	15	82
Akron Indians	1-4-3	.200	23	89
Racine Tornadoes	1-4-0	.200	8	92
Columbus Tigers	1-6-0	.143	26	93
Canton Bulldogs	1-9-3	.100	46	161
Hammond Pros	0-4-0	.000	3	56
Louisville Colonels	0-4-0	.000	0	108

Providence Steam Roller—1927

YEAR: 1927
HEAD COACH: Jimmy Conzelman (coach/player)

234   Appendix: Year-by-Year Results, Team Rosters and Statistics

LEAGUE: NFL
HOME STADIUM: Cycledrome
SCHEDULE/RESULTS OF GAMES:
Regular season NFL record: 8-5-1; 5th-place finish
Overall record: 9-5-1
Points For: 105 (7.5/game)
Points Against: 88 (6.3/game)

1927 Schedule/Results

Date	Opponent	Site	Game Score	H/A	Attendance
09/18	New London Sub-Base	Cycledrome	W 44-0	H	-------
09/25	New York Giants	Cycledrome	L 0-8	H	7,500
10/02	Buffalo Bisons	Cycledrome	W 5-0	H	3,500
10/09	Chicago Bears	Cycledrome	Canceled	H	-------
10/16	Pottsville Maroons	Cycledrome	L 3-6	H	7,500
10/23	Dayton Triangles	Cycledrome	W 7-0	H	6,500
10/29	at Frankford Yellow Jackets	Frankford Stadium	W 20-7	A	5,000
10/30	Frankford Yellow Jackets	Cycledrome	W 14-0	H	9,000
11/06	at Chicago Bears	Wrigley Field	T 0-0	A	15,000
11/08	at New York Giants	Polo Grounds	L 0-25	A	38,000
11/13	Duluth Eskimos	Cycledrome	W 13-7	H	7,500
11/20	Cleveland Bulldogs	Cycledrome	L 0-22	H	12,000
11/24	at Pottsville Maroons	Minersville Park	L 0-6	A	4,000
11/27	New York Yankees	Cycledrome	W 14-7	H	10,000
12/03	at New York Yankees	Archbold Stadium	W 9-0	A	5,000
12/04	Pottsville Maroons	Cycledrome	W 20-0	H	1,500

Team Roster (24)

Player	Position	GP/GS	WT	HT	College
Jimmy Conzelman	WB-S-HB-TB-DH	14/6	175	6-0	Washington-St. Louis
Bill Cronin	TB-DH-HB-LB-WB-S	9/3	182	5-10	Boston College
Jack Cronin	TB-DH-HB-S-FB-LB	12/3	178	5-11	Boston College
Dinger Doane	FB-LB-TB-DH	5/2	190	5-10	Tufts
Jack Fleischmann	OG-DG	14/12	184	5-6	Purdue
Mike Gulian	OT-DT	2/1	205	6-0	Brown
Al Hadden	FB-LB-DH-HB-WB-S	10/7	186	5-8	Washington & Jefferson
Joe Kozlowsky	OT-DT-OG-DG	12/8	201	5-10	Boston College

Player	Position	GP/GS	WT	HT	College
Jim Laird	OG-DG	14/12	194	6-0	Colgate
Bulger Lowe	OE-DE	11/6	180	5-11	Lafayette, Fordham
Ed Lynch	E-T	11/10	191	6-0	Catholic
Dave Mishel	HB-TB-DH-WB-S	4/3	182	5-9	Brown
Grattan O'Connell	OE-DE	2/2	185	5-11	Boston College
Curly Oden	TB-S-HB-LB-FB-DH	13/11	163	5-6	Brown
Al Pierotti	C-MG-OG-DG-OT-DT	14/11	199	5-10	Washington & Lee
Bill Pritchard	FB-LB-HB-DH	12/9	185	5-10	Penn State
Orland Smith	OT-DT-OG-DG	13/9	203	5-11	Brown
Gus Sonnenberg	OT-DT	14/11	196	5-6	Dartmouth, Detroit Mercy
Jack Spellman	OT-DT-OE-DE	14/10	201	5-10	Brown
Jim Stifler	OE-DE	2/1	175	5-10	Brown
Bull Wesley	C-MG	10/4	190	6-1	Alabama
Abe Wilson	G-TB	14/12	192	5-10	Washington
George Wilson	TB-HB-FB-LB-DH	14/12	200	5-10	Washington
Lloyd Young	FB-LB	3/2	190	6-1	Macalester, North Dakota

Scoring

Player	Rush TD	Rec TD	PR TD	Tot TD	XP	FG	Safety	TPs
Jimmy Conzelman	1	3		4				24
George Wilson	4			4				24
Gus Sonnenberg			0		7	3		16
Curly Oden	1	1		2				12
Bill Pritchard	1			1	3			9
Bill Cronin		1		1				6
Jack Cronin			1	1				6
Ed Lynch		1		1				6
Team Totals	7	5	2	14	10	3	1	105
Opponent Totals				13	5	1	1	88

Score by Quarter	1	2	3	4	Total
Steam Roller	7	38	40	20	105
Opponents	21	20	16	31	88

NFL Standings—1927

Team	W-L-T	W-L%	PF	PA
New York Giants	11-1-1	.917	197	20
Green Bay Packers	7-2-1	.778	113	43
Chicago Bears	9-3-2	.750	149	98
Cleveland Bulldogs	8-4-1	.667	209	107
Providence Steam Roller	8-5-1	.615	105	88
New York Yankees	7-8-1	.467	142	174
Frankford Yellow Jackets	6-9-3	.400	152	166
Pottsville Maroons	5-8-0	.385	80	163
Chicago Cardinals	3-7-1	.300	69	134
Dayton Triangles	1-6-1	.143	15	57
Duluth Eskimos	1-8-0	.111	68	134
Buffalo Bisons	0-5-0	.000	8	123

Providence Steam Roller—1928

YEAR: 1928
HEAD COACH: Jimmy Conzelman (coach/player)
LEAGUE: NFL
HOME STADIUM: Cycledrome
SCHEDULE/RESULTS OF GAMES:
Regular-season NFL record: 8-1-2; 1st-place finish—NFL Champions
Overall record: 11-1-2
Points For: 128 (11.6/game)
Points Against: 42 (3.8/game)

1928 Schedule/Results

Date	Opponent	Site	Game Score	H/A	Attendance
09/23	Long Island Warlow A.C.	Cycledrome	W 48-0	H	-------
09/30	New York Yankees	Cycledrome	W 20-7	H	5,000
10/07	Frankford Yellow Jackets	Cycledrome	L 6-10	H	8,000
10/14	Dayton Triangles	Cycledrome	W 28-0	H	7,000
10/21	at New York Yankees	Yankee Stadium	W 12-6	A	8,000
10/28	Pottsville Maroons	Cycledrome	W 13-6	H	8,000
11/04	Detroit Wolverines	Cycledrome	W 7-0	H	8,500
11/10	*Pere Marquette*	Braves Field	W 14-7	A	-------
11/11	*Pere Marquette*	Cycledrome	W 20-0	H	6,000
11/17	at Frankford Yellow Jackets	Frankford Stadium	T 6-6	A	15,000

Appendix: Year-by-Year Results, Team Rosters and Statistics 237

Date	Opponent	Site	Game Score	H/A	Attendance
11/18	Frankford Yellow Jackets	Cycledrome	W 6–0	H	12,000
11/25	New York Giants	Cycledrome	W 16–0	H	13,000
11/29	Pottsville Maroons	Minersville Park	W 7–0	A	10,000
12/02	Green Bay Packers	Cycledrome	T 7–7	H	10,500

Team Roster (19)

Player	Position	GP/GS	WT	HT	College
Jimmy Conzelman	BB-S-FB-LB	4/3	175	6–0	Washington-St. Louis
Bill Cronin	DH-OE-LB-FB-WB	9/1	182	5–10	Boston College
Jack Cronin	TB-DH-WB-OE-DE	8/5	178	5–11	Boston College
Jack Fleischmann	OT-DT-OG-DG	11/6	184	5–6	Purdue
Al Hadden	FB-LB-WB-DH	9/7	186	5–8	Washington & Jefferson
Frank "Duke" Hanny	OE-DE	11/10	199	6–0	Indiana
Norm Harvey	OE-DE	9/4	196	6–0	Detroit Mercy
Perry Jackson	OT-DT	10/7	202	6–1	Southwestern Oklahoma State
Jim Laird	OG-DG	8/0	194	6–0	Colgate
Curly Oden	BB-S-TB-DH	11/9	163	5–6	Brown
Milt Rehnquist	OG-DG-OT-DT-C-MG	11/11	229	6–0	Bethany (Kansas)
Jim Simmons	WB-DH-FB-LB-DT	8/4	186	6–0	Southwestern Oklahoma State
Clyde Smith	C-MG	11/11	181	5–10	Missouri
Orland Smith	OT-DT	9/2	203	5–11	Brown
Gus Sonnenberg	OT-DT-TB-DH	11/10	196	5–6	Dartmouth, Detroit Mercy
Jack Spellman	OT-DT-OE-DE	11/10	201	5–10	Brown
Art "Pop" Williams	FB-LB-WB-TB-DH	7/5	205	6–0	Connecticut
Abe Wilson	OG-DG-OT-DT	9/5	192	5–10	Washington
George Wilson	TB-WB-DH	11/11	200	5–10	Washington

Scoring

Player	Rush TD	Rec TD	Int TD	Tot TD	XP	FG	TPs
George Wilson	5			5			30

238 Appendix: Year-by-Year Results, Team Rosters and Statistics

Player	Rush TD	Rec TD	Int TD	Tot TD	XP	FG	TPs
Curly Oden	1	3		4	3		27
Art Williams	3	1		4			24
Jack Cronin	3			3			18
Jimmy Conzelman	2			2	1		13
Gus Sonnenberg					7	1	10
Duke Hanny			1	1			6
Team Totals	12	6	1	19	11	1	128
Opponent Totals				6	3	1	42

Score by Quarter	1	2	3	4	Total
Steam Roller	32	43	21	32	128
Opponents	0	13	13	16	42

NFL Standings—1928

Team	W-L-T	W-L%	PF	PA
Providence Steam Roller	8-1-2	.889	128	42
Frankford Yellow Jackets	11-3-2	.786	175	84
Detroit Wolverines	7-2-1	.778	189	76
Green Bay Packers	6-4-3	.600	120	92
Chicago Bears	7-5-1	.583	182	85
New York Giants	4-7-2	.364	79	136
New York Yankees	4-8-1	.333	103	179
Pottsville Maroons	2-8-0	.200	74	134
Chicago Cardinals	1-5-0	.167	7	107
Dayton Triangles	0-7-0	.000	9	131

Providence Steam Roller—1929

YEAR: 1929
HEAD COACH: Jimmy Conzelman (coach/player)
LEAGUE: NFL
HOME STADIUM: Cycledrome
SCHEDULE/RESULTS OF GAMES:
Regular-season NFL record: 4-6-2; 7th-place finish
Overall record: 5-6-2
Points For: 107 (8.9/game)
Points Against: 117 (9.8/game)

Appendix: Year-by-Year Results, Team Rosters and Statistics

1929 Schedule/Results

Date	Opponent	Site	Game Score	H/A	Attendance
09/22	West Weymouth Union A.C.	Cycledrome	W 37-0	H	6,000
09/29	Dayton Triangles	Cycledrome	W 41-0	H	8,500
10/06	New York Giants	Cycledrome	L 0-7	H	14,000
10/13	Orange Tornadoes	Cycledrome	W 7-0	H	10,000
10/20	Buffalo Bisons	Cycledrome	T 7-7	H	8,500
10/27	at New York Giants	Polo Grounds	L 0-19	A	25,000
11/05	at Staten Island Stapletons	Thompson Stadium	T 7-7	A	10,000
11/06	Chicago Cardinals*	Kinsley Park	L 0-16	H	8,500
11/09	at Frankford Yellow Jackets	Frankford Stadium	L 0-7	A	6,000
11/10	Frankford Yellow Jackets	Cycledrome	L 6-7	H	-------
11/17	Minneapolis Red Jackets	Cycledrome	W 19-16	H	8,500
11/24	Boston Bulldogs	Cycledrome	W 20-6	H	-------
11/28	at Boston Bulldogs	Braves Field	Canceled	A	-------
12/01	Green Bay Packers	Cycledrome	L 0-25	H	6,500

*First NFL Night Game

Team Roster (21)

Player	Position	GP/GS	WT	HT	College
Jimmy Conzelman	QB-S-LB-OE-DE-OH-DH	9/2	175	6-0	Washington-St. Louis
Bill Cronin	DH-DE-OE-LB-FB-OH	10/7	182	5-10	Boston College
Jack Cronin	QB-DH-FB-OH-OE-DE-LB	12/5	178	5-11	Boston College
Jack Fleischmann	OG-DG	12/12	184	5-6	Purdue
Art Garvey	OG-DG-OT-DT	9/7	234	6-1	Notre Dame
Archie Golembeski	C-MG-OG-DG	8/5	182	5-10	Holy Cross
Al Hadden	OE-DE-FB-LB	9/7	186	5-8	Washington & Jefferson
Frank "Duke" Hanny	OE-DE-OT-DT	11/7	199	6-0	Indiana
Norm Harvey	C-MG-OT-DT-OG-DG	8/2	196	6-0	Detroit Mercy
Perry Jackson	OT-DT-OE-DE-TB-DB	7/5	202	6-1	SW Oklahoma St.

240 Appendix: Year-by-Year Results, Team Rosters and Statistics

Player	Position	GP/GS	WT	HT	College
Lou Jennings	C-MG	2/2	230	6-3	Haskell Indian, Centenary
Jack McBride	FB-LB-OH-DH	12/6	185	5-11	Syracuse
Warren McGuirk	OT-DT	12/10	200	5-11	Boston College
Milt Rehnquist	OE-DE-C-MG	8/7	229	6-0	Bethany (Kansas)
Orland Smith	OT-DT-OG-DG	10/4	203	5-11	Brown
Jack Spellman	OT-DT-OE-DE	12/11	201	5-10	Brown
Hust Stockton	OH-DH	1/0	193	5-11	Gonzaga
Gibby Welch	QB-S-OH-DH-FB-LB	12/10	178	5-11	Pittsburgh
Art "Pop" Williams	FB-LB-S-QB-OH-DH	12/8	205	6-0	Connecticut
Abe Wilson	OG-DG-OT-DT-C-MG	10/3	192	5-10	Washington
George Wilson	QB-S-OH-DH	12/12	200	5-10	Washington

Scoring

Player	Rush TD	Rec TD	Tot TD	XP	FG	TPs
Art Williams	6	1	7			42
Gibby Welch	2	4	6			36
Jimmy Conzelman		1	1			6
Jack Cronin	1		1			6
Jack McBride	·			6		6
George Wilson	1		1			6
Lou Jennings				4		4
Duke Hanny					1	1
Team Totals	10	6	16	11	0	107
Opponent Totals			17	9	2	117

Score by Quarter	1	2	3	4	Total
Steam Roller	41	41	6	19	107
Opponents	27	27	19	44	117

NFL Standings—1929

Team	W-L-T	W-L%	PF	PA
Green Bay Packers	12-0-1	1.000	198	22
New York Giants	13-1-1	.929	312	86
Frankford Yellow Jackets	10-4-5	.714	129	128

Appendix: Year-by-Year Results, Team Rosters and Statistics 241

Team	W–L–T	W–L%	PF	PA
Chicago Cardinals	6–6–1	.500	154	83
Boston Bulldogs	4–4–0	.500	98	73
Staten Island Stapletons	3–4–3	.429	89	65
Providence Steam Roller	4–6–2	.400	107	117
Orange Tornadoes	3–5–4	.375	35	80
Chicago Bears	4–9–2	.308	119	227
Buffalo Bisons	1–7–1	.125	48	142
Minneapolis Red Jackets	1–9–0	.100	48	185
Dayton Triangles	0–6–0	.000	7	136

Providence Steam Roller—1930

YEAR: 1930
HEAD COACH: Jimmy Conzelman (coach/player)
LEAGUE: NFL
HOME STADIUM: Cycledrome
SCHEDULE/RESULTS OF GAMES:
Regular-season NFL record: 6–4–1; 5th-place finish
Overall record: 10–4–1
Points For: 90 (8.2/game)
Points Against: 125 (11.4/game)

1930 Schedule/Results

Date	Opponent	Site	Game Score	H/A	Attendance
09/14	West Weymouth	Cycledrome	W 59–0	H	4,014
09/17	Quincy Trojans	Cycledrome	W 28–0	H	3,100
09/21	Brooklyn Professionals	Cycledrome	W 63–0	H	4,800
09/28	New York Giants	Cycledrome	L 7–27	H	12,000
10/01	Frankford Yellow Jackets	Cycledrome	W 14–0	H	3,500
10/05	Newark Tornadoes	Cycledrome	W 14–0	H	4,500
10/09	Brooklyn Dodgers	Cycledrome	Canceled	H	-------
10/12	Chicago Cardinals	Cycledrome	W 9–7	H	13,000
10/16	at Newark Tornadoes	Newark Schools Stadium	Canceled	A	-------
10/19	Staten Island Stapletons	Cycledrome	W 7–6	H	5,000
10/26	at New York Giants	Polo Grounds	L 0–25	A	10,000
11/02	Brooklyn Dodgers	Cycledrome	W 3–0	H	-------
11/08	at Frankford Yellow Jackets	Frankford Stadium	L 7–20	A	4,000

242 Appendix: Year-by-Year Results, Team Rosters and Statistics

Date	Opponent	Site	Game Score	H/A	Attendance
11/09	Frankford Yellow Jackets	Cycledrome	T 7-7	H	-------
11/16	Portsmouth Spartans	Cycledrome	Canceled	H	-------
11/23	Minneapolis Red Jackets	Cycledrome	W 10-0	H	-------
11/27	at Brooklyn Dodgers	Ebbets Field	L 12-33	A	8,000
11/30	at Pere Marquette	Braves Field	W 6-0	A	1,500

Team Roster (26)

Player	Position	GP/GS	WT	HT	College
Jack Cronin	QB-FB-DH-OH-S-LB	10/3	178	5-11	Boston College
Forrest Douds	OT-DT	9/7	216	5-10	Washington & Jefferson
Bud Edwards	OH-DH-FB-LB	9/3	190	5-11	Brown
Herb Eschbach	C-MG	7/4	190	6-0	Penn State
Weldon Gentry	OG-DG	4/0	195	5-10	Arkansas, Oklahoma
Al Graham	OG-DG	9/9	211	6-0	None
Al Hadden	OH-DH-FB-LB	9/4	186	5-8	Washington & Jefferson
Tony Holm	OH-DH-FB-LB	3/2	214	6-1	Alabama
Perry Jackson	OT-DT	10/5	202	6-1	Southwestern Oklahoma State
Joe Kozlowsky	OT-DT-OG-DG	8/2	201	5-10	Boston College
Ted Kucharski	OE-DE	8/0	185	6-1	Holy Cross
Tony Latone	FB-LB-OH-DB	11/7	195	5-11	None
Jack McArthur	C-MG-OT-DT	4/0	211	5-11	St. Mary's (CA)
Warren McGuirk	OT-DT	11/8	200	5-11	Boston College
Herb Meeker	QB-S-OH-DH-FB-LB	11/3	145	5-3	Washington State
Curly Oden	QB-S-OH-DH-FB-LB	10/6	162	5-6	Brown
Forrest "Frosty" Peters	QB-S-OH-DH	12/8	183	5-10	Montana State, Illinois
Frank Racis	OG-DG	11/6	200	6-0	None
Milt Rehnquist	OG-DG	10/7	229	6-0	Bethany (Kansas)
Al Rose	OE-DE	11/11	201	6-3	Texas
Ray Smith	C-MG	10/7	195	5-10	Tulsa, Missouri
Gus Sonnenberg	OT-DT	1/0	196	5-6	Dartmouth, Detroit Mercy

Appendix: Year-by-Year Results, Team Rosters and Statistics   243

Player	Position	GP/GS	WT	HT	College
Jack Spellman	OE-DE	11/10	201	5–10	Brown
Dutch Webber	OE-DE	1/1	190	6–2	Kansas State
Art "Pop" Williams	S-QB-OH-DH	11/8	205	6–0	Connecticut
Herm Young	OE-DE	3/0	178	5–11	Detroit Mercy

Scoring

Player	Rush TD	Rec TD	KR TD	Int TD	Tot TD	XP	FG	TPs
Frosty Peters	1			1	2	7	2	25
Tony Latone	3				3			18
Butch Meeker		1	1		2	1	1	16
Art Williams	2				2			12
Bud Edwards		1			1			6
Frank Racis				1	1			6
Herm Young		1			1			6
Curly Oden					0	1		1
Team Totals	6	3	1	2	12	9	3	90
Opponent Totals				19	11			125

Score by Quarter	1	2	3	4	Total
Steam Roller	20	27	16	27	90
Opponents	13	40	34	38	125

NFL Standings—1930

Team	W–L–T	W–L%	PF	PA
Green Bay Packers	10–3–1	.769	234	111
New York Giants	13–4–0	.765	308	98
Chicago Bears	9–4–1	.692	169	71
Brooklyn Dodgers	7–4–1	.636	154	59
Providence Steam Roller	6–4–1	.600	90	125
Staten Island Stapletons	5–5–2	.500	95	112
Chicago Cardinals	5–6–2	.455	128	132
Portsmouth Spartans	5–6–3	.455	176	161
Frankford Yellow Jackets	4–13–1	.235	113	321
Minneapolis Red Jackets	1–7–1	.125	27	165
Newark Tornadoes	1–10–1	.091	51	190

Appendix: Year-by-Year Results, Team Rosters and Statistics

Providence Steam Roller—1931

YEAR: 1931
HEAD COACH: Ed Robinson (coach)
LEAGUE: NFL
HOME STADIUM: Cycledrome
SCHEDULE/RESULTS OF GAMES:
Regular-season NFL record: 4-4-3; 6th-place finish
Overall record: 15-4-3
Points For: 78 (7.1/game)
Points Against: 127 (11.5/game)

1931 Schedule/Results

Date	Opponent	Site	Game Score	H/A	Attendance
09/06	Boston Collegians	Cycledrome	W 20-0	H	------
09/13	Quincy Trojans	Cycledrome	W 34-7	H	------
09/20	Weymouth	Cycledrome	W 66-0	H	------
09/27	New York Giants	Cycledrome	L 6-14	H	8,000
10/04	Frankford Yellow Jackets	Cycledrome	T 0-0	H	------
10/10	at Frankford Yellow Jackets	Baker Bowl	W 6-0	A	3,000
10/11	Bridgeport All Stars	Cycledrome	W 67-7	H	------
10/18	Cleveland Indians	Cycledrome	L 6-13	H	6,000
10/25	at Green Bay Packers	City Stadium	L 20-48	A	6,000
10/27	at Buffalo Bears	Bison Stadium	W 6-0	A	------
11/01	at Staten Island Stapletons	Thompson Stadium	T 7-7	A	4,000
11/08	Brooklyn Dodgers	Cycledrome	W 7-0	H	4,000
11/15	Staten Island Stapletons	Cycledrome	W 6-0	H	2,000
11/21	Cleveland Indians	Cycledrome	W 13-7	H	------
11/22	Watchemoket All Stars	Cycledrome	W 27-0	H	2,000
11/22	Speedways of Cranston	Cycledrome	W 32-0	H	2,000
11/22	Natick Sacred Hearts	Cycledrome	W 7-0	H	2,000
11/22	East Providence Townies	Cycledrome	W 12-0	H	2,000
11/26	Green Bay Packers	Cycledrome	L 7-38	H	5,000
11/29	at New York Giants	Polo Grounds	T 0-0	A	18,000
12/05	at Waterbury Bearcats	Fitton Field	W 65-0	A	3,000
12/13	at Memphis Tigers	Hodges Field	W 12-6	A	1,000

Team Roster (24)

Player	Position	GP/GS	WT	HT	College
Sky August	OH-DH-QB-S	7/1	180	5-11	Villanova

Player	Position	GP/GS	WT	HT	College
Fred Dagata	FB-LB	1/0	187	5–10	Providence
Bud Edwards	OH-DH-FB-LB	9/4	190	5–11	Brown
Herb Eschbach	C-MG	4/1	190	6–0	Penn State
Weldon Gentry	OG-DG	7/4	195	5–10	Arkansas, Oklahoma
Royce Goodbread	OH-DH-FB-LB	4/2	207	5–11	Florida
Al Graham	OG-DG	11/10	211	6–0	None
Tex Irvin	OT-DT-FB-LB	10/9	225	6–0	Davis & Elkins
Jack McArthur	OG-DG-OT-DT-DE	9/3	211	5–11	St. Mary's (CA)
Herb Meeker	QB-S-OH-DH	9/3	145	5–3	Washington State
Curly Oden	QB-S-OH-DH	11/4	162	5–6	Brown
Oran Pape	OH-DH-QB-S	11/7	180	5–11	Iowa
Lew Pope	OH-DH-QB-S	8/3	196	6–0	Purdue
George Pyne	OT-DT	2/1	218	5–11	Holy Cross
Milt Rehnquist	OG-DG	2/0	229	6–0	Bethany (Kansas)
Al Rose	OE-DE	11/11	201	6–3	Texas
Joe Schein	OT-DT	11/11	212	5–10	Brown
Dexter Shelley	OH-DH-QB-S	8/5	191	5–11	Texas
Ray Smith	C-MG	10/10	195	5–10	Tulsa, Missouri
Alex Sofish	OG-DG	11/8	200	6–2	Grove City
Jack Spellman	OE-DE	11/10	201	5–10	Brown
Herb Titmas	QB-S-OH-DH	11/5	165	5–8	Syracuse
Art "Pop" Williams	S-QB-OH-DH	8/2	205	6–0	Connecticut
Lee Woodruff	FB-LB	11/7	202	6–0	Mississippi

Scoring

Player	Rush TD	Rec TD	PR TD	Oth TD	Tot TD	XP	FG	TPs
Lee Woodruff	4				4	1		25
Oran Pape	1	2			3			18
Al Rose		2		1	3			18
Curly Oden			1		1			6
Herb Titmas		1			1			6
Dexter Shelley					0	4		4
Herb Meeker					0	1		1
Team Totals	5	5	1	1	12	6	0	78
Opponent Totals					19	13	0	127

Score by Quarter	1	2	3	4	Total
Steam Roller	0	33	13	32	78
Opponents	55	40	0	32	127

NFL Standings—1931

Team	W-L-T	W-L%	PF	PA
Green Bay Packers	12-2-0	.857	291	87
Portsmouth Spartans	11-3-0	.786	175	77
Chicago Bears	8-5-0	.615	145	92
Chicago Cardinals	5-4-0	.556	120	128
New York Giants	7-6-1	.538	154	100
Providence Steam Roller	4-4-3	.500	78	127
Staten Island Stapletons	4-6-1	.400	79	118
Cleveland Indians	2-8-0	.200	45	137
Brooklyn Dodgers	2-12-0	.143	64	199
Frankford Yellow Jackets	1-6-1	.143	13	99

Steam Roller All-Time Leading Scorers: 1925-1931

Scoring (Alpha Order)

Player	Rush TD	Rec TD	PR TD	KR TD	Fbl TD	Oth TD	Tot TD	XP	FG	Safety	TPs
Dutch Connor							0	2			2
Jim Conzelman	1	6					7	1			43
Bill Cronin		1					1				6
Jack Cronin	4		1				5				30
Bud Edwards		1					1				6
Franny Garvey					1	1	2	1			13
Archie Golembeski		1			2		3	1			19
Duke Hanny						1	1	1			7
Lou Jennings							0	4			4
Jack Keefer	2						2	3			15
Jim Laird	3						3	2	3		29
Tony Latone	3						3				18
Ed Lynch		1					1				6
Red Maloney					1		1	4	3		19
Jack McBride							0	6			6
Butch Meeker		1		1			2	2	1		17
Curly Oden	8	4	5				17	4			106

Appendix: Year-by-Year Results, Team Rosters and Statistics 247

Player	Rush TD	Rec TD	PR TD	KR TD	Fbl TD	Oth TD	Tot TD	XP	FG	Safety	TPs
Oran Pape	1	2					3				18
Frosty Peters	1				1		2	7	2		25
Bill Pritchard	1						1	3			9
Frank Racis					1		1				6
Al Rose		2			1		3				18
Dexter Shelley							0	4			4
Gus Sonnenberg							0	14	4		26
Jack Spellman					1		1				6
Fred Sweet							0	1	2		7
Herb Titmas		1					1				6
Gibby Welch	2	4					6				36
Cy Wentworth	2		1				3	3	1		24
Art Williams	11	2					13				78
George Wilson	10						10				60
Lee Woodruff	4						4	1			25
Herm Young		1					1				6
Safeties										4	8
Team Totals	53	27	6	2	4	6	98	64	16	4	708
Opponent Totals							101	61	10	3	703

Score by Quarter	1	2	3	4	Total
Steam Rollers	126	247	162	173	708
Opponents	158	185	117	243	703

Scoring (Points Order)

Player	Rush TD	Rec TD	PR TD	KR TD	Fbl TD	Oth TD	Tot TD	XP	FG	Safety	TPs
Curly Oden	8	4	5				17	4			106
Art Williams	11	2					13				78
George Wilson	10						10				60
Jim Conzelman	1	6					7	1			43
Gibby Welch	2	4					6				36
Jack Cronin	4		1				5				30
Jim Laird	3						3	2	3		29
Gus Sonnenberg							0	14	4		26
Frosty Peters	1				1		2	7	2		25
Lee Woodruff	4						4	1			25
Cy Wentworth	2		1				3	3	1		24

Player	Rush TD	Rec TD	PR TD	KR TD	Fbl TD	Oth TD	Tot TD	XP	FG	Safety	TPs
Archie Golembeski		1			2		3	1			19
Red Maloney					1		1	4	3		19
Tony Latone	3						3				18
Oran Pape	1	2					3				18
Al Rose		2				1	3				18
Butch Meeker		1		1			2	2	1		17
Jack Keefer	2						2	3			15
Franny Garvey					1	1	2	1			13
Bill Pritchard	1						1	3			9
Duke Hanny					1		1	1			7
Fred Sweet							0	1	2		7
Bill Cronin		1					1				6
Bud Edwards		1					1				6
Ed Lynch		1					1				6
Jack McBride							0	6			6
Frank Racis					1		1				6
Jack Spellman					1		1				6
Herb Titmas		1					1				6
Herm Young		1					1				6
Lou Jennings							0	4			4
Dexter Shelley							0	4			4
Dutch Connor							0	2			2
Safeties										4	8
Team Totals	53	27	6	2	4	6	98	64	16	4	708
Opponent Totals							101	61	10	3	703

Steam Roller All-Time Leaders

Seasons Played

Jack Spellman—7
Curly Oden—6
Jack Cronin—4
Al Hadden—4

Joe Kozlowsky—4
Jim Laird—4
Milt Rehnquist—4
Art "Pop" Williams—4

Games Played

Jack Spellman—81
Curly Oden—66
Jack Cronin—42

Jim Laird—42
Joe Kozlowsky—41

Points Scored

Curly Oden—106
Art "Pop" Williams—78
George "Wildcat"
  Wilson—60
Jimmy Conzelman—43
Gibby Welch—36

Jack Cronin—30
Jim Laird—29
Gus Sonnenberg—26
Frosty Peters—25
Lee Woodruff—25

Most Touchdowns

Curly Oden—17
Art "Pop" Williams—13
George "Wildcat"
  Wilson—10

Jimmy Conzelman—7
Gibby Welch—6
Jack Cronin—5

Touchdown Passes

George "Wildcat"
  Wilson—13
Dexter Shelley—3

Jack McBride—2
Frosty Peters—2
Curly Oden—2

Most Extra Points

Gus Sonnenberg—14
Frosty Peters—7
Jack McBride—6
Red Maloney—4

Curly Oden—4
Lou Jennings—4
Dexter Shelley—4

Most Field Goals

Gus Sonnenberg—4
Jim Laird—3

Red Maloney—3

Head Coaching Records

Jimmy Conzelman	26–16–6	.604
Archie Golembeski	6–5–1	.542
Ed Robinson	4–4–3	.500
Jim Laird	5–7–1	.423

All-Time Providence Steam Roller Record Versus Each NFL Opponent

Boston Bulldogs

Record: 1-0-0

November 24, 1929	Boston Bulldogs 6 @ Providence Steam Roller 20

250 Appendix: Year-by-Year Results, Team Rosters and Statistics

Brooklyn Dodgers

Record: 2-1-0

November 2, 1930	Brooklyn Dodgers 0 @ Providence Steam Roller 3
November 27, 1930	Providence Steam Roller 12 @ Brooklyn Dodgers 33
November 8, 1931	Brooklyn Dodgers 0 @ Providence Steam Roller 7

Brooklyn Lions

Record: 1-0-0

September 26, 1926	Brooklyn Lions 0 @ Providence Steam Roller 13

Buffalo Bisons

Record: 2-0-1

November 8, 1925	Buffalo Bisons 0 @ Providence Steam Roller 10
October 2, 1927	Buffalo Bisons 0 @ Providence Steam Roller 5
October 20, 1929	Buffalo Bisons 7 @ Providence Steam Roller 7

Canton Bulldogs

Record: 1-0-0

November 11, 1926	Canton Bulldogs 2 @ Providence Steam Roller 21

Chicago Cardinals

Record: 1-1-0

November 6, 1929	Chicago Cardinals 16 @ Providence Steam Roller 0
October 12, 1930	Chicago Cardinals 7 @ Providence Steam Roller 9

Chicago Bears

Record: 1-0-1

December 9, 1925	Chicago Bears 6 @ Providence Steam Roller 9
November 6, 1927	Providence Steam Roller 0 @ Chicago Bears 0

Cleveland Bulldogs

Record: 0-1-1

November 29, 1925	Cleveland Bulldogs 7 @ Providence Steam Roller 7
November 20, 1927	Cleveland Bulldogs 22 @ Providence Steam Roller 0

Cleveland Indians

Record: 1-1-0

October 18, 1931	Cleveland Indians 13 @ Providence Steam Roller 6
November 21, 1931	Cleveland Indians 7 @ Providence Steam Roller 13

Appendix: Year-by-Year Results, Team Rosters and Statistics 251

Columbus Tigers

Record 1-0-0

| October 10, 1926 | Columbus Tigers 0 @ Providence Steam Roller 19 |

Dayton Triangles

Record: 3-0-0

October 23, 1927	Dayton Triangles 0 @ Providence Steam Roller 7
October 14, 1928	Dayton Triangles 0 @ Providence Steam Roller 28
September 29, 1929	Dayton Triangles 0 @ Providence Steam Roller 41

Detroit Wolverines

Record: 1-0-0

| November 4, 1928 | Detroit Wolverines 0 @ Providence Steam Roller 7 |

Duluth Eskimos

Record: 1-0-1

| November 28, 1926 | Duluth Eskimos 0 @ Providence Steam Roller 0 |
| November 13, 1927 | Duluth Eskimos 7 @ Providence Steam Roller 13 |

Frankford Yellow Jackets

Record: 7-8-3

October 3, 1925	Providence Steam Roller 0 @ Frankford Yellow Jackets 7
November 22, 1925	Frankford Yellow Jackets 7 @ Providence Steam Roller 20
December 13, 1925	Frankford Yellow Jackets 14 @ Providence Steam Roller 6
October 30, 1926	Providence Steam Roller 7 @ Frankford Yellow Jackets 6
October 31, 1926	Frankford Yellow Jackets 6 @ Providence Steam Roller 3
December 11, 1926	Providence Steam Roller 0 @ Frankford Yellow Jackets 24
October 29, 1927	Providence Steam Roller 20 @ Frankford Yellow Jackets 7
October 30, 1927	Frankford Yellow Jackets 0 @ Providence Steam Roller 14
October 7, 1928	Frankford Yellow Jackets 10 @ Providence Steam Roller 6
November 17, 1928	Providence Steam Roller 6 @ Frankford Yellow Jackets 6
November 18, 1928	Frankford Yellow Jackets 0 @ Providence Steam Roller 6
November 9, 1929	Providence Steam Roller 0 @ Frankford Yellow Jackets 7
November 10, 1929	Frankford Yellow Jackets 7 @ Providence Steam Roller 6
October 1, 1930	Frankford Yellow Jackets 0 @ Providence Steam Roller 14
November 8, 1930	Providence Steam Roller 7 @ Frankford Yellow Jackets 20
November 9, 1930	Frankford Yellow Jackets 7 @ Providence Steam Roller 7
October 4, 1931	Frankford Yellow Jackets 0 @ Providence Steam Roller 0
October 10, 1931	Providence Steam Roller 6 @ Frankford Yellow Jackets 0

Green Bay Packers

Record: 0-4-1

December 6, 1925	Green Bay Packers 13 @ Providence Steam Roller 10
December 2, 1928	Green Bay Packers 7 @ Providence Steam Roller 7
December 1, 1929	Green Bay Packers 25 @ Providence Steam Roller 0
October 25, 1931	Providence Steam Roller 20 @ Green Bay Packers 48
November 26, 1931	Green Bay Packers 38 @ Providence Steam Roller 7

Kansas City Cowboys

Record: 0-1-0

November 14, 1926	Kansas City Cowboys 22 @ Providence Steam Roller 0

Los Angeles Buccaneers

Record 0-1-0

November 7, 1926	Los Angeles Buccaneers 7 @ Providence Steam Roller 6

Minneapolis Red Jackets

Record: 2-0-0

November 17, 1929	Minneapolis Red Jackets 16 @ Providence Steam Roller 19
November 23, 1930	Minneapolis Red Jackets 0 @ Providence Steam Roller 10

New York Giants

Record: 2-10-1

October 11, 1925	New York Giants 0 @ Providence Steam Roller 14
November 15, 1925	Providence Steam Roller 12 @ New York Giants 13
October 3, 1926	New York Giants 7 @ Providence Steam Roller 6
November 21, 1926	Providence Steam Roller 0 @ New York Giants 21
September 25, 1927	New York Giants 8 @ Providence Steam Roller 0
November 8, 1927	Providence Steam Roller 0 @ New York Giants 25
November 25, 1928	New York Giants 0 @ Providence Steam Roller 16
October 6, 1929	New York Giants 7 @ Providence Steam Roller 0
October 27, 1929	Providence Steam Roller 0 @ New York Giants 19
September 28, 1930	New York Giants 27 @ Providence Steam Roller 7
October 26, 1930	Providence Steam Roller 0 @ New York Giants 25
September 27, 1931	New York Giants 14 @ Providence Steam Roller 6
November 29, 1931	Providence Steam Roller 0 @ New York Giants 0

New York Yankees

Record: 4-0-0

November 27, 1927	New York Yankees 7 @ Providence Steam Roller 14
December 3, 1927	Providence Steam Roller 9 @ New York Yankees 0

Appendix: Year-by-Year Results, Team Rosters and Statistics 253

| September 30, 1928 | New York Yankees 7 @ Providence Steam Roller 20 |
| October 21, 1928 | Providence Steam Roller 12 @ New York Yankees 6 |

Orange/Newark Tornadoes

Record: 2-0-0

| October 13, 1929 | Orange Tornadoes 0 @ Providence Steam Roller 7 |
| October 5, 1930 | Newark Tornadoes 0 @ Providence Steam Roller 14 |

Pottsville Maroons

Record: 5-4-0

October 4, 1925	Providence Steam Roller 6 @ Pottsville Maroons 0
October 18, 1925	Pottsville Maroons 34 @ Providence Steam Roller 0
October 24, 1926	Pottsville Maroons 0 @ Providence Steam Roller 14
November 25, 1926	Providence Steam Roller 0 @ Pottsville Maroons 8
October 16, 1927	Pottsville Maroons 6 @ Providence Steam Roller 3
November 24, 1927	Providence Steam Roller 0 @ Pottsville Maroons 6
December 4, 1927	Pottsville Maroons 0 @ Providence Steam Roller 20
October 28, 1928	Pottsville Maroons 6 @ Providence Steam Roller 13
November 29, 1928	Providence Steam Roller 7 @ Pottsville Maroons 0

Rochester Jeffersons

Record: 1-0-0

| November 1, 1925 | Rochester Jeffersons 0 @ Providence Steam Roller 17 |

Staten Island Stapletons

Record: 2-0-2

November 5, 1929	Providence Steam Roller 7 @ Staten Island Stapletons 7
October 19, 1930	Staten Island Stapletons 6 @ Providence Steam Roller 7
November 1, 1931	Providence Steam Roller 7 @ Staten Island Stapletons 7
November 15, 1931	Staten Island Stapletons 0 @ Providence Steam Roller 6

Providence Steam Roller All-NFL Selections

Year	Player	Position	Selection
1925	Gerry "Red" Maloney	End	Second Team
1925	Dolph Eckstein	Center	Second Team
1925	Shirley "Cy" Wentworth	Halfback	Second Team
1926	Olaf "Curly" Oden	Halfback	Second Team
1927	Jack Fleischmann	Guard	First Team
1927	Joe Kozlowsky	Tackle	First Team

Year	Player	Position	Selection
1927	Gus Sonnenberg	Tackle	First Team
1927	Olaf "Curly" Oden	Quarterback	First Team
1927	Edward Lynch	End	Second Team
1927	George "Wildcat" Wilson	Halfback	Second Team
1928	Clyde Smith	Center	First Team
1928	George "Wildcat" Wilson	Halfback	First Team
1928	Olaf "Curly" Oden	Quarterback	Second Team
1928	Milton Rehnquist	Guard	Second Team
1928	Gus Sonnenberg	Tackle	Second Team
1929	Milton Rehnquist	Guard	First Team
1929	Gibby Welch	Halfback	Second Team
1931	Al Graham	Guard	Second Team
1931	Al Rose	End	Third Team

Pearce B. Johnson's All-Time Providence Steam Roller Squad

Position	Player	Years with Providence
Ends	Gerry "Red" Maloney	1925
	George "Bull" Lowe	1925, 1927
	Jack Spellman	1925–1931
Tackles	Gus Sonnenberg	1927–28, 1930
	Joe Kozlowsky	1925–27, 1930
Guards	Milton Rehnquist	1928–1931
	Jack Fleischmann	1927–1929
Center	Clyde Smith	1930–1931
Quarterback	Olaf "Curly" Oden	1925–28, 1930–31
Halfbacks	George "Wildcat" Wilson	1928–29
	Shirley "Cy" Wentworth	1925–26
	Jack Cronin	1927–30
Fullbacks	Jim Laird	1925–28
	Art "Pop" Williams	1928–31

Providence Steam Roller Players in Pro Football Hall of Fame

- Jimmy Conzelman
- Fritz Pollard

Appendix: Year-by-Year Results, Team Rosters and Statistics 255

Year-by-Year Starting Lineups

Year	Record	Backfield	Offensive Line	Special Teams
1931	4-4-3	TB—Deck Shelley	LE—Al Rose	PR—Al Rose
		FB—Lee Woodruff	LT—Tex Irvin	KR—Al Rose
		BB—Herb Titmas	LG—Al Graham	K—Dexter Shelley
		WB—Oran Pape	C—Ray Smith	
			RG—Alec Sofish	
			RT—Joe Schein	
			RE—Jack Spellman	
1930	6-4-1	TB—Frosty Peters	LE—Al Rose	PR—Milt Rehnquist
		FB—Tony Latone	LT—Forrest Douds	KR—Milt Rehnquist
		BB—Curly Oden	LG—Milt Rehnquist	K—Frosty Peters
		WB—Pop Williams	C—Ray Smith	
			RG—Al Graham	
			RT—Warren McGuirk	
			RE—Jack Spellman	
1929	4-6-2	TB—Abe Wilson	LE—Al Hadden	PR—Milt Rehnquist
		FB—Jack McBride	LT—Duke Hanny	KR—Milt Rehnquist
		BB—Gibby Welch	LG—Hec Garvey	K—Jack McBride
		WB—Pop Williams	C—Milt Rehnquist	
			RG—Jack Fleischmann	
			RT—Warren McGuirk	
			RE—Jack Spellman	
1928	8-1-2	TB—Wildcat Wilson	LE—Duke Hanny	PR—Jim Simmons
		FB—Al Hadden	LT—Gus Sonnenberg	KR—Jim Simmons
		BB—Curly Oden	LG—Milt Rehnquist	K—Gus Sonnenberg
		WB—Bill Cronin	C—Clyde Smith	
			RG—Jack Fleischmann	
			RT—Arnie Shockley	
			RE—Jack Spellman	
1927	8-5-1	TB—Abe Wilson	LE—Ed Lynch	PR—Gus Sonnenberg
		FB—Bill Pritchard	LT—Gus Sonnenberg	KR—Gus Sonnenberg
		BB—Curly Oden	LG—Jack Fleischmann	K—Gus Sonnenberg
		WB—Al Hadden	C—Al Pierotti	
			RG—Jim Laird	
			RT—Orland Smith	
			RE—Jack Spellman	
1926	5-7-1	TB—Cy Wentworth	LE—Franny Garvey	PR—Frank Seyboth

256 Appendix: Year-by-Year Results, Team Rosters and Statistics

Year	Record	Backfield	Offensive Line	Special Teams
		FB—Jim Laird	LT—Joe Kozlowsky	KR—Frank Seyboth
		BB—Curly Oden	LG—Jack Donahue	K—Cy Wentworth
		WB—Jack Spellman	C—Dolph Eckstein	
			RG—Lloyd Young	
			RT—Mike Gulian	
			RE—Archie Golembeski	
1925	6-5-1	TB—Cy Wentworth	LE—Franny Garvey	PR—Nate Share
		FB—Jim Laird	LT—Joe Kozlowsky	KR—Nate Share
		BB—Curly Oden	LG—Nate Share	K—Red Maloney
		WB—Al McIntosh	C—Dolph Eckstein	
			RG—Archie Golembeski	
			RT—Mike Gulian	
			RE—Red Maloney	

Chapter Notes

Introduction

1. David S. Neft, Richard M. Cohen, and Jordan Deutsch, *Pro Football: The Early Years, An Encyclopedic History 1895–1959* (Ridgefield, CT: Sports Products, 1978), 35.
2. Harold Claassen, *The History of Professional Football, Its Great Teams, Games, Players and Coaches* (Englewood Cliffs, NJ: Prentice-Hall, 1963), 3.
3. Claassen, *History of Professional Football*, vii.

Chapter One

1. Dennis Kennedy, "He Was There for the Kickoff," *Observer Life*, July 14, 1994, 1B.
2. Kennedy, "He Was There for the Kickoff."
3. Tom Emery, "Way Before the Patriots, Providence Fans Enjoyed Title Ride with Steam Roller," *Providence Journal*, February 1, 2015, Travel Section 1.
4. Bill Parrillo, "In 1928, 'Super Bowl' Was the Talk of R.I., Providence Steam Roller Won NFL Title," *Providence Journal Bulletin*, December 28, 1988, D-11.
5. Kennedy, "He Was There for the Kickoff."
6. Jonathan Hock, Pearce B. Johnson Interview with NFL Films, October 4, 1991.
7. "Clay Hills Steam Rollers Battle to Scoreless Tie," *Hartford Courant*, October 18, 1920, 14.
8. "Along the Sidelines," *Providence Journal*, October 21, 1924, 21.
9. "Roller Flattens Marines; 49–0 Score," *Providence Journal*, November 17, 1924, 6.
10. Bob Gill, "Providence Starts Rolling, 1924," *The Coffin Corner*, vol. 17, no. 4 (1995), 4.
11. Dick Reynolds, *The Steam Roller Story* (Self-Published in Providence, 1989—In the Rhode Island Historical Society Collection), 7.
12. "Cycledrome Opening Attracts 9000 Crowd: Verkeyn Wins Main Event of 30 Miles: Belgian Leads from Start to Finish in Grind Behind Motors—Gastman Makes Hit—Meyer Captures Sprint Match," *Providence Journal*, June 3, 1925, 7.
13. John Eisenberg, *The League, How Five Rivals Created the NFL and Launched a Sports Empire* (New York: Basic Books, Hachette Book Group, 2018), 37.

Chapter Two

1. Staff Correspondent, "Leading Pro Elevens to Show Wares Here," *Providence Journal*, August 3, 1925, 7.
2. "National Grid Circuit Opens Season Sunday," *News-Record*, September 19, 1925, 5.
3. "Pro Football Soon Under Way," *Providence Journal*, September 12, 1925, 11.
4. "Wentworth Brilliant in One-Side Contest," *Providence Journal*, September 21, 1925, 6.
5. Robert L. Wheeler, "That Old Steam Roller ... in infancy ... in lusty prime ... in decline," *Providence Sunday Journal*, November 11, 1956, 21.
6. Wheeler, "That Old Steam Roller ... in infancy ... in lusty prime ... in decline," 21.

7. David Fleming, *Breaker Boys, The NFL's Greatest Team and the Stolen 1925 NFL Championship* (New York: ESPN Books, A Division of ESPN Publishing, 2007), 94.
8. "Fumbles Cost Maroons Game; Steam Rollers Outplayed," *Pottsville Republican*, October 5, 1925, 7.
9. "Fumbles Cost Maroons Game; Steam Rollers Outplayed," 7.
10. Providence Steam Roller vs New York Giants game program, October 11, 1925, Providence Steam Roller Club, 1925, 1.
11. Providence Steam Roller vs New York Giants game program, 1.
12. Fleming, *Breaker Boys, The NFL's Greatest Team and the Stolen 1925 NFL Championship*, 117.
13. Wheeler, "That Old Steam Roller ... in infancy ... in lusty prime ... in decline," 21.
14. Wheeler, "That Old Steam Roller ... in infancy ... in lusty prime ... in decline," 21.
15. "Pro Football All Business," *Boston Globe*, November 30, 1925, 11.
16. Neft, Cohen, and Deutsch, *Pro Football: The Early Years, An Encyclopedic History 1895–1959*, 35.
17. Ira Morton, *The Red Grange Story: An Autobiography*, as told to Ira Morton (Urbana: University of Illinois Press, 1957 and 1981), Kindle Edition, 9.
18. Staff Correspondent, "Grange Stopped; Roller Defeats Chicago 9–6," *Providence Journal*, December 10, 1925, 1.
19. Staff Correspondent, "Grange Stopped; Roller Defeats Chicago 9–6," 1.
20. Wheeler, "That Old Steam Roller ... in infancy ... in lusty prime ... in decline," 24.
21. "Steam Rollers Lose to Yellow Jackets," *Boston Globe*, December 14, 1925, 10.
22. "Roller Team Lauded at Annual Banquet, *Providence Journal*, February 21, 1926, 23.
23. "Oden Is Outstanding Figure in Triumph," *Providence Journal*, October 25, 1926, 6.
24. "Wentworth Misses Attempt for Point," *Providence Journal*, November 8, 1926, 6.
25. "Pottsville Topples Steam Roller 8 to 0," *Providence Journal*, November 26, 1926, 8.
26. Claassen, *The History of Professional Football, Its Great Teams, Games, Players and Coaches*, 48.
27. "Pottsville's Late Drive a Winner," *Boston Globe*, October 17, 2017, 19.
28. "Touchdown in Last Period Gives Roller 13–7 Victory," *Providence Journal*, November 14, 1927, 6.
29. Robert Searing, "In 1907, Syracuse University opens Archbold Stadium, called then the 'greatest athletic arena in America,'" Syracuse.com—https://www.syracuse.com/living/2021/09/in-1907-syracuse-university-opens-archbold-stadium-called-then-the-greatest-athletic-arena-in-america.html#:~:text=On%20September%2025%2C%201907%2C%20the%20Syracuse%20Orange%20varsity,in%20America%2C"%20by%20some%20in%20the%20national%20press.
30. "Roller Downs Yankees, 9–0, in Syracuse Benefit Battle," *Providence Journal*, December 4, 1927, 21.

Chapter Three

1. "Sport Comment," *Buffalo News*, July 9, 1928, 13.
2. John R. Hess, Jr., "National Football League Near Dissolution," *Providence Journal*, August 26, 1928, 22.
3. Hock, Pearce B. Johnson Interview.
4. Hock, Pearce B. Johnson Interview.
5. Hock, Pearce B. Johnson Interview.
6. John R. Hess, Jr., "Williams Splits New York Line for First Touchdown," *Providence Journal*, October 1, 1928, 6.
7. Hess, "Williams Splits New York Line for First Touchdown," 6.
8. Rachel Slade, "The High-Rise Cliffhanger, Inside the Decades-Long Saga of Rhode Island's Landmark Skyscraper, The Superman Building," *Yankee Magazine*, July/August 2022, 108.
9. Wheeler, "That Old Steam Roller ... in infancy ... in lusty prime ... in decline," 22.
10. John R. Hess, Jr., "Miners' Drive for Tie Game Stopped on Three-Yard Line," *Providence Journal*, October 29, 1928, 6.
11. Hess, "Miners' Drive for Tie Game Stopped on Three-Yard Line," 6.
12. Reynolds, *The Steam Roller Story*, 19.
13. Fred Knight, "Curly Oden Sprints 40 Yards for Score with Wilson Pass," *Providence Journal*, November 19, 1928, 6.

14. Knight, "Curly Oden Sprints 40 Yards for Score with Wilson Pass," 6.
15. Associated Press, "Protests Decision in Steam Rollers' Game," *Boston Globe*, November 21, 1928, 24.
16. Bill Parrillo, "In 1928, 'Super Bowl' was the talk of R.I., Providence Steam Roller won NFL Title," *Providence Journal Bulletin*, December 28, 1988, D-11.
17. Parrillo, "In 1928, 'Super Bowl' was the talk of R.I., Providence Steam Roller won NFL Title," D-11.
18. Pearce B. Johnson, *Professional Football in Rhode Island and its National Connections* (Pearce B. Johnson self-published, Providence, RI, 1994), 17.
19. Reynolds, *The Steam Roller Story*, 24.
20. Neft, Cohen, and Deutsch, *The Scrapbook History of Pro Football, 1893–1979*, 42.
21. Reynolds, *The Steam Roller Story*, 26.
22. John R. Hess, Jr., "First—and Second Guesses," *Providence Journal*, December 3, 1928, 7.
23. Fred Knight, "Providence Stages 72-yard Spectacular Scoring March," *Providence Journal*, December 3, 1928, 6.
24. Hess, Jr., "First—and Second Guesses," 7.
25. Reynolds, *The Steam Roller Story*, 29.
26. Reynolds, *The Steam Roller Story*, 29.
27. Reynolds, *The Steam Roller Story*, 26.
28. "Conzelman Is Selected Most Valuable Player by Rollers," *Providence Journal*, December 5, 1928, 9.
29. "Conzelman Is Selected Most Valuable Player by Rollers," 9.
30. Reynolds, *The Steam Roller Story*, 29–30.
31. "Conzelman Is Selected Most Valuable Player by Rollers," 9.
32. Reynolds, *The Steam Roller Story*, 22.
33. Dan Daly and Bob O'Donnell, *The Pro Football Chronicle* (New York: Macmillan 1990), 34.

Chapter Four

1. "Football Body Bars Wrestler," *Spokesman-Review*, June 30, 1929, 24.
2. Albert W. Keane, "Calling 'Em Right," *Hartford Courant*, August 3, 1929, 14.
3. "Ernie Nevers to Play with Chicago Cards," *Green Bay Press-Gazette*, July 30, 1929, 11.
4. Frank Korch, "Fifth of a series of articles on clubs in the National Football League and their prospects for the season," *Collyer's Eye* (Chicago), September 28, 1929, 12.
5. John R. Hess, Jr., "Friedman's Passing Features 75 yard Touchdown Drive, *Providence Journal*, October 7, 1929, 7.
6. John R. Hess, Jr., "New York Capitalizes Breaks to Score Two Touchdowns," *Providence Journal*, October 28, 1929, 7.
7. "Air Attack Gives Giants Triumph Over Grid Rivals," *Brooklyn Daily Eagle*, October 28, 1929, 23.
8. John R. Hess, Jr., "6000 Fans See Chicago Ace Flash in Scoring Rampage," *Providence Journal*, November 7, 1929, 12.
9. Hess, Jr., "6000 Fans See Chicago Ace Flash in Scoring Rampage," 12.
10. Paul Tanier, "Deflategate, Roaring 20's Style: New England's 1st Controversial NFL Champions," Bleachereport.com, May 19, 2015.
11. Hess, Jr., "Come from Behind to Score 3 Touchdowns for Victory," 7.
12. Johnny Blood, "My Greatest Thrill in Pro Football," Green Bay Packers 1933 game program, 10.
13. Blood, "My Greatest Thrill in Pro Football," 10.
14. John R. Aborn, "Smother West Weymouth Eleven in Exhibition Game," *Providence Journal*, September 15, 1930, 8.
15. John R. Aborn, "Rollers Beat Quincy Trojans 28 to 0 in Floodlight Game," *Providence Journal*, September 18, 1930, 11.
16. John R. Aborn, "Clicks off Nine Touchdowns, 42 Points in Second Half," *Providence Journal*, September 22, 1930, 9.
17. John R. Hess, Jr., "Local Pro Team Wins Third Straight at Cycledrome," *Providence Journal*, October 13, 1930, 7.
18. F. C. Matzek, "His Dropkick in 3rd Period Features Defensive Battle," *Providence Journal*, November 3, 1930, 7.
19. "Dazzling Plays Thrill Crowd at Philadelphia," *Providence Journal*, November 9, 1930, 29.
20. Bob Curran, *Pro Football's Rag Days* (New York: Bonanza Books, a division of Crown, 1969), 53.

21. John R. Hess, Jr., "Former Brown Head Coach to Succeed Jim Conzelman," *Providence Journal*, February 15, 1931, 25.
22. "Sportlets by Jack," *Iowa City Press-Citizen*, September 14, 1931, 9.
23. Curran, *Pro Football's Rag Days*, 113.
24. John R. Hess, Jr., "Stubborn Defence Stops 3 Roller Scoring Threats," *Providence Journal*, October 5, 1931, 7.
25. John R. Hess, Jr., "Roller Goes Into Air for 6–0 Victory in Final 35 Seconds," *Providence Journal*, October 11, 1931, 27.
26. John R. Hess, Jr., "Devastating Aerial Attack Features Offence of Locals," *Providence Journal*, October 26, 1931, 5.
27. "87-Yard Run Robs Bears of Chance to Tie Providence," *Buffalo Evening News*, October 28, 1931, 27.
28. Curran, *Pro Football's Rag Days*, 61.
29. "3000 See Roller Win at Worcester," *Providence Journal*, December 6, 1931, 29.

Epilogue

1. Henry F. Reilly, "I Remember the Steam Roller," *Providence Journal*, 1962, 11.
2. Bob Dick, "Steamroller pros, '28 grid champs, cited at ceremony," *Providence Journal*, November 29, 1982, A-13.
3. "Conzelman Is Selected Most Valuable Player by Rollers," *Providence Journal*, December 5, 1928, 9.

A Steam Roller Who's Who

1. "Jimmy Conzelman," Pro Football Hall of Fame, https://www.profootballhof.com/players/jimmy-conzelman/.
2. "Adolph W. Eckstein," Brown University Athletic Hall of Fame, https://brownbears.com/honors/hall-of-fame/adolph-w-eckstein/557, 1.
3. Buddy Thomas, "Looking Back: Carl Etelman, unstoppable force," *Standard-Times*, February 6, 2004, https://www.southcoasttoday.com/story/sports/2004/02/07/looking-back-carl-etelman-unstoppable/50292644007/.
4. "Tufts Eleven Will Show Tomorrow How It Has Responded to Casey's Coaching," *Boston Globe*, September 29, 1922, 19.
5. "Mian Gulian," Brown University Athletic Hall of Fame, https://brownbears.com/honors/hall-of-fame?hof=503.
6. "Bridgeport Defeats Williams 6–0," *Bridgeport Telegram*, November 6, 1922, 14.
7. "Healey's Eleven Headed for 1922 State Championship; To Play Williams on Sunday," *Bridgeport Telegram*, October 31, 1922, 6.
8. Reynolds, *The Steam Roller Story*, 10.
9. "Joe Kozlowsky," Boston College Varsity Club Hall of Fame, https://bceagles.com/honors/varsity-club-hall-of-fame/joe-kozlowsky/145.
10. "Don Miller," Pro Football Foundation—College Football Hall of Fame, https://footballfoundation.org/hof_search.aspx?hof=1374.
11. "Olaf G. H. Oden," Brown University Athletic Hall of Fame, https://footballfoundation.org/hof_search.aspx?hof=1374.
12. "Oran Pape Memorial Bridge," Iowa Department of Transportation, https://iowadot.gov/autotrails/special-designations.
13. "Walter Irvin 'Pard' Pearce," Staley Museum, https://www.staleymuseum.com/staleys-bears-20-21/pard-pearce/.
14. Associated Press, "Krivik Revives Drop Kicking as Modern Art," *Schenectady Gazette*, October 14, 1945, 22.
15. Neil Lanctot, *Negro League Baseball: The Rise and Ruin of a Black Institution* (Philadelphia: University of Pennsylvania Press, 2008), 433.
16. John M. Carroll, *Fritz Pollard: Pioneer in Racial Advancement* (Urbana: University of Illinois Press, 1998), 4.
17. "Joseph Schein, Teacher, Militant, Athlete, Dies," *Providence Journal*, May 29, 1969, 26.
18. Reynolds, *The Steam Roller Story*, 10.
19. "Smith Resigns as C. of E. Coach; No Successor Picked," *New College Life* (Emporia, Kansas), February 2, 1935, 1.
20. "Orland F. Smith," Brown University Athletic Hall of Fame, https://brownbears.com/honors/hall-of-fame?hof=172.
21. "Gibby Welch has signed up with Providence," *Coshocton Tribune*, September 25, 1929, 4.
22. "College Captains: Welch of Pittsburgh," *Decatur Daily Review*, October 15, 1927, 4.

23. Dick Hudson, "Gibby Welch Was a Great One, *Charleston Daily Mail*, January 26, 1956.

24. Marion County High School Football History—Guin, Alabama, https://www.facebook.com/mchsfootballhistory/posts/119107766436967/, April 28, 2020.

25. "Williams Will Not Return to Conn. Aggies," *Hartford Courant*, September 6, 1928, 14.

26. "George 'Wildcat' Wilson," National Football Foundation—College Football Hall of Fame, https://footballfoundation.org/hof_search.aspx?hof=1440.

Bibliography

Books

Anderson, Lars, *The First Star: Red Grange and the Barnstorming Tour That Launched the NFL* (New York, NY: Random House, 2009).
Benter, Michael D., *The Badgers: Milwaukee's NFL Entry of 1922-1926* (Haworth, NJ: St. Johann Press, 2013).
Carroll, John M., *Fritz Pollard: Pioneer in Racial Advancement* (Urbana: University of Illinois Press, 1998).
Claasen, Harold, *The History of Professional Football: Its Great Teams, Games, Players and Coaches* (Englewood Cliffs, NJ: Prentice-Hall, 1963).
Cope, Myron, *The Game That Was* (Cleveland: The World Publishing Company, 1970).
Crippen, Kenneth R., *The Original Buffalo Bills: A History of the All-American Football Conference Team, 1946-1949* (Jefferson, NC: McFarland, 2010).
Curran, Bob, *Pro Football's Rag Days* (New York: Bonanza Books, 1969).
Eisenberg, John, *The League: How Five Rivals Created the NFL and Launched a Sports Empire* (New York: Basic Books, Hachette Book Group, 2018).
Fleming, David, *Breaker Boys: The NFL's Greatest Team and the Stolen 1925 NFL Championship* (New York: ESPN Books, A Division of ESPN Publishing, 2007).
Gill, Bob, and Tod Maher, *Outsiders: Minor League and Independent Football 1923-1950* (Haworth, NJ: St. Johann Press, 2006).
Gill, Bob, Steve Brainerd, and Tod Maher, *Outsiders II: Minor League and Independent Football 1951-1984* (Haworth, NJ: St. Johann Press, 2010).

The Granite, 1925 and 1926 (Durham: University of New Hampshire, 1925).
Greenberg, Murray, *Passing Game: Benny Friedman and the Transformation of Football* (New York: PublicAffairs, 2008).
Holy Cross Men's Basketball Fact Book 2018-2019 (Worcester, MA: College of the Holy Cross, 2018).
Illinois Football Media Guide, 2004 (Urbana: University of Illinois, 2004).
Jumbo Book 1925 (Tufts University Yearbook) (Medford, MA: Tufts University, 1925).
Lanctot, Neil, *Negro League Baseball: The Rise and Ruin of a Black Institution* (Philadelphia: University of Pennsylvania Press, 2008).
Laudati, Peter, *Scrapbook of Providence Steam Roller Club*—at the Rhode Island Historical Society (Providence, RI: Self-published, 1977).
Lester, Robin, *Stagg's University: The Rise, Decline & Fall of Big-Time Football at Chicago* (Champaign: Illini Books Edition, 1999).
Morton, Ira, *The Red Grange Story: An Autobiography*, as told to Ira Morton (Urbana: University of Illinois Press, 1957 and 1981, Kindle Edition).
Neft, David S., Jordan A. Deutsch, and Richard M. Cohen, *Pro Football: The Early Years, An Encyclopedic History 1895-1959* (Ridgefield, CT: Sports Products, Inc., 1978).
Neft, David S., Richard M. Cohen, and Rick Korch, *The Football Encyclopedia* (New York: St. Martin's Press, 1994).
Nowlin, Bill, and Bob Brady, *Braves Field: Memorable Moments at Boston's Lost Diamond* (Phoenix: SABR, 2015).
O'Donnell, Bob, and Dan Daly, *The Pro

Football Chronicle (New York: Collier Books, Macmillan, 1990).
Peterson, Robert W., Pigskin: The Early Years of Pro Football (New York: Oxford University Press, 1997).
Providence Steam Roller Game Programs, 1925 to 1931 (Providence: Providence Steam Roller Club, 1925–1931).
Reynolds, Dick, The Steam Roller Story (Providence: Self-published, 1989).
Reynolds, Dick, and Pearce B. Johnson, Professional Football in Rhode Island and Its National Connection (Providence: Self-Published, 1989).
Smith, Don R., and Mike Rathet, Their Deeds and Dogged Faith (New York: Rutledge Books, Balsam Press, Inc., 1984).
Trotter, Jake, I Love Oklahoma/I Hate Texas (Chicago: Triumph Books, August 2012).
Willis, Chris, Old Leather: An Oral History of Early Pro Football in Ohio, 1920–1935 (Lanham, MD: The Scarecrow Press, 2005).

Newspapers and Magazine Articles

Aborn, John R., "Clicks off Nine Touchdowns, 42 Points in Second Half," Providence Journal, September 22, 1930.
Aborn, John R., "Rollers Beat Quincy Trojans 28 to 0 in Floodlight Game," Providence Journal, September 18, 1930.
Aborn, John R., "Smother West Weymouth Eleven in Exhibition Game," Providence Journal, September 15, 1930.
"Air Attack Gives Giants Triumph Over Grid Rivals," Brooklyn Daily Eagle, October 28, 1929.
"Along the Sidelines," Providence Journal, October 21, 1924.
Associated Press, "A.E. Golembeski," Lewiston Daily Sun, March 10, 1976.
Associated Press, "Former Brown Grid Star Fatally Injured in Auto Accident," Record-Journal, April 3, 1930.
Associated Press, "Grange is pushed for spotlight," Anniston Star, January 17, 1926.
Associated Press, "Grange's star dimmed; Wilson outplays him," Albuquerque Journal, January 25, 1926.
Associated Press, "Krivik Revives Drop Kicking as Modern Art," Schenectady Gazette, October 14, 1945.
Associated Press, "Pro Grid Season Successful," Spokesman Review, February 13, 1928.
Associated Press, "Protests Decision in Steam Rollers' Game," Boston Globe, November 21, 1928.
Baker, Paul, "Forgotten Stadiums: The Cycledrome," December 8, 2020, https://oldstadiumjourney.com/forgotten-stadiums-the-cycledrome/.
"Benkert Captures 1924 Scoring Title," New York Times, October 1, 1924.
Blood, Johnny, My Greatest Thrill in Pro Football, Green Bay Packers 1933 game program.
"Bridgeport Defeats Williams 6–0," Bridgeport Telegram, November 6, 1922.
"Captain Wentworth Runs Wild as New Hampshire Beats Lowell 47–0," The New Hampshire, Vol. 14, No. 6, November 9, 1923.
Carroll, Bob, "The Impact of Red Grange on Pro Football," The Coffin Corner, Vol. 20, No. 2, 1998.
Carroll, Bob, "Steamrollered," The Coffin Corner, Vol. 31, No. 2, 2009.
"Clay Hills Steam Rollers Battle to Scoreless Tie," Hartford Courant, October 18, 1920.
"College Captains: Welch of Pittsburgh," Decatur Daily Review, October 15, 1927.
"Conzelman Is Selected Most Valuable Player by Rollers," Providence Journal, December 5, 1928.
"Cycledrome Opening Attracts 9000 Crowd: Verkeyn Wins Main Event of 30 Miles: Belgian Leads from Start to Finish in Grind Behind Motors—Gastman Makes Hit—Meyer Captures Sprint Match," Providence Journal, June 3, 1925.
Daley, Arthur J., "Londos Keeps Title by Pinning Pierotti," New York Times, July 31, 1931.
"Deaths and funerals," Vincennes Sun-Commercial, December 31, 1982.
Dick, Bob, "Steamroller pros, '28 grid champs, cited at ceremony," Providence Journal, November 29, 1982.
"87-Yard Run Robs Bears of Chance to Tie Providence," Buffalo Evening News, October 28, 1931.
Emery, Tom, "Way before the Patriots, Providence fans enjoyed title ride with Steam Roller," Providence Journal, January 31, 2015.

Bibliography

"Enterprise All Cape Team," *Falmouth Enterprise*, September 8, 1927.

"Ernie Nevers To Play with Chicago Cards," *Green Bay Press-Gazette*, July 30, 1929.

"Falmouth Locals," *Falmouth Enterprise*, November 15, 1928.

"Football Body Bars Wrestler," *Spokesman-Review*, June 30, 1929.

"'Gibby' Welch Has Signed Up in Providence," *Coshocton Tribune*, September 25, 1929.

"Gibby Welch Is Entered for Pitt in Penn Relay," *Lima News*, April 19, 1928.

"Gibby Welch Selected as Head Coach at Morris Harvey College: Former Pitt Star Coaches Football; Parkersburg Star Named to All-America Team in 1927," *Charleston Daily Mail*, July 16, 1931.

Gill, Bob, "Providence Starts Rolling," *The Coffin Corner*, Vol. 17, No. 4, 1995.

Gill, Bob, "Struggling to Stay on the Black," *The Coffin Corner*, Vol. 15, No. 5, 1993.

"Gran's manager makes pro offer to Huskies star," *The Pittsburgh Post*, January 28, 1926.

"Grat O'Connell's Funeral Will Be Held on Monday," *Hartford Courant*, March 15, 1942.

"Grid Iron Squad Honored," *New York Times*, December 19, 1916.

Hallahan, John J., "Pro Football All Business," *Boston Globe*, November 30, 1925.

Hamel, Michael, "Pittsburgh Steelers Make Rhode Island Their Summer Home, 1964 to 1966," https://smallstatebighistory.com/pittsburgh-steelers-rhode-island/, 2017.

"Healey's Eleven Headed for 1922 State Championship; To Play Williams on Sunday," *Bridgeport Telegram*, October 31, 1922.

Hess, John R., Jr., "Come from Behind to Score 3 Touchdowns for Victory," *Providence Journal*, November 18, 1929.

Hess, John R., Jr., "Devastating Aerial Attack Features Offence of Locals," *Providence Journal*, October 26, 1931.

Hess, John R., Jr., "First—and Second Guesses," *Providence Journal*, December 3, 1928.

Hess, John R., Jr., "Friedman's Passing Features 75-yard Touchdown Drive," *Providence Journal*, October 7, 1929.

Hess, John R., Jr., "Local Pro Team Wins Third Straight at Cycledrome," *Providence Journal*, October 13, 1930.

Hess, John R., Jr., "Miners' Drive for Tie Game Stopped on Three-Yard Line," *Providence Journal*, October 29, 1928.

Hess, John R., Jr., "New York Capitalizes Breaks to Score Two Touchdowns," *Providence Journal*, October 28, 1929.

Hess, John R., Jr., "Roller Goes into Air for 6–0 Victory in Final 35 Seconds," *Providence Journal*, October 11, 1931.

Hess, John R., Jr., "6000 Fans See Chicago Ace Flash in Scoring Rampage," *Providence Journal*, November 7, 1929.

Hess, John R., Jr., "Williams Splits New York Line for First Touchdown," *Providence Journal*, October 1, 1928.

Hogrogian, John, "The Hartford Blues, Part 1," *The Coffin Corner*, Vol. 4, No. 8, 1982.

Hogrogian, John, "The Hartford Blues, Part 2," *The Coffin Corner*, Vol. 4, No. 9, 1982.

Hogrogian, John, "Rhode Island's Pro Football Champions—1928 Providence Steam Roller," *Rhode Island History*, published by the Rhode Island Historical Society, Volume 36, No. 4, November 1977.

Hogrogian, John, "The Steam Roller," *The Coffin Corner*, Vol. 2, No. 3, 1980.

Hoover, Brett, and Stephen Eschenbach, "Fritz's Fame," *Brown Alumni Magazine*, March/April 2005.

Hudson, Dick, "Gibby Welch Was a Great One," *Charleston Daily Mail*, January 26, 1956.

"Jack and Bill Cronin Coaching at LaSalle," *Boston Globe*, September 15, 1927.

John Thomas Obituary, *Chicago Tribune* (Chicago, IL), August 21, 1977.

"Joseph Schein, Teacher, Militant, Athlete, Dies," *Providence Journal*, May 29, 1969.

Keane, Albert W., "Calling 'Em Right," *Hartford Courant*, August 3, 1929.

Kelly, Billy, "Before and After," *Buffalo Courier*, October 3, 1927.

Kennedy, Dennis, "He was there for the kickoff," *Observer Life*, July 14, 1994.

Knight, Fred, "Curly Oden Sprints 40 Yards for Score with Wilson Pass," *Providence Journal*, November 19, 1928.

Knight, Fred, "Providence Stages 72-yard Spectacular Scoring March," *Providence Journal*, December 3, 1928.

Korch, Frank, "Fifth of a series of articles

on clubs in the National Football League and their prospects for the season," *Collyer's Eye*, September 28, 1929.

"Kozlowsky Named Cambridge Director of Physical Education," *Boston Globe*, December 18, 1953.

"Kucharski Resigns as LHS Principal," *Fitchburg Sentinel*, March 2, 1965.

"League Pennant Comes to Falmouth," *Falmouth Enterprise*, September 5, 1929.

"Live Tips and Topics," *Boston Globe*, May 2, 1931.

Matzek, F. C., "His Dropkick in 3rd Period Features Defensive Battle, *Providence Journal*, November 3, 1930.

"The Men Who Make the Argosy," *Argosy*, August 16, 1930.

Monahan, Bob, "Holy Cross' Hop Riopel," *Boston Globe*, September 5, 1966.

Moshier, Jeff, "Terriers and Green Devils Grid Rivals for Past 17 Years," *Evening Independent*, November 1, 1932.

"National Grid Circuit Opens Season Sunday," *News-Record*, September 19, 1925.

"New Short Stop and Old Twirler on Local Diamond," *Falmouth Enterprise*, July 31, 1930.

Obituary—Tony Holm, *Chicago Tribune*, July 17, 1978.

"Oden is Outstanding Figure in Triumph," *Providence Journal*, October 25, 1926.

O'Leary, James, "Martin Throws Pair of Rivals at Arena," *Boston Globe*, December 8, 1932.

Pacitti, Tony, "The Lost World of Providence Sports," *Providence Monthly*, May 19, 2016, https://providenceonline.com/stories/the-lost-world-of-providence-sports,19181.

Parascenzo, Marino, "Famed Pitt football star Gibby Welch dies at 79," *Pittsburgh Post-Gazette*, February 11, 1984.

Parrillo, Bill, "In 1928, 'Super Bowl' was the talk of R.I., Providence Steam Roller won NFL Title," *Providence Journal Bulletin*, December 28, 1988.

"Peabody Strengthened for Peres Tomorrow," *Boston Globe*, November 27, 1926.

Pierotti, Albert, "Chelsea Teacher, All-America, 67," *Boston Globe*, February 13, 1964.

"Pottsville Topples Steam Roller 8 To 0," *Providence Journal*, November 26, 1926.

"Pottsville's Late Drive a Winner," *Boston Globe*, Oct 17, 1917.

"Pro Football All Business," *Boston Globe*, November 30, 1925.

"Pro Football Soon Under Way," *Providence Journal*, September 12, 1925.

Providence Steam Roller vs New York Giants game program, October 11, 1925, Providence Steam Roller Club, 1925.

"Pyne rejects pay cut and gets cut," *The Vindicator*, August 23, 2001.

"Reds Defeat Chicago Cards," *Cincinnati Enquirer*, November 13, 1933.

Reilly, Henry F., "I Remember the Steam Roller," *Providence Journal*, 1962.

"Rocca-Perez Headline Tonight's Mat Program," *Kingston Daily Freedom*, September 28, 1960.

"Roller Downs Yankees, 9–0, in Syracuse Benefit Battle," *Providence Journal*, December 4, 1927.

"Roller Flattens Marines; 49–0 Score," *Providence Journal*, November 17, 1924.

"Roller Team Lauded at Annual Banquet," *Providence Journal*, February 21, 1926.

Schubert, Bill, "Jimmy Conzelman," *The Coffin Corner*, Vol. 19, No. 1, 1997.

Searing, Robert, "In 1907, Syracuse University opens Archbold Stadium, called then the 'greatest athletic arena in America,'" Syracuse.com—https://www.syracuse.com/living/2021/09/in-1907-syracuse-university-opens-archbold-stadium-called-then-the-greatest-athletic-arena-in-america.html#:~:text=On%20September%2025%2C%201907%2C%20the%20Syracuse%20Orange%20varsity,in%20America%2C"%20by%20some%20in%20the%20national%20press.

"Shelley Rites Tomorrow," *Austin American-Statesman*, December 18, 1968.

Slade, Rachel, "The High-Rise Cliffhanger, Inside the Decades-Long Saga of Rhode Island's Landmark Skyscraper, The Superman Building," *Yankee Magazine*, July/August, 2022.

"Smith Resigns as C. of E. Coach; No Successor Picked," *New College Life*, February 2, 1935.

"Sport Comment," *Buffalo News*, July 9, 1928.

"Sportlets by Jack," *Iowa City Press-Citizen*, September 14, 1931.

Sportsman, "Live Tips and Topics," *Boston Globe*, September 21, 1926.

Staff Correspondent, "Grange Stopped; Roller Defeats Chicago 9–6," *Providence Journal*, December 10, 1925.

Staff Correspondent, "Leading Pro Elevens to Show Wares Here," *Providence Journal*, August 3, 1925.
"Steam Rollers Lose to Yellow Jackets," *Boston Globe*, December 14, 1925.
"Stockton and Bross Use Football Just as If It Was a Baseball," *Spokane Daily Chronicle*, November 22, 1923.
"Stockton Put on All-Star Eleven," *Spokesman-Review*, December 18, 1923.
"Stockton's Record Still Stands; Was Scoring Backfield Marvel," *Spokane Daily Chronicle*, November 7, 1931.
Tanier, Paul, "Deflategate, Roaring 20's Style: New England's 1st Controversial NFL Champions," Bleachereport.com, May 19, 2015.
Thomas, Buddy, "Looking Back: Carl Etelman, unstoppable force," *Standard-Times*, February 6, 2004, https://www.southcoasttoday.com/story/sports/2004/02/07/looking-back-carl-etelman-unstoppable/50292644007/.
"3000 See Roller Win at Worcester," *Providence Journal*, December 6, 1931.
"Touchdown in Last Period Gives Roller 13-7 Victory," *Providence Journal*, November 14, 1927.
"Tufts Eleven Will Show Tomorrow How It Has Responded to Casey's Coaching," *Boston Globe*, September 29, 1922.
United Press International, "Red Grange Arrives at Portland: Ears Have Giant Linemen," *Albany Democrat-Herald*, January 27, 1926.
"Wade's Warriors Play Tough Ones," *Evening Herald*, November 4, 1929.
"Walter Scott Macphee '22," *Princeton Alumni Weekly*, Princeton University Press, May 19, 1980.
"Warren P. McGuirk, was athletics director at UMass Amherst; at 75," *Boston Globe*, February 21, 1981.
"Wentworth Brilliant in One-Side Contest," *Providence Journal*, September 21, 1925.
"Wentworth Misses Attempt for Point," *Providence Journal*, November 8, 1926.
Wheeler, Robert, L., "That Old Steam Roller...in infancy...in lusty prime... in decline," *Providence Sunday Journal*, November 11, 1956.
"Williams Will Not Return to Conn. Aggies," *Hartford Courant*, September 6, 1928.
"Wrestling: How is it done?" *Newsweek*, November 22, 1954.

Wright, Frank, S., "Goodbread is one of Gators' Chief Threats," *St. Petersburg Times*, September 29, 1929.
"WSU Football 'Great,' Butch Meeker, is Dead," *Spokane Chronicle*, December 28, 1960.
Yohe, Steve, "A Study of Danno O'Mahoney," https://1wrestlinglegends.com.

Newspapers

Akron Beacon Journal (Akron, OH)
Albany Democrat-Herald (Albany, OR)
Anniston Star (Anniston, AL)
Arizona Republic (Phoenix, AZ)
Athol Daily News (Athol, MA)
Austin American-Statesman (Austin, TX)
Bangor Daily News (Bangor, ME)
Battle Creek Enquirer (Battle Creek, MI)
Belleville News-Democrat (Belleville, IL)
Bennington Evening Banner (Bennington, VT)
Berkshire Evening Eagle (Pittsfield, MA)
Billings Gazette (Billings, MT)
Boston Globe (Boston, MA)
Bridgeport Telegram (Bridgeport, CT)
Brooklyn Citizen (Brooklyn, NY)
Brooklyn Daily Eagle (Brooklyn, NY)
Brooklyn Times Union (Brooklyn, NY)
Buffalo Courier (Buffalo, NY)
Buffalo Evening News (Buffalo, NY)
Buffalo News (Buffalo, NY)
Buffalo Times (Buffalo, NY)
Charleston Daily Mail (Charleston, WV)
Chicago Tribune (Chicago, IL)
Cincinnati Enquirer (Cincinnati, OH)
Collyer's Eye (Chicago, IL)
Coshocton Tribune (Coshocton, OH)
Courier-Post (Camden, NJ)
Daily News (Canonsburg, PA)
Daily News (Mount Carmel, PA)
Daily News (New York, NY)
Daily Olympian (Olympia, WA)
Dayton Daily News (Dayton, OH)
Dayton Herald (Dayton, OH)
Democrat and Chronicle (Rochester, NY)
Des Moines Register (Des Moines, IA)
Detroit Free Press (Detroit, MI)
Eugene Guard (Eugene, OR)
Evening Bulletin (Providence, RI)
Evening Herald (Klamath Walls, OR)
Evening Herald (Pottsville, PA)
Evening Independent (St. Petersburg, FL)
Evening News (Harrisburg, PA)
Falmouth Enterprise (Falmouth, MA)

268   Bibliography

Fitchburg Sentinel (Fitchburg, MA)
Frederick Press (Frederick, OK)
Granite Monthly Magazine (Durham, NH)
Green Bay Press-Gazette (Green Bay, WI)
Hartford Courant (Hartford, CT)
Herald-Press (St. Joseph, MI)
Holyoke Daily Transcript and Holyoke Telegram (Holyoke, MA)
Indianapolis Star (Indianapolis, IN)
Intelligencer Journal (Lancaster, MA)
Iowa City Press-Citizen (Iowa City, IA)
Journal Herald (Dayton, OH)
Kansas City Times (Kansas City MO)
Lancaster Intelligence Journal (Lancaster, PA)
Lancaster New Era (Lancaster, PA)
Lansing State Journal (Lansing, MI)
Latrobe Bulletin (Latrobe, PA)
Lewiston Daily Sun (Lewiston, ME)
Lexington Leader (Lexington, KY)
Lima News (Lima, OH)
Lincoln Journal Star (Lincoln, NB)
Lindsborg Progress (Lindsborg, KS)
Los Angeles Times (Los Angeles, CA)
Marshfield News-Herald (Marshfield, WI)
Meriden Record (Meriden, CT)
Minneapolis Journal (Minneapolis, MN)
Minneapolis Star Tribune (Minneapolis, MN)
Morning Call (Allentown, PA)
Morning Call (Paterson, NJ)
Morning News (Wilmington, DE)
Mount Carmel Item (Mount Carmel, PA)
New College Life (Emporia, KS)
New York Times (New, York, NY)
New-Record (Neenah, WI)
Newport Daily News (Newport, RI)
News Gazette (Champaign, IL)
News-Herald (Franklin, PA)
Norman Transcript (Norman, OK)
North Adams Transcript (North Adams, MA)
Odessa-American (Odessa, TX)
Ogden Standard-Examiner (Ogden, UT)
Palm Beach Post (West Palm Beach, FL)
Philadelphia Inquirer (Philadelphia, PA)
Pittsburgh Daily Post (Pittsburgh, PA)
Pittsburgh Post (Pittsburgh, PA)
Pittsburgh Post-Gazette (Pittsburgh, PA)
Plain Dealer (Cleveland, OH)
Pottsville Republican (Pottsville, PA)
Press Journal (Vero Beach, FL)
Princeton Alumni Weekly (Princeton, NJ)
Providence Journal (Providence, RI)
Quad City Times (Davenport, IA)
Reading Times (Reading, PA)
Record-Journal (Meriden, CT)
Richland Beacon News (Rayville, LA)
Rutland Daily Herald (Rutland, VT)
St. Louis Star and Times (St. Louis, MO)
St. Petersburg Times (St. Petersburg, FL)
Salina Journal (Salina, KS)
Salt Lake City Tribune (Salt Lake City, UT)
San Francisco Examiner (San Francisco, CA)
San Pedro News-Pilot (San Pedro, CA)
Schenectady Gazette (Schenectady, NY)
Shamokin News-Dispatch (Shamokin, PA)
South Bend Tribune (South Bend, IN)
Spokane Chronicle (Spokane, WA)
Spokesman-Review (Spokane, WA)
Springfield Daily News (Springfield, OH)
Standard-Speaker (Hazelton, PA)
Standard-Times (New Bedford, MA)
Standard-Union (Brooklyn, NY)
Star Press (Muncie, IN)
Star Tribune (Minneapolis, MN)
Stevens Point Journal (Stevens Point, WI)
Sunday News (Lancaster, PA)
Tacoma Daily Ledger (Tacoma, WA)
Tampa Bay Times (Tampa Bay, FL)
Tennessean (Nashville, TN)
Terre Haute Tribune (Terre Haute, IN)
The Times (Munster, IN)
Vincennes Sun-Commercial (Vincennes, IN)
Vindicator (Youngstown, OH)
Wichita Eagle (Wichita, KS)
Yonkers Herald (Yonkers, NY)
Yonkers Statesman (Yonkers, NY)

Websites

Ainsworth Sports All-time Colgate football player rankings, www.Ainsworth sports.com/football_player_rankings_by_college_ny_colgate.htm.

Ainsworth Sports All-time Dartmouth football player rankings, www.ainsworthsports.com/football_player_rankings_by_college_nh_dartmouth.htm.

Ainsworth Sports All-time Syracuse University player rankings, www.ainsworth sports.com/football_player_rankings_by_college_ny_syracuse.htm.

Armed Forces Colgate Football Memorabilia Collection—Jim Laird, www.colgatefootballcollection.com/armed-forces.html.

Armenia, Estacio, "Mike Gulian, o

primeiro armenio na NFL," https:// estacaoarmenia.com.br/56737/mike-gulian-o-primeiro-armenio-na-nfl/.
Art in Ruins, Providence Cycledrome— https://artinruins.com/property/cyclodrome/.
Baseball Reference—Frank Seyboth, https://www.baseball-reference.com/register/player.fcgi?id=seybot001fra.
Baseball Reference—Jack Fleischmann, https://www.baseball-reference.com/register/player.fcgi?id=fleisc001jac.
Baseball Reference—Jack Keefer, https://www.baseball-reference.com/register/player.fcgi?id=keefer001jac.
Baseball Reference—Waddy MacPhee, https://www.baseball-reference.com/players/m/macphwa01.shtml.
Bobbs-Merrill Company archives finding aids—Burt Shurtleff, https://webapp1.dlib.indiana.edu/findingaids/view?doc.view=entire_text&docId=InU-Li-VAC 1799.
Boston College Varsity Club Athletic Hall of Fame—Grattan O'Connell, https://bceagles.com/honors/varsity-club-hall-of-fame/grattan-o-connell/147.
Boston College Varsity Club Athletic Hall of Fame—Jack Cronin, https://bceagles.com/honors/varsity-club-hall-of-fame/john-cronin/167.
Boston College Varsity Club Athletic Hall of Fame—Joe Kozlowsky, https://bceagles.com/honors/varsity-club-hall-of-fame/joe-kozlowsky/145.
Brown Bears Football—All-Decade Teams, http://www.brownbears.com/sports/m-footbl/spec-rel/081703aaa.html.
Brown University Athletic Hall of Fame—Bert Shurtleff, https://brownbears.com/honors/hall-of-fame/bertrand-l-shurtleff/150.
Brown University Athletic Hall of Fame—Bud Edwards, https://brownbears.com/hof.aspx?hof=559.
Brown University Athletic Hall of Fame—Curly Oden, https://brownbears.com/hof.aspx?hof=255.
Brown University Athletic Hall of Fame—Dave Mishel, https://brownbears.com/hof.aspx?hof=322.
Brown University Athletic Hall of Fame—Dolph Eckstein, https://brownbears.com/honors/hall-of-fame/adolph-w-eckstein/557.
Brown University Athletic Hall of Fame—Fritz Pollard, https://brownbears.com/honors/hall-of-fame/fredrick-d-pollard/242.
Brown University Athletic Hall of Fame—Jack Spellman, https://brownbears.com/honors/hall-of-fame/john-f-spellman/181.
Brown University Athletic Hall of Fame—Mike Gulian, https://brownbears.com/honors/hall-of-fame/mian-gulian/503.
Brown University Athletic Hall of Fame—Orland Smith, https://brownbears.com/honors/hall-of-fame/orland-f-smith/172.
Brown University Football Letter Winners, https://brownbears.com/sports/2018/5/8/brown-varsity-lettermen-football.aspx?id=2650.
College Football Data Warehouse, Fordham Game-by-Game-Results, https://web.archive.org/web/20110708133218/http://www.cfbdatawarehouse.com/data/div_iaa/patriot/fordham/yearly_results.php?year=1935.
College Football Hall of Fame—Wildcat Wilson, https://footballfoundation.org/hof_search.aspx?hof=1440.
Dartmouth College "Wearers of the Green" Athletics Hall of Fame—Chick Burke, https://dartmouthsports.com/honors/wearers-of-the-green/charles-f-chick-burke/2061.
Dartmouth College "Wearers of the Green," Athletics Hall of Fame—Red Maloney, https://accessibility-13.sidearmsports.com/honors/wearers-of-the-green/geralds-red-maloney/2065.
Deaths, Dartmouth Alumni Magazine, March 1998, https://archive.dartmouthalumnimagazine.com/article/1998/3/1/deaths.
Deaths (Mike Gulian), Brown Alumni Monthly, March 1970, https://archive.org/stream/brownalumnimonth706brow/brownalumnimonth706brow_djvu.txt.
Find a Grave—Bert Shurtleff, https://www.findagrave.com/memorial/103804076/bertrand-leslie-shurtleff.
Find a Grave—Dave Mishel, https://www.findagrave.com/memorial/126833841/dave-mishel.
Find a Grave—Don Miller, https://www.findagrave.com/memorial/64976335/don-miller.
Find a Grave—Duke Hanny, https://www.

findagrave.com/memorial/175025388/frank-mathew-hanny.
Find a Grave—Hec Garvey, https://www.findagrave.com/memorial/20666921/arthur-aloysius-garvey.
Fordham University 2019 Football Media Guide—Bulger Lowe, https://s3.amazonaws.com/sidearm.sites/fordham.sidearmsports.com/documents/2019/8/26/FordFB19.pdf.
George H. "Bulger" Lowe Award, https://gocrimson.com/news/2013/12/6/12_6_2013_1161.
Georgetown Blue and Gray Gridmen Trample Over Furman for a 20–0 Victory, https://repository.library.georgetown.edu/bitstream/handle/10822/1041246/GTA_Hoya_v006_1924-25_n006.pdf.
Georgetown Football History Project—Fred Sheehan, https://www.hoyafootball.com/players/captains.htm.
Georgetown Surprises Penn Team Holding Them to a 3–0 Victory, https://repository.library.georgetown.edu/bitstream/handle/10822/1041247/GTA_Hoya_v006_1924-25_n007.pdf.
"Gus Sonnenberg captures World Championship," https://classicwrestlingarticles.wordpress.com/2013/07/26/gus-sonnenberg-captures-world-championship/.
The Guy with the GumShoes, Cecil "Honk" "Tex" Irvin, The College Years, https://web.archive.org/web/20151024154957/http://www.deleonhandbook.com/De_Leon_Handbook/Irvin_2.html.
Holy Cross Baseball Archives, https://goholycross.com/sports/2020/7/24/holy-cross-baseball-archives.aspx?path=base.
IMDb—Gus Sonnenberg, https://www.imdb.com/name/nm0814397/.
IMDb—Rockin' the Blues, https://www.imdb.com/title/tt0049687/.
The Internet Wrestling database—Jack Spellman, https://classicwrestlingarticles.cagematch.net/?id=2&nr=25339&page=4&s=100.
Jack McBride—NFL Career NFL Statistics, https://www.jt-sw.com/football/pro/players.nsf/ID/00680013.
LA84 Foundation, "Gridiron Nostalgia: Heroes of 1927, https://digital.la84.org/digital/collection/p17103coll10.
Marion County High School Football History—Guin, Alabama, https://www.facebook.com/mchsfootballhistory/posts/119107766436967.
Nahmias, Leah, "Providence's Lost Stadium: The Providence Cycledrome and the City's Sporting Past," https://artinruins.com/property/cycledrome/.
National Football Foundation, Don Miller, College Football HOF, https://footballfoundation.org/hof_search.aspx?hof=1374.
National Football Foundation, Jim Crowley, College Football HOF, https://footballfoundation.org/hof_search.aspx?hof=1371.
New England's First NFL Champions, https://trophylives.wordpress.com/2014/02/22newenglands.first-nfl-champions/.
New York Giants Football Records, www.luckyshow.org/football/NYGiants.htm.
New York Yankees Football Records, www.luckyshow.org/football/NYYanks3.htm.
News Gazette (Champaign, IL), "Happy Birthday, Ron Guenther, http://www.news-gazette.com/sports/illini-sports/other/2011-10-01/happy-66th-ron-guenther.html.
Officer Down Memorial Page—Oran Pape, https://www.odmp.org/officer/10343-patrolman-oran-h-pape.
"Oran Pape Memorial Bridge," Iowa Department of Transportation, https://iowadot.gov/autotrails/special-designations.
People Pill—Royce Goodbread, https://peoplepill.com/people/royce-goodbread.
Pro Football Archives, https://www.profootballarchives.com, various players and the Providence Steam Roller 1925–1931.
Pro Football Archives, Providence Steam Roller—1925, https://www.profootballarchives.com/1925nflpro.html.
Pro Football Archives, Providence Steam Roller—1926, https://www.profootballarchives.com/1926nflpro.html.
Pro Football Archives, Providence Steam Roller—1927, https://www.profootballarchives.com/1927nflpro.html.
Pro Football Archives, Providence Steam Roller—1928, https://www.profootballarchives.com/1928nflpro.html.
Pro Football Archives, Providence Steam Roller—1929, https://www.profootballarchives.com/1929nflpro.html.
Pro Football Archives, Providence Steam Roller—1930, https://www.profootballarchives.com/1930nflpro.html.

Bibliography 271

Pro Football Archives, Providence Steam Roller—1931, https://www.profootball archives.com/1931nflpro.html.

Pro Football Hall of Fame decade of the 1920s—http://www.profootballhof. com/history/decades/1920s/providence. aspx.

Pro Football Hall of Fame—Fritz Pollard, https://www.profootballhof.com/ players/fritz-pollard/.

Pro Football Hall of Fame—Jimmy Conzelman, https://www.profootballhof. com/players/jimmy-conzelman/#-player-full-bio.

Pro Football Reference, https://www.profootball-reference.com, various players and the Providence Steam Roller 1924–1931.

Pro Football Reference, Providence Cycledrome, https://www.pro-football-reference.com/stadiums/PRV00.htm.

Pro Football Reference, Providence Steam Roller, https://www.pro-football-reference.com/teams/prv/ (and several other pages including each year of the team).

Professional Football Researchers Association's Hall of Very Good—Tony Latone, www.profootballresearchers.org/hall-of-very-good-2021.html.

Professional Wrestling Hall of Fame, https://www.pwhf.org.

Providence Steamrollers basketball history, https://nbahoopsonline.com/teams/ Xdefunct/ProvidenceSteamrollers/ index.html.

Reaching for the Brass Ring: A Portrait of Doan's 1937 Baseball School—Frosty Peters, http://www.hotspringsbaseball trail.com/untold-stories/reaching-brass-ring-portrait-doans-1937-baseball-school/.

Rhode Island Heritage Hall of Fame—Jack Spellman, https://riheritagehalloffame. com/John-Spellman/.

Rhode Island Hockey Hall of Fame—James E. Dooley, http://www.RIHHOF. com/judge-james-e-dooley/.

Rhode Island Hockey Legacy, https:// www.rihockeylegacy.com/richard-j-dennis-post.html, various pages.

Rhode Island Sports Chronicle—Joe Braney, https://www.risportschronicle. com/speed-braney.html.

Rhody on the Roller, https://www.risports chronicle.com/rhody-on-the-roller.html.

Small State/Big History, A Bicycle Paradise: Peter Laudati, Vincent Madonna and the Providence Cycledrome, 1925–1934, https://smallstatebighistory.com/ a-bicycle-paradise-peter-laudati-vincent-madonna-and-the-providence-cycledrome-1925-1934/.

Sports Reference—College Football, https://www.sports-reference.com/cbb/, various players and teams.

Sports Reference—John Spellman, http:// www.sports-reference.com/olympics/ athletes/sp/john-spellman-1.html.

Staley Museum—Pard Pearce, https:// www.staleymuseum.com/staleys-bears-20-21/pard-pearce/.

SWOSU Alumni Association Athletic Hall of Fame—Arnold Shockley, http://www. swosu.edu/alum-foun/alumni/award/ ath-hof-bios/shockley-arnold.asp.

SWOSU Alumni Association Athletic Hall of Fame—Jim Simmons, https://web. archive.org/web/20151011004050/http:// www.swosu.edu/alum-foun/alumni/ award/ath-hof-bios/simmons-je.aspx.

SWOSU Alumni Association Athletic Hall of Fame—Perry Jackson, https://web. archive.org/web/20130828044317/http:// www.swosu.edu/alum-foun/alumni/ award/ath-hof-bios/jackson-jp.aspx.

Tufts Now, "Integrating Football—in 1916," https://now.tufts.edu/2016/12/12/ integrating-football-1916.

UMass Athletics Hall of Fame—Warren McGuirk, https://umassathletics.com/ honors/hall-of-fame/warren-pmcguirk/ 95.

UNH Wildcats Hall of Fame—Cy Wentworth, https://unhwildcats.com/sports/ 2015/7/23/Development_0723150850. aspx.

University of Texas Sports Hall of Honor—Dexter Shelley, https://texassports. com/sports/general/roster/dexter-shelley/1579.

UW Football Coaching History, https:// washington_ftp.sidearmsports.com/ old_site/pdf/m-footbl/9_08FBMG.pdf.

Washington State Honors Hall of Fame—Butch Meeker, https://wsucougars.com/ honors/hall-of-fame/butch-meeker/1127.

Washington University Husky Hall of Fame—Wildcat Wilson, https://www. uwtyeeclub.com/big-w-club/the-husky-hall-of-fame/inductees-by-sport/.

Weldon Gentry Obituary, https://www.

newspapers.com/clip/94093974/
obituary-for-weldon-c-gentry/.
WrestlingData.com—Blue Sun Jennings, https://www.wrestlingdata.com/index.php?befehl=bios&wrestler=4030&bild=1&details=7.
WVU Sports Hall of Fame—Fred Graham, https://wvusports.com/honors/wvu-sports-hall-of-fame/fred-graham/156.

Other

Hock, Johnathan A., Oral History Interview with Pearce B. Johnson, October 4, 1991, NFL Films.

Laudati, Peter, His personal papers—In the Rhode Island Historical Society Collection.

Index

Abbott, Fay 59
Abramson, George 33
Acme Packing 12
Adelphia Hotel 80
Akron Indians (NFL) 174, 233
Akron Pros (NFL) 4, 12, 32, 33, 40, 52, 162, 190, 191, 192, 193, 207, 230
All-America Football Conference (AAFC) 149, 195
All-Bridgeport 156, 163
All-Hartford 14
All-New Britain 29, 144, 163
Ambulance Quintet of Pawtucket 13
American Association 190
American Chain 13, 14, 15
American Football Association 221
American Soccer League 13
American Wrestling Association 209, 211
Anderson, Hunk 35, 36
Andrews Field 24
Annenberg, Ivan 82
Anthracite League 172, 192, 196, 207, 208
Apponaug 12
Arcadia Ballroom 75, 76, 208
Arena Football League 141
Archbold, John D. 65
Archbold Stadium 65, 66, 137, 234
Ashland Armco Yellow Jackets 169
Assumption College 197
Atlantic City Convention Hall 140
Atlantic Coast Football League (ACFL) 140
August, Sky 122, 124, 132, 133, 143, 244
Avedesian, Firpo 15

Bacchus, Carl 62, 78
Bacon, Frank 17
Badgro, Red 117
Baker Bowl 126, 244
Basketball Association of America (BAA) 140, 144

Baseball Hall of Fame 14
Bates College 184, 191
Behman, Bull 81
Belden, Bunny 116
Benkert, Heinie 178
Berkley Oval 13
Berry, Charlie 37, 45
Bethany (KS) College 196
Bethlehem Bears 193
Big Green of Maple Grove, PA 154
Billings Poly Institute 189
Biltmore Hotel (Providence) 69, 89, 90, 208
Bison Stadium (Offermann) 129, 244
Blood, Johnny 51, 62, 108, 124, 132
Bloodgood, Al 49, 50, 62, 63, 83
Bogue, George 115
Bomar, Lynn 31, 42
Boston, Massachusetts 33–37, 44, 80, 84, 120, 137
Boston Arena 191, 209
Boston Braves (MLB) 137, 175, 191
Boston Braves, Boston Redskins and Washington Redskins (NFL) 134, 135, 136, 139, 196, 197, 211, 224, 225
Boston Bulldogs (AFL/NFL) 84, 96, 98, 99, 107, 110, 148, 154, 162, 163, 167, 168, 170, 173, 174, 176, 177, 179, 180, 186, 187, 190, 196, 203, 213, 219, 220, 221, 223, 239, 241, 249
Boston Celtics (NBA) 10
Boston College 14, 40, 55, 97, 101, 147, 148, 149, 150, 151, 170, 180, 181, 184, 185, 197
Boston College Athletic Hall of Fame 148, 170, 185
Boston Collegians 124, 244
Boston Fitton A.C. 14, 135
Boston Garden 94
Boston Patriots *see* New England Patriots
Boston Red Sox (MLB) 11, 131

273

Boston Tigers 14
Boston University 122, 127, 154, 155, 169, 184, 205
Bowser, Paul 209
Brady, Tom 137
Braney, Joe 14, 15, 23, 42, 143–144, 228, 231
Braves Field 33, 35, 80, 120, 137, 228, 236, 239, 242
Braxton, Garland 175
Bridgeport All Stars 127, 244
Britton, Earl 36, 59
Brooklyn College 145
Brooklyn Dodgers (MLB) 186
Brooklyn Dodgers (NFL) 109, 110, 115, 117, 118, 120, 123, 130, 153, 157, 159, 178, 179, 189, 190, 198, 201, 221, 241, 242, 243, 244, 246, 250
Brooklyn Horsemen (AFL) 156, 200
Brooklyn Lions (NFL) 39, 40, 41, 42, 145, 157, 185, 231, 233, 250
Brooklyn Professionals 112, 241
Brown University 2, 8, 9, 12, 14, 23, 24, 40, 42, 55, 63, 86, 91, 109, 122, 127, 130, 139, 152, 153, 154, 161, 169, 179, 183, 184, 185, 186, 191, 193, 198, 199, 202, 203, 205, 206, 210, 211, 212, 214, 215
Brown University Athletic Hall of Fame 152, 154, 161, 169, 184, 186, 193, 203, 206, 211
Brown University Field 24, 139, 140
Bruder, Doc 46, 59
Brumbaugh, Carl 159
Bryan, Johnny 36
Buckman, Neal 140
Budd, Johnny 45, 46, 59, 78
Buffalo All-Americans (NFL) 27, 39, 162, 171, 172
Buffalo Bears 129, 244
Buffalo Bills (NFL) 140
Buffalo Bisons (NFL) 30, 31, 57, 69, 96, 97, 100, 101, 110, 165, 177, 208, 210, 214, 228, 230, 234, 236, 239, 241, 250
Buffalo Prospects 172
Buffalo Rangers (NFL) 233
Burke, Chick 14, 24, 25, 26, 40, 144, 228
Burnett, Dale 112, 113, 117

Calac, Pete 49
Caldwell, Bruce 83
Calverley, Ernie 140
Cambridge A.A. Bulldogs 13
Camp, Walter 192, 193, 215
Campbell, Glenn 117, 125
Canadian-American Hockey League 9, 10
Canisius College 129
Canton Bulldogs (NFL) 4, 39, 40, 49, 52, 95, 171, 172, 174, 184, 185, 206, 207, 230, 231, 233, 250
Carlisle Industrial School 28
Carr, Joseph F. 22, 24, 47, 48, 69, 82, 96, 110, 118, 123
Carr, Harlan 57
Casey, Steve "Crusher" 209
Catholic University 174
Cavanaugh, Major Frank 170
Cawthon, Rainey 159
Caywood, Les 113
Centenary College 98, 168
Centre College 206
Chamberlin, Guy 5, 25, 26, 45, 59, 95, 139
Charlotte Bantams (AFL) 165
Chicago Bears (NFL) 4, 12, 32, 33–37, 52, 53, 55, 57, 58, 61, 68, 69, 75, 78, 97, 111, 124, 137, 139, 146, 149, 153, 154, 156, 157, 162, 164, 183, 188, 189, 192, 223, 228, 230, 233, 234, 236, 238, 241, 243, 246, 250
Chicago Bulls (AFL) 160
Chicago Cardinals (NFL) 37, 96, 102, 103, 104, 110, 115, 125, 135, 136, 137, 138, 146, 147, 151, 152, 160, 165, 166, 187, 189, 190, 194, 195, 201, 202, 213, 230, 233, 236, 238, 239, 241, 243, 246, 250
Chicago Cubs (MLB) 61, 188
Chicago Rockets (AAFC) 149
Chicago Staleys see Chicago Bears
Christensen, George 124
Cianci, Vincent A., Jr. 139
Cincinnati Reds (NFL) 194, 224
City Stadium 244
Clark, Algy 127
Clark, Dutch 124
Clark, Potsy 124
Clarke, Howard 16
Classical High School (Providence) 11, 40, 179, 185, 186, 187
Clay Hills 13
Cleveland Browns (NFL) 195
Cleveland Bulldogs (NFL) 22, 32, 39, 48, 53, 54, 62, 63, 69, 70, 183, 196, 197, 204, 205, 217, 228, 230, 234, 236, 250
Cleveland Indians (NFL) 123, 127, 128, 129, 130, 131, 134, 171, 174, 184, 198, 216, 224, 244, 246, 250
Cleveland Panthers (NFL) 13, 17, 48
Cleveland Tigers (NFL) 150, 190, 191
Clinton Oval 13
Cochrane, Mickey 14
Colgate University 15, 65, 135, 171, 172
College Football Hall of Fame 103, 149, 183, 224
College of Emporia 205
Colonial Baseball League 9

Index 275

Colorado Avalanche (NHL) 12
Columbus Panhandles (NFL) 15
Columbus Tigers (NFL) 29–30, 43, 44, 52, 169, 185, 208, 210, 213, 228, 230, 231, 233, 251
Coney Island Velodrome 191
Connecticut Huskies 136
Connecticut Yankees 135
Connolly, James G. 91
Connor, Dutch 14, 16, 17, 18, 24, 25, 26, 27, 28, 29, 144–145, 229, 230, 246, 248
Conzelman, Jimmy 5, 52, 53, 55, 56, 57, 58, 59, 60, 61, 62, 64, 65, 66, 67, 68, 71, 72, 73, 74, 75, 77, 78, 79, 80, 81, 88, 89, 90, 91, 92, 95, 98, 99, 100, 104, 105, 106, 107, 109, 111, 112, 121, 122, 123, 138, 145–147, 150, 155, 162, 165, 167, 175, 202, 207, 208, 233, 234, 235, 236, 237, 238, 239, 240, 241, 246, 247, 249, 254
Coppen, Charles, B. 7–9, 11, 12, 22, 24, 25, 32, 35, 38, 40, 52, 68, 78, 91, 92, 98, 109, 110, 111, 121, 122, 123, 133, 136
Corcoran, Bunny 16, 17
Cornsweet, Al 127, 131
Crabtree, Clyde 118, 159
Cranston Stadium 139
Creighton, Milan 136
Cronin, Bill 55, 56, 57, 62, 68, 71, 80, 81, 92, 98, 101, 106, 109, 148, 234, 235, 237, 239, 246, 248, 255
Cronin, Jack 55, 57, 65, 66, 68, 71, 72, 75, 80, 81, 83, 84, 85, 86, 92, 98, 99, 101, 102, 104, 106, 108, 112, 113, 120, 122, 138, 139, 147–148, 234, 235, 237, 238, 239, 240, 242, 246, 247, 248, 249, 254
Crowley, Jim 33, 148–149, 182, 183, 229
Crowther, Rae 213
Cycledrome 1, 3, 6, 10, 18, 19, 20, 21, 22, 23, 24, 28, 30, 31, 32, 33, 36, 37, 38, 39, 42, 45, 46, 47, 49, 50, 51, 52, 53, 56, 57, 58, 59, 60, 62, 64, 67, 72, 76, 77, 78, 80, 81, 82, 84, 87, 88, 89, 96, 97, 100, 102, 103, 104, 107, 108, 109, 110, 111, 112, 115, 116, 119, 121, 123, 124, 127, 130, 131, 135, 136, 137, 139, 228, 231, 234, 236, 238, 241, 244

DaGata, Fred 124, 125, 126, 149, 245
Dartmouth College 3, 14, 23, 54, 144, 162, 163, 176, 184, 208
Dartmouth "Wearers of the Green" Athletics Hall of Fame 144, 176
Davis, Ernie 65
Davis & Elkins College 122, 166, 167
Day, Herschel "Rip" 193
Dayton Triangles (NFL) 17, 53, 59, 73, 75, 96, 98, 99, 109, 110, 159, 160, 164, 168, 169, 177, 194, 213, 217, 219, 223, 230, 233, 234, 236, 238, 239, 241, 251
Dean Academy 143, 144, 147, 180, 184
Decatur Staleys *see* Chicago Bears
Dempsey, Jack 5
Denver Bears 176
Denver Broncos (NFL) 140
Detroit Lions (NFL) 195
Detroit Panthers (NFL) 18, 54, 57, 58, 68, 146, 147, 150, 155, 162, 165, 175, 208, 210, 230, 233
Detroit Wolverines (NFL) 69, 70, 78, 79, 88, 96, 221, 223, 236, 238, 251
Diehl, Wally 74, 104, 159
Dilweg, LaVern "Lavvie" 5, 69, 85, 124, 128, 132
Doane, Dinger 40, 58, 68, 150, 234
Dole, Sumner 221
Donahue, Jack 47, 49, 50, 55, 150–151, 231, 256
Dooley, James E. 9–10, 38, 40, 69, 92, 123, 134
Dorais, Gus 213
Dorchester American Legion 13
Dorsett, Tony 218
Douds, Forrest 109, 115, 118, 120, 122, 151–152, 242, 255
Dowler, Tommy 135
Doyle, Ed 57
Driscoll, Paddy 5, 37, 52, 57, 61, 69
Dubienny, Jack 129
Duluth Eskimos (NFL) 51, 53, 62, 69, 148, 231, 233, 234, 236, 251
Duluth Kelleys (NFL) 230
Dunn, Red 108, 124, 128
Dunne, James E. 91, 98
Durfee High School 40, 149
Durham Bulls 200
Dyche, Schubert 189

E.M. Lowe's Drive-In Theatre 10–11, 136
East Providence Townies 131, 244
East-West Shrine Game 151, 153, 182, 189, 201
Eastern League 11, 176, 190, 191, 193
Eastern Shore League 200
Ebbets Field 120, 242
Eckstein, Dolph 23, 26, 27, 36, 37, 42, 44, 49, 55, 138, 139, 152–153, 229, 231, 253, 256
Edwards, Bud 109, 113, 116, 117, 118, 120, 124, 130, 132, 139, 153–154, 242, 243, 245, 246, 248
Elliott, Doc 32
Emerson, Ox 124
Englemann, Wuert 128

Index

Erickson, Hal 106
Ernst, Jack 78, 113
Eschbach, Herb 154, 242, 245
Etelman, Carl 154–155, 162, 231

Feather, Tiny 78, 99, 112
Federal League of Baseball 9
Fenway Park 15
Fitchburg State College 171
Fitton Athletic Club 154
Fitton Field 133, 244
Fitzgibbon, Paul 132
Flaherty, Jack 123
Flaherty, Ray 213
Flanagan, Hoot 29
Fleischmann, Jack 54, 67, 68, 71, 79, 81, 87, 92, 100, 103, 109, 138, 155, 234, 237, 239, 253, 254, 255
Flenniken, Mack 115, 116, 125
Florida State League 190
Fordham University 14, 33, 40, 143, 144, 149, 170, 173, 174, 177
Forst, Dutch 49, 156, 232
Fort Adams 11
Foster, Wally 31
Four Horsemen of Notre Dame 21, 24, 33, 37, 149, 183
Frankford Stadium 25, 46, 51, 59, 80, 96, 104, 228, 231, 234, 236, 239, 241
Frankford Yellow Jackets (NFL) 16, 17, 22, 25, 26, 27, 32, 36, 37, 39, 45, 46, 47, 51, 52, 53, 59, 60, 70, 74, 75, 79, 80, 81, 82, 85, 88, 97, 99, 104, 105, 106, 110, 113, 114, 118, 119, 120, 122, 123, 126, 127, 134, 137, 158, 159, 160, 161, 162, 163, 165, 169, 171, 174, 178, 182, 186, 189, 194, 196, 198, 207, 213, 223, 230, 231, 233, 234, 236, 237, 238, 239, 240, 241, 242, 243, 244, 246, 251
Frankford Yellow Jackets (pre–NFL) 150, 174
Friedman, Benny 54, 62, 63, 70, 78, 79, 99, 101, 102, 111, 112, 113, 117, 121, 124, 132, 184
Fry, Wes 65

Garvey, Franny 23, 26, 27, 28, 36, 45, 46, 49, 55, 157, 229, 232, 233, 239, 246, 248, 255, 256
Garvey, Hec 97, 109, 156–157, 239, 255
Gehrig, Lou 11, 74, 76
Gentry, Weldon 117, 122, 126, 127, 131, 157–158, 242, 245
George, Ed Don 209
Georgetown University 101, 163, 200, 201
Georgetown University Athletic Hall of Fame 201
Georgia Tech 120, 183

Gilberton Catamounts 192, 193, 207
Gipp, George 156
Golembeski, Archie 14, 18, 22, 23, 26, 27, 28, 30, 31, 32, 39, 43, 44, 45, 47, 49, 55, 97, 100, 138, 144, 158, 228, 229, 230, 232, 233, 239, 246, 248, 249, 256
Gonzaga University 160, 212, 213
Goodbread, Royce 122, 124, 158–159, 245
Graham, Al 109, 115, 118, 120, 125, 126, 133, 159–160, 242, 245, 254, 255
Graham, Fred 160, 232
Grange, Red 5, 32–36, 39, 55, 64, 66, 69, 72, 111, 137, 139, 149, 165, 182, 192, 213, 215, 218, 223
Great Lakes Naval 145
Greater New York Circuit 178
Green Bay Packers (NFL) 12, 33, 69, 70, 73, 84, 85, 86, 87, 89, 96, 97, 107, 108, 110, 111, 117, 120, 122, 123, 124, 128, 129, 132, 133, 137, 147, 149, 156, 164, 186, 187, 198, 201, 202, 208, 213, 217, 223, 228, 230, 233, 236, 237, 238, 239, 240, 243, 244, 246, 252
Grove, Roger 128
Grove City College 122, 207
Gulian, Mike 23, 42, 44, 45, 49, 50, 51, 109, 139, 161–162, 229, 232, 234, 256
Guyon, Joe 5

Hadden, Al 54, 56, 67, 68, 75, 77, 78, 79, 80, 81, 84, 87, 92, 98, 103, 115, 162, 234, 237, 239, 242, 248, 255
Hagberg, Swede 100, 101
Hagenbuckle, Vern 51, 162–163, 232
Hagerty, Jack 61, 112
Haines, Hinkey 28, 42, 43, 50, 62, 83
Halas, George 5, 58, 69, 111, 146, 162, 188
Halicki, Ed 104, 105, 106, 119
Hall of Very Good 138, 173
Hamas, Steven 100
Hamer, Tex 17, 25, 26, 27, 45, 46, 47
Hammill, Ching 26, 163, 229
Hammond Pros (NFL) 52, 193, 230, 233
Hanny, Duke 57, 68, 71, 80, 81, 92, 109, 138, 164, 237, 238, 239, 240, 246, 248, 255
Harris A.C. 13
Hartford Blues (NFL) 19, 39, 44, 51, 157, 175, 177, 182, 184, 207, 217, 231, 233
Harvard University 36, 40, 44, 154, 155, 161, 179, 180, 184, 193
Harvey, Norm 68, 71, 77, 92, 164–165, 237, 239
Haskell Indian Nations University 168, 215
Hathaway, Russ 17
Haycraft, Ken 106

Index

Hazelton Mountaineers 143
Hein, Mel 123
Hendrian, Dutch 28
Hennessey, J.T. 58
Henry, Gwinn 205
Henry, "Pete" Wilbur 57, 95
Herman, Babe 21
Hill, Charley 50
Hobart College 65
Hodges Field 133, 244
Hogan, Paul 43
Holm, Tony 109, 112, 113, 114, 116, 165–166, 242
Holy Cross College 14, 18, 23, 25, 26, 36, 55, 110, 133, 156, 157, 158, 170, 195, 197
Holy Cross Varsity Club Hall of Fame 197
Homan, Two Bits 52, 105, 106, 213
Hope Field 13
Houser, Ken 57
Howard, Dosie 79
Hubbard, Cal 56, 57, 83, 124
Huffine, Ken 17
Hughitt, Tommy 117
Hummel, Swede 51, 166, 232
Humphries, Jimmy 158

Imlay, Tut 47
Indian Packing Company 12
Indiana State University 160
Indiana University 87, 164
Industrial Trust Company skyscraper (Superman building) 73
International League 188
Interstate Football League 153
Irvin, Tex 122, 124, 125, 127, 166–167, 245, 255

Jackson, Don 82
Jackson, Perry 68, 69, 71, 79, 81, 92, 98, 115, 122, 167–168, 202, 237, 239, 242
Jennings, Lou 98, 99, 100, 138, 168, 240, 246, 248, 249
Jerry Wolman Sports Hall of Fame 143
Joesting, Herb 106, 118, 119, 120
Johnson, Caroline (Mrs.) 71, 79, 80, 84, 85, 86, 87, 89, 90
Johnson, Pearce B. 2, 8, 9, 11, 12, 22, 68, 71, 72, 85, 89, 90, 93, 109, 110, 111, 135, 138, 139, 140
Jolley, Al 100
Jones, Ben 59
Jordan, Hunk 11
Joseph, Red 131

Kaer, Mort 126
Kansas City Athletics (MLB) 200

Kansas City Blues (NFL) 197, 217
Kansas City Cowboys (NFL) 49, 50, 63, 166, 197, 204, 205, 217, 230, 231, 233, 252
Kansas State University 216, 217
Kassel, Chuck 103
Keefer, Jack 40, 41, 42, 43, 45, 46, 47, 48, 50, 55, 109, 139, 169, 232, 246, 248
Kelly, "Wild Bill" 105, 120
Kendrick, Jim 30
Kenneally, George 63, 64
Kennedy, John F. 35
Kennedy, Joseph P., Jr. 35
Kennedy, Robert F. 35
Kenosha Maroons (NFL) 188, 189
Kessler, Bob 140
Kezar Stadium 223
Kinsley Park 11, 13, 14, 15, 16, 17, 18, 96, 103, 108, 137, 239
Kirkleski, Frank 58, 59, 63, 67, 100, 113
Kitzmiller, Dutch 125, 132
Koplow, Lou 169, 232
Koppisch, Walter 30, 50
Korean War 221
Kostos, Tony 119
Kotal, Eddie 33, 85
Kowalski, George 11
Kozlowsky, Joe 14, 23, 26, 27, 28, 36, 44, 47, 49, 62, 67, 68, 107, 109, 118, 170, 229, 232, 234, 242, 248, 253, 254, 256
Kucharski, Ted 110, 112, 114, 122, 170–171, 242

Lafayette College 173
Laird, Jim 15, 16, 17, 18, 22, 26, 31, 32, 33, 36, 37, 38, 39, 40, 41, 42, 46, 49, 51, 55, 57, 59, 62, 63, 68, 81, 92, 97, 171–172, 229, 230, 232, 235, 237, 246, 247, 248, 249, 254, 255, 256
Lake Forest College 181
Lambeau, Curly 5, 33, 69, 84, 85, 97, 110, 124, 128
LaSalle Academy 122, 138, 144, 148
Latone, Tony 27, 29, 37, 45, 59, 67, 78, 84, 107, 110, 111, 112, 113, 114, 115, 116, 117, 120, 121, 122, 138, 172–173, 242, 243, 246, 248, 255
Laudati, Madeline 71
Laudati, Peter 1, 9–11, 13, 18, 20, 71, 73, 92, 110, 136
Layden, Elmer 183
Lee, Eric 11
Lehigh University 180
Lester, Pinky 14, 15, 16, 17, 18, 42, 51, 138, 173, 232
Lewellen, Verne 66, 69, 85, 87, 108, 124
Lewis, "Strangler Ed" 91, 94, 209

278 Index

Lidberg, Cully 108
Lombard College 166
Lombardi, Vince 149
Long Island Warlow A.C. 70, 72, 236
Los Angeles Buccaneers (NFL) 39, 47, 48, 49, 52, 69, 70, 177, 231, 233, 252
Los Angeles Memorial Coliseum 223
Los Angeles Wildcats (AFL) 55, 222, 223, 224
Louisville, Colonels (NFL) 39, 233
Londos, Jim 211
Lowe, Bulger 16, 26, 55, 68, 173–174, 229, 235, 254
Lowell Tech 220
Loyola University-New Orleans 133
Ludlow, Ivan 208
Lyman, William "Link" 95
Lynch, Ed 54, 56, 57, 58, 60, 65, 67, 68, 174–175, 235, 246, 248, 254, 255
Lynn Papooses 200

Macalester (ND) College 225
MacKinnon, Jack 86
MacPhee, Waddy 40, 175–176, 232
Mahoney, Dan 11
Major League Baseball (MLB) 7, 131
Maloney, Red 23, 26, 27, 32, 33, 35, 36, 37, 40, 107, 176–177, 229, 246, 248, 249, 253, 254, 256
Manning, Jim 40, 41, 42, 177, 232
Marks, Larry 86, 87
Marshall, Bobby 192
Mathews, Dixie 135
Mathys, Charles 33, 149
Maul, Tuffy 47, 48
McArthur, Jack 115, 177–178, 242, 245
McBride, Jack 28, 31, 43, 50, 56, 57, 61, 62, 83, 97, 99, 100, 101, 102, 105, 107, 109, 118, 120, 178–179, 240, 246, 248, 249, 255
McCrillis, Ed 107, 179, 232
McDonough, Jack 11, 48, 52
McGlone, Joe 40, 41, 42, 180, 232
McGoldrick, Hugh 180, 229
McGraw, John 175
McGuirk, Warren 97, 103, 115, 118, 122, 138, 180–181, 240, 242, 255
McIntosh, Al 22, 23, 25, 181, 229, 232, 256
McLaughry, Tuss 24, 154, 206
Meeker, "Butch" Herb 110, 111, 112, 113, 114, 115, 116, 119, 120, 124, 130, 131, 132, 133, 182, 242, 243, 245, 246, 248
Melrose Park 11, 13
Memorial Stadium (Univ. of Illinois) 34
Memphis Tigers 133, 157, 165, 189, 201, 224, 244

Mercer, Ken 60, 74
Metacomet Golf Club 38
Michalske, Mike 65, 124
Michigan State University 149
Middlebury College 163
Miller, Don 33, 182–183, 229
Milstead, Century 83
Milwaukee American Legion 156
Milwaukee Badgers (NFL) 146, 147, 150, 190, 191, 193, 230, 233
Milwaukee Nighthawks 164
Minersville Park 27, 228, 231, 234, 237
Minneapolis Marines (NFL) 16
Minneapolis Red Jackets (NFL) 95, 96, 106, 118, 119, 120, 123, 159, 172, 187, 221, 225, 239, 241, 242, 243, 252
Mishel, Dave 63, 68, 127, 130, 139, 183–184, 235
Molenda, Bo 132
Mollinet, Lou 59, 60
Montana State University 189
Moore, Bucky 133
Moore, Dinty 58
Moran, Hap 45, 84, 112, 113
Morris Harvey College 218
Morrissey, Richard 209
Mount Pleasant High School 139–140
Mount Vernon Cardinals 221
Mullen, Dave 15
Muller, Brick 47, 48
Munn, Wayne "Big" 94
Murphy Tommy "Kid" 21
Murtaugh, Mickey 61

Nagurski, Bronco 111
Narragansett Park 10
Nashua Millionaires 200
Natick Sacred Hearts 131, 244
National Basketball Association (NBA) 140
National Basketball League (NBL) 140
National Hockey League (NHL) 7
Naval Academy 167
Nesser, Al 50, 57, 83
Nevers, Ernie 5, 51, 52, 62, 69, 96, 103, 115, 139
New Britain, CT Squad 13, 14
New England Circuit 140
New England League 200
New England Patriots (NFL) 89, 137, 139, 141, 195
New England Pro Football Conference 140
New England Steam Rollers 141
New Hampshire University Hall of Fame 145

Index 279

New Haven Blues 15
New Jersey Circuit 178, 199
New London Boys Club 135
New London Sub-Base 16, 22, 25, 41, 56, 180, 228, 231, 234
New Orleans/Utah Jazz (NBA) 12, 213
New York Brickley Giants (NFL) 150, 171, 190, 191
New York Brown Bombers 193
New York Giants (MLB) 175, 197, 200
New York Giants (NFL) 18, 21, 22, 23, 28, 29, 31, 32, 39, 42, 43, 50, 56, 57, 61, 67, 69, 78, 82, 83, 85, 96, 97, 99, 100, 101, 102, 110, 111, 112, 113, 117, 120, 121, 123, 124, 125, 126, 132, 139, 147, 156, 157, 165, 166, 167, 169, 196, 197, 204, 217, 218, 219, 220, 225, 228, 230, 231, 233, 234, 236, 237, 238, 239, 240, 241, 243, 244, 246, 252
New York University (NYU) 102, 129
New York Yankees (MLB) 35, 74, 76, 197
New York Yankees (AFL/NFL) 40, 53, 64, 65, 66, 68, 69, 70, 72, 73, 76, 77, 95, 97, 137, 147, 156, 164, 165, 175, 176, 177, 178, 179, 194, 195, 196, 198, 204, 217, 218, 221, 234, 236, 238, 252, 253
Newark Field Club 16
Newark Schools Stadium 241
Newark Tornadoes *see* Orange Tornadoes
Newport Naval Training Station 15
Newport Torpedo Station 14
Nicholson File 7, 13
Noble, Dave 33, 47, 48
Norman, Will 78
North Carolina Pre-Flight School 149
Northeast Football Hall of Fame 143
Northeastern State University 204
Northern Arizona University 181
Norwich University 145, 171
Nydall, Mally 106, 120

Oakland Raiders (NFL) 140
O'Boyle, Harry 85, 87
O'Connell, Grattan 55, 184–185, 235
Oden, Curly 14, 15, 16, 18, 22, 25, 30, 41, 42, 43, 44, 45, 46, 48, 49, 50, 52, 56, 57, 58, 59, 60, 62, 65, 67, 68, 73, 78, 79, 80, 81, 83, 84, 86, 87, 89, 91, 92, 97, 109, 113, 116, 117, 120, 126, 127, 128, 130, 131, 138, 139, 153, 185–186, 198, 208, 223, 229, 232, 235, 237, 238, 242, 243, 245, 246, 247, 248, 249, 253, 254, 255, 256
Oehlrich, Arnie 74, 82
Offermann, Frank, J. 129
Ohio State University 131, 183
Ohio Valley League 169, 217

Oklahoma City Chiefs 158
O'Neill, Red 25
Oorang Indians (NFL) 208
Orange A.C. 200
Orange/Newark Tornadoes (NFL) 95, 100, 114, 115, 116, 123, 159, 172, 175, 177, 178, 182, 189, 199, 217, 239, 241, 243, 253
Orient Heights 12
Outlet Company 12
Owen, Steve 57, 83

Pacific Coast League 14, 188
Pape, Oran 122, 124, 125, 126, 127, 128, 129, 130, 131, 132, 133, 186–187, 245, 247, 248, 255
Parksley Spuds 200
Passaic Red Devils 153
Paterson Miners 140, 141
Paterson Panthers 178
Pawtuxet A.C. 8, 13
Pearce, Pard 11, 40, 187–189, 229
Penn State University 28, 55, 154, 194, 218
Pere Marquette 15, 17, 18, 80, 110, 120, 121, 135, 136, 151, 216, 236, 242
Peters, Frosty 109, 111, 113, 114, 115, 116, 118, 119, 120, 121, 122, 182, 189–190, 225, 242, 243, 247, 249, 255
Pharmer, Art 118, 119, 126
Philadelphia Athletics (MLB) 14, 126
Philadelphia Eagles (NFL) 139, 195, 206, 224, 225
Philadelphia Phillies (MLB) 175
Philadelphia Yellow Jackets 136
Piedmont League 155, 200
Pieri, A.R. 10, 13, 144
Pierotti, Al 55, 57, 68, 107, 138, 190–191, 235, 255
Pinckert, Ernie 135
Pitt Stadium 218
Pittsburgh Pirates (NFL) *see* Pittsburgh Steelers
Pittsburgh Steelers (NFL) 140, 151, 152, 165, 166, 224
Pittsfield Hillies 176, 191
Plansky, Tony 101, 102
Pohlman, John 191, 229
Pollard, Fritz 12, 32, 33, 36, 40, 109, 138, 139, 191–193, 229, 254
Polo Grounds 31, 50, 61, 62, 85, 101, 102, 117, 121, 132, 175, 228, 231, 234, 239, 241, 244
Pope, Lew 122, 124, 125, 132, 135, 193–194, 245
Portland Beavers 14
Portsmouth Spartans (NFL) 110, 119, 120, 123, 124, 126, 133, 151, 160, 164, 165, 166,

168, 189, 190, 201, 202, 217, 220, 242, 243, 246
Potts, Daddy 47
Pottsville Maroons (NFL) 18, 22, 26, 27, 28, 29, 37, 39, 44, 45, 50, 51, 52, 58, 59, 63, 64, 66, 67, 70, 77, 78, 80, 83, 84, 85, 96, 107, 110, 111, 147, 150, 172, 173, 176, 185, 195, 196, 208, 223, 228, 230, 231, 233, 234, 236, 237, 238, 253
Presnell, Glenn 124
Princeton University 40, 154, 175, 176, 215
Pritchard, Bill 53, 55, 56, 57, 58, 59, 60, 68, 194–195, 235, 247, 248, 255
Pro Football Hall of Fame 1, 2, 9, 19, 88, 91, 92, 93, 103, 105, 123, 132, 138, 139, 145, 213, 254
Professional Football Association 140
Professional Wrestling Hall of Fame 139, 209
Providence, City of (Renaissance City) 3, 5, 7, 8, 9, 10, 11, 13, 19, 20, 21, 22, 24, 28, 48, 58, 74, 75, 76, 81, 91, 96, 119, 141
Providence Civic Center 139, 141
Providence Clam Diggers/Gold Bugs 13, 20
Providence College 18, 26, 39, 44, 97, 124, 149, 158, 216
Providence Colored All Stars 14
Providence Grays 11, 13, 190
Providence Huskies 136
Providence Journal 2, 8, 9, 11, 12, 15, 17, 20, 22, 25, 31, 36, 44, 45, 51, 57, 62, 66, 73, 78, 81, 82, 86, 87, 88, 100, 101, 103, 106, 112, 115, 116, 118, 122, 126, 127, 128, 133, 138
Providence Reds *see* Rhode Island Reds
Providence Steamrollers (BAA) 140, 144
Purdue University 54, 122, 155, 193, 194
Pyle, C.C. 223
Pyne, George, Jr. 195, 245

Quincy A.A. Trojans 13, 112, 124, 241, 244

Racine Legion (NFL) 190, 191, 215
Racine Tornadoes (NFL) 39, 233
Racis, Frank 78, 84, 107, 110, 115, 122, 195–196, 242, 243, 247, 248
Randall, Red 184
Randels, Proc 63
Rapp, Bob 43
Reading Aces 188
Rederick, Ben 57
Redman, Gus 17
Rehnquist, Milt 69, 71, 78, 81, 87, 89, 92, 97, 103, 108, 115, 118, 196–197, 237, 240, 242, 245, 248, 254, 255

Rhode Island Auditorium 13, 144
Rhode Island Heritage Hall of Fame 148, 211
Rhode Island Historical Society 1, 2, 23, 29, 34, 37, 38, 39, 66, 70, 86, 90, 111, 114, 125
Rhode Island Reds 9, 10, 144, 186
Rice, Grantland 183
Riopel, Hop 25, 26, 27, 40, 197, 229
Ring, Jimmy 175
Robb, Harry 207
Robb, Stan 49
Robertson, Everett 11
Robinson, Ed 24, 122, 124, 125, 127, 137, 244, 249
Rochester Colts 188
Rochester Jeffersons (NFL) 16, 30, 39, 156, 171, 172, 175, 207, 210, 214, 228, 230, 253
Rock Island Independents (NFL) 39, 146, 147, 230
Rockford Rox 188
Rockne, Knute 5, 87, 121, 156, 183, 213
Rodriquez, Kelly 119
Roepke, Johnny 74, 75
Rose, Al 115, 120, 125, 126, 130, 131, 132, 133, 197–198, 201, 216, 242, 245, 247, 248, 254, 255
Rose Bowl 24, 47, 122, 146, 183, 193, 212, 218, 224
Roslindale American Legion 13
Rushton, Sam 136
Rust, Reggie 135
Rutgers University 178
Ruth, Babe 5, 11, 35, 76
Ryan, Cassie 100

Sacramento Senators 188
St. Alphonsus A.A. 154
St. Louis Cardinals (MLB) 74, 126
St. Louis Cardinals (NFL) 89
St. Mary's (CA) 177
Salemi, Sam 77
Salt Lake City Bees 188
Samson, Seneca 44, 198–199, 232
San Francisco 49ers (NFL) 140
San Francisco Giants (MLB) 200
San Francisco Tigers 223
Schaffnit, Pete 48
Scharer, Eddie 64
Schein, Joe 122, 125, 135, 199, 245, 255
Schmidt, Kermit 135
Schreiner Institute 167
Scott, Bob 40, 48, 199, 232
Scott, Phil 100
Sedbrook, Len 99, 101, 102, 112, 113
Seyboth, Frank 199–200, 232, 255, 256

Index

Share, Nate 23, 26, 28, 200, 229, 256
Sheard, Shag 30
Sheehan, Fred 200–201, 229
Shelley, Dexter 126, 127, 128, 129, 130, 131, 133, 198, 201–202, 245, 247, 248, 249, 255
Shenandoah Presidents 196
Shenandoah Yellow Jackets 196
Shibe Park 37
Shockley, Arnie 68, 69, 98, 167, 168, 202, 204, 255
Shurtleff, Bert "Mad Murdock" 14, 15, 23, 26, 36, 40, 107, 138–139, 202–203, 229
Simendinger, Ken 156
Simmons, Jim 62, 70, 71, 72, 73, 74, 75, 78, 81, 92, 97, 203–204, 237, 255
Sisson, Charles P. 91, 141
Smith, Clyde 69, 70, 71, 73, 77, 78, 86, 87, 89, 92, 97, 138, 204–205, 206, 237, 254, 255
Smith, Orland 55, 57, 62, 68, 71, 77, 79, 92, 109, 138, 139, 205–206, 235, 237, 240, 255
Smith, Ray 115, 118, 120, 126, 132, 135, 205, 206, 242, 245, 255
Smyth, Lou 30, 36, 206–207, 232
Snell, George 42
Sofish, Alec 122, 207–208, 245, 255
Sonnenberg, Gus 54, 57, 58, 59, 60, 62, 65, 66, 67, 68, 71, 73, 74, 75, 78, 79, 81, 83, 84, 86, 87, 89, 90, 92, 93, 94, 95, 96, 97, 98, 109, 116, 138, 139, 208–210, 211, 235, 237, 238, 242, 247, 249, 254, 255
South Dakota State University 128
Southwest Oklahoma State University 68, 167, 168, 202, 203, 204
Southwest Oklahoma State University Alumni Association Athletic Hall of Fame 168, 202, 204
Spanish-American War 8
Speedways of Cranston 131, 132, 244
Spellman, Jack 14, 15, 23, 26, 27, 28, 30, 41, 42, 47, 49, 57, 62, 68, 71, 75, 77, 78, 81, 83, 87, 92, 100, 103, 109, 115, 118, 120, 121, 126, 127, 130, 131, 135, 138, 139, 208, 210–211, 229, 230, 232, 235, 237, 240, 243, 245, 247, 248, 254, 255, 256
Spellman, Larry 128
Spicer, Frankie 21
Springfield College 186
Stagg, Amos Alonzo 215
Staff, Spike 11, 12, 14, 211–212, 229
Staley Starch Company 12
Stamford All-Collegians 25
Stanford University 51, 103, 183, 218
Stanley, Happy 20
Stark, Doug 1
Staten Island Stapletons (NFL) 95, 102, 103, 109, 116, 129, 130, 157, 171, 172, 177, 187, 224, 239, 241, 243, 244, 246, 253
Steam Roller Five 144
Sternaman, Ed 111
Sternaman, Joey 36, 57, 69
Stifler, Jim 42, 51, 184, 212, 232, 235
Stockton, Hust, Jr. 32, 45, 46, 52, 59, 74, 81, 82, 99, 107, 212–213, 217, 219, 240
Stockton, John 213
Stramiello, Mike 120
Strong, Ken 102, 103, 116, 129, 130
Stuhldreher, Harry 21, 24, 25, 183
Super Bowl XXXVI 89, 137
Sutherland, Jock 218
Swarthmore College 181
Sweet, Fred 14, 26, 30, 31, 42, 49, 214, 229, 230, 232, 247, 248
Syracuse University 12, 14, 28, 43, 48, 59, 65, 122, 143, 144, 178, 216

Talbot, John 214–215, 232
Tampa Bay Buccaneers (NFL) 195
Tampa Bay Lightning (NHL) 12
Tanner, Bob 118
Texas Legion Hall of Honor 198
Thomas, John 215, 229
Thomas, Mildred 215
Thomas, Rex 42, 78, 117
Thomason, Stumpy 120
Thompson Stadium 102, 129, 239, 244
Thorpe, Jim 5, 28, 40, 49, 53
Tiernan, Young 21
Titmas, Herb 122, 124, 125, 130, 131, 198, 216, 245, 247, 248, 255
Tobin, Elgie 12–13
Tonry, Babe 16
Torpedo Station 13
Triggs, Jack 216, 232
Tryon, Eddie 65, 69
Tufts University 12, 23, 58, 150, 154, 155, 190, 200
Tully, George 60
Tulsa Oilers (AFL) 194
Tunney, Gene 5
Turville, Charles 20
Twin-County Football League 143

Union Quakers 150, 171
Union Station 84
United States Army 159, 161, 163, 169, 171, 174, 186, 195
United States Navy 145, 149, 163, 167, 173, 176, 181, 188, 201, 203
University of Alabama 40, 109, 165, 166, 220
University of Arkansas 157

University of Buffalo 194
University of California 47
University of Chicago 215
University of Connecticut 25, 70, 163, 220, 221
University of Detroit 110
University of Detroit Mercy 164, 165, 208, 225
University of Florida 158, 159
University of Illinois 33, 34, 189
University of Iowa 122, 186
University of Jamestown (ND) 215
University of Massachusetts 138, 181
University of Massachusetts Hall of Fame 181, 206
University of Michigan 34, 54, 169, 184
University of Minnesota 106
University of Mississippi 122, 224
University of Missouri 204, 205, 206
University of Nebraska 48, 49, 218
University of New Hampshire 14, 15, 22, 144, 145, 184, 219, 220
University of New Hampshire Wildcats Hall of Fame 220
University of Norwich 26, 38
University of Notre Dame 4, 11, 21, 24, 37, 87, 121, 148, 149, 156, 182, 183, 213
University of Oklahoma 157, 158, 201
University of Peabody 151, 190
University of Pennsylvania 25, 187, 188, 201, 220
University of Pittsburgh 28, 72, 97, 217, 218
University of Rhode Island 23, 181
University of Southern California 182
University of Tennessee 159
University of Texas 126, 197, 198, 201
University of Texas Sports Hall of Honor 201
University of Tulsa 206
University of Vermont 199, 200
University of Washington 3, 55, 222, 224
University of Washington Husky Hall of Fame 224
University of West Virginia 100, 101, 160, 218
University of West Virginia Athletics Hall of Fame 160
Urban, Luke 149

Van Horn, Charlie 57
Velodrome 231
Verkeyn, Charles 20
Villanova University 122, 143, 156
Vokaty, Otto 127, 131
Voss, Tillie 164
Vreeland, Swede 14, 16

Washington & Jefferson University 54, 109, 151, 162
Washington & Lee University 55, 190
Washington Redskins *see* Boston Braves
Washington Senators (NFL) 207
Washington State Honor Hall of Fame 182
Washington State University 110, 123, 182, 193, 212
Washington University (St. Louis, MO) 145, 146
Watchemoket All Stars 131, 244
Waterbury Bearcats 132, 133, 244
Waterbury Blues 17, 18, 25, 156
Waterbury Brasscos 191
Webber, Dutch 87, 113, 216–217, 243
Webster, John *see* John Thomas
Weimer, Chuck 101, 131
Weir, Ed 52, 74, 81
Welch, Gibby 72, 73, 76, 77, 97, 98, 99, 100, 101, 106, 107, 108, 109, 213, 217–218, 240, 247, 249, 254, 255
Welsh, Jim 50
Wentworth, Cy 21, 22, 24, 25, 26, 27, 28, 30, 31, 33, 35, 36, 37, 41, 42, 44, 47, 48, 49, 50, 55, 107, 219–220, 229, 232, 233, 247, 253, 254, 255, 256
Wentz, Barney 27, 29, 45
Wesley, Bull 40, 42, 46, 49, 59, 65, 68, 220, 232, 235
West Point Field Artillery 21, 22, 24, 25, 228
West Weymouth Union A.C. 97, 98, 111, 124, 125, 239, 241, 244
Westenberg, Marvin (The Shadow) 209
Western League 176
Western Union 76
Weston Field 13
Whelan, Ed 8
White, Byron "Whizzer" 139
Wiberg, Ossie 78, 112
Williams of New Haven, CT 13, 14, 40, 41, 156, 231
Williams, Pop 70, 71, 72, 73, 74, 75, 78, 79, 80, 81, 92, 99, 102, 103, 106, 107, 108, 113, 114, 120, 121, 124, 127, 132, 133, 135, 138, 220–221, 223, 237, 238, 240, 243, 245, 247, 248, 249, 254, 255
Williams, Roger 7
Willis, Chris 8
Wilson, Abe 55, 68, 77, 92, 109, 138, 222, 224, 235, 237, 240, 255
Wilson, Mike 104, 105
Wilson, Mule 61, 112, 113, 117, 129
Wilson, Round House 21
Wilson, Wildcat 55, 56, 57, 59, 60, 61, 62,

63, 64, 65, 66, 67, 68, 70, 71, 72, 74, 75, 76, 77, 78, 79, 80, 81, 83, 84, 87, 89, 90, 91, 92, 98, 99, 100, 101, 102, 103, 104, 105, 106, 108, 109, 128, 138, 139, 145, 174, 217, 222–224, 235, 237, 240, 247, 249, 254, 255
Winston Salem Twins 155
Winters, Sonny 15
Wise, William 55
Woodruff, Jim 101
Woodruff, Lee 122, 124, 125, 126, 127, 130, 131, 132, 133, 224–225, 245, 247, 249, 255
Workman, Hoge 131
World Series 74, 76, 126, 175
World War I 5, 13, 156, 164, 169, 171, 172, 173, 174, 180, 186, 188, 203, 215

World War II 143, 145, 146, 149, 159, 161, 163, 167, 169, 171, 173, 176, 181, 190, 195, 208, 211, 221
Wray, Lud 135
Wrigley Field (Cubs Park) 34, 53, 61, 234
Wycoff, Doug 61, 116

Yale University 83, 184, 193
Yankee Stadium 76, 236
Young, Herm 110, 113, 114, 115, 225, 243, 247, 248
Young, Lloyd 28, 30, 41, 47, 50, 56, 225, 229, 232, 235, 256
Youngfleish, Frank 50
Youngstrom, Swede 52

www.ingramcontent.com/pod-product-compliance
Lightning Source LLC
Chambersburg PA
CBHW032033300426
44117CB00009B/1040